ENGELS
A REVOLUTIONARY LIFE

ENGELS

A REVOLUTIONARY LIFE

A Biography of Friedrich Engels

John Green

ENGELS: A REVOLUTIONARY LIFE
John Green

First Published in India 2013

ISBN 978-93-5002-224-5

Published in agreement with Artery Publications, London
For publication and sale only in the Indian Subcontinent
(India, Pakistan, Bangladesh, Nepal, Maldives,
Bhutan and Sri Lanka)

Published by
AAKAR BOOKS
28 E Pocket IV, Mayur Vihar Phase I, Delhi 110 091
Phone : 011 2279 5505 Telefax : 011 2279 5641
info@aakarbooks.com; www.aakarbooks.com

Printed at
Mudrak, 30 A Patparganj, Delhi 110 091

Acknowledgements

Any book of this nature depends on the support, help and advice of many individuals and organisations. I cannot thank all who have contributed by name, but hope they will not be offended if I have not included them below.

I particularly wish to thank the Norman Melburn and Barry Amiel Trust for their generous financial support towards this project. The Engels Museum in Wuppertal, the Institute of Social History in Amsterdam, the Marx Memorial Library in London and The Working Class Movement Library in Salford always responded promptly and helpfully to my queries. To Dr. Uwe de la Motte, formerly of the Institut für Marxismus-Leninismus in Berlin, I owe deep gratitude for granting me access to his library of works by Marx and Engels and for his clarification of Hegel's philosophic impact on 19th century Germany. I also wish to say a big thank you to Michal Bończa, Bob Dixon, Robin de la Motte and Richard Murgatroyd who all read early drafts and pointed out some glaring mistakes and inconsistencies. They all made insightful suggestions for improvement. Michal Boncza was also invaluable in transforming the bare text into a well-designed book. I am also grateful for the support of my daughters, Galina and Siski Green, who gave me useful advice and made perceptive comments from the perspective of a younger generation.

As with my previous books, this project would not have left the starting blocks without the stimulus and unstinting support of Bruni de la Motte, who is also my most stringent but indispensable critic. She read the biography in its various drafts and suggested numerous corrections and improvements. However, I am alone responsible for the final text and any shortcomings or errors it may contain.

To the memory of my parents, Marguerite and Norman,
and my brother, Bob, whose lives were inspired
by the dream of socialism

CONTENTS

'Only he who does nothing makes no mistake,
apart from the mistake of doing nothing.'
Vladimir Lenin

'Caminante, no hay camino, se hace camino al andar'
(Wanderer, there is no path; in walking we make the path)
Antonio Machado

Introduction

In the 1980s I was involved in making a commemorative documentary on the life of Karl Marx for German television and we found ourselves filming in Chetham's Library, Manchester. We wished to shoot footage of one of the reports by the Factory Inspectorate that Marx may have perused here. On leafing through one of the volumes, I was amazed to find some lightly pencilled notes in the margins that turned out to be in Engels' own hand. From that moment on I have always been intrigued by him, overshadowed as he has been by his more famous friend and collaborator; I wondered what drove this privileged young man to commit social suicide by throwing in his lot with industrial workers and their struggle for emancipation. This short biography is an attempt to help answer that question and to bring Friedrich Engels alive for others who know little or nothing about him.

It is always dangerous to compare an individual from one historical era with one in another, but in the case of Friedrich Engels, a comparison with Che Guevara is too obvious and tempting to ignore. His life has an uncanny resemblance to that of Che Guevara, apart from the, albeit important, fact that he didn't die young – a prerequisite for being turned into an icon in the way that Che has been. Like Guevara, he too rejected a comfortable, privileged background, espousing the lot of the poor and the oppressed. It may be difficult to imagine the similarity when you see photographs of the older Engels, looking much more like an avuncular Charles Dickens than a dashing Che. But in the few youthful photos left to us, he does appear to have a remarkable physical resemblance – the good looks, wispy beard and long hair. He was tall with a trim, athletic figure and he stares out at us with that confident challenging look. In his twenties, like Che Guevara, he penned radical poetry and dreamed of transforming the world; he also fought with a small band of revolutionary 'guerrilleros' in the wooded hills of southern Germany against the might of the Prussian Army. He was hounded across Europe by the Prussian state, was placed top of its most wanted list, charged with high treason, and he was harassed and spied upon. For many years, he was obliged to lead two separate lives: one as a respectable middle class businessman and the other as a semi-conspiratorial militant. At the time, he was acknowledged as the undisputed leader, alongside Marx, of the burgeoning revolutionary socialist movement in Europe and was largely responsible for the setting up of militant cells of workers and intellectuals in most European countries.

Despite the huge intellectual contribution he made during his lifetime, he was no stuffy academic figure; he made no secret of his love of the sensual and carnal, and certainly indulged the pleasures of life to the full, alongside his earnest research. Unlike his friend Marx, he was very much a 'man of action' and a practical activist as well as an intellectual.

History is unkind to those who play second fiddle or who are overshadowed by greater personalities. Sometimes they may have made as significant a contribution as their more famous colleagues, but history obscures them from posterity's view. It is also a sad reality that our society seems to crave individual heroes and ignores the fact of collective achievement, even though no discoveries are ever made by one individual alone.

Emilie du Châtelet, Voltaire's mistress, was reckoned by him to have a better mind and only her status as a woman kept her out of the limelight. Her contribution to Voltaire's own thought, mathematical science in France during the 18th century and our understanding of energy were invaluable. She has been largely eclipsed by history.

Alfred Russell Wallace, a contemporary of Darwin, contributed almost as much as the latter to establish the existence of an evolutionary process, but who knows his name today? He independently proposed a theory of natural selection which actually prompted Darwin to publish his own more developed and researched theory sooner than he had intended to avoid the danger of being eclipsed by Wallace. The same goes for Rosalind Franklin, the physical chemist whose work laid the basis for Watson and Crick to crack the molecular structure of DNA, but they won Nobel Prizes, she didn't.

But perhaps one of the most neglected of such historical figures is Friedrich Engels, the compatriot and lifetime collaborator of Karl Marx. Numerous books, pamphlets and essays have been written about Marx, but biographical studies of Engels and his contribution to 'Marxist' thought are hardly plentiful. He himself, in typically self-effacing manner, said towards the end of his life: 'All my life I did what I was made for, that is playing second fiddle and I believe I acquitted myself tolerably well. And I was happy in having so excellent a first violin as Marx.'

Marx and Engels hit it off from the time of their first real meeting in Paris and became intimate friends and collaborators on almost everything they did in connection with the international workers' movement and the development of the theory that we now term 'Marxism'.

Engels is often dismissed simply as the 'wealthy capitalist' who kept the Marx family from descending into absolute penury, but this attitude does him a profound disservice; he was undoubtedly Marx's intellectual equal and made a significant creative contribution not only through his own writings, but to many that they jointly published, as well as to many of those published under Marx's name alone. He was, perhaps like those other 'second fiddles' mentioned above, an extremely modest and self-effacing man and these qualities are hardly those to facilitate elevation into the historical pantheon.

His few, no doubt well-intentioned, biographers carry a certain amount of responsibility for having buried him under the dust sheets of history: we have had verbose academic studies as well as hagiographies, neither of which has helped our fuller understanding of the man or offered us entertaining reading. There have been at least 13 biographies, but the classic one is Gustav Mayer's two-volume biography written in the 1930s and only published in English in 1936 in an abridged form. The only really in-depth Engels biography written in English is the one published in 1974 by W. O. Henderson.

I have tried to remove much of the historical dust, in order to reveal the man of flesh and blood hidden beneath, someone we can readily identify with and who comes alive through his passionate historical intervention. I have provided only as much historical background as I felt was necessary in order to follow the stages of his life and the significance of his various actions and writing, but without overburdening the reader.

With this biography, I make no claims to have discovered vital new material about Engels' life or that I am providing radically new insights. It is more an attempt to rescue the man Friedrich Engels from the suffocating embrace of academia and to remove the layers of clutter and detailed overload that have kept him hidden.

I have also tried to highlight the more important of his ideas and overcome certain misunderstandings as to his role as Marx's collaborator and populariser. I have tried to tease out the aspects of his life and work that have relevance for us today and could be of interest to a post-communist generation who either know little or nothing about him, or have been put off by his association with the flawed and often repressive states that claimed to be governed by the principles he and Marx elaborated. There have also been numerous attempts, since his death, to appropriate his name and work as a justification for the programmes and actions of a number of leftist sects, which have also served to sully his reputation.

I hope to show that, in both his life and work, he was motivated primarily by a deep humanity and revulsion of oppression and exploitation everywhere. During a period of heightened nationalism and xenophobia, he remained a true internationalist, even though he retained strong emotional and cultural ties to the country of his birth, Germany. He was a democrat who saw the liberation of the working classes as a precursor and prerequisite for the liberation of all mankind.

I believe that whatever one's political persuasions or opinions on communism and communists, about engineering history or building utopias, Engels' life is of interest because his ideas were revolutionary and he was an honest, principled and passionate man whose every action was taken on behalf of his fellow human beings. Whether he was misguided in his conclusions, I will leave readers to judge for themselves.

I have written this biography in the present tense rather than, as is the norm, in the past. This may disconcert some readers, but I feel that this tense will communicate the immediacy of his life and the revolutionary events that accompanied it in a more intimate way than the distancing past tense could have done.

I found Gustav Mayer's pioneering *Friedrich Engels- Eine Biografie* as well as *Friedrich Engels – Dokumente seines Lebens*, edited by Manfred Kliem invaluable sources. An abridged version of Mayer's book has been published in English. I made full use of the collected works of Marx and Engels (published in 43 volumes as the *Marx-Engels-Werke* by Dietz Verlag, Berlin), as well as a whole number of other sources, some of which are listed in the select bibliography. The translations of Marx's and Engels' works in English are available in *The Collected Works of Marx and Engels* (50 volumes). In this book, all translations from Engels' and Marx's letters and other writings from the original German are my own.

Chapter One (1820-1840)
A wild seed

On 28 November 1820, Friedrich Engels Sr. is exceedingly proud: his young wife has presented him with his first child – a healthy son. Like many first sons at that time, he too is named after his father. The succession and the future of the family textile company, he feels, should now be secure. Admiring his new-born, the father can hardly envisage that this son will become, in class terms, his mortal enemy.

Engels jr. is born, only two years after Marx, and 31 years after the French Revolution plunged Europe into convulsions and inspired generations of radicals. In the following year Napoléon dies, but during Engels' lifetime Europe is still experiencing the aftershocks of the revolution and undergoing a vast and radical restructuring. There is a permanent revolutionary, and counter-revolutionary, atmosphere, catalysed by the rapid social and industrial changes that are taking place, particularly in Britain, and their repercussions on the rest of Europe. However, Engels' childhood and early youth offer us few clues at all as to how and why he becomes transformed into a passionate revolutionary. His family is loving and supportive, he is born with a silver spoon in his mouth, and the society in which he grows up is devout and upstanding. However the world he enters has been changed irrevocably by the cataclysmic revolution of 1789.

Before the revolution, continental Europe during the eighteenth century, in terms of everyday life, had more in common with the 15th or 16th centuries than with the 20th. Structural and economic change was still proceeding at a very slow pace and industry remained largely traditional. Technology had not yet been affected by scientific discovery and society was still firmly hierarchical, with small groups enjoying privilege and power; the aristocracy ruled supreme, underpinned by a powerful church. The mass of the population was still rural, with the middle classes and artisans concentrated in the small towns. Armies were relatively small and dynastic rather than national in allegiances. Before 1789 no continental state could boast a parliament and republican ideas were scarcely voiced.

The overriding factor precipitating change was undoubtedly the Declaration of the Rights of Man by the French revolutionary government in 1789. Throughout Europe events in France had elicited sympathy, admiration and hope among the oppressed as well as among the more educated and enlightened. The proclamation of universal rights shattered once and for all the concept of a fixed and hierarchical society. By the early eighteen hundreds traditional social structures had changed almost beyond recognition in much of western Europe, largely as a consequence of the tremors resonating from that revolution and partly as a result of Britain's dramatic industrialisation and colonial expansion, offering an alternative path out of feudal ossification.

In the year of Engels' birth, Europe is still very much divided by an invisible vertical fault-line between an eastern feudal area and a western one, still largely traditional but struggling to come to terms with the new revolutionary challenge. Industrialisation, mass conscript armies and reformed administrative structures, new political concepts and national aspirations are beginning to transform the old Europe of entrenched monarchies supported by a privileged nobility on the back of a servile peasantry.

Engels enters the world in Barmen, a small, staid and provincial town with a population of under 40,000 located astride the banks of the River Wupper north of Solingen, in the Rhineland. The town is characterised by a concentration of textile mills. Engels' father is the owner of a cotton mill, and his mother Elise (née van Haar), is the daughter of a rector and grammar school headmaster, and has no occupation outside the home, as is the norm in bourgeois households. His devout family has him christened in the Protestant Reformed Church in Elberfeld on 18 January.

Ferdinand Freiligrath, later dubbed the 'poet of the revolution' and to become one of Engels' close friends, describes the town as, 'a cursed nest, prosaic, small-townish, sombre and reviled, like no other'. It certainly has no revolutionary tradition but, because of its concentration of textile factories, is often dubbed 'Germany's Manchester'.

It is, at the time Engels is growing up, a typically conservative, largely Protestant, town. His family, having been in the local textile business for generations, enjoys high esteem. The family has been innovative and diligent, and his great grandfather introduced the first mechanical lace making techniques to the area in 1775. They carry out the middle class rituals, like all their peers: dressing formally in black suits or dresses, and attending church service on Sundays; the only entertainment being a singsong around the piano with the family and perhaps close friends at weekends. Though Engels' mother is hardly an exemplary pietist - she plays dressing-up games with the children, and when Engels reaches 20, she gives him the Christmas present he has requested, the complete works of Goethe, which is not the kind of reading the pious deemed suitable for young Christian gentlemen.

Engels himself, in 1839, describes Barmen in the following way:

> The narrow Wupper river propels its ruddy waves, sometimes rapidly, sometimes hesitantly, between the smoky factories and between the bleaching sheds, decked in skeins of fabric thread; but its deep redness derives not from some massacre, as it's only the pens of theologians that do battle here and garrulous old women, arguing over trifles; and it's not red in embarrassment about the doings of the people, although, truly, there would be good reason to be, but is due only to the many Turkish-red dye factories...[1]

He goes on to illustrate how different Barmen is from other parts of Germany, and here, in this short excerpt, we see clearly the stylistic germ of his classical work, *The Condition of the Working Class in England* which he is to write as a 25 year old in 1845:

> You won't find a trace of that sparkling, active folk life that you find almost everywhere else in Germany...an awful destitution envelops the lower classes, particularly among the factory workers in Wuppertal; syphilis and lung diseases dominate to an extent that is hard to believe; in Elberfeld alone, out of 2,500 school-age children, 1,200 don't attend school, but grow up in

> the factories, so that the factory owner doesn't need to replace them with grown-ups who'd have to be paid double the pay. The rich factory owners, though, have elastic consciences and if one or more children are allowed to go to the dogs there won't be any pious soul sent to hell, particularly since, every Sunday, they all traipse off to church. It is also generally accepted that among factory owners, the most pious treat their workers the worst, hold down their pay in all sorts of ways, using the excuse of removing temptation from them to spend their wages on drink; and these are the self-same individuals who, when the election of the pastor comes round, use bribes to get their man elected.[2]

His family is well off, its wealth based on several generations of cotton mill owners. In 1837 his father expands the business, entering a partnership with the Ermen brothers to create a larger company with mills in Manchester (founded in 1837) and in Engelskirchen (opened in 1841). Establishing a branch of the firm in Britain gives it access not only to British markets, but also to a more advanced technological expertise.

The name Engels is known throughout Germany and abroad long before Engels jr. made it synonymous with Marxism and communism. Cotton reels and silk thread and other haberdashery articles already carried the name of the firm 'Ermen & Engels, Manchester' and 'Ermen & Engels, Engelskirchen'. Barmen, unlike most other, still semi-rural towns in Germany, experienced an early industrialisation. It is the textile trades in Rhineland and Silesia that are the seeds of future capitalist industrial development in Germany. One of the most successful firms engaged in the manufacture of colours and pharmaceutical products is the Elberfeld firm of Bayer, founded in 1863, which is destined to become one of the world's most powerful chemical companies by the twentieth century.

His family's politics are strictly conservative and nationalist, and their social views largely conformist, despite their social philanthropy. It is this latter aspect which undoubtedly rubs off on the young Friedrich. Already his great grandfather and thereafter his grandfather, had built housing for some of their key workers and an elementary school for their children. Of special significance is that his great grandfather's firm, Caspar Engels & Sons, never used child labour, an exception at the time. And in 1807, at the beginning of the administrative crisis caused by local and state indebtedness as a result of the obligatory Napoleonic taxes, Caspar Engels became one of the leading lights in a poor association whose aim was to privately maintain social payments which had, up to then, been the responsibility of the Barmen city council. In the aftermath of the Napoleonic wars, central Europe was suffering economic dislocation.

In the hunger years of 1816/17 Caspar Engels set up a corn association to sell cheap cereals to the poor, and Engels' own father continued this tradition. Of course such philanthropy did nothing to change the thinking, methods or essence of the system and in many ways it strengthened the Engels family business, but it would have certainly sown the seeds for a humanitarian outlook in the young Engels.

His father is, according to family reports quite stern but bright and with a healthily independent approach to life, being also of good humour and generally likeable; Engels jr. appears to have inherited a similar makeup. Most of the family are musically inclined and his father plays both the bassoon and cello, and chamber concerts are a regular feature in the family home. Engels, though, appears to have no strong musical inclinations. During his business travels in Switzerland, Italy and England, Engels' father also visits the theatre. Such 'frivolity' is considered sinful by the pietists and he is regularly criticised by them for this. The Engels family, however, amply compensates for such deviation by making generous contributions to the Reformed (Protestant) Church in Barmen, which they attend.

Engels always feels much closer to his mother than to his father and his eight siblings (four sisters and four brothers) apparently feel the same. She has a bubbly personality, is sensitive and very musical and has enjoyed a balanced, humanitarian education in her father's household. With her strong emotions, she is the polar opposite of her sober husband. Engels values her 'wonderful depth of feeling' and can never reconcile himself to his father's untrammelled dominance in the home, so that his mother 'never enjoyed any independence with father around'.

Engels is the only member of the family who strays from the straight and narrow; all his brothers enter the family business and his sisters marry local businessmen; they all remain conformist and conservative in their political outlook. There appears to be no straightforward explanation as to why he alone should espouse socialism.

Early boyhood

The house in the Brucherstrasse, where Engels and his siblings come into the world and in which he spends his childhood, is a commodious, four-storey, slate-faced house in the centre of the town. After his parents die, the family will move to the nearby small town of Engelskirchen, and the house itself is to be destroyed by Allied bombing in 1943. Where it stood, there is now a commemorative plaque on which is engraved: 'Here stood the house in which the great son of our town, Friedrich Engels, was born. He is the co-founder of scientific socialism'.

As a youngster, he is particularly close to his three and a half years' younger sister, Marie, with whom he later corresponds in an often light mocking tone, during his sojourns in Bremen and Berlin. They agree not to write less than four pages each time to each other. In later years he develops more intimate ties to his brother, Emil, who often defends Engels against his critics within the family who are outraged at his socialist views. He also maintains reasonably amicable relations with his brother Hermann, but avoids politics when corresponding with him.

His early years, if not light-hearted or idyllic, are relatively harmonious, but in the years of maturity his relations with the family become increasingly and permanently strained largely as a result of his militant politics. A few months before his death he summed up his relationship with his 'really pious and arch reactionary family' during his lifetime with the words that are also valid for his relationships with everyone: 'One can remain good friends on a personal level despite political differences.'

From his early childhood we have little detail, but we know these years are largely defined by his mother because his father, fully occupied with the expanding business, has little leisure time to devote to the family. Possibly because of this, the children often spent long periods with their mother's parents in Hamm. There, Engels develops a particularly close relationship with his grandfather, a rector and grammar school headmaster, who reads classical stories to the small boy and helps him with his homework. His love and respect for Gerhard van Haar is revealed in a poem he gives him on New Year's Day, written as a 13 year old:

Oh you dear grandfather, who always greeted us with kindness
Who always helped us when we were stuck in our work

And told us such lovely stories when you were with us...

Now I wish you, grandfather, a happy New Year
A long life, much joy and little sorrow
All this is wished you, from your loving grandchild.[3]

A completely different influence is exercised by his uncle, Pastor Karl Snethlage. He is an immediate neighbour to the family and the children spend many hours in his home. Through him Engels and his siblings are introduced to a strict and pious belief system – and a rather different world from that at home or at their grandparents. Some of this piousness certainly left its mark on the young Engels, but not in the way its most ardent adherents would have wished: 'of that ecstatic piety,' he says in 1839, 'about which I heard preached so often from the pulpit, but never felt any of it; my religion was and is calm, blissful peace...'

In 1828, the year the great romantic composer, Franz Schubert, dies aged 31, Engels begins school. He attends the elementary school in Barmen until he is 14 years of age. The school is, he tells us, 'in the hands of a narrow- and small-minded board of governors (on which Engels' father sits), that chose, in the main, only the pious as teachers'. But he is grateful for the 'riveting lessons in physics and chemistry' he receives which equip and provide him with 'an invaluable basis for my further scientific education.' This sound scientific grounding he is given at the school, compared with the Biblical creationism he has imbibed from his uncle Snethlage, causes him already at this tender age to question the varying interpretations of reality. How can he reconcile the comforts he enjoys at home with the abject poverty of his father's workers which he observes daily on his way to school? We don't know what he thinks at this time, but a remark he records his teacher making that 'the poor go to the drinking den and the gentlefolk go to their club', reveals an early awareness of class difference.

In 1834 he transfers to the evangelical Gymnasium (grammar school) in the neighbouring town of Elberfeld. This is in accordance with the Engels family tradition: the eldest son would be sent to the grammar school, where he would obtain a sufficiently rounded education for his future role of taking on the family firm. So that Engels won't have to take the long walk to school twice daily, he is provided with lodgings in Elberfeld, at the house of the school's provisional headmaster, Dr. Hantschke, and afterwards in the evangelical hostel run by the same Hantschke. The school, according to Engels, is acknowledged as one of the best in Prussia.

Long before German unification in 1871, its educational system had won widespread admiration throughout Europe, and it was well deserved. The German states enjoyed a level of literacy higher than any other European country at the time and German higher education was the best in the world. During the twenties, when Engels is going to school, there is one child in school for every eight adults in the population, whereas in England it is only 1 to 16 and in France, 1 to 30. Prussia has an illiteracy rate of under 10% - quite phenomenal in Europe at this time.[4] Thus, we can imagine the thorough schooling Engels will be privileged to receive. He has 34-36 lessons in the week, and apart from mathematics, physics, anthropology, biology and geography, the students are offered a broad curriculum in the humanities: Latin, Greek and Hebrew, German, French, religious instruction and history, which includes that of the antique world.

The school in Barmen laid stress on the sciences, here the emphasis is on languages, and Engels is able to demonstrate his real talents. He is clearly a very bright student (although in the first year in Elberfeld his marks are not outstanding) and does well in all subjects, but particularly languages. Here he is not only given a thorough, all-round education, but is also taken beyond the realms of Old Testament creationism that is taught in most schools. His immersion in the works of the Greek philosophers, Latin scholars and the literature of Voltaire, Montesquieu and Molière certainly help broaden his cultural horizons.

His father notes this rapid development of his son's education, with a certain concern, because his own basic schooling, doesn't allow him to keep up. In a letter to his wife in 1835, he writes:

> Friedrich brought home only mediocre marks last week. Outwardly, he is, as you know, better behaved, but despite his earlier strict chastisement, he doesn't seem to learn obedience, even out of fear of punishment. I also had another worry today, when I found in his desk a smutty book from the lending library, a story of chivalry from the thirteenth century. Odd, that he leaves such books in his cupboard without a care. God willing, I hope he keeps his disposition, but I often worry about

> this, otherwise fine, boy.' His father reiterates this concern at the end of the same letter: 'Once again, I hope the loving God will give the boy his protection to ensure his character is not ruined. Up to now he has developed a worrying thoughtlessness and lack of character alongside his otherwise sympathetic attributes.[5]

Do we detect here that his father already senses that his son may not fit in with his plans and slip obediently into the business career mapped out for him? It certainly indicates that Engels is developing an independence of mind and, from his father's point of view, a perhaps too-critical approach to life. Influences from outside the family are having their effect and it is evident that he is slowly drawing away from his father's ideology. His basic character, however, is clearly derived from both his parents: his father's rationality and his mother's jollity. His emerging social conscience also grows out of the family tradition – he often gives his small amounts of pocket money to the poor, as we know from what other family members relate. In Engels' last school report he is characterised as 'a modest, honest and easy-going young man...diligent and keen to gain an all-round education. He is particularly praised for his proficiency in languages'.

For some years his father seems reconciled to his completing the Abitur (German A-level equivalent) and going on to university to read political economy or a similar, applicable discipline. But just nine months before Engels is due to sit his final exams, his father, quite suddenly, determines that he shall leave school and embark on business training straight away. Does he perhaps fear losing his son to the academic world? The decision comes as a stark blow to Engels, who is clearly not interested in a business career, but is drawn to the humanities, philosophy and science and is keen to go to university along with his school friends. He is highly inquisitive and his mental horizons lie far beyond the confines of business. It is impossible for him to argue – a decision taken by the pater familias is binding.

To learn the ropes in his father's business, he is placed, to begin with, in the Barmen headquarters as a junior clerk, where he stays for a year, before being dispatched to Bremen to complete his training. In the Barmen company he shadows his father, picking up the way the business is run. He also enjoys the perk of accompanying his father on business trips to London, Amsterdam and Rotterdam.

These trips, though, hardly compensate for the drudgery in the office, so he bites his tongue and knuckles under, staying with the firm Friedr. Engels & Co. from September 1837 until July 1838.

His father has grandiose plans for a German-English family firm and Engels is being groomed to become the future boss. He is to learn not only general business skills, but study European textile production techniques and marketing. Engels' brother Herman is destined to become the financial wizard, the third son, Emil, is to train as a machine specialist and drive forward the mechanisation of the company. Finally, Rudolf, the youngest, is to become a specialist textile expert, particularly in cottons and silks. The family roles are thus mapped out, the drama written; it only has to be acted out. But Engels isn't keen on his pre-determined role; he lacks the necessary interest and commitment, and he has his own private aspirations.

We have little written evidence from this time about his general views on life, as we do for Karl Marx, or what his private aspirations are. Although very early on he reveals his identification with the goal of German unity and admits to his sister, Marie, that the only colours he likes are 'black, red and gold' [the colours of a German nation not yet born] and quotes a verse from a banned student song extolling freedom. But from the 17 year-old Marx we have a more profound expression of his world view. Still at school, he writes the following in his A-level exam essay on choosing a profession:

> But the chief guide which must direct us in the choice of a profession is the welfare of mankind and our own perfection. It should not be thought that these two interests could be in conflict, that one would have to destroy the other; on the contrary, man's nature is so constituted that he can attain his own perfection only by working for the perfection, for the good, of his fellow men.
>
> If he works only for himself, he may perhaps become a famous man of learning, a great sage, an excellent poet, but he can never be a perfect, truly great man.
>
> History calls those men the greatest who have ennobled themselves by working for the common good; experience acclaims as happiest the man who has made the greatest number of people happy; religion itself teaches us that the ideal being whom all strive to copy sacrificed himself for the sake of mankind, and who would dare to set at nought such judgments?

> If we have chosen the position in life in which we can most of all work for mankind, no burdens can bow us down, because they are sacrifices for the benefit of all; then we shall experience no petty, limited, selfish joy, but our happiness will belong to millions, our deeds will live on quietly but perpetually at work, and over our ashes will be shed the hot tears of noble people.[6]

This view of life reveals not only an incredible maturity, but also an early humanitarian outlook and sense of service to the community. It is perhaps reasonable to assume that Engels was having not dissimilar thoughts. He is certainly unhappy about leaving full-time education to enter business, as the subsequent slaking of his thirst for intellectual stimulation while in Berlin testifies. While his friends go off to university and will be able to study the latest philosophical and historical publications and debate the new ideas in the relaxed atmosphere of their chosen academies, he is to spend his valuable time slaving over an office desk, snatching spare hours to explore these worlds on his own.

He takes to writing poetry and socialising with his former school comrades before they leave for university. He is animated by the Barmen poetry circle which centres around the young free-thinking poet Ferdinand Freiligrath. Freiligrath, also a businessman, later becomes a leading radical, and a close friend of both Marx and Engels. He collaborates with them on the radical *Rheinische Zeitung* and is persecuted and imprisoned by the Prussian state for his revolutionary activities and writings.

Engels, like the young Marx, dreams of becoming a poet and fills at least one exercise book of poems, but after the previous experience of his father going through his desk, this time he keeps them well hidden, at his friend's house. He soon recognises that his poetic talent is not sufficient to win him any laurels. He clearly feels he can only really be himself in these circles with his friends, where they smoke, drink, debate, tell jokes and have a good laugh.

In the thirties, Germany is going through a feverish intellectual period, a confrontation of minds, pro- or anti-authority. The great French revolution of 1789 demonstrated to the ruling elites of Europe that any relaxation of tight control in any area of life could spell another challenge to their power. The Holy Alliance, a coalition of Russia, Austria and Prussia, created in 1815, has managed, with considerable difficulty, to restore the old order, but how long will it hold? The forces of revolution have been subdued, but the fetters on society re-imposed by the old order are being rattled once again. It becomes clear to increasingly broader sections of society that change must come. But those calling for change come largely from among a small elite of well-educated and often privileged middle class individuals, including a significant number of still marginalised Jews.

Germany is not yet a united nation, but a mish-mash of smaller statelets, with Prussia as the dominant one. They are divided by archaic customs barriers, different legal systems and governmental structures, but united by a common language and culture. There is a yearning, particularly among the well-educated younger generation, for a united Germany, but as a democratic republic. For many, particularly those like Engels and his friends, who come from the more liberal, French-influenced, Rhineland, freedom from Prussian dominance is an almost visceral goal. All these ideas, while not yet mainstream, deeply affect the young intellectuals with whom Engels socialises in Barmen. All the other siblings remain firmly in the fold and pursue the sort of lives and careers expected of them by their conservative parents. He is the only one of the family who will reject his bourgeois upbringing and become a socialist.

Flying the nest

In 1838 he is sent to Bremen, in northern Germany, to complete his business training, while almost all his school friends go off to university. There, he is still not allowed to stray from the straight and narrow; his father ensures that he is quartered in the Christian household of Pastor Treviranus. The window of his small room looks out on an alley and late in the evening things get rather noisy, he tells his sister: 'the cats squeal, the dogs bark, the ghosts laugh and howl and rattle the windows of the house opposite'. When he stays up after eleven o'clock, he watches the lamplighter, who also lives in the alley, going on his rounds. In Bremen he is to work as commercial apprentice to the trading company of the Consul Heinrich Leupold, which is involved in the export of German linen to America and the import of coffee and cigars.

He writes many an entertaining letter from Bremen to his former school friends, the brothers, and pastor's sons, Friedrich and Wilhelm Graeber, as well as to his sister, Marie. He is not only unhappy, but also bored, he tells them, although the letters appear to contradict this downbeat assessment and reflect his wide ranging interests and activities. They are also invariably illustrated with his witty thumbnail sketches, caricaturing himself and his friends. To the Graeber brothers he laments:

> If I didn't have this incredibly lively correspondence with all of you in Berlin, Bonn, Barmen and Elberfeld, how would I be able to kill the interminable time that I sit in the office, without being able to read?[7]

However, he takes it all with good humour. In an ironical letter he explains his work thus:

> Do you know what super fine medium blend ordinary Domingo coffee is? That is again one of those profound concepts that one comes across in businessmen's philosophy and that are beyond the reach of your mental capabilities. Super fine medium blend ordinary Domingo coffee is coffee you buy from the island of Haiti, which has a light tinge of green, but is usually grey and in which for every ten good beans, there are four bad ones, six stones and a half ounce of dirt, dust etc.

What he doesn't like doing is having to pack crates of samples for foreign customers:

> Think yourself lucky that you have nothing to do with crates of samples! ...It's madness and first class chaos. You can spend the whole day in the packing sheds next to the open windows, in this cold, just packing linen. That's awful, and it's a total waste of time.[8]

In another letter, he makes no concealment of his fervent republicanism and his disdain of monarchs who 'bathe in the people's blood':

> I expect anything good only of that prince whose ears are boxed right and left by his people and whose palace windows are smashed by the stones flung by the revolution.[9]

It is during his stay in Bremen that he begins his real struggle to be free of religion. His letters to the brothers, Friedrich and Wilhelm

Graeber show this clearly. He now completely rejects orthodox religion, and hates the 'damned tubercular, fireside pietism', he says vehemently in one of his letters. He adopts to begin with a liberal form of supernaturalism, but increasingly tends towards rationalism. He tells his friend Wilhelm Graeber that from now on, he 'can only accept something as Godly if it can be rationally justified'. He cannot reconcile himself to the fact that, as far as he is concerned, the Bible is full of contradictions, which clearly indicates that human beings have co-written it and not the omnipotent hand of God. His period in Berlin the following year will consolidate this trend to secularism and eventually lead him to atheism.

Bremen, of course, is one of the bustling and wealthy Hansa towns, where trade and commerce flourish. It is also, at that time, the port from which most of Germany's poor, destitute and adventurous emigrants sail, many to the New World. He certainly savours the more liberated atmosphere in this city, on the safer side of the black and white frontier posts that denote the Prussian state boundary. With its more liberal censorship and the opportunity of obtaining books banned elsewhere, Bremen offers its young guest untold treasures. As a Hanseatic city, it enjoys the status of an independent state, largely free of Prussian interference. Here Engels utilises this newly discovered freedom to carry out a lively, if non-remunerative, smuggling trade, sending to his friends back home books that are banned there.

He is so frustrated with his daily routine that he turns to literary pursuits to exercise his mind and give him a sense of real purpose. His writing at this time reveals a freshness and a natural facility with language; it is so full of life and strong ideas that he readily finds editors willing to publish what he writes. His first journalistic work is published, under the pseudonym, Friedrich Oswald, in the *Telegraph für Deutschland [Telegraph for Germany]* in 1839, when he is only 19. It is a critical review of a work by the philosopher and publisher of the paper, Karl Gutzkow, but it leads to the publication of further essays, travel reports and poems. He uses the name Oswald to hide his real identity. If potential publishers found out how young he was, it would preclude his having anything else published, and if his family saw his by-line it would have shocked them to see Engels 'demeaning himself' by writing for a newspaper. Gutzkow reports that he has to edit his pieces for the Telegraph, 'taking out the personal comments that were too harsh', but that later Engels refuses to have his pieces tampered with. At this time, he still views aesthetics and style as more important than content or subject matter, but this is slowly changing. He maintains his dreams of perhaps becoming a professional writer and, like Shelley, leading the battle for freedom with his poetry.

He is fascinated by shipping, foreign trade and emigration, and is taken on a guided tour of one of the emigration ships in Bremerhaven. This causes him to reflect on why so many of his fellow Germans are prepared to leave their homeland for the uncertainty of foreign parts. He writes an article about this for the *Morgenblatt für gebildete Leser [Morning Paper for Educated Readers]* and speaks of the uncertain position of the German peasant, trapped between serfdom and independence, the strict laws of inheritance and the fickleness of patrimonial justice. He is also horrified by the third class berths on board, where men, women and children are bedded alongside each other like close-fitting paving stones, the healthy next to the sick. In this, his first article for the *Morgenblatt,* we find Engels already observant and perceptive of social relations.

In July 1839 he is out enjoying himself in a rowing boat on the river during stormy weather and uses this as a metaphor in a poem he writes in celebration of the anniversary of the German July Revolution of 1830. He describes it as 'the most beautiful expression of the people's will since the wars of freedom' against Napoleon, and warns the dukes and kings of Germany of the fate that befell Charles X, the last of the great Bourbon kings of France, who was forced to flee the revolution in 1830 and died in exile. In the poem, his eye sweeps 'with angry courage' over the Hanoverian river bank, where 'the people look up with penetrating eyes and the sword sits uneasily in its scabbard'. He asks the king who has broken his promise of constitutional reform, 'do you sit as secure on your golden throne, as I in my rocking boat?' He is soon arguing that there can be no valid opposing argument to the people being involved in state power, abolishing censorship, doing away with special rights for the aristocracy and for full rights for Jews.

In another letter he writes to the Graeber brothers in Barmen, on 13 November 1839, he castigates them for not writing: 'If you don't write today, I'll mentally castrate you…let me be with your damned Christian sophistry; no, rather a good pagan than a bad Christian'. In the same letter, he then pens a passionate poetic plea for revolutionary action:

> The sentimental little songs go unheard and the resounding hunting horn awaits a hunter to blow the rallying call for a hunt on tyrants, in the tree tops God's storm is roaring and Germany's youth stands ready in the grove, swords clanging, raising their goblets brim-full; from the mountains glimmer the burning castles, the thrones shake, the altars shudder and God calls through the gale and storm, forwards, forwards, who will oppose us?

These are the Shelley-esque and hyperbolic romantic sentiments of youth, but nonetheless stated with conviction. This tone is not exceptional in his letters to the Graeber brothers. He also writes a cycle of poems, 'An Evening', which again show clear resonances of Shelley - a poet he admires tremendously and plans to translate. The poem is also published in the *Telegraph*.

His republican spirit now finds unrestrained expression even in his letters to his sister. When Marie, who is now in a genteel Pensionat [girls' finishing school] in Mannheim, writes to him proudly that she has been presented to the Grand Duchess von Baden, he replies brusquely: 'When you are next introduced to such a Royal Highness, tell me only whether she is pretty or not, I have no other interest in such personalities'.

Although he is very much on his own, belonging to no clearly defined political circle of like-minded young men, and having to hack his own way forward out of the thicket, he is imbibing new ideas like a man with a dreadful thirst and is slowly but surely developing his own unique outlook. He is straining at the traces and complains, in one of his letters, that he spends his time copying correspondence, but not having the time to write anything of his own. He seems to get on well with Heinrich Leupold, his boss, and the latter even allows him to drink beer in the office, but there is no doubt that he is far from behaving like an exemplary trainee. Despite his complaint above, he does manage to make time to write to friends and his sister Marie quite regularly. He even has time to draft literary projects, plans for the future and to doodle cartoon sketches, some of which have survived. On one of them he portrays himself lounging in his hammock, smoking a cigar, in the warehouse attic. As soon as his boss leaves the premises, he retreats to this attic refuge to 'smoke a cigar, to swing in the hammock and sometimes to take a nap'.

He tells his sister, Marie, that 'I continue to practise my singing and composing regularly' and even sends her samples of his compositions. He joins a choir and also goes to concerts and is a great admirer of Beethoven. After one such concert he writes:

> What a symphony [Beethoven's C minor] it was last night! You never heard anything like it in your whole life if you don't know this wonderful work. What despairing discord in the first movement, what elegiac melancholy, what a tender lover's lament in the adagio, what a tremendous, youthful, jubilant celebration of freedom by the trombone in the third and fourth movements![10]

In addition, he also brushes up on his languages, extending his knowledge to Spanish, Portuguese, Italian, Dutch, alongside English and French. In a letter to Marie he brags that he can now converse in 25 languages; certainly, at this time, a wild exaggeration.

In these months in Bremen, he remains as physically active as ever: 'Recently I swam in the Weser River and left the other guys floundering away behind me,' he trumpets to her. 'I managed to cross it four times without pausing, something few in Bremen will be able to imitate.' In winter, when the river is frozen over, he goes ice-skating. In his letters to Marie he invariably portrays himself as the loveable ruffian: 'I've now bought myself a couple of swords and fencing gloves, because I wasn't prepared to fight in my kid gloves'. He also takes dancing lessons to 'allow my stiff legs to learn a little grace', and begins riding, which becomes a life-long passion, galloping off with his friend Roth into the countryside outside the town. He socialises with the other apprentices and office staff, but is clearly far more advanced than most of them in so many ways, including his working knowledge of several languages, but also his wide cultural interests and debating skills.

In October 1840, he reports that he has formed a Bremen moustache club. This is no doubt as a riposte to his landlord, Pastor Treviranus, who comes by one morning and says he looks 'quite revolting' and demands that he shaves. Engels refuses point blank: '...now I shall not shave until I have a moustache as black as a raven', he tells Marie. 'I have sent out a circular to all young men capable of growing a moustache, telling them that it is high time to shock all the Philistines and grow a moustache...everyone who is brave enough to challenge the Philistines and grow a moustache was asked to sign. Soon I had a dozen moustachioed lads in the club.' Facial hair adornment, particularly among younger men, is deemed to be socially egregious, so growing moustaches is a juvenile form of protest against the prevailing conservatism. His father promises him a set of razors, but he will not use them 'out of principle', he says.

A month later, when the moustache club comes together to celebrate its jubilee, Engels finds that some have already been forced by their bosses 'to hack off those criminal appendages...those that arrived without their moustaches were obliged to paint them on.'

After spending a year and half in Bremen, obligatory military service looms before him. All young men have to face this on 1 January of the year in which they reach 20. In his unfinished work on *The Role of Force in History* which he is writing forty years later, he says that 'the wealthy could easily get out of military service', but he refuses to contemplate such a way out. His father is prepared to pull the necessary strings for him, but here, probably for the first time, he puts his foot down and opposes his father. He despises those young men, he says, who 'fear cold water like a rabid dog and see it as a badge of honour to dodge military service.' Engels isn't going to be one of these, and reports punctually to the military conscription office in Barmen. His medical shows him to be healthy and with 'a strong body', making him highly suitable for the artillery. He is also well over the minimum height requirements of five feet, four inches for guardsmen in the artillery (he is in fact six feet – very tall for that time), so that's where he is instructed to report. On the basis of his final, excellent grammar school report, which is deemed the equivalent of a school-leaving certificate, he will only be required to serve one year.

He doesn't, though, have to serve immediately, and in the intervening months, he accompanies his father again on a business trip to England, via Holland, to London, Liverpool and to Manchester where the family firm of Ermen & Engels is based. This is only his second trip to Britain, and he reports it romantically in an essay 'Landscapes' that is published in the *Telegraph für Deutschland:*

> You who complain of the prosaic dullness of railways without ever having seen one should try travelling on the one from London to Liverpool. If ever a land was made to be traversed by railways it is England. No dazzlingly beautiful scenery, no colossal mountain masses, but a land of soft rolling hills which

> has a wonderful charm in the English sunlight, which is never quite clear. It is surprising how various are the groupings of the simple figures; out of a few low hills, a field, some trees and grazing cattle, nature composes a thousand pleasant landscapes. The trees, which occur singly or in groups in all the fields, have a singular beauty that makes the whole neighbourhood resemble a park. Then comes a tunnel, and for a few minutes the train is in darkness, entering into a deep cutting from which one is suddenly transported again into the midst of smiling, sunny fields.
>
> At another time the railway track is laid on a viaduct traversing a long valley; far below it lie towns and villages, woods and meadows, between which a river takes its meandering course; to the right and left are mountains which fade into the background, and the valley is bathed in a magical light, half-mist and half-sunshine. But you have hardly had time to survey the wonderful scene before you are carried away into a bare cutting and have time to recreate the magical picture in your imagination. And so it goes on until night falls and your wearied eyes close in slumber.
>
> Oh, there is rich poetry in the counties of Britain! It often seems as if one were still in the golden days of merry England and might see Shakespeare with his fowling-piece moving stealthily behind a hedge on a deer-poaching expedition, or you might wonder why one of his divine comedies is not actually taking place on this green meadow. For wherever the scenes are supposed to occur, in Italy, France or Navarra, his baroque, uncouth rustics, his too-clever schoolmasters, and his deliciously bizarre women, all belong basically to merry England and it is remarkable that only an English sky is suited to everything that takes place. Only some of the comedies, such as A Midsummer Night's Dream, are as completely adapted to a southern climate as Romeo and Juliet, even in the characters of the play.[11]

In May, he accompanies his father again on a business trip to Italy. This second long business trip is certainly not for relaxation and rest, though such an impression might be adduced from his essay 'Lombardian impressions' published in the Young Hegelian magazine, *Athenäum*. He and his father travel by post-chaise to the main centres of silk and cotton production in Switzerland, Lombardy and Milan, then one of Europe's biggest silk markets. This certainly gives Engels an overview of the textile trade on a European level.

The odd thing about this young trainee is that alongside his training, he is equally diligent as a journalist, a poet, essayist and literary critic. He does all this not, of course, under his own name, but under the already established pseudonym Friedrich Oswald. Oswald's writing can be read regularly in some of Germany's most prestigious newspapers, including the famous *Augsburg Allgemeine Zeitung* alongside such luminaries as Heinrich Heine and Alexander von Humboldt.

We know little detail of the sort of intellectual life Engels experiences in Bremen, but in a letter to friends before he leaves, he says, contradicting his earlier remarks: 'Here I've been able to read a great deal, particularly the sort of literature that you'd never be allowed to publish here, totally liberal ideas etc., critiques of the old Hanoverian Billy-goat [Ernst August, King of Hanover]'. It is very likely that he has already come across the revolutionary writings of his contemporary and Rhineland compatriot, Georg Büchner. The latter had been influenced by the utopian communist theories of Francois-Noël Babeuf and Claude Henri de Saint-Simon (1813-37). There is no evidence that the two men ever met, but it would not have been surprising given their common geographical and political affinities. While Büchner was completing his studies in Giessen he established a secret society dedicated to revolution. With the help of the evangelical theologian Friedrich Weidig he published a pamphlet 'Der Hessische Landbote', a revolutionary tract attacking social injustice in the Grand Duchy of Hesse. For this, he and Weidig are charged with treason. Weidig is arrested, tortured and dies in prison in Darmstadt; Büchner is able to flee across the border to Strasbourg, but dies of typhoid at the age of only 23.

Engels has also used his spare time to deepen his knowledge of languages, history and philosophy. He also has his first book published, by Brockhaus & Avenarius, in Leipzig and Paris: *Das Leben, Charakter und Philosophie des Horaz. Ein Dialog [The Life, Character and Philosophy of Horace – a Dialogue]*. His first published poem, 'The Beduinen' [The Bedouins 1838], had already been printed in the *Bremische Conversationsblatt [Bremen Conversational Paper]*. His keen interest in writing and in journalism has clearly been well established, although he is still only 20 years of age.

At the end of March 1841, he concludes his training with Heinrich Leupold in Bremen, and bids farewell to the town in a manner that lends credence to his 'ruffian' image, with two duels, as related in a letter to his friend, Friedrich Graeber:

> I am now fencing furiously and will soon hack you all to pieces. I have had two duels here in the last four weeks. The first fellow has retracted the insulting words of 'stupid boy' which he said to me after I gave him a box on the ear, and the slap is still unexpiated. I fought with the second fellow yesterday and gave him a real beauty above the brow, running right down from the top, a really first-class prime.[12]

He has not only made enemies, but also a number of friends during his stay and has enjoyed a rather relaxed life, although it hasn't provided him with the intellectual stimulus he so desperately seeks. He tells his sister in March, shortly before his departure: 'I thank God that I can now leave this tedious nest, in which you can only fence, eat, drink, sleep and slog – voilà tout'. He yearns for the time to be able to study fulltime and not have to waste it anymore in the soul-destroying routines of business. He hopes that after completing his year's military service, his father will then let him go to university.

CHAPTER TWO (1841-1842)

Soldiering for the King

Towards the end of September 1841 Engels takes the post-chaise to Berlin to undertake his obligatory military service as a dutiful Prussian citizen, and reports for duty on 1 October. In the previous weeks he has been dreading the ordeal of wasted hours marching up and down Berlin's wide avenues, but this dread is compensated by the thought that he'll be able to take advantage of the intellectual opportunities in the Prussian capital.

Of a thousand conscripts only 25 are 'one-year men', like Engels. In the regulations it states that the one-year men are permitted to undertake activities 'in furtherance of their careers, in so far as they do not conflict with the needs of the service'. He is excited about the prospect of being able to attend lectures at Berlin's Friedrich Wilhelm's University (today the Humboldt University). At this time the university is a renowned centre of struggle between the different philosophical schools and an exciting focus of debate on existential questions.

On arrival he is met by his friends, Friedrich Plümacher and Gustav Feldmann, with whom he has corresponded during his time in Bremen, and they will introduce him to Berlin city life and culture. He is here at a crucial time. The year 1841 is one of the most exciting for a long time - a stormy revolutionary process is taking place within Prussian philosophical radicalism. In Germany such philosophical debates are the equivalent of torrid party political feuds in other countries, like Britain. This one heralds a conflict the like of which Germany has not seen since Luther nailed his theses to Wittenberg's cathedral portal and ushered in the Reformation in 1517.

To begin with Engels is quartered in the barracks on the Kupfergraben, only a short walk from the university – the citadel of Berlin's intellectual life. When he enters its lofty portals for the first time, he feels a deep sense of humility and privilege to be able to sit in its hallowed auditorium among the full-time students. Now is his opportunity to test his hard-earned auto-didactic learning and supplement his ideas.

During this year, despite the intellectual rewards, he never warms to this most Prussian of all cities, with its monumental, neo-classical buildings, its wide avenues, exercise squares and military aura. In later life he will say that whenever he hears the name 'Berlin' he again feels sand between his toes: 'the poetry of nature is missing: sand, sand, sand!!' This refers to the fact that Berlin was built in a glaciated basin, ringed by shallow lakes and with an extremely sandy soil, which, when whipped up by the winds, penetrates every crevice and crack.

It is not only the sand that irritates him in Berlin, but also its gritty citizens. They are a little like the proverbial Cockneys, with sharp and witty tongues, but also a down-to-earth vulgarity. Whenever he hears a Berlin dialect being spoken, he says, he hears the 'snotty bark of my Prussian lieutenant in my ear'. The Berlin cuisine, too, offers no prandial recompense. He consumes it largely in the barracks, and it is, for him, the epitome of poverty and lacking in imagination. In 1888 during his journey to America on the steamship, *City of Berlin,* he will tell Eduard Bernstein that: 'Berlin has never seemed so beautiful to me as on this *City of Berlin*'!

As a one-year conscript, he is obliged to pay for his own uniform, his upkeep and that of his service horse. However, his father has agreed to cover all the costs of his conscription year in Berlin. To begin with he resists moving into private lodgings, but he finds the military routine and privations in the barracks incredibly tedious and they circumscribe his freedom to follow more worthwhile pursuits. Although he can lodge there for free, with cheques from home, arriving regularly and punctually, he is soon able to move out and find more comfortable private lodgings in Dorotheen Strasse. He also takes advantage of other special privileges enjoyed by one-year conscripts, which include the services of a young batman, as well as special leave and the right to continue with his studies. He clearly has time, too, to visit the theatre, the opera and concerts. At a recital by Franz Lizst, he is particularly moved by the pianist's demonic and expressive playing and includes a sketch of him in one of his letters home.

It takes him a full three months to settle down in the city, before he feels in the mood to write his first letter home. Of course, much of his time is taken up with parading back and forth in the exercise yards and often in front of the king. 'I really can't do any more of this damned marching up and down the Schlossplatz (Palace Square),' he writes to his sister. (He would, no doubt, have chuckled at the irony of it being renamed 'Marx-Engels Platz' by the post war socialist government of the German Democratic Republic).

So, from October 1841 until 30 September 1842, like a reluctant peacock, he has to parade in the plumage of the Prussian king. He describes for his sister Marie his new blue uniform with its black collar, decorated with two yellow stripes, red reversed-out coat tails and epaulettes ribbed with white. 'I can tell you,' he says, 'it makes me feel really pompous – I could be put on an exhibition stand. Recently I totally disconcerted the poet Rückert [whose poetry was given world renown in Schubert's and Mahler's song versions], who is here at the moment and I really annoyed him. I sat right at the front when he gave a reading here and the poor fellow could only concentrate on my burnished buttons and was really thrown'. Very soon, though, Engels becomes a bombardier and is obliged to wear a new uniform with gold braid and a blue collar with red piping. He again continues to upbraid his sister for her obsequiousness to the aristocracy (she had begged him to tell her if he had already been introduced to the king): 'what are you chattering in your letter about "Old Fritz" [the Prussian king] and young "Fritzchen Wilmchen" [the king's son]? You women should not get involved in politics about which you understand nothing'.

Towards the end of his year, Engels also has the companionship of a dog. 'It's a handsome young spaniel…and quite crazy,' he writes to his sister, Marie. 'He has a great talent for boozing and if I go to a restaurant in the evening, he always sits near me and has his share, or makes himself at home at everybody else's table…He is an excellent swimmer but too crazy to learn any tricks. I have taught him one thing. When I say "Namenloser" [Nameless] (that's his name) "there's an aristocrat!" he goes wild with rage and growls hideously at the person I show him.[13]

Despite finding the chores of conscript life difficult to bear, Engels accepts them with stoicism, utilising the opportunity to pick up important military knowledge, which he later exploits in his acclaimed articles on military tactics and strategy as well as in his temporary career, in 1848, as a revolutionary soldier. In this pursuit he is undoubtedly encouraged by his Company Commander, Herr von Wedell, of whom Engels retains fond memories, and later refers to him as 'my old captain'. He is given a thorough grounding in artillery techniques, particularly at the hands of First Lieutenant von Platen and Second Lieutenant Schmidt. This training is utilised fifteen years later when he writes on military equipment and tactics for the *New American Encyclopaedia*, which in terms of military knowledge at the time is highly competent.

Engels hates all the rigorous and pointless exercising, even though he is spared the worst of it. He speaks of the big 'Wart Feld' exercise square as a place, 'where you sink up to your knees in sand and it has the peculiar property of being electric. When the Twelfth Infantry Household Artillery, to which I belong, arrives there, and is negatively charged, the positive and negative electricity clashes and creates mayhem and chaos in the air, attracting all the clouds. Otherwise,' he moans, 'how can I explain that it always rains or snows when our company is on the square?'

Alongside his square-bashing, which leaves him little time during the day for other pursuits, he certainly makes full use of his evenings off after the strenuous daily training, to slip into lectures at the university. In 1842 he writes:

> The most important aspect of Berlin and what differentiates the Prussian capital from other cities, is its university. I don't mean the imposing facades on the Opera Square, not the Anatomy and Mineralogy Museum, but the numerous lecture halls with their erudite and pedantic professors, witty and serious students, young and old with moss-encrusted academic heads... [He goes on to bemoan the apathy he perceives at other German universities, but praises Berlin as a counterpoint] ...Berlin boasts representatives of all points of view among its academic staff and thus makes a lively polemic possible and provides the student with an illuminating and clear overview of contemporary tendencies.[14]

Despite being a member of his majesty's armed forces, Engels throws himself into the intellectual maelstrom of university life, and is particularly excited by the ideas of Hegel, which he sees as a direct challenge to the old order. He attends lectures whenever he can get away from his eternal parading, although not legitimately as he is not a registered student, but an interloper. And, if he can't attend certain lectures that interest him, he borrows other students' notes. We know, for instance, from the Young Hegelian and later philosophical historian, Kuno Fischer, that in writing his polemical pamphlet against Schelling's revelational philosophy, Engels uses the notes of fellow students.

Schelling was parachuted into his professorial post in Berlin by the Prussian king, largely in order to combat the 'dangerous militancy' of the followers of Hegel. He was a renowned conservative, promoting a mystical, classically-based philosophy that provided an intellectual bolster for the reactionaries of the Prussian state. This infuriates the followers of Hegel. Engels is so incensed that he writes a furious rebuttal of Schelling's ideas.

We do know about some of the lectures Engels attends, but little about who he meets and what he learns at the university. From the letters he writes to his sister we glean scant information in this direction. They are couched in big brother bravado and at a level he deems suitable for her; of his own inner thoughts, political ideas and turmoil he reveals little. We do know, though, that his main interest is in the great philosophical debates of the time and he attends those lectures which feed into that interest. Among the students who would have sat alongside him at the time are Søren Kierkegaard, Jacob Burckhardt and Mikhail Bakunin, as well as several other Russian revolutionaries, although it is unknown whether he gets to know any of them or has any contact at all. Marx, who studied philosophy at the university from 1836-41, left the city only a few months before Engels' arrival.

Prussia at this time is a virtual police state. Political parties are still forbidden and secret agents are everywhere sniffing for any signs of dissidence and rebellion. Despite the philosophical debates at the university, Berlin, too, is characterised by this stifling atmosphere. It is an affront to any free-thinking young man or woman, and Engels feels this acutely. One way of attempting to get around the bans and censorship is for like-minded individuals to form or join literary, philosophical or musical circles, where a relatively relaxed atmosphere allows heretical ideas to be aired. As public political debate and opposition to the powers that be are out of the question, such issues can only be raised publicly under the guise of philosophical positioning. The rulers only fear ideas when 'they grip the masses' as Marx later phrases it; as long as they are confined to small, ineffective groups of students and professors, they are largely tolerated. Thus, various groups rallied around leading academic or intellectual figures. Engels and other young radicals are particularly attracted to the ideas of Georg Hegel, the foremost German idealist philosopher. Although he had died ten years earlier, his ideas are still resonating strongly in 1841, particularly in Berlin among the young intellectuals seeking alternatives to the rigid irrationality of the Prussian state and perhaps sensing the underlying seismic rumblings among the people.

In his student days, Hegel had been an avid supporter of the French Revolution, but in his mature years, as professor and rector of the university in Berlin, he became an upholder of the constitutional Prussian monarchy. For him, the French Revolution was significant because it introduced the concept of individual political freedom into European societies for the first time in recorded history, even though it later descended into terror. Hegel's remarks on the French revolution led the poet Heinrich Heine to call him 'The Orléans of German Philosophy'.[15]

Although Hegel's philosophy is considered one of the most complex of all philosophies, this apparently proved no barrier to the young Engels. Hegel's goal was to provide an all-encompassing, systematic theory of the universe. The revolutionary in his philosophy was his method of thinking: his use of the dialectic. The concept of dialectics (first developed by the ancient Greeks) was elaborated by Hegel, whose dynamic model of nature and history gave it a new lease of life. 'To properly comprehend and perceive the dialectical is of absolute importance. It is, in essence, the principle of all movement, all life and all activity in reality,' he said. It is undoubtedly this holistic approach and the revolutionary use of the dialectical method which most inspire Engels. Hegel believed that his method could be applied to explain and systematize the whole universe. For him the dialectic was a manifestation of what he termed the 'Weltgeist' (world spirit). He believed that human reason, the human mind, was a manifestation of God, but his God had little in common with the God of the Christian tradition.

Using the dialectical method, he formulated a theory which propounded general laws of development in nature, society and thought. He maintained that historical conditions are only transitory stages in social development, from a lower to a higher form of civilisation; what today has a justified existence, tomorrow will die and be replaced by something new. The dialectical method as a general developmental theory meant that there were no fixities, no absolute truths. And it is this idea that gave his philosophy such an explosive resonance. Society, in his view, was not something fixed, but the transient result of an ongoing conflict between opposing or contradictory forces. Hegel argued that the state must always be rational, and at the time it is this concept particularly that attracts the revolutionary students who are daily confronted by the perceived irrationality of the Prussian state and society in general.

However, Hegel's philosophy contained a central contradiction. He considered that the basis for all reality lay in the development of ideas, culminating in the 'absolute idea', which would find its expression precisely in the establishment of a reforming Prussian state. He viewed the evolution of nature, humankind and social relations as based in the development of ideas. The intellect develops and in an irreversible process drives history forwards. Marx and Engels are, later, to turn Hegel upside down and put him 'from standing on his head, firmly back on his feet', as they expressed it. Contrary to Hegel, they will maintain that ideas arise out of material being and that consciousness is simply an expression of a particularly highly developed form of material - the human brain, an interpretation first made by Ludwig Feuerbach.

Hegel argued that in the objective world, as in the mind, dialectical conflict or contradiction would eventually lead to a state of absolute perfection; each new synthesis approaches and eventually culminates in the fulfillment of divine will. For Marx and Engels, on the other hand, each new synthesis inevitably approaches and eventually culminates in the utopian goal of Communism, where conflict (class struggle) will be resolved. Marx and Engels believed that the dialectic worked not because of divine will represented in human reason, but that it was firmly based in the natural struggles taking place in the material world.

This central contradiction in Hegel's philosophy, mentioned above, leads directly to the establishment of two groups of Hegelians – the revolutionary Young Hegelians, to which Marx and Engels belong, and the conservative, Old, or Right, Hegelians. The former place emphasis on the dialectical method and see Hegel's philosophy as implicitly anti-feudal and anti-religious; while the Old Hegelians use his philosophy to justify the Prussian state as the realisation of the 'absolute idea'; they advocate a Protestant orthodoxy and the political conservatism of the post-Napoleonic restoration period.

Hegel's influence was immense both within philosophy and in the sciences. Throughout the 19th century many chairs of philosophy around Europe were held by Hegelians. He was particularly influential on the work of Ludwig Feuerbach, another key philosophical source for Marx and Engels, but also on the existential philosophers, Kierkegaard and, in the 20th century, on Jean-Paul Sartre. By the 1850s, after less than a generation, Hegel's philosophy will be suppressed and even banned by the Prussian autocrats. His philosophy amounted to a direct challenge to the fixities of both entrenched religion and the Prussian monarchy. By emphasising the primacy of reason and underlining the dynamics of change through dialectical processes, he implicitly undermined the ideological foundations of the traditional hierarchies.

Today, Hegel is probably more significant historically for what his ideas achieved politically, through the interpretations of others, than philosophically. He provided a new generation with an arsenal of ideas with which to do battle. The Young Hegelians embraced his ideas, but divested them of their Prussian accoutrements. They also saw themselves as the successors of the French Encyclopaedists, followers of the leading Enlightenment figures, Voltaire and Diderot.

It is Karl Friedrich Werder who probably first introduces Engels to Hegelian philosophy. Werder's lectures are very popular and provoke keen debates among the students, and it is Werder who opens the attack in 1841 on Friedrich Wilhelm Schelling who had been given a professorship at the university by the Prussian king. Engels throws himself into the stormy debate between the pro- and anti-Hegelians and, after hearing the inaugural lecture by Schelling, the chief critic of Hegel's thought, he immediately writes two brochures, published anonymously, and an article for the *Telegraph*, in which he sets out his arguments against the 'dead' Schelling and for the 'living' Hegel. These find significant resonance in liberal circles. Arnold Ruge, a leading Young Hegelian, says of them, that 'this engaging, personable young man has overtaken all the old donkeys in Berlin'. He praises the liveliness and clarity of his brochures, but remarks tellingly that the writing is a characteristic product of youth, as revealed in its rich metaphorical prose. He actually thought at the time that the attack was the work of Bakunin.

It is astounding that a youngster who hasn't even completed his secondary schooling, has never attended university before, has the temerity to challenge the leading philosophical representative of the conservatives in this citadel of intellectualism, in such a public fashion and with such panache. In concluding his polemic, Engels describes how thrilling he finds this newly discovered truth; it has opened up a completely new mental world for him. His writings at this time also clearly reveal the influence of the German materialist philosopher, Ludwig Feuerbach.

Engels waxes lyrically about the new life he envisions:

> The world that was so foreign to us and nature, whose hidden powers frightened us like spooks, are now related to us and have become something natural. The world that we all felt was a prison, now reveals itself in its true form, as a wonderful kingly palace, in which we can all enter and leave, poor and rich, the high and low.[16]

With the publication of these two brochures, Engels has conclusively broken the thread that still bound him to the beliefs of his youth and his family. He is also no longer content with the contemplative constructions adopted by many of his fellow Young Hegelians. He has now become an avowed revolutionary, seeking to link philosophy with surrounding social reality.

In later years, he writes in Robert Owen's *The New Moral World* that Professor Ruge was one of the first to characterise the Young Hegelians as atheists (thus taking Hegel's thinking a step further than the man himself had dared). It is the Young Hegelians who imbue Hegelism with more humanity; they are attemping to transform a rather difficult, formalised and abstract philosophy into a world-changing one. In a satirical poem he writes together with Edgar Bauer, attacking the religious fundamentalists, he provides an uncompromising sketch of himself:

> ...That tall and long-legged stepper
> Is Oswald, coat of grey and trousers shade of pepper;
> Pepper inside as well, Oswald the Montagnard;
> A radical is he, dyed in the wool, and hard.
> Day in, day out, he plays upon the guillotine a

Single solitary tune and that's a cavatina
The same old devil-song; he bellows the refrain:
Formez vos batallions! Aux armes citoyens!

In this same poem, he also refers to Marx and, although he hasn't met him at this time, he clearly admires his stance :

A swarthy chap from Trier, a marked monstrosity.
He neither hops nor skips, but moves in leaps and bounds
Raving aloud. As if to seize and then pull down
To earth the spacious tent of Heaven up on high,
He opens wide his arms and reaches for the sky.[17]

He has won his own liberation victory over old ideas and feelings, thanks overwhelmingly to Hegel, but also to Feuerbach. During the second half of 1841 he has been avidly studying the latter's *Essence of Christianity*. This new found sense of purpose and joy at being at the centre of such a profound philosophical debate is supremely palpable. His years of isolation, of mole-like digging for knowledge have now been left behind. However, Marxist philosophy, as propounded by Marx and Engels from the 1840s onwards, will be based firmly in Hegel's philosophy that influenced them both separately in Berlin. They adopt Hegel's system of dialectics but, reject its idealistic base, substituting materialism in its stead.

With his fellow 'Freier', the Free Ones, those radical students and intellectuals who are calling for a new Germany, he celebrates this new-found optimism in typically student fashion. In the coffee houses and drinking dens of Berlin he and his friends debate, carouse and drink heartily to the new dawn. Words alone are not enough anymore, they jump on the tables and, with youthful fervour, demand immediate action.

In 1842 the reactionary Prussian government drives the revolutionary academic and Hegelian, Hugo Bauer, a close friend of Marx, from Bonn University, under the guise of defending Christian values. In Prussia, such action against a tenured academic is unprecedented. It provokes outrage among the young intellectuals. At the same time Engels is a close friend of Hugo's brother, Edgar, who is also in Berlin. Together with Edgar Bauer[18] and under his pseudonym Oswald, he writes a poetic skit on the whole affair, called 'The

Atheist Troop'. In this work they reject what they see as eternal and pointless debate and demand action. The poem is published in 1842, and is deemed so significant that several papers reprint it. Engels is undoubtedly already on the radical wing of the group, but is very soon to outgrow the views of his student friends.

It is around this time, too, that Engels starts writing for the radical *Rheinische Zeitung,* based in Cologne. Although a provincial newspaper, it has a readership and significance beyond the Rhineland, soon becoming the leading oppositional journal in Germany. Its radical iconoclasm and mocking of all things petty bourgeois lend it a high profile reputation among radical intellectuals. The correspondence from Berlin comes almost exclusively from the Young Hegelians who see the *Rheinische Zeitung* as 'their paper', and they literally bombard the editors with their articles. Under the editorship of Moses Hess, later widely acknowledged as the 'father of German socialism', it is increasingly taking up a socialist position and distancing itself ideologically from the ideas of the Young Hegelians.

Once Engels completes his year's service as a bombardier in Berlin, his company commander writes that he has left a good impression both 'in his personal behaviour, as well as in his military performance'. At the beginning of October 1842 he leaves his unit and the circle of the 'Freien' in which he's enjoyed many a jovial hour and a great deal of intellectual stimulus, to embark on a very different life both personally and politically.

Once he has received his demob certificate, he leaves Berlin without delay. On his way back to Barmen, he stops off in Cologne to see Rave, Hess and Rutenberg, the editors of the *Rheinische Zeitung,* most probably in the hope of establishing a post as permanent correspondent for the paper. At this time Marx is not in Cologne; he begins work there as political editor on the paper a short time later, so the two men again just miss meeting each other. Moses Hess is the paper's editor-in-chief, and he appears to be impressed by the political maturity of the young Engels with whom he holds detailed discussions on a whole range of contemporary matters. These talks represent, in terms of Engels' intellectual development, a clear break from the student climate in Berlin.

He is an 'anno 1 revolutionary and he left me as the most avid of communists,' writes Moses Hess, editor at the *Rheinische Zeitung,* glowingly to his friend Berthold Auerbach after Engels' visit to the paper's editorial office. Of course, Hess flatters himself in thinking it is he alone who has turned Engels into a communist, but undoubtedly his articles on communism in the *Rheinische Zeitung* have influenced the young man considerably. Hess's account of their meeting also no doubt facilitates the first meeting between Engels and Marx in November. Later, in 1843, Engels does give Hess the credit for first introducing him and his circle to communism.

Hess is the first to suggest publicly that socialism has to be the real goal of any meaningful revolutionary movement. He comes to this conclusion, though, from a different path to the Hegelians. He feels it is time to transfer the new won freedoms in science and theory into reality. He is also the first to point out that an idealistic philosophy even on the part of its most advanced adherents is always going to lag behind real life and only in communism can society find its logical goal.

Clearly Engels' family will by now have got wind of his increasing political radicalism, and it is likely that his father is keen to remove him from the 'dangerous' influences now spreading through Germany. To send him to work in the jointly-owned company in Manchester would seem the most logical step, as he will be able to keep an eye on the firm in the family's interest and will be out of reach, they imagine, of his radical and iconoclastic comrades.

From family members we do know that Engels sr. had awaited his son's return from Berlin with impatience. He wants him urgently to study the more advanced 'English commercial methods', in order to introduce them speedily to the factory in Engelskirchen. Thus, it is decided to install him in Manchester as 'General Assistant', a higher status position than he has occupied up to now. This will also mean that he won't be completely tied to the office as he was in Bremen, so the idea does have its attractions for him.

The autumn of 1842, in Barmen, sees Engels busilly preparing for his departure to Manchester to complete his business training. Whether he thinks of other career possibilities, we don't have any firm evidence, but it is highly probable that he has. The idea of spending a year or two in England and being able to study the country and its people is no doubt a seductive interim proposition to the 22 year old. He views it as an opportunity to continue his political activities at arm's length from the family. Of course, it also conveniently postpones the difficulty of having to find his own means of subsistence.

He departs towards the end of November 1842, and travels with great expectations, because it is in England that he expects, from what he has heard and read, the industrial working class movement to be much more advanced than it is in either Germany or France. He feels his own country is in 'a condition of archaic apathy, and is still in its social infancy, is not even a proper society, there's no life, no consciousness, no action!' From this point of view alone, he looks forward to his English sojourn and to be able to immerse himself in a more promising political situation.

On his way to the 'sceptered isle' he again stops over at the *Rheinische Zeitung* in Cologne and offers to become its English correspondent. He arrives at a critical moment, when the paper is about to break completely with the Young Hegelians in Berlin, because the paper, under Hess's and now Marx's influence, has moved on politically and views the group as mired in outdated philosophic attitudes. The Young Hegelians are largely concerned with ideas in themselves, whereas Marx, Hess and their supporters are concerned about changing society in a socialist direction. They intend to make the paper more a forum for political discussion and action than for abstract philosophising.

It is at this crucial juncture that Marx and Engels meet for the first time, albeit fleetingly. Marx is only two and half years older than Engels and also from the Rhineland, the son of a Jewish lawyer who converted to Protestantism. He is cultured and liberal in outlook.

Engels, tall, with military bearing and challenging clear blue eyes stands for the first time before the raven-haired, swarthy and stockier Marx, whose ebony eyes spark dangerously like lit coals. Apart from their beards, they have little in common physically, and Marx is in little doubt that they don't in terms of their ideas either. Although Engels admires Marx, the latter views him suspiciously, despite Hess's praise, imagining him still as a died-in-the-wool Young Hegelian and a representative of that chattering clique of Berlin students. This cool, if not frosty, reception brings the two men no closer together.

CHAPTER THREE (1842 – 1845)

Love in the satanic mills

The period between 1815 and 1848, before Engels arrives in Britain, was one of unprecedented social change and upheaval in the country, particularly in the towns, accompanied by widespread and popular unrest. When the young Victoria was crowned in 1837 most of her subjects still lived in the countryside, but by the close of the century 80 percent will be living in towns.

The great international economic slump of 1837-42 had brought hunger and mass unemployment to the industrial areas. Various reasons have been given for the slump: the incurrence of large state debts due to the construction of canals and railroads; expansion of credit; unfavourable trade balances and a frenzy of land speculation, in the USA particularly. The 1837 panic lasted four years, and in this period many a fortune was made and lost. Against this background, strikes and agitation against the draconian Poor Law, for the introduction of a ten hour day, for parliamentary reform and trade union rights were spreading. Those with their fingers on the pulse felt that the country really was on the brink of revolution.

The Chartist movement, the largest democratic mobilisation of working people Europe had ever seen, was galvanising the nation. Its success was made possible by the dense concentrations of industrial workers in the big urban centres which facilitated organisation, solidarity and rapid communications. The seeds of this movement were sown only six years before Engels comes to Manchester.

It was the realisation by leading radicals that little headway would be made on essential reform without some form of unity and national campaign that led to the birth of Chartism. Parliament was corrupt, the majority of the population had no vote and electoral boundaries were outdated and took no account of the massive growth of urban populations. In 1836 James Lovett and his comrades in the small London Working Men's Association (LWMA) met to formulate a list of national demands, around which a campaign for democratic rights could be launched. Several 'missionaries' from the LWMA then toured the country during 1837 and, after holding meetings in public houses and halls, managed to establish more than 100 local WMAs in the larger towns. New radical papers were also launched, above all the *Northern Star*, to spread information about the campaign.

Already strikes, mass agitation and demonstrations, sometimes violent, had broken out in all the big industrial towns, like Birmingham, Newcastle, Glasgow and Manchester. Working people were growing impatient for change. In early 1837 a meeting was called, which formulated a petition in the form of a six point Charter of demands, around which the movement could rally and campaign. The six demands laid out in the Charter were for: Equal electoral districts; the abolition of property qualifications for MPs; universal manhood suffrage; vote by ballot; payment of MPs and annual parliaments. These six points were not so much an end in themselves as the key to the ushering in of a new era, a source of hope for radical change and betterment. They were embraced avidly by the industrial workers who saw in them the political means of solving their own economic grievances; the Charter was taken to heart by the mass of working people like nothing before.

Chartism was hardly a clear-headed and united organisation and was often confused about where it wanted to go, but by 1838 it had come to represent working people as an independent force, whereas on the continent the industrial workers were still holding on to the 'tail of the bourgeoisie'. It brought three separate strands of agitation together: the anti-Poor Law movement, the London Working Men's Association and the Birmingham-based Political Unions, which had campaigned actively for political reform up until the passing of the Reform Act of 1832. The government and ruling circles were increasingly worried about the revolutionary potential of the movement and there were underground mutterings of armed uprising. So, in near panic, the government struck first, banning meetings and arresting leading Chartist figures, leading to bloody clashes between police and demonstrators in several big cities. It was, after all, only 49 years since the French Revolution had sent terrifying shudders through the elites of Europe, and the government was well aware that radicalism and rebellion could rapidly sweep through the urban slums like flames through a timber yard if left uncontrolled.

Chartism would not have experienced such a rapid rise had it not been built on previous civil rights struggles and consciousness. Tom Paine's *Rights of Man*, published in 1791 had become deeply embedded in the consciousness of all those concerned with liberty, and was a blueprint for republicans and those demanding justice in following decades. This, in its turn, had its roots in the ferment of the English Revolution which had overthrown the monarchy and unleashed a wide-ranging debate on social justice and democracy, expressed particularly radically by the demands of the Levellers and Diggers, rank-and-file groups from Cromwell's New Model Army.

The Corresponding Act forbade the creation of national political or union organisations with local branches, so organising around the Charter was difficult. The Chartist press helped fill the breach as organising focus and fount of information, promoting unity and helping to bind the movement nationally. The *Northern Star*, the paper for which Engels is later to write, had a circulation of almost 11,000 in 1838, rising to 48,000 by the spring of 1839.

In 1839 the first Chartist Convention was held. It comprised delegates sent from various parts of the country and followed a series of speech-making tours by the LWMA and leaders of the revived Political Unions. The aim of the Convention was to organise support for the national Petition and see it safely through parliament.

The rapid growth of the Chartist movement represented a widespread and rising consciousness of rights that were being denied and of the need to organise to obtain them. Although it was led, in the main, by middle class radicals, its adherents were largely made up of ordinary workers. What gave the Chartist movement its strength, was that it managed to draw together the different strands of struggle: those campaigning for parliamentary reform, for better working conditions, union rights or the right to vote. It united working people in a way no movement before had been able to do.

Conditions in Britain during the late thirties and early forties were the worst for generations, with widespread unemployment – it was the longest and deepest crisis of British capitalism. The international economic downturn had hit manufacturing industry particularly severely. The depth of this crisis and its impact on working people was clearly reflected in the death rate. From its high peak of over 33 per 1,000 around 1730 it had fallen steadily, but by 1840 had risen once again to almost 21 per 1,000. The situation led to intensified agitation on the part of those organisations concerned with social welfare and rights for working people.

As the campaign gathered strength, but without tangible results, the demands grew, particularly among the miners, for armed insurrections. In Newcastle ironworkers were already forging weapons and in Leeds there was talk of procuring arms.

Because of the enormous size of the movement and the widespread support it had won by 1838 victory seemed close and many believed the Charter would be won in a few months or, at most, years. In its support there were gatherings of a size not seen in Britain before. A large meeting in Glasgow in 1838 was followed by one of 80,000 in Newcastle, 100,000 in Bradford and 200,000 in Birmingham, but the most impressive was the rally in Manchester where, it is estimated, up to 250,000 attended. The latter was almost certainly the largest political rally ever held in the country. The Chartist movement was the first to utilise the new weapon of large-scale political demonstration and assembly, with banners and placards.

As the time approached for the presentation of the first petition to parliament, the mood hardened on both sides. Arguments raged between those insisting on peaceful and legal means and those who said the movement should be prepared to use force if the petition were ignored. The government, of course, was not watching idly as this movement mushroomed and became increasingly radical in its demands; they were frightened and spurred to take more drastic action, realising that previous measures had not been enough. Troops were despatched to the big industrial areas; a proclamation was made declaring the carrying of arms illegal and preparations were made to enrol special constables from the moneyed classes. Again, arrests were made of Chartist leaders. Parliament, predictably, rejected the petition on 12 July 1839 and this provoked angry riots in Birmingham and other big cities.

The Combination Acts of 1799 and 1800 were still in force and these prohibited the formation of trade unions in all industries, although many illegal combinations had been established and subterfuges, like the setting up of Benefit Societies, to get around the legislation, were being used. At this time the links between the Convention and the inchoate unions were almost non-existent. So when the Convention met again on 16 July and decided to call a general strike, it was doomed to fail. Consequently, it called instead for token strikes and although there was a good response to this, the government saw the calling off of the general strike as a weakness and went on the offensive, arresting scores of Chartists, including many in the leadership. In frustration, plans were being laid by Chartist groups for a concerted uprising towards the end of that same year. In South Wales a revolt of the miners was put down by troops with fourteen killed and dozens wounded. If this uprising had been successful it would undoubtedly have sparked similar ones throughout the country.

During 1840, Chartist leaders both inside and outside prison did some hard thinking about tactics. The movement began to revive at the end of the year with a closer unity with the trade union movement. As a result, at its Manchester conference in 1840, the National Charter Association was formed and this was to become the prototype of a truly working class party in Britain. Its constitution had to be carefully framed in order to avoid an immediate government crackdown.

With the release of Chartist leaders from prison there was a revival of the movement, and by the end of 1841 it had 282 branches and in the following year claimed a membership of 50,000. A new petition, with over three million signatures, was presented in May 1842, but was again summarily rejected by parliament. This rejection again led to increased anger and demand for more radical action among working people.

In August 1842, only a few months before Engels' arrival in Britain, the first general strike in the country takes place. It begins as a movement of resistance to the imposition of wage cuts in the mills, and becomes known as the 'Plug Riots' (because some striking workers stopped production by pulling out the boiler plugs from the steam engines in their factories). What begins as a series of strikes in the industrial districts, starting in the Midland coalfield, eventually spreads to the textile industry in Lancashire and Yorkshire and will eventually involve nearly half a million workers. It lasted a whole month, representing the biggest single exercise of working class strength in nineteenth century Britain.

The Anti-Corn Law League, formed by Cobden and Bright in

1839, also grew rapidly into a mass movement, galvanising large numbers of people in meetings and demonstrations, but was not as class-based as the Charter movement. Its demands were not radical in the way those of the Chartists were, but it vied with the Chartist Movement for support. However, in the industrial areas of the north, it was vehemently opposed by Chartists and found no widespread support among the working classes.

Although the Whigs had managed to push through the Reform Act in 1832 against the entrenched opposition of the landed gentry, represented by the Tories, this had not been enough to placate the mass of the people. It had merely tinkered with the corrupt electoral system, which was still overwhelmingly weighted in favour of the under-populated countryside and landowning interests. The Corn Laws, introduced in 1815, and supported by the landowners, had kept the price of corn artificially high by taxing imports. This meant that working people had to pay high prices for wheat and bread. The Corn Laws were the last significant victory for the old landowning class, but were opposed by working people as well as the big industrialists, as higher corn prices meant that wages could not be reduced any further if their workers were to survive.

The workshop of the world

This is to be Engels' first lengthier sojourn in England, when he stays from the beginning of December 1842 until August 1844. It is during this intensive period that he is able to correct a number of his misconceptions about the country, based largely on his reading and hearsay. He will arrive at a crucial juncture, just as the great slump is coming to an end, and the Chartist movement is at its height. The coming 21 months in England will have a similar impact on his thinking as the Paris years do on Marx. Both have emerged from the school of German philosophy and both draw similar conclusions after their periods spent abroad; Marx incorporates the French revolutionary experience into his thinking and Engels the English industrial and economic system.

In 1828 his elder contemporary, the poet Heinrich Heine, who Engels will meet in Paris in 1846, wrote from London:

> Send a philosopher to London, but not on your life a poet! Send a philosopher there and stand him at the corner of Cheapside and he will learn more there than from all the books

> of the last Leipzig fair. All human waves roar around him, a sea of new thoughts will rise before him, and the Eternal Spirit which hovers upon its waters will breathe upon him. The most hidden secrets of the social order will suddenly be revealed to him. He will hear the pulse of the world beat audibly, and see it visibly – for if London is the right hand of the world, its active mighty right hand, then we may regard the street which leads from the Exchange to Downing Street as the world's radial artery.

If Engels did read this essay he would have also taken to heart Heine's following words:

> The stranger who wanders through the great streets of London and does not chance right into the quarters in which the common people live, sees little or nothing of the dire misery there. Only here and there, at the entrance of some dark alley, a ragged woman stands mutely with a suckling babe at her exhausted breast, and begs with her eyes. Perhaps if those eyes are still beautiful, one glances into them and shrinks back at the world of wretchedness to be found here. The common beggars are all old people, generally blackamoors, who stand at the corners of the streets clearing pathways – a very necessary thing in muddy London – and ask for coppers in return. It is only in the dark night that poverty, with her fellows, vice and crime, glides from her lair. She shuns the daylight all the more carefully, since her wretchedness contrasts so glaringly with the pride of wealth which struts about everywhere...[19]

This might be exaggeratedly poetic and lurid, but it certainly conveys a vivid picture of what will have confronted Engels before he travels on to Manchester. It is the greatest financial centre in the world, in a country exporting more capital and drawing in more investment income from abroad than any other. It is also Britain's main centre of trade and commerce; its East End docks unloading dozens of ships each day with goods pillaged from the colonies, and its narrow thoroughfares jam-packed with carriages pressing the bustling cosmopolitan populace, who are trying to dodge the horses' hooves and the iron-bound wheels of the vehicles.

We cannot be certain that Engels has read Heine's travel essays from England, before he arrives this time, but it is highly probable as he is already a great admirer of the poet's works. These images certainly set the scene for what will confront Engels in Manchester and inspire his most famous work: *The Condition of the Working Class in England.* His first visit here was with his father in 1837, but that short stay only provided him with a fleeting acquaintance with the country; now he has the opportunity to get to know it in depth. To begin with, he does view England through Prussian eyes, although coloured by his readings of Disraeli and Dickens. Only slowly, as he is confronted with the realities, does he, over time, shed many of his inaccurate preconceptions.

Already in Bremen, Engels had been developing a sense of an inner mission, but here the crass poverty and misery of British towns shocks him violently. It convinces him unutterably that 'obtuse selfishness' is a fundamental principle of capitalism and as long as it remains so, there will be social war. Britain is 'a country like no other' in the world, in which steam power and machinery have revolutionised the production process, in which railways and steam ships shrink the distances and in which the chasm between rich and poor is unprecedented. Britain's most important industry at the time Engels arrives is the textile industry, with its main centres in Lancashire and Yorkshire, and Liverpool as the biggest cotton market in the world. Manchester, the second largest town in England, is the centre of cotton spinning and it is here that Engels is based.

Manchester is a new kind of city in which the formation of a radically new human world is taking shape. Next to London it is Britain's most important city, the embodiment of the new industrial capitalist age. It impresses him with the immensity of its industrialisation. Barmen, his home town is also a place dominated by textile mills, but in comparison it is a village, with around 40,000 inhabitants, whereas Manchester has over 300,000. Already by 1830, there are over 560 cotton mills in Lancashire as a whole, employing more than 110,000 workers, of whom 35,000 are children, some as young as six years of age. The dense pall of smoke from factory chimneys and the workers' hovels hangs permanently over the city; the damp seeps into one's bones; the noise and clatter of machinery and hobnail boots on cobblestones provide the day's music and set its rhythms. The streets between the packed working class tenements are open sewers. At this time, life expectancy in Manchester is around 26 years, the lowest figure since the years of the plague. It is at the same time a hellish and exciting city. This is the reality that confronts this young man from a provincial and straight-laced small town in the Rhineland.

Only 12 years before Engels' arrival in Manchester, the first regular passenger steam train began running between Manchester and Liverpool, engendering enormous excitement and terror. And by 1842 the railways have become a permanent fixture, completely transforming communications and travel; canal construction is going on apace and new technologies are being introduced into the cotton industry. Manchester is certainly a thrilling centre of the modern age. He arrives in the wake of a momentous upsurge of working class militancy, and is excited by the demonstrations of working class strength he hears and reads about. He has experienced nothing like it in Germany and he is impatient for the revolution to happen and this sometimes colours his interpretation of life, before experience and maturity teach him more patience and greater realism. Despite the mass Anti-Corn Law and Chartist movements, he can't imagine the British aristocracy, who see their social rule threatened, giving it up voluntarily, not until, as he puts it, 'the knife is at their throat'.

What confounds him about life in the cities is that 'everywhere there is a barbaric indifference, an egoistic hardness, on the one hand, and a nameless misery on the other, everywhere social warfare...everywhere mutual plundering under the protection of the law'. Nowhere else in the world has the artisan been marginalised by machines and replaced by a mass proletariat to the extent that he witnesses here in Britain. Engels is awed and horrified by the modern industrial system and refuses to accept that this is how society is destined to be. He finds it extremely offensive that the overwhelming majority of his fellow human creatures should be condemned to live in squalor, poverty and humiliation. Few thinkers of his generation see this new proletariat as anything other than a faceless mass, cowed, uneducated and incapable of achieving a better life. Many descriptions by observers and writers at the time portray their situation as a given, as one would describe animals in the wild; to invoke sympathy perhaps but seldom revolutionary change.

In Barmen, Engels has had little direct contact with workers, but in Manchester he will mix with them on an individual basis and will be impressed and encouraged by what he experiences; he will witness their resilience and recognise their potential strength. He becomes determined to understand how industrial capitalism functions, how the system has developed and what mechanisms could transform it. In Manchester Engels has 'his nose rubbed in it' as he later characterises his confrontation with crass class relations. This first-hand experience leads him to a greater understanding of how far economic realities and class struggle determine history. Previous historians had paid little heed to these factors. He also recognises clearly how these class and economic relations determine the party political forces: in England the Tory Party represents the old landed gentry and the Whigs the rising bourgeoisie or middle class.

Marx hasn't yet seen Manchester or experienced the industrial world first-hand, but he too is dissatisfied with the society he sees around him, refusing to accept it as God-given. He sets about examining society from a philosophical point of view. In their own way both men reach similar conclusions, but from different points of departure.

During the big general strike in July 1842, in response to the increased misery and depressed wages, Manchester has been at the centre of protest. When Engels arrives in December, the working classes are still animated by the events. This incendiary atmosphere captures his imagination and he is led into over-quick predictions of impending revolution on the back of working class action. However it isn't only Engels who feels the revolution is battering at the door, but many in ruling circles and even their paper, *The Times*, fears the impending explosion. The memories of the French Revolution still haunt the middle classes, as reflected succinctly in Elizabeth Gaskell's novel *Cranford*, in which Lady Ludlow remarks: 'If our lower orders have the edge tools [literacy] given to them, we shall have the terrible scenes of the French Revolution acted over again in England. When I was a little girl, one never heard of the rights of men, one only heard of the duties.'[20]

Not unlike Lady Ludlow, but with joy rather than fear, Engels sees in the general strike the initial spark of the revolution to come, but he seriously underestimates the braking action of entrenched social and political forces. The subsequent trials of the Chartist leaders who were involved in the 1842 strike, also demonstrate clearly to him that the poor are not judged by 'their peers' but by their born enemies.

Not long after Engels' arrival in Manchester, however, the

economic crisis peters out and many of the factory owners now feel able to make concessions and buy off sections of the working class. It is the beginning of a great capitalist expansion, the only hiccup being the short slump that takes place in 1847-48. From the mid-1840s onwards there is a significant improvement in wages and conditions of the skilled and organised workers, and this serves to dampen militancy. Nevertheless, abject poverty is still very much the norm: as the *Manchester Times* reports in July of that same year, 'the hungry and half-clothed men and women are stalking through the streets begging for bread'.

He came with great expectations of the English working class, after everything he has heard about the Chartist movement and English militancy. To begin with he is to be sorely disappointed: the English proletariat is not straining at the leash, preparing the revolution as he has imagined. They have no clear vision of a different society. He can't get over the fact that the English have not even the most elementary understanding of philosophy and don't consider this as a lack. He finds it incomprehensible that they act only in accordance with empirical experience and in an exceedingly practical way and ignore the great ideas. He only begins to understand this attitude once he has studied British history in more detail. He is most exercised about the fact that the English can't see 'that the so-called material interests can never become independent leading forces in history, but that they are consciously or unconsciously always at the service of a principle, that pulls the thread of historical progress'. He is also amazed at British religiosity – even the most educated individuals believe in miracles, and scientists twist their research to conform to religious sensibilities and the idea of creation.

With the government ignoring Chartist demands, there are increasing calls from the radicals for a different approach. For the Chartists, the right to vote has been central to their demands. However, when it becomes increasingly clear that a common franchise for all adult citizens is not about to be granted, sections of the movement become more ready to listen to those who argue that class struggle against the owners of capital is necessary, something Engels wholeheartedly approves of and supports. On the other hand, the ideas for a peaceful road to socialism as promulgated by Robert Owen are also gaining support.

Engels embraces the Chartist movement and is firmly convinced that it will, once it gains a more profound understanding of class forces, indeed initiate revolution. He is, though, still a little confused, based on his experience in Germany, by the fact that it has few intellectual supporters or leaders. The intellectuals, apparently, have no belief in the Chartist Movement or the working classes as offering a potential for social transformation.

Engels' first articles on England for the *Rheinische Zeitung* (under his usual pseudonym), in 1842, are written very much in the style of Hess. He still believes at this time a number of the clichés he has imbibed about England: that the land owners are more powerful here than on the continent and that German industry is already a threat to the British even in its home markets. In his youthful enthusiasm, he has a premonition of great social change whenever a strike breaks out. Only when he begins to study British constitutional issues does he begin to change his tune significantly and is forced to recognise that the country has a freedom of assembly, unknown elsewhere on the continent, as well as the right to form campaigning organisations and working men's groups, making it very different to Germany or France.

To begin with he uses what free time he has to study contemporary English literature, as well as the various newspapers in order to deepen his familiarity with his newly adopted country. A few years later, he also reads George Eliot, born only one year before he was, and admires her perceptive understanding of Victorian society. Eliot herself becomes a friend of Robert Owen, but it is unlikely she ever meets Engels. Although, interestingly, Eliot is fluent in German and undertakes the first translation into English of Feuerbach's critical work, *The Essence of Christianity*.

Shelley is one of his literary heroes already in Germany. The poet's hatred of piousness and the monarchy immediately struck a deep chord with him. Now in Shelley's own country, he begins to translate his poem, *Queen Mab* into German. He is also very much influenced by Thomas Carlyle's description of English social conditions in the latter's book, *Past and Present* published in 1843. Carlyle writes under the influence of the Cromwellian ideological tradition, bemoaning the fact that materialism has now become the world view and utilitarianism the ethic of the ruling class; society has been atomised, mammon rules with brutal dominion over all social relations. He sees an idle land-owning aristocracy and a bourgeoisie wholly servile to mammon; parliamentary representation is based on bribery and religion is fragmented; individuals are isolated from each other. Engels later describes Carlyle's work as the only really worthwhile book he reads during his time in Manchester. Carlyle had in fact visited Manchester in October 1838, a month before Charles Dickens made the same journey. Both were equally horrified by the ugliness of the city, the noise and misery. Dickens addressed a gathering at the Athenaeum, a Manchester club to which working men could belong and use the library, and of which Engels later becomes a member. During Dickens' visit, the idea for a new novel came to him and he noted, 'What I have seen has disgusted and astonished me beyond all measure. I mean to strike the heaviest blow in my power for these unfortunate creatures…' His blow is, though, some time in coming – in fact 15 years later with his novel *Hard Times*.

Engels is rapidly realising that he will have to deepen his knowledge of economics, which is perhaps even more vital to him than literature and philosophy if he is to fully grasp the historical process taking place under a rapidly advancing capitalist system. In this sense, his profession as a businessman will be of great value, giving him insights others don't have.

To begin with, Engels takes lodgings in a furnished house in the centre of Manchester, but will later move into his own rented accommodation. His workplace lies in the commercial centre and, as General Assistant, he has his office in Southgate, but is often in the factories too, fascinated by the production process. Ermen & Engels have cotton mills, warehouses and offices in Manchester, Salford, Eccles and Bolton. From his office in Manchester, he only has about a quarter of a mile to the stock exchange, where he is often obliged to conduct business, and is not far from the Victoria Mills, belonging to Ermen & Engels, in Weaste, on the River Irwell.

Work at the office is strenuous, particularly because Peter Ermen, the chairman of the company, is hard on himself and his underlings. As Engels is his 'right hand', the man's moods are offloaded on to him first. Peter Ermen's brother, Anton, in a letter from 1834, writes about 'Peter's slave-driving methods' and about the fact that he has to rise at 6.00 am and then after a ten hour day in the office, go off to night school to improve his English and study cotton production techniques, so that he is never home before 9 or 10 in the evening. This gives some inkling of what Engels has to contend with.

From his letters, he reveals little detail of his daily work or of factory life in general, but we do gather that there is frequent conflict with his nominal boss – Peter Ermen. The latter makes no secret of the fact that he only keeps him on 'out of loyalty to the father'. Peter's brother, Anton, provides the family's assessment of Engels with the words: 'He worked for the firm as little as he could get away with and spent most of his time at political meetings and on studying the social conditions in Manchester.' He couldn't be based in a better place than Manchester to observe and learn about working class attitudes, their conditions of life and struggles; and it is this aspect of life in Britain that especially fascinates him. The north, and particularly Lancashire, is also the main stronghold of Chartism, even though its origins were in London among the thinking, radical artisans.

Engels declares that the Charter's six points 'were enough to overthrow the whole English constitution, queen and lords included. Chartism,' he writes, 'is of an essentially social nature, a class movement. The six points which for the radical bourgeoisie are the end of the matter...are for the proletariat a mere means to further ends. "Political power our means, social happiness our end" had now become the clearly formulated war cry of the Chartists.' As in most movements, the Chartists, too, engender their own right and left wings, and Engels identifies with the latter. The left is characterised by a much clearer conception of socialism, to which they devote their efforts, seeing the achievements of the Charter's points as only a step along the road. The popular and fiery orator Fergus O'Connor represents the centre ground, but is invariably supported by the left against the right. Leaders of the more radical forces are the Irishman Bronterre O'Brien and, later, Ernest Jones and George Julian Harney, the editor of the Chartist paper, *Northern Star*. These men, however, never achieve the mass popularity of O'Connor himself, who was the original founder of the *Northern Star*.

Engels' first personal contacts with Chartism are through George Harney and James Leach. Leach is a factory worker in Manchester, who has quite a following among working men in the city; he is elected onto the Chartist Association's provisional executive at its first convention. He also helps Engels in his researches into working conditions in Manchester and is quoted several times in his book, *The Condition of the Working Class in England*.

Engels pays a visit to Harney in 1843, shortly before the latter is to move the National Charter Association headquarters from Leeds to London. His visit is important also in shaping Harney's political future. The two men hit it off immediately as Harney later reveals:

> I knew Engels; he was my friend and occasional correspondent over half a century. It was in 1843 that he came over from Bradford to Leeds and enquired for me at The Northern Star office. A tall, handsome young man, with a countenance of almost boyish youthfulness, whose English, in spite of his German birth and education, was even then remarkable for its accuracy. He was largely given to hospitality, but the principal charm at his hospitable board was his own 'table talk' and the 'good Rhine wine', his felicitous conversation and genial wit. He was himself laughter-loving and his laughter was contagious. A joy-inspirer, he made all around him share his happy mood of mind.[21]

Harney is three years older than Engels and a man with a rich political background. He is one of those who demands action rather than words; a man after Engels' own heart. However, the unsuccessful strike of 1842 does lead Harney to begin to question this attitude. He is also one of those Chartist leaders with a less blinkered or insular outlook and is a genuine internationalist, unlike the overwhelming majority of Chartists who have only a dim awareness of any affinity between their struggle and those on the continent. He is a revolutionary by sentiment as well as conviction, and his distaste of organised religion also endears him to Engels. He welcomes with alacrity Engels' offer to write on continental matters for his paper. Engels will also write many pieces for Harney's Democratic Review in the fifties, all anonymously.

Harney is an orphan who went to the Naval School in Greenwich, leaving school at fourteen to go to sea. Two years later, he leaves the Navy to work as a shop boy for the publisher Henry Hetherington, the publisher of *The Poor Man's Guardian* paper, edited by the Chartist leader, Bronterre O'Brien. The paper challengingly carries on its title page the words: 'published contrary to law' i.e. the publisher refuses to pay stamp duty, arguing that this compromised the freedom of the press. Harney is imprisoned three times before he is out of his teens for selling an 'illegal' journal. He is addicted to flaunting his 'red cap of liberty' at public meetings and, later, Marx and Engels are to nick-name him 'Citizen Hip-hip-hurrah' with reference to his unfailing, but indiscriminate readiness to applaud all manner of revolutionary sentiment.

Engels is clearly the more intellectual of the two men, but despite their very different backgrounds the two hit it off immediately. Harney, though, remains basically an empirical socialist, largely indifferent to theoretical systems, while Engels, true to the German tradition, bases his thinking more on theoretical and philosophic principles. These different approaches lead to a later cooling of the friendship between the two. In the meantime, Engels and George Harney conduct an extensive correspondence on the problems within the Chartist and the English working class movements (although only Harney's letters survive) and Engels also maintains good contacts with leading members of the German proletarian emigration groups in London and is keeping abreast of events in mainland Europe.

Harney provides a restraint on Engels' youthful enthusiasm in these early years. When Engels waxes lyrical about the revolutionary potential he perceives in Britain and on the realisation of the Charter demands, Harney reins him in with his sober assessment. He tells him, he doesn't foresee a revolution in Britain in the lifetime of either of them, nor is he convinced about achieving the demands of the Charter in the short-term. And in a discussion about the possible use of force to achieve working class demands, he writes: 'English people are the most unmilitary, indeed anti-military people on earth'. He clearly knows his own people a lot better than this young and enthusiastic German.[22]

By his forties he has become somewhat disillusioned with the political movement in Britain and moves to the USA, before returning to settle in Jersey among French refugees from the 1848 revolution. Engels pays him a visit there in 1857 and describes this in one of his letters to Marx, in which he says he 'went pubbing' with Harney and that 'he seems damn'd glad to have retired from big politics to his small royaume des aveugles [kingdom of the blind]'.[23]

Engels goes on to establish a warm relationship also with Robert Owen, and soon starts writing articles for both the *Northern Star* and *The New Moral World*, the paper of the English Owenites. He also attends workers' meetings as often as he can and, in one of his letters, he captures vividly the feel of such a gathering, in Manchester's Hall of Science:

> While the English state church is up to other things, the socialists have taken up the cause of workers' education and have achieved an enormous amount; to begin with you can't be more amazed when sitting with workers in the Science Hall and listening to them talking about political, religious and social matters with clear consciousness...the workers today possess well-bound, excellent translations of French philosophy from the last century, most have the Social Contract by Rousseau, the Systems of Nature and several works by Voltaire in penny pamphlet form, and journals dealing with the debates around communist fundamentals, as well as the works ofThomas Paine and of Shelley in cheap editions. Then come the Sunday lectures which are avidly attended. When I go to the communists' hall in Manchester, which seats 3000, it is packed to the gunwales every Sunday...These meetings take the form of a church service; there is a choir, accompanied by an orchestra, and they sing from the gallery, hymns about social issues, often with sacred melodies but with communist texts, and everyone stands to join in. Then the lecturer gets on the platform...and gives his speech amid lots of laughter, because the English sense of humour punctuates these speeches with blasts of fresh air...[24]

During this period from 1842 to '44 Engels' thinking undoubtedly matures and he becomes more confident. He redoubles his efforts, utilising his renowned affability, to establish firm relations with other leading Chartists and the socialist lecturers in Manchester, as well as with leading German progressives in the city. In his discussions with the Chartists, he attempts to convince them that only through socialism can working people realise their political emancipation, and he introduces the Owenites to the ideas of continental socialism and communism. He himself is also on a steep learning curve and attempting to plumb the English character. He is amazed, he writes later, 'that most of them [the English socialists] were very little informed about the social movements taking place in other parts of the continent.' Britain was then and still is today, largely cut off from, and ignorant of, what is happening on the ground in the neighbouring European countries. What Engels is able to pass on from his wider experience, is undoubtedly invaluable as far as expanding the horizons of these socialist leaders is concerned, and convincing them that the battle for socialism can more easily be achieved by collaborating with their fellow workers in other countries.

The working classes in the mid 19th century may be downtrodden, many living in abject misery and ignorance, but there is, among many, also a thirst for knowledge and education. There is a widespread awareness that the world doesn't have to be the way it is, indeed shouldn't be this way. Many, particularly the more skilled workers, are actively searching for answers to their queries and looking for solutions to the seemingly unbridgeable social contradictions; the established churches are largely silent on these matters, or actively collaborate with the mill owners, and so socialism, particularly with a quasi-religious aura, has an attractive appeal. It offers the poor, those with little hope or prospect of betterment, the idea that a different society is feasible.

He notes already the high levels of self-education among sections of the workers in Manchester, particularly those involved in Chartist or socialist groups. Many of these have set up their own libraries and reading rooms, and also attempt to provide their children with 'a proletarian education'. They are so feared by the establishment that it sets up its own counter educational centres, the Mechanics Institutions, in order to pull workers away from such radical hot-beds. Engels is more than ever convinced that the achievement of political democracy alone cannot relieve the misery of the working classes; only the abolition of private property can do that. Although admiring the Chartists and influenced by their ideas, he feels that they have an exaggerated estimation of the effectiveness of pure political means. He is convinced, however, that they will come to recognise this themselves sooner or later and that objective circumstances will drive them into the arms of socialism. Political democracy, he feels, is an oxymoron, a 'hypocrisy' and a 'theology'; only economic justice can deliver real democracy.

At this time he is still hoping to complete a translation of Proudhon's work, *What is Property?*, for the British movement. There is no comparable treatise available in English at the time that demonstrates with such intellectual acuity and theoretical rigour what the essence of private property is and so thoroughly exposes its contradictoriness. Proudhon's anarchist theory is clearly still influential on Engels and he is becoming increasingly aware that the state is an expression of the class character of society. He is also, to his own surprise, beginning to realise that the economic forces in society are more potent than political ones. Proudhon's writings convince him that the most powerful element in history, the germ and decisive reason for all revolutions, are economic forces; that the state doesn't determine the structure of society but vice versa.

He is also desperate to convince English workers that a strictly legal revolution will not be possible, and uses the experience of the French 'July Revolution' of 1830 to underline his arguments. Even the self-professed socialists he meets have not even a fragmentary idea of what their fellow socialists on the Continent are doing or thinking. To address this ignorance, he writes an article for Owen's *New Moral World* in November 1843, with the title, 'The Progress of Social Reform on the Continent'. This leads to a regular correspondence in the *New Moral World* and also in Harney's *Northern Star*. In France, he explains, Communist groups were formed after the July Revolution, once the workers realised that it was not enough to bring about a change in the structure of the state only. First the overthrow of the existing social order is necessary if they are to change their conditions fundamentally.

Engels has great respect for one of the French leaders, Étienne Cabet. He notes that Cabet, whose views are very similar to Robert Owen's, emphasises the need, in a future communist state, to secure individual freedoms, precisely those which their opponents accuse the communists of jeopardising. Engels explains why the communists there are republicans and feel the need to set up secret organisations and are not frightened of using force to reach their goals. But he is strongly against such secret societies, whose de facto illegality, he feels, unnecessarily gives the actions of their persecutors a mantle of legality.

The Chartists, Engels finds, know only about English socialism, particularly as propounded by Robert Owen, but have no inkling of German communism or French ideas about socialism, so trying to differentiate between the two terms, socialism and communism, would only confuse them, so he uses them interchangeably at this time. In an article in Owen's *New Moral World* he explains that the French constitution and laws sanction the oppression of the poor by the rich and make the creation of communist colonies following the British example impossible. Engels tries to demonstrate to British workers that they can only gain justice and freedom through the introduction of communism. He doesn't hide his anger over the fact that the French still identify communism with Christianity. He attacks this position as 'false consciousness' and doesn't want to see himself, he remarks, having escaped the religiosity of his father's household, being embraced by it again through the back door of communism.

The Chartist movement in Britain doesn't even broach the question of wealth distribution, which irks Engels. He argues that this big question should be placed at the centre of the movement's demands. As long as only political-democratic demands remain central, this vital question will be left unresolved. The Chartists' main demand is a democratisation of state power, not its revolutionary transformation. Even if one goes back to Paine, Locke, Rousseau or Cobbett, the demands are always based on the demand for 'natural rights'. The young and passionate German is convinced that only if the English proletariat would follow the blueprint of the German radical philosophers, would they have the necessary tools to take state power. However, there is little concept of class struggle in Britain at this time; the radical movements are driven by idealism and a strong ingrained sense of 'natural' justice, often biblically based. The only genuinely socialist movement in the country is that initiated by Robert Owen, also from idealistic principles.

Owen has always been associated with the co-operative movement in the public mind, but his contribution to the political debate at this time is invariably overlooked. In the 1830s Owenism as an organised movement assumed a mainly propagandist character. There were a series of Co-operative Congresses, followed by Socialist Congresses. Owenite branches were set up in many towns all over Britain and a number of full-time 'missionaries' employed to lecture and help organise groups. Leaflets, journals and pamphlets were produced in large numbers. Owenites also had their own permanent meeting places, commonly known as Halls of Science, like that in Manchester.

In two and half years, during the thirties, two million Owenite tracts were circulated and in Manchester one thousand were distributed at public meetings every Sunday; in London 40,000 were given away; 50,000 copies of Owen's manifesto were sold. A number of his works were translated into German, Polish and Welsh.[25] As a result of all this, socialist and secularist ideas were widely circulated and had a profound influence on what Engels called the 'most educated and solid elements' of the working class. In succeeding years Owen's ideas became more abstract and remote from reality and his influence waned.

Owen felt that the key to solving the social inequities and crass discrepancies between rich and poor in the industrial system was better planning and leadership on a co-operative and solidarity basis to overcome the conflict between the different class interests. He felt that greed and selfishness needed to be overcome and a new economic principle established based on a 'new moral world order'. He set up socialist or co-operative colonies both in Britain and the USA to demonstrate how his ideas would work. Although none of them was successful in the long term, they did lead to the worldwide co-operative movement, still flourishing and with us today. It was however unable to challenge seriously the capitalist system.

Owen's views are strongly rooted in 18th century rationalism and British pragmatism, and are very different from Engels' and Marx's philosophy-based utopianism, although he does, like Engels, believe that the history of human irrationality is coming to an end and that a rebirth of intellectual idealism is imminent. Emotionally they are both drawn to socialism as the solution to social discord, but over which path to take in order to get there, they diverge significantly.

Manchester's 'Hall of Science', built by Owenites at Campfield, contained, according to a contemporary observer 'the finest and most spacious lecture hall in town'. Owen's Sunday educational meetings there are attended by thousands, and Engels is often present. For this young man from censorious Barmen they must have been a real eye-opener: free and open debate on all manner of subjects, unthinkable in his home town with its fear of dissidence and its draconian censorship.

Engels always gives due respect to Owen as a genial socialist and initiator of significant progress in the social field, that followed his campaigning, but also because he is the first of his kind to go 'against his own class'. He is 50 years Engels' senior and a mill owner, who has discovered his own path to socialism. Engels is impressed, too, by his courageous stand against church hypocrisy and the fact that he dares 'name marriage, religion and private property as the precursors of all misery since the beginning of the world'. Owen's followers, he feels, are the only ones who dare to use their minds as far as religion is concerned. He praises the English socialists for their open struggle against the different religious sects, particularly vis-à-vis the French, who he feels still conceive of their socialism as rooted in religion, with their devotion to Saint-Simon.

The condition of the working class

Engels is not long in Manchester before he begins investigating social and political relations, particularly the living and working conditions of England's working people. He studies the works of the economists Adam Smith, David Ricardo, Jean-Baptiste Say, John Ramsay McCulloch and James Stuart Mill. We are seeing in his intellectual development a gradual step by step approach to materialism and communism up to 1844. It is here, during this, his first longer stay in Manchester, that Engels undergoes a transformational political education, culminating in his eventual conviction that materialism and 'scientific communism' are the solutions to social conflict and injustice.

Engels' father had hoped he would spend his time studying English manufacturing methods, so that the best could be adopted in Barmen; however, Engels is only really interested in the socio-political aspects of the factory system, not in how better to make money.

In an article for the *Rheinische Zeitung*, he describes the situation as he sees it in England:

> In the cotton districts most people are employed, in Manchester there is probably only one unemployed worker for every ten employed, in Bolton and Birmingham the ratio is probably similar, and when the English worker is employed, he is content. And he can be, certainly if he's a cotton worker, and if he compares his lot with that of his German and French counterparts. There the worker has hardly enough to survive on potatoes and bread; lucky he who has meat once a week. Here he eats beef daily and, for his money, gets as good a roast as the wealthiest in Germany. Twice a day he has tea and still has money left over to take a glass of porter at noon and in the evening a brandy with water. That's the life style of most workers in Manchester for working 12 hours a day. But how long will that last! With the slightest tremor in the business world, thousands of workers will be on the dole.[26]

The first hand investigation he carries out of the lives of working people in Manchester could never have been done without the help and collaboration of Mary Burns. Mary is a spirited and vivacious 19 year-old daughter of a dyer who works in one of the local mills.

Her laughing flirtatiousness and proletarian confidence fascinates Engels from the first moment he sees her, but we don't know how or where their meeting takes place. She may have caught his eye selling refreshments at one of the political meetings in the Owenite Hall of Science or she may have been a domestic in one of the neighbouring houses. It is unlikely she is working in one of the mills at this time, as Engels' description of the girls who work in the Ermen & Engels mills is not conducive to such a conclusion: 'In the throstle room of the cotton mill at Manchester in which I was employed, I do not remember to have seen one single tall, well-built girl; they were all short, dumpy and badly formed, decidedly ugly in the whole development of the figure'.

He takes an immediate fancy to Mary and they soon strike up a relationship. Engels, always with an eye for attractive girls, is captivated by her effervescent character and pretty face. Although she can barely read or write and has virtually no schooling, she is clearly bright and street-wise. She also has a ready sense of humour and brings a light-hearted touch into Engels' life that would be dominated otherwise by office monotony and a somewhat ascetic bachelordom. Once they become close friends, she also takes on the role of his guide and companion on many a jaunt through the working class areas. Without her, he would undoubtedly have found it difficult to gain access to working families – a well dressed young man wandering down their streets alone would look very odd and he would have been suspected of being up to no good. With Mary, Engels is able to explore behind the facades of the high streets, where the factory workers live. She also takes him around 'Little Ireland', lying within a bend of the River Medlock by the Oxford Road, and to Irish Town, close to the valley of the River Irk, where most Irish immigrants live in the most squalid conditions.

In all the great towns, as census figures show, migrants from the rural areas outnumbered those born there. An important part of this group was the Irish – in 1841 there were 133,000 in Lancashire alone. And between 1841 and '51 it was estimated that half a million more came to England. They played a double part – on the one hand, out of desperation, they were prepared to accept much lower wages and conditions than the natives, but on the other, they brought a tradition of struggle and took readily to trade unionism. The Irishman, Fergus O'Connor became perhaps the outstanding individual figure of Chartism as well as the embodiment of its contradictions. In 1847, as the first Chartist, he was elected to parliament, as MP for Nottingham.

The friendship between Engels and Mary Burns very soon blossoms into intimacy and they become a couple, although never marrying. Engels considers marriage a bourgeois institution anyway, but is also keen to maintain his bachelor status in order to remain free to pursue his gypsy political life and not become tied down by family commitment. He writes about Mary to his family, but their reaction to the liaison and the possibility of his marrying a simple working class girl is predictable outrage. Their attitude may also have influenced his decision not to marry. It is, though, no doubt, largely through her that Engels is able to gain a fuller and deeper understanding of what it means to be working class. His later book, *The Condition of the Working Class in England*, may never have been completed without her influence and it would certainly have lacked its sense of intimacy and first-hand knowledge.

There is almost no information about Mary available. As she was virtually illiterate, she wrote no letters, so there is no evidence from that source either. The correspondence between Engels and Marx or with third parties makes scarce a mention of her. Engels' friend Georg Weerth, later, in a poem he dedicates to her (see excerpt on p.102), writes of her selling oranges from a stall on the Liverpool docks and sending money home to Ireland to assist the struggle for freedom there. Whether this is based in reality or is simply poetic imagination we don't know. In a letter to his mother he describes her 'bold, black looks' and her 'blood was warm and quick'. Eleanor Marx, in a letter to the leading German social democrat, Karl Kautsky will describe her as' pretty, witty and charming'. From these few laconic sketches, it is not difficult to imagine why Engels feels immensely attracted to her.

Before Engels writes his *Condition of the Working Class in England*, the radical social changes wreaked by the industrial revolution have been largely ignored in the wider public sphere. Although there had been a number of detailed studies undertaken, like the series of reports issued by the Poor Law Commissioners in 1835-47, culmina - ting in the publication of Edwin Chadwick's *Report on the Sanitary Conditions of the Labouring Population in 1842*, these did not reach a wide readership. Even Joseph Adshead's book, *Distress in Manchester: Evidence of the State of the Labouring Classes in 1840-42*, only looks at the situation in terms of poverty, disease and death. The social change wrought by the industrial revolution had been apocalyptic. According to the British economist Adam Smith, of around half a million people working in the spinning mills, almost 200,000 of them were women, 160,000 children and only 158,000 men. The implication of such statistics for family life and the position of women in society has far-reaching repercussions in the political as well as the social sphere.

Engels' singular achievement with his study is to link this misery with the rise of capitalism, to reveal the intrinsic connectedness and to indicate a solution. His book is, for most people, a revelation. In it he exposes the harsh underlying realities behind the enormous wealth creation that no one is keen to address; they are to remain hidden, like naked female flesh, from public view. In his book, Engels describes how mid 19th century society in England is characterised primarily by the enormous chasm that exists between the bourgeoisie and proletariat. Engels describes the 'two nations' thus: 'The bourgeoisie has more in common with all other nations on earth than with the workers who live immediately next to it. The workers speak different dialects, have other ideas and thoughts, other customs and ethical principles, other religions and politics than the bourgeoisie. They are completely different peoples...' [27] In the same year -1845 - Disraeli corroborates Engels' portrayal in his novel, *Sybil or the Two Nations.*

The *Factories Inquiry Commission Report (1833)* on which Engels bases much of his findings would only be read by a few parliamentarians and academics at most. Disraeli would also no doubt have consulted them while researching his own novel. In general the areas of art and literature well into the mid-nineteenth century totally ignored the lives of the industrial masses. Elizabeth Gaskill's novel, *Mary Barton,* acknowledged as probably the first novel to have a working class hero and set in Engels' Manchester, is written only in 1848; Thomas Martin Wheeler's novel *Sunshine and Shadow,* probably the first complex political working class novel to be published in Britain, is serialised in Harney's *Northern Star* in 1850, and Dickens' *Hard Times* appears in 1854, the same year that John Snow discovers that cholera – the scourge of urban slum living – is spread by contaminated water.

Virtually the only painting of the period which even attempted to portray manual work was Ford Maddox Brown's 'Work' completed in 1856, depicting workmen digging up a Hampstead street. Maddox Brown's fellow Pre-Raphaelites preferred to escape into the romantic certainties of medieval chivalry than confront their contemporary reality; August Doré began his engravings of inner-city life only in the sixties.

In *The Condition of the Working Class in England*, which he writes up later, after his return to Barmen, Engels describes factory working conditions unsentimentally but vividly, and backs up his own observations and opinions with detailed factual material culled from the *Factories Report*. The Commission had been set up by the government of the time in response to increasing agitation about the appalling conditions in the country's factories and how these conditions were impacting on social life.

Sir David Barry, one of the surgeons who did some of the research for the *Factories Report*, wrote about the effects of exceedingly long working hours, and is quoted by Engels:

> He noted deformities caused by the overwork, especially flattening of the foot, which he frequently observed. In cases, in which a stronger constitution, better food, and other more favourable circumstances enabled the young operative to resist this effect of a barbarous exploitation, we find, at least, pain in the back, hips, and legs, swollen joints, varicose veins, and large, persistent ulcers in the thighs and calves. These affections are almost universal among the operatives. The reports of Stuart, Mackintosh, and Sir David Barry contain hundreds of examples; indeed, they know almost no operative who did not suffer from some of these affections; and in the remaining reports, the occurrence of the same phenomena is attested by many physicians...
>
> Commissioners Stuart, Mackintosh and Sir David Barry use the strongest wording when describing the health implications of mill work and the little care most factory owners take for the girls who do it... The use of narcotics to keep the children still is fostered by this infamous system, and has reached a great extent in the factory districts. Dr. Johns, Registrar in Chief for Manchester, is of the opinion that this custom is the chief source of the many deaths from convulsions...
>
> Another effect of flax spinning is the specific twisting of the shoulder, i.e. the projection of the right-hand shoulder blade

> which comes about due to the nature of the work...the continuous bending in this work and the low siting of the machines have led to a short stature...Apart from these debilities and the crippling of workers and their limbs, they are also endangered in another way. Working between the machines results in a significant number of accidents, of a more or less serious nature and, for the workers, often result in their being unable to continue working. The most common accidents are those where part of a finger is damaged, less often the whole finger, part of, or the whole, hand, an arm etc. after being trapped in the cogs and crushed... even with minor accidents, tetanus often infects the wound, and death soon follows. In Manchester, apart from the many cripples you see – one is missing a part or the whole of his arm, another his foot, the third half his leg – you think you are living in the midst of an army that has just returned from the front.[28]

In his book, Engels describes the attitude of a typical Manchester citizen of the moneyed classes: 'I once accompanied such a bourgeois gentleman into Manchester and spoke with him about the terrible conditions in the working class areas and told him I had never seen such a badly built city. The man listened to me calmly and then, on reaching the corner of the road where he left me, he said: "And, yet there is a great deal of money made here, good day!" 'This short incident captures in a nutshell the confident indifference of 'John Bull' to the suffering of his fellow human beings.

The dwellings for the thousands of workers the industrial expansion required were not planned, but thrown up in the most haphazard way, as densely as possible. He describes how he wanders through the labyrinth of filthy back passages, miniscule courtyards, where pigs are kept, stepping through the slime of excrement and garbage. The stench makes him want to retch. The cramped and damp homes are filled with children and adults, clothed in rags, several to a room, with scarcely any furniture. It is easy to get lost here; there are no landmarks or clear pathways. 'When I re-read my description [as portrayed in his *The Condition of the Working Class in England]*,' he says, 'I have to admit that, far from exaggerating, I fall short by far of portraying it graphically enough: the filth, the depravity and inhabitability...' Engels' younger contemporary, the Berlin artist Heinrich Zille, expressed the situation unforgettably, when he said: 'housing can shatter you just as surely as an axe'.

In this book, he wants to do more than paint a local picture; he is looking for something that typifies the system that can become a symbol for the general. In his daily research he gets to know Manchester undoubtedly more intimately than most of its own inhabitants.

Interestingly, among the wealthiest of the Lancashire mill owners during Engels' stay in Manchester is one Sir Robert Peel, father of the Tory prime minister, who is also a partner in his father's firm. Peel is one of those who campaigned for the earlier Factory Acts of 1802 and 1819, to ameliorate the lot of the workers, but they have clearly had only limited effect. Engels, at this time, sees the Tories as the English equivalent of the Prussian Junkers he knows from home, and fails to recognise a significant philanthropic strand in their politics, despite their entrenched conservatism.

In his first six months in Manchester, Engels' social intercourse is almost entirely with such bourgeois 'gentlemen', as those described above, to whom he is expected to pay his respects and cultivate amicable relations in the interests of the business. As soon as he has gone through the motions, though, he throws himself into the work he loves most, investigating the impact of capitalist industry on the working people and relating that to his developing political ideas.

The businessmen and middle classes he meets find a ready, and conscience-salving explanation for the repeated crises and misery in Malthus's popular theory that populations naturally outgrow the means to feed and clothe them. But anyone interested in improving society refuses to accept Malthusian determinism, considering it fatalistic and wrong-headed. Engels, too, rejects his 'infamous and base doctrine' passionately; he can't see how the enormous potential offered by science and industry cannot be harnessed to bring happiness and plenty to all mankind. For him this theory is even more absurd than the living absurdity of the contradiction between rich and poor. He refuses to believe that the world is not capable of feeding everyone. However, he is not satisfied to simply reject Malthusianism on an ethical basis only, but is determined to refute it on the basis of economic facts.

Manchester is a quintessentially northern English town, in the 1800s, but it also has a sizeable German population and it isn't difficult for Engels to make contact with immigrants of similar political persuasions to his own. In 1843, he meets leaders of the underground German workers' organisation, Bund der Gerechten (League of the Just), Karl Schapper, Joseph Moll und Heinrich Bauer. Later that year, in December he meets the German revolutionary and writer, Georg Weerth, while the latter is travelling through England, and they become intimate friends.

Of course there are German factory owners too, like Ermen, and they are no different from their English counterparts in the way they treat their workers, but they do differ in terms of their education and are more open to outside ideas. They love books, paintings and, above all, music, putting on cultural events on a regular basis. For instance at the home of Peter Ermen, Engels finds a well-stocked library and the old man is not averse to attending social occasions. Most of these businessmen emigrated from southern Germany and particularly from the Rhine area towards the end of the 18th century, and in family circles they hold on to their Germanic culture, even if they appear to be acclimatised Englishmen to the outside world. But Engels doesn't feel at home in their world either. He expresses this sentiment clearly in his dedication to 'The Working Classes of Great Britain' of his book, *The Condition of the Working Class in England*:

> Working Men!
> To you I dedicate a work, in which I have tried to lay before my German Countrymen a faithful picture of your condition, of your sufferings and struggles, of your hopes and prospects. I have lived long enough amidst you to know something about your circumstances; I have devoted to their knowledge my most serious attention, I have studied the various official and non-official documents as far as I was able to get hold of them - I have not been satisfied with this, I wanted more than a mere abstract knowledge of my subject, I wanted to see you in your own homes, to observe you in your everyday life, to chat with you on your condition and grievances, to witness your struggles against the social and political power of your oppressors.
> I have done so: I forsook the company and the dinner-parties, the port-wine and champaign [sic] of the middle-classes, and devoted my leisure-hours almost exclusively to the intercourse with plain Working-Men; I am both glad and proud of having done so. Glad, because thus I was induced to spend many a happy hour in obtaining a knowledge of the realities of life -

> many an hour, which else would have been wasted in fashionable talk and tiresome etiquette; proud, because thus I got an opportunity of doing justice to an oppressed and calumniated class of men who with all their faults and under all the disadvantages of their situation, yet command the respect of every one but an English money-monger; proud, too, because thus I was placed in a position to save the English people from the growing contempt which on the Continent has been the necessary consequence of the brutally selfish policy and general behaviour of your ruling middle-class.[29]

Although he enjoys the company of Mancunians, he has little fondness for their grimy city. He sometimes longs for the more bucolic environs of his homeland, for the calmer and more idyllic life on the Rhine, particularly when the seasons change. In autumn, he visualises the hillsides golden with the autumnal colours of the vines, the grape harvesting and jovial drinking in the small 'Weinstuben' (wine cellars). While in Manchester, whether autumn or spring, the skies are invariably gun-metal grey and the rain pelts down for days on end; the outpourings from the factory chimneys darken the sky even more and an acrid miasma hangs over the city like a pestilential blanket. Then Engels dreams, as he writes to his uncle, August, of springtime back home and the musical gatherings: 'Now one knows only too well that it will be green on the Rhine, the crystal clear wavelets of the river, rippling under the breath of spring; nature will be clad in its Sunday best and everyone at home will be preparing for the musical outing. They will leave tomorrow and I won't be there!'

However, once he develops his contacts and friendships with other revolutionaries and working people in Manchester, he slowly begins to savour his time there despite the smoke and rain, and his nostalgia is momentarily dissipated. During 1843, with the help of his new Manchester friends and Georg Weerth, he is able devote himself even more to researching working class life and the conditions under which the people live and work.

He and Weerth are already acquainted from their time at the *Neue Rheinische Zeitung*, where Weerth was also a temporary editor. The latter happens to be working in Yorkshire while Engels is in Manchester and he often journeys over from Bradford to enjoy 'many a lively Sunday' with Engels and talk politics or go horse racing and take long walks. He is also employed in the textile trade, as a company representative, but like Engels, his chief interests are writing and politics. He pens numerous articles and essays about England and the working class, but his style is more personal and novelistic than Engels'. In his first months in England he writes that he has never done a better thing for himself than coming to the island and seeing with his own eyes, 'all this misery and also all the means to remove it'. Side by side he sees, 'the basest villainy and 'the soundest world movement'. Engels describes Weerth as 'the first and most significant poet of the proletariat.' Weerth calls Engels the 'German philosopher' and feels pity for him, 'buried in that dark city'.

His verse from 1844 onwards takes on an increasingly social aspect, no doubt strongly influenced by his vivid impressions of the north. As can be seen clearly in these two stanzas from his poem 'The Cannon Forger':

> He goes – but in his angry soul
> He bears, the sullen moan,
> The guns his hands have fashioned roll
> Their thunder tone.
>
> He slowly speaks, "The time is near,
> Ye thrice accursed crew –
> The guns, that put your foes in fear,
> We'll turn on you.[30]

He is also much affected by Engels' views, just as his more famous compatriot, Heinrich Heine is by Marx. Weerth dies tragically young, in 1856, aged 34, from a malarial infection while on business in Havana, Cuba.

Towards the end of this first period of his stay in Britain, Engels gradually comes to the conclusion that Chartism and the small English socialist movement in their present forms can never lead the workers to socialism. The Chartists, he now feels, are lagging, ideologically and are less developed, than the sprouting socialist groups, but he recognises that they are led by 'real proletarians who represent the proletariat'. The socialists are more advanced ideologically but, in the main, they come from the middle class and there seems little hope, in the short term, of them being able to coalesce with the working classes. Engels strongly recommends that the two need to amalgamate and then, 'the working class will really be the rulers of England', he maintains.

In the summer of that same year, 1843, he takes advantage of a visit to London to make a quick journey to the continent. In Ostend he meets up with the social revolutionary poet, Georg Herwegh and the liberal literary critic and historian, Georg Gervinus, to discuss political issues and publishing opportunities for his writings. Herwegh has already worked on the *Rheinische Zeitung* and has written its poetic manifesto and Gervinus is one of the seven professors from Göttingen whom Engels admires for joining the protest in 1837 against the Crown Prince's refusal to accept a new, more liberal constitution in the kingdom of Hanover. Such discussions help him develop and refine his own ideas. Engels has a continental perspective of the situation in Britain and sees the class struggle as a dialectical one, each separate national struggle complementing and contributing to the others. The coallescence between his knowledge of Hegel's philosophy, French utopianism and now British economic theory and practice turns him into a proto-materialist and 'scientific' communist even before Marx has reached this stage.

Already in February 1843, Marx had left the *Rheinische Zeitung* and withdrawn to his study, frustrated by censorship and the limited impact of the paper. He begins work on his *Economic and Philosophic Manuscripts*, the foundation stone for *Capital* later. Engels announces his own newly won insight on the role played by economics in an article published in Owen's *The New Moral World* in 1843. Engels emphasises later that he and Marx could never have developed the ideas and theory of what subsequently becomes known as historical materialism without the input of the founders of French socialism, Saint Simon and Charles Fourier together with German philosophers like Kant, Fichte and Hegel. He stresses that only 'when the political and economic conditions in France and England are subjected to a German-dialectical critique can real results be achieved.' And, it is certainly true, that without the utopian seeds sown by the early French socialists, subjected to the rigorous nurture of German rationality and scientific discipline and then planted into the Industrial realities, particularly of English 19th century capitalism, there would have been no Marxist theory; these are its three main sources.

During his early years in England Engels angrily writes: 'It is something that is taken for granted in Germany but you can't knock it into the heads of the obstinate Britons, that so-called material interests can never be seen as self-sufficient, guiding goals, but that they always serve, subconsciously or consciously, a principle which guides historical progress.' This reflects an attitude that must have often frustrated and infuriated Engels, Marx and the other German communists: the German approach to life is largely philosophically-based and rational, whereas the British tend to be much more down-to-earth. They adopt a more pragmatic approach to problems and issues; philosophic speculation they find difficult to digest and are invariably suspicious of it. The reason for this difference in character and attitude to life is probably anchored in Britain's relative isolation from continental Europe where the ferment of ideas more easily crosses borders and invigorates political movements.

It is his confrontation in Manchester with the realities of Victorian capitalism that crystallises Engels' thinking on historical materialism. 'It was in Manchester,' he writes, 'where I was hit in the face by the economic realities which in the historical narrative to date have played either no role or were dismissed. At least in the modern world, though, they are a decisive historical force and the basis of today's class contradictions in those countries where industry is most highly developed e.g. as in England...' He develops these ideas, based on this new discovery, in an essay, 'Outlines of a Critique of Political Economy' which he writes during 1843 and it is published at the end of February 1844 [in the *Deutsch-Französische Jahrbücher*]. Later, in a biographical sketch on Karl Kautsky, he writes that this article was important 'because it represented the first attempt to base socialism on political economy'. He is already fully conversant with the ideas of leading economists like Adam Smith and Ricardo, whom he subjects to a thorough criticism, just as he tears apart the theories of Malthus. He ridicules the traditional economists' 'Law' of supply and demand – what are we to think of a law which produces periodic crises, he asks, rather than rely on such a fickle mechanism, wouldn't it be better to plan. He also challenges the idea of capital being a separate entity from labour – it is the product of labour i.e. merely labour in a different form, he argues. This short essay is the first attempt to fuse Hegelian dialectics with the new economic discoveries. In typically Engels fashion it is lucid, erudite and incisive, with almost Swiftian wit.

Marx admits later that it was this work that stimulated his own ideas and obliged him to examine more closely the role of economics, a subject he knew next to nothing about at the time. It triggers a correspondence between the two that eventually blossoms into a full-blooded friendship. It can justly be seen as the first exploration of the ideas that later form the basis for Marx's *Capital.* Even for us today, this short tract, which Engels wrote as a 24-year old, has amazing resonances as it unrelentingly exposes the debilities of capitalism that are still immanent. Though, interestingly, the word 'capitalism' as a description of the system of property ownership is not once mentioned in it; the term only comes into use later. The excerpt below from his *Outlines of a Critique of Political Economy* illustrate the fundamental truth of his analysis:

> "Have we overthrown the barbarism of the monopolies?" [here the term 'monopoly'refers to the dominance by individual nation states of certain sectors of trade or production] Exclaim the hypocrites. "Have we not carried civilisation to distant parts of the world? Have we not brought about the fraternisation of the peoples, and reduced the number of wars?" Yes, all this you have done – but how! You have destroyed the small monopolies so that the one great basic monopoly, property, may function the more freely and unrestrictedly. You have civilised the ends of the earth to win new terrain for the deployment of your vile avarice. You have brought about the fraternity of the peoples – but the fraternity is the fraternity of thieves. You have reduced the number of wars – to earn all the bigger profits in peace, to intensify the utmost enmity between individuals, the ignominious war of competition!

He also lambasts the idea of owning land as akin to taking away people's means of survival: 'To make earth an object of huckstering – the earth which is our one and all, the first conditions of existence – was the last step towards making oneself an object of huckstering'.[31] This is an argument the environmental movement will later take up to challenge the very idea of land ownersip. Engels' essay may be rather basic – it is after all only exploratory – but it raises crucial questions that still need addressing today: the contradiction between labour and capital, and the unequal appropriation and distribution of profits; it demonstrates the corrosive effect of the system on individuals, on family cohesion and society as a whole. Importantly, Engels also examines the different definitions of value and the crucial difference between price and value. Looking at the role of competition, he writes:

> By dissolving nationalities, the liberal economic system had done its best to universalise enmity, to transform mankind into a horde of ravenous beasts (for what else are competitors?) who devour one another just because each has identical interests... [And later:] We have seen that in the end everything comes down to competition, so long as private property exists. It is the economist's principal category – his most beloved daughter, whom he ceaselessly caresses – and look out for the Medusa's head which she will show you![32]

How contemporary those sentences sound in a time of takeovers by predatory private equity funds and globalised capital!

Although Engels is still a relative greenhorn in economic theory, he is, in his own words later, 'still somewhat proud of my first theoretical work of sociology'. This work represents the first attempt to define the subject matter of what will become Marxist political economy; it also exemplifies the turning around of Hegel's idealistic dialectics (as Marx put it: turning Hegel from standing on his head, firmly onto his feet), the proof that economic relations are nothing more than relations between human beings. As relations between human beings, they can be changed by mankind to create a more just society, leading eventuallly to the abolition of private property, which in any case will become a historical necessity. In a second article, 'The Situation in England', Engels describes the nub of the matter as the future of work and argues that the bourgeoisie is not only incapable of moulding the future history of mankind, but should be hindered from attempting to do so.

When, in 1844 at the end of August he leaves England, he is in possession of a whole new array of ideas and concepts about the connections between classes and the state. He is more aware of the immense social repercussions of the industrial revolution and has clearer ideas about the future, which he believes is already being carried in the womb of triumphant capitalism. As Marx is reaching similar conclusions to Engels, expressed in his own articles in the

Jahrbücher, he initiates an avid correspondence with Engels.

Between 1843 and '45 both Engels and Marx are, independently, in their thinking still very much under the influence of Ludwig Feuerbach[33], although both adopt different ways of tackling the same subject matter. Marx puts 'human emancipation' at the centre of his work and sees the 'inhuman' era of history as a consequence of the system of private property and workers' alienation from their work; Engels goes further, seeing communism as the necessary outcome of economic developments, particularly as a result of the industrial revolution. Their correspondence around the ideas expressed in the *Jahrbücher* has, as yet, not led to a lengthier meeting between the two men. However, Engels' return to Germany once his 'training period' is over makes it possible for him to arrange a stop-over in Paris, for ten days, where Marx is temporarily ensconced. This time, despite the nervousness of both men, the frostiness of their first meeting is immediately transformed into a warmth that will suffuse their relationship throughout the following, difficult decades. They could not contain their excitement and exhilaration at finding in each other the collaborator of which they could only dream; the identity of their thinking is almost uncanny.

This is the moment when he and Marx embark on their deep and unbreakable friendship and collaboration. From now on their lives will be like one; every political shift, every event and idea will be shared and their own views synchronously developed. Each of them, independently, has a clear vision of the goal and also the means of attaining that goal. They both realise also that only together will they be able to master the enormous task facing them. It is amazing that this bond between two such great thinkers and personalities will stand the test of time, and the great body of their work can only be properly understood when viewed as an organic whole.

For these few days he hoped to be able to forget the 'awful pewter-coloured skies' and the Lancashire smog, to enjoy the seductive sensuality of Paris. The city with its joie de vivre, the myriad memories of its world-shaking revolution and, of course, the pretty mademoiselles is dear to his heart. But the family in Barmen is impatient for his return and there is so much to talk over with Marx in the short time allotted to him, so such delights have to be postponed. He spends his short time locked in serious debate with Marx. He also manages to meet and hold discussions with the Russian anarchist, Mikhail Bakunin and other radical exiles.

These discussions elate him more than any jovial evenings in the cafes and bars or trips to the theatre could have ever done. To realise that he and Marx have been thinking along similar lines and have, in effect, done the groundwork for the establishment of a new theory of historical development is a tremendously exciting discovery. Although many disagreed then, and still do, their discovery is as ground-breaking as Darwin's discovery of evolution. Up till this point, history has been seen as either an unravelling of divine purpose or a series of events determined and brought about by great historical figures, with the mass of the people as mere backdrop.

From this time on, economics and industrial capitalism becomes central to Marx's research. Engels, though, has a great advantage over him, in that he is fully conversant with English politics and commerce. He now has first hand experience of large industrial processes and has been able to make detailed observations of a modern proletariat, how it actually exists as a class. In this sense, he is the ideal partner for Marx, who brings the ability of abstract thinking, generalising and systematic rigour to refine the ideas and goals they both have. Even in the area where Marx achieves his greatest fulfilment – political economy – Engels is, to begin with, very much the feeder. It is undoubtedly he also who pushes Marx in the direction of investigating the role of private property and the contradiction between the humane phraseology of capitalism's apologists and the inhuman practice of the free market system. It is Engels who explains to him the role of economic crises, capital accumulation and concentration.

Paul Lafargue, Marx's son-in-law, later relates that Engels told him, 'that when he met Marx in the Café de la Régence, one of the first centres of the 1789 revolution, Marx raised with him for the first time the idea of economic determinism within his theory of historical materialism.' Engels himself says of this meeting: 'We were in complete agreement on all theoretical issues, and from this date on we began our collaborative work.'

The few days Marx and Engels are meeting in Paris coincides with the arrival of a German literary journal containing a biting article by their erstwhile student friend, Bruno Bauer in response to their essays in the *Französische Jahrbücher*. They discuss bringing out a small pamphlet in reply. This will be their first collaborative effort. Engels immediately puts pen to paper, writing a first draft for what has been agreed will be a slender brochure. Marx, though, elaborates this into a full-length book. It may be that Marx did this to avoid the strict censorship laws which were aimed at publications of fewer than twenty pages. It also underlines the different approach of the two new friends: Engels always prepared to dash off a quick and short riposte, Marx determined to mine every idea to the full. So what began as a modest pamphlet becomes a more fundamental settling of accounts with their philosophic consciences: *The Holy Family or a Critique of Critical Criticism*. It is a rather prolix criticism – over 200 pages – of the Hegelian idealism of Bruno Bauer and his followers [Bauer is a theologian, philosopher and historian, and a former student of Hegel's]. In his preface, Marx writes: 'Real humanism in Germany has no worse enemy than *spiritualism* or *speculative idealism*, which in place of the *individual human being* places "*self-consciousness*" or "*spirit*"; the spirit is what animates, the flesh is no use'. In a sense *The Holy Family* provides a sketchy outline for the *Manifesto of the Communist Party*, they will write later. *The Holy Family* is a heavy salvo against philosophical idealism (the belief in a non-material force or deity).

When he receives a copy in March 1845 in Barmen, Engels is horrifed by its title, fearing the potential repercussions if his pious family get wind of it. In a letter to Marx, he also expresses his surprise that he has turned their proposed pamphlet into a rather weighty tome: 'That you have expanded the 'Critical Critique' to 20 pages [printers' sheets] was surprising enough for me,' he says, but then consoles himself that, 'it is good so and in this way more can be got across to interested parties, for goodness knows how long it would otherwise have lain in a drawer of your writing desk'.[34]

The original title of their joint work was simply *A Critique of Critical Criticism* but the publisher, on his own initiative, gives it the rather more alluring title of *The Holy Family*, finding it more epigrammatic and sensational. The title *The Holy Family* is a sarcastic reference to the group of idealist philosophers around Bruno Bauer. It represents the new dialectical materialism's first resolute skirmish with idealist philosophy.

Back in Barmen

After leaving Paris, Engels then goes on to Cologne, where he stays another three days, clearly on Marx's instructions, to brief members of the 'Cologne Circle', before continuing his journey to Barmen. On arrival, the 'prodigal son' is spared a grilling from his family, as they are all up to their necks in the arrangements for his sister Marie's wedding to Emil Blank. Emil Blank, according to Engels, is a communist, so it would appear surprising and most incongruous that the family is prepared to see one of their daughters married to one of the 'devil's servants'. However, Engels' description is perhaps more wishful thinking than hard fact. Blank has apparently expressed socialist sympathies and taken out a subscription to the *Neue Rheinische Zeitung*, but one hears nothing of a left-wing political nature after his marriage to Marie; he enters commerce and settles down to an orderly bourgeois life like the other male members of the family.

Engels uses the breathing space to renew contact with his old school friends and is surprised how radicalised they've become: 'they've really started to revolutionise their family affairs and give their elders a proper dressing down if they put on aristocratic airs with their servants or workers – and that really is something in patriarchal Elberfeld,' he writes. He is also amazed at the transformation that has taken place in the area during his short absence - further industrialisation, a more civilised political climate and the factory owners have begun to address some of the social grievances of the workers as a consequence of the weavers' revolt in Silesia that same year, 1844. This was commemorated in Heine's incisive and bitter poem, *The Silesian Weavers*, which concludes:

Doomed be the king, the rich man's king,
Who would not be moved by our suffering,
Who tore the last coin out of our hands,
And let us be shot by his blood-thirsty bands...We weave;
we weave.

Doomed be the fatherland, false name,
Where nothing thrives but disgrace and shame,
Where flowers are crushed before they unfold,
Where the worm is quickened by rot and mold...We weave;
we weave.
The loom is creaking, the shuttle flies;
Nor night nor day do we close our eyes.
Old Germany, your shroud's on our loom,
And in it we weave thy threefold doom; ...We weave;
we weave!

The starving weavers in Silesia caused quite a stir throughout Germany when they rose up against their unbearable conditions, as did the Bohemian calico printers in the spring of 1844. For the first time in ages attention is drawn to neglected social conditions of working people. Newspapers throughout the country begin printing articles on the need for social reform. The situation has again become more unsafe. Engels writes: 'there has been a steep increase in crime, robbery and murder as a response to the old social structures. The streets of an evening are very unsafe, the bourgeoisie is beaten up, attacked at knifepoint and robbed; and if the proletarians here develop under the same laws as those in England, they'll soon recognise that this behaviour, as individuals, using force as a form of protest against the social order is useless and the only real way is to protest together through communism'. He clearly understands that acts of random violence and petty crime are a valid expression of alienation from society and of anger at the crass disparities in wealth, but he also knows that such actions are meaningless without political leadership and conscious collective action. The elite is in a state of anxiety and even fear at what is bubbling beneath the surface. Only shortly before Engels' return, on 26 July 1844, a disgruntled civil servant, Ludwig Tschech, achieves minor historical infamy by attempting to assassinate King Wilhelm IV and his consort in Berlin. Such an event only serves to increase the tension.

Back in Barmen, Engels is clearly determined to give up a businessman's career once and for all and to join Marx in devoting himself full-time to revolutionary work. But he knows he can't just confront his family with such a decision, even though he is itching to return to Marx. He realises that it will take a few months to slowly acclimatise them to his wishes. When, however, he realises his father will never countenance such action, he throws himself into completing his book on the conditions of the English working class.

Once his sister's wedding is over, he is subjected to a serious talking to: '...persuasive advice from my brother-in-law and the tragic faces of my old folks obliged me to submit to the 'horse trading' [Engels uses this demeaning term invariably when he talks about the business world] again and I spent several days slogging in the office.' He says he is also persuaded to knuckle down in the office again as he's begun a love affair with a Barmen girl, about which we have no further details.

> But I was disconsolate even before I began to work,' he bemoans, 'Barmen is so awful, I don't just have to be a bourgeois, but a factory owner into the bargain, and actively engaged in battle with the proletariat. A few days in my old man's factory has confronted me once again with the awfulness of it all, as I'd somewhat overlooked this aspect. I had of course reckoned on spending only so long in this horse-trading as suited me, then write some illegal tract which would anger the police, only to slip over the border in suitably quiet fashion. But I can't even stand it that long. If I didn't have the daily reminder of the most atrocious tales from English society in my book [Condition of the Working Class in England], I think I would go somewhat stale, but that at least keeps my blood on the boil...Enough! At Easter I'm leaving. On top of it all, the flabby life in a fundamentalist Christian Prussian family – I can't take it any more; I might grow into a German Philistine and then smuggle philistinism into the communist movement.[35]

Here, in these few remarks we can almost physically identify with Engels' complete desolation and frustration. Here is a young man, enflamed by the new revolutionary philosophical ideas of his time, raring to get out there and change the world, yet being forced into the straitjacket of small-town business. This is the 'cri de coeur' of every adventurous young man, trapped in the daily routine of a 9-5 office job, even though Engels has the enviable advantage of being the boss's son.

From mid-November 1844 until mid-March '45, he completes his manuscript, on top of his work in the office and undertaking business trips on behalf of his father's firm to Cologne, Düsseldorf and Westphalia, which he of course also utilises to renew his contacts with old friends and to proselytise for the communist cause. Prussian police records, in true German fashion, archived meticulously, tell us that he is often to be seen at Schloss Holte near Bielefeld, 'where all the revolutionary elements come together.'

Despite doing his duty in the office, his father still accuses him of laziness every time he is caught poring over his manuscript. In a letter to Marx, he says that he is unable to visit, 'otherwise my family would break with me.' Like Marx, Engels occupies himself in these months not only with English matters, and shares with Marx all his thoughts. 'We should bring out a small brochure,' he writes, 'on the practicalities of ushering in communism and to provide a popular description of communist practice in England and America; we should bring out a magazine to illustrate the social misery and expose the bourgeois regime, as well as set up a library with the best works of foreign socialist writers'.

At this time Marx is still working on his book project, a critique of political economy (published under the title: *Economic and Philosophic Manuscripts*) and Engels drives him unremittingly: 'Make sure you get your book on political economy finished, even if you remain dissatisfied with much of it, that's neither here nor there, the mood is conducive and we must strike while the iron is hot...now is the time.'[36]

Engels is not only an impatient driver but can also be a most patient helper. He offers Marx some advice on what should be included in the *Manuscripts*. After reading a book by Max Stirner, titled *Der Einzige und sein Eigenthum* [*The Individual and his Property]* which takes up Jeremy Bentham's ideas on egoism, Engels sees a dialectical irony in the idea. He recommends that it should be built into their theory: the idea that it can also be egoistic to fight for a better society, because you aren't happy in the old one and can only see your own fulfilment and everyone else's, in a new, communist one.

Engels realises he has to make the goal of liberating the working class his own cause first, if it is to mean anything. In this vein he writes to Marx in Cologne:

> First we have to make this thing our own egoistic thing, before we can do anything about it and, in this sense, we are, apart from any material aspirations we may have, communists out of egoism, and as egoists we want to be human beings not just individuals. That's the way to answer the fellow [Stirner]. In the second place he must be told that in its egoism the human heart is of itself, from the very outset, unselfish and self-sacrificing, so that he finally ends up with what he is combating. These few platitudes will suffice to refute the one-sidedness. But we must also adopt such truth as there is in the principle. And it is certainly true that we must first make a cause our own, egoistic cause, before we can do anything to further it – and hence that in this sense, irrespective of any eventual material aspirations, we are communists out of egoism also, and it is out of egoism that we wish to be human beings, not mere individuals.[37]

It is interesting that Engels here appears to be promoting a more idealistic than purely materialist position i.e. man is intrinsically good. He is deliberately emphasising, in a dialectical way, the idea of individual motivation and that it should be 'natural' to desire a better society, because only in such a society can one realise one's own potential. This idea in no way invalidates the apparent contradiction between Engels' characterisation of capitalist society as 'egoistic' or selfish.

Hand in hand with the theoretical work goes practical agitation. As the working class movement appears static, Engels attends all sorts of meetings which are called to discuss social issues and seizes the few legal opportunities to introduce communist ideas. He has significant success in this work and, as an illustration, writes to Marx about a meeting in Elberfeld where 'we defeated the pious with the help of the rationalists, with an overwhelming majority - everything Christian was deleted from the statutes. I really savoured the absolutely laughable scene of the rationalists trying to uphold their theoretical Christianity with their practical atheism'.

Strengthened by their success at such gatherings, Engels and other comrades decide to hold their own public meetings in the largest hall, in Elberfeld's top inn, the Zweibrücker Hof. 'At the first meeting we had 40, at the second 130, and at the third at least 200 people,' he tells Marx proudly. In a lecture at one of these meetings, he relates how successful communist groups have already been set up in America. These are probably the first such socialist meetings to be held on German soil. The Wuppertal poet, Adolf Schults, who is present at one of them, gives us a flavour:

> In order to give the whole event an innocuous cover, a girl harpist is booked so that it can be presented as a musical-declamatory evening's entertainment. After it begins with the harpist, poems by two local poets on social issues are read to get the audience in the right mood, then Hess and Friedrich Oswald [Engels' cover name] speak, but neither is an accomplished speaker, so they have little impact.

It is left to the local theatre director and comic dramatist to defend the present order and to argue the impossibility of communism. A lively, even heated debate follows. While Hess describes communism for the audience as a natural law of love and assures them that revolution can be avoided if one helps humanitarianism to victory, Engels, who knows his home patch, feels it is more effective to appeal to the intellect of his audience, to their practical sense, to their business-schooled minds. He attempts to explain the senselessness of free competition, which by ignoring the need to better organize production and distribution, leads to crises and chaos, destroys the existence of the lower middle classes, concentrates capital and leads to sharpening class conflict and finally a necessary reordering of society.

As may be imagined, these meetings are reported in minute detail to the Rhineland president, Freiherr von Spiegel-Borlinghausen, by the mayor of Elberfeld. Among other things these communists discussed, he reports, was the 'unholy institute of marriage'! In the Mayor's report, Engels is often quoted and described as; 'Herr Frd. Engels, the eldest son of the highly esteemed father, the businessman Friedr. Engels senior. Engels' use of the pseudonym 'Oswald' is clearly no barrier to his being recognised by some of the local people. Also present at the meeting, the Mayor reports, is the lawyer, Dr. Wesendonk who states that 'communism was a truth, whose forward march could not be stopped'.[38]

Most of Engels' middle class contemporaries no doubt find it incomprehensible that such privileged young men should support a movement to overthrow the very social structures which provide them with their advantages. It is probably just as difficult for someone today in Western Europe to understand fully how middle class individuals like Engels and Marx could identify so readily with the working class and throw in their lot with it. The working class in western Europe and North America today is a less clearly defined, nebulous entity and certainly no longer has an aura of romance about it. The vast industries which spawned the working class in its classic incarnation, and as Marx and Engels experienced it, have disappeared, at least in the more highly developed nations.

To be able to understand their fascination, it is perhaps necessary to remind ourselves of the social realities of that time. Europe is slowly emerging from an era of feudalistic dynasties and most countries are run on authoritarian lines by a moneyed and privileged elite, with censorship, severe limitations on the freedom of speech and draconian laws to enforce them. These ruling elites represent a narrow class interest and are ossified in their outlook. They are opposed not only by the rising bourgeoisie; the new industrial working class, increasing with the industrialisation of the towns, also represents a new and potent force in society. Of course, it is largely uneducated, ignorant and vulgar; it is debased by poverty and overcrowding in slum conditions, and drink and debauchery are often the only forms of escape. However, within this mass, there are also increasing numbers of individuals who refuse to accept their lot, who educate themselves and who become politically and socially active. Although the overwhelming majority of the bourgoisie will certainly not see any common ground between its own aspirations and those of the working class, a tiny number of the more enlightened do. Middle class intellectuals like Marx and Engels, who fret under the constraints of the old society, see the working class as the only vital social force potentially capable of pushing through the sort of changes they themselves seek. There is, in addition, the romance of a Bohemian life, of mixing with the 'salt of the earth' and discarding the useless clutter of bourgeois rituals and hypocritical, sanctimonious behaviour.

Both Engels and Hess, when addressing the meetings in Elberfeld, speak somewhat cautiously, given the middle class public they have before them and the climate of suspicion and censorship. In Mayor von Carnap's report (quoted above) he leaves out what Engels actually says, probably to protect the reputation of Engels' father and also, no doubt, because he and Engels Sr. both work together and hold interests in a railway company.

The mayor, in concluding his report, writes that he is convinced that the citizens who attend these meetings are too honourable to be, and intelligent enough not to be, snared by the rebellious talk, but if such discussions continue, he writes, 'I would not wish to take responsibility for the consequences among the lower orders in a factory town like ours'.

Needless to say, after the Mayor's report, the government Landrat [Regional Governor] for Elberfeld and Privy Councillor, Graf von Seyssel d'Aix, having got wind of what is happening, decides to clamp down on these activities. We know from Schults that Engels intended to talk about the realisability of communism at the fourth meeting, but because of the ban this never takes place. He publishes the speech he intended to give later in the *Rheinische Jahrbücher* and in his closing sentences he gives a significant assurance that no one envisages introducing communism overnight and against the will of the nation, but nevertheless the future belongs to it, and the developmental road of all civilised nations leads to it.

At the same time the Police President enquires of the President-in-Chief of the Rhineland whether he thinks one would be able to rely on the loyalty of the military in the case of rebellion, but the latter thinks he is referring to 'communist influence' and replies that he has no worries that the communists have any influence at all on the troops and has noted no communist activities in the Rhine area. He also feels, he says, 'that such influence is improbable as it would find no suitable terrain, because the lower classes are very much beholden to the Catholic clergy whose hierarchical tendency stands in such contrast to the teachings of the communists, such that one could view the Catholic Church as a reliable antidote to such poison. And,' he goes on, 'it isn't the proletariat in the Rhineland that is the problem but the educated, and dissatisfied, middle classes'. Such is the confidence of the ruling elite, despite the warning signs. This assessment, no doubt, has a large element of veracity in it – the Wuppertal and Elberfeld populace is very devout and they salve their consciences in church every Sunday.

The owner of the Zweibrücker Inn is told he is forbidden to allow his premises to be used in the future for communist meetings, on pain of losing his licence to operate. Engels is also given to understand, that if he goes ahead with the planned fourth meeting, he will be arrested and charged. A report about the 'communist agitation in the Rhineland' is also sent to Berlin and as a result the Home Office minister there, von Arnim-Boytsenburg, bans all such meetings in the area, 'to prevent the spread of communist ideas in the factory towns of Elberfeld-Barmen, which would be incalculably dangerous'.

After the banning of the meetings, Engels is kept under particular scrutiny by the Prussian police. The Police Director submits reports of his journey through the Rhine and Westphalia and mentions Engels' activities: 'Friedrich Engels, from Barmen, is a thoroughly trustworthy man, but he has a son, who is a died-in-the-wool communist and travels around as a writer; it's possible his name is Friedrich too.' He is named in another police report as one of the leaders of the communist party.

In his conclusion to the Elberfeld lectures, Engels again defines the social ideal that absorbs him and has made him into a communist. His desire is that everyone should have the opportunity to freely develop their human essence, to interact with their neighbours on a human level, without having to fear powerful crises affecting their lives. He is prepared to devote his life to the communist ideal, he avows, because he views communism as the realisation of his own humanitarian goal. 'The really human life, with all its requirements and needs' he assures the fearful in his audience, 'we have no wish to destroy, but in fact we wish to enable the opposite to come about'. Engels confirms the exclusivity of the meetings by admitting to Marx that, 'all Elberfeld and Barmen was there, from the moneyed aristocracy to the épicerie; only the proletariat was not represented'.

Engels' family protests strongly about his communist activities. In March the book he has co-written with Marx is to be seen in an Elberfeld bookshop, and this makes Engels even more anxious. *The Holy Family* will 'cause me more conflict with my parents, who are already irritated as it is.' he writes to his friend. He is also surprised to see his name above Marx's on the title page, as he has contributed little more than a tenth of the text.

As long as his father is kept unaware of the book, he can be expected to keep his promise of letting his son attend Rhineland's Friedrich-Wilhelm's University in Bonn to study business finance, from Easter 1845, as Engels hopes to do. He will be admitted to study there because he fulfils the minimal entrance requirements. Although he has no 'Abitur', he has completed a grammar school education and his military service. There is, though, no record of his registering at the university. In a letter to Marx, in Brussels, he writes:

> At the moment I'm living a real dog's life here. Because of the meetings and the "debauched" character of several of our local communists with whom I, of course, socialize, the whole religious fanaticism of my old man is discovered anew and is made worse by my declaration of giving up a business career, and with my appearing publicly as a communist, he's developed a glittering bourgeois fanaticism too. Just imagine my position.

It is worthwhile quoting more fully from this letter and what he goes on to tell Marx, as it vividly reflects the restrictive, pious family climate that is suffocating him:

> All my letters are checked, because the family thinks it's all communist post. They put on this holier-than-thou expression – it drives me so crazy, I just have to get out of the way. I sit in my room and work, on communism of course - they know that – then they pull the same faces. I can't eat, drink, sleep, not even fart without being confronted with those damned "baby Jesus-like" expressions. If I go out or stay at home, keep quiet or speak, laugh or not, I can do what I will and immediately my old man puts on this outrageous expression. On top of all that, he is so stupid he thinks both communism and liberalism are 'revolutionary' lumping them together and then he makes me responsible, despite my protestations, for all the outrageous speeches of the English bourgeoisie in Parliament. And, to top it all, we've now entered the holy season in the house, as one of my brothers and a sister were confirmed eight days ago. Today the whole tribe are prancing off to evening mass – the Corpus Christi has done his works – the woeful faces this morning outdid everything... Yesterday evening I was with Hess talking about communism till two in the morning. Strong hints, of course, that I should have been in my bunk. Finally they build up courage enough to ask where I was. "With Hess". "With Hess! God on high!" Pause, build up of Christian despair on their faces. "What society you've chosen!" sighs etc. It's enough to drive one mad. You have no idea of the malice in this Christian witch hunt for my soul. My old man now only needs to find out about the existence of the Critical Critique and he'll turf me out of the house.[39]

Again, all Engels' despair is given full vent in this letter. One cannot help but deeply sympathise with his lot; and his worst premonitions are soon to be fulfilled.

Eventually he is forced out of the house, so taking up a university place is now out of the question. He rapidly, though, comes to terms with the new situation and, with the little money he has, he leaves to join Marx in Brussels. He is also fleeing an unhappy love affair with a Barmen girl, who has apparently rejected his advances. At this time he appears to have no plans to return to Manchester, so it has to be assumed that he considers his affair with Mary Burns to be over.

His time of voluntary exile has begun and he is free of harassment by the police back home. Marx is already on the wanted list and can no longer re-enter Germany, but Engels is still spared that indignity and can return at will, but he has no desire to do so, 'as long as the bourgeoisie talked politics but still went to church (and) what the proletariat was doing, who knows?' Despite everything, he is able to complete *The Condition of the Working Class in England* and this is published in Leipzig in 1845. Although being ostensibly about Britain, its explosive combination of descriptions of poverty and oppression with the ideas of revolutionary socialism is immediately clear to any intelligent reader in Germany. In it Engels discusses the problems of a modern city, of industrial work, alientation and poverty and how these can be overcome. In many ways it remains a contemporary discussion. It is received as a bombshell. By combining sober factual material gleaned from the *Factories and Mines Inspectorate Reports* with his own keen observations and political understanding, Engels has thrown down a gauntlet to the home-grown mill owners.

Hearing about Marx's precarious financial situation in his Brussels exile, Engels offers him, 'with profound pleasure', any royalties paid on his book, so that, 'the swine will at least not be granted the pleasure of placing you in financial embarrassment by their infamy'.

The book's later publication in English has no less a profound impact than it had in Germany. After all, few read or even knew about the reams of factory inspectors' reports, but distilled and brought to public knowledge in an easily digestable book, which also underlines the inchoate power of the working class and its revolutionary potential, it represents an incendiary mixture. In his foreword to the German edition he says that it was conceived only as a first chapter to a more comprehensive work on the social history of England, but that the importance of the subject matter obliged him to publish it separately.

Karl Kautsky comments perceptively: '...For the first time the necessity of fusing socialism and the workers' movement was discussed. With this book, we have the beginning of theoretical socialism. It is based largely, if only partially consciously, on the same foundation as is the *Communist Manifesto*, which is written two years' later...Engels sees not just misery, as the socialists of his time do, but the germs of a higher social structure which it carries within its womb. Later generations who will grow up in the intellectual atmosphere of modern socialism will find it difficult to imagine what an achievement the 24 year-old Engels notched up with his book, at a time when the suffering of the working class was either denied or bemoaned, but not investigated as a link in the historical process.'

Engels argues that as long as the owning classes show no inclination for freedom themselves, and also oppose the self-liberation of the workers by every means, then the workers will be forced to undertake the social revolution by themselves. But he passionately believes that communism is 'an issue for humanity not just for the workers'. Interestingly, he argues, in the conclusion to his book, that to the extent the proletariat adopts communist and socialist elements as its own, then to the same extent will the coming revolution see less blood-letting, acts of revenge and anger, 'because the communist understands that the individual bourgeois cannot behave otherwise in the present circumstances'. In this way, he feels, a communist organisation would be able to contain the brutality of the revolution, before it devolves into terror as the 1789 French one did, and would eventually bring it under control.

The authorities take no action against Engels' book, but when his friend Moses Hess and others attempt to publish similar social criticism in a new paper for working people, the authorities come down like a ton of bricks. It is marginally acceptable to publish a book which only a few middle class individuals will purchase, but to have those same ideas in a cheap paper intended for the lower classes could only inflame matters even more. In Germany publishing anything of even a liberal tinge, never mind radical, is still virtually impossible; censorship is everywhere and the rulers tolerate no deviation from the hegemonic ideology. Engels admits later that he had little idea at the time of what real theoretical research work really meant and had learnt first hand from Marx how to work'. However with his good practical sense and myriad connections, he has, in many ways, a higher profile than Marx, and is viewed by many in the contemporary workers' movement at this time as the theoretical leader.

What Engels learns in Manchester about the dehumanising process of industrial capitalism, about economic crises, the relationship of wages to profit, the population theories of Malthus and the dominating force of private property lead him to put economics centre stage. He is convinced that only by overcoming the hegemony of capitalist production can working people and mankind as a whole be set free. These ideas are to become the basis of 'scientific socialism', and he is the first to discover them. With his usual modesty, he says that Marx finally gave these ideas their focus. 'Marx stood higher, saw further and had a better and quicker overview than all others,' he said.

What Marx achieves through philosophical and historical deduction, Engels does through looking at the economic realities in England and from his political practice, although Marx is clearly more advanced in terms of the level and incisiveness of his concept formation.

Chapter Four (1845 – 1848)
Exile and the Communist Manifesto

Among the middle classes of Wuppertal the rumour circulates for weeks that Friedrich Engels, who stood up and spoke so forthrightly at communist meetings, has, as the better part of valour, chosen to escape overnight to America.

For Engels himself, now safely in Brussels, feelings are mixed; on the one hand, he is overjoyed to escape the pettiness and oppressive home atmosphere and to be with his friend Marx, but on the other he feels a certain sadness on having to leave his close comrades in the Rhineland and his 'Heimat', the homeland, so dear to most Germans. He moves into lodgings close to Marx and soon has, safe in his wallet, the emigration permit from His Majesty's Belgian Government which allows him to reside in Belgium until he should decide to emigrate to the USA. He probably obtains this on Marx's advice, as he himself has already considered moving there. America is a pioneering and profoundly democratic country with a burgeoning industry, as well as with a now sizeable population of German and other European émigrés. It would provide a fertile soil for revolutionary activities they feel. However, in the end, neither of them takes advantage of the opportunity, as Brussels is also an ideal city in which a communist political programme for the coming revolution can be elaborated without outside interference, and it is a suitable place for them to continue their theoretical work, at least in the short term.

Brussels is characterised by a tranquil, almost provincial atmosphere. Founded on the bourgeois freedoms gained in the revolution of 1830, the upper middle class and the clerical hierarchy hold the reins of power tightly in their hands; there are no signs of even an inchoate workers' movement. Clearly the government feels no threat from a small, motley group of German radicals, though the police still keep tabs on them.

Both Marx and Engels live only a short walk away from the 'Bois Sauvage', a hotel for foreigners where most of the German emigrants end up staying. Marx himself has lived here with his whole family since he was expelled from Paris. Other émigrés, including the poet Ferdinand Freiligrath and Heinrich Bürgers, who came with him, still live there. In early 1845, though, Marx moves into one of the Brussels suburbs and within a week a group of progressive and democratically-minded German émigrés, as well as several Belgians and Poles form a small colony around him. The Belgian police records reveal that Engels took a house next to Marx from May 1845.

Engels relates that when he met up with Marx in the spring of 1845, Marx 'had already drafted the basis of his theory of historical-materialism and we sat down to work on the details of this newly won perspective, in its various ramifications'. Although Engels gives Marx the credit of being the first to elaborate this theory, Marx himself emphasises how far Engels had developed the basic ideas, independently: 'Friedrich Engels...came to the same conclusion as I had, but via a different process. Once he arrived in Brussels in the spring of 1845 we decided to elaborate our opposition to the ideology of German philosophy and, in fact, to draw a line under our previous philosophical mentality'. [40]

Engels, using Brussels as his base, is keen to travel to other European countries to cement links with the workers' movements there. In June 1845 he is also determined to visit the Rhineland again, and to utilise the fact that his sister Marie is now married to 'the communist' Emil Blank. It would provide an ideal fig leaf for him to carry out more agitational work for the communist cause. He is at this time, still somewhat of a hot-head, impatient for change and regrets that 'we can only rely on writing pens and that we can't implement our thinking directly with our hands or, if needs be, with our fists'. He seriously believes that neither he nor his compatriots will live to 50. At Marx's 50th birthday celebration in 1868, he recalls: 'What youthful enthusiasts we were 25 years' ago, when we prided ourselves on being beheaded well before we reached this age.' This is very reminiscent of Che's remarks and his selfless heroism at the same age. In a letter to his old friend Julio Castro in 1959, Che writes: 'This experience of ours is really worth taking a couple of bullets for. [If you *do* come,] don't think of returning, the revolution won't wait. A strong hug from the one who is called and whom history will call…' [41]

Engels belatedly discovers that his Belgian permit is only valid for travel to other countries, not to return to Germany, whence he has come. In addition, as the poet Georg Weerth writes to his mother, 'he is fallen out terribly with his family; they see him as Godless and notorious, and his wealthy father refuses to give him another penny. But I know this son as a supremely good person who has a rare understanding and intelligence, and exerts enormous efforts, day and night in fighting for the welfare of the working classes'.

For the summer of 1845 he plans another trip to England to collect material for his new book about the development of English industrial society. He manages to undertake this journey, despite a shortage of money, and Marx accompanies him, travelling via London to Manchester. Another motivation, no doubt, is also to see Mary Burns again and perhaps persuade her to accompany him back to Brussels. He explains his trip to the family by saying he has to return to Manchester to collect some books he left there.

For both Marx and Engels it is a memorable journey, and what was intended as a short stay, is extended to six weeks. For the two of them to be alone together, fancy free and under no outside pressures, it is a real holiday. He later recalls his friend sitting in the alcove of Chetham's Library in Manchester. There, the surrounding, leaded and stained-glass windows filter the light, making even the dismal weather outside appear sunny. Engels also takes the opportunity of this short trip to re-establish his links with the left wing of the Chartist movement and introduce Marx to Harney, Owen and his other close friends. For Marx, this is his first opportunity to see English industrial capitalism first hand and to immerse himself in the literature dealing with the Island's economy.

During July and August they occupy themselves intensively with the English economy and history. Engels manages to fill three exercise books full of dense text as a result of this short visit and enjoys a 'wonderful time' researching collaboratively with his great friend. In London they hold more talks with George Harney and the leaders of the secret League of the Just, the forerunner of the League of Communists. They also help in the organisation of an international society of 'Fraternal Democrats' which is consolidated by radicals from a number of countries, after they have left. It is an organisation which remains in existence up to 1859. Harney, from the English side, is an incredibly reliable force and has a vital input into the organisation which comprises 130 Germans, 40 Scandinavians, 20 Hungarians, Poles, Russians, Italians, Swiss, Belgians, French, English and individuals from other countries. It also gives a focus for the propagation of their ideas on communism.

On their journey back from Manchester to London, and then on to Brussels, they are accompanied this time by Engels' partner, Mary Burns, whom he has persuaded to join him. She stays at Engels' side for a whole year, until August 1846. It is a happy, if not an easy year. Mary's sunny character and her bubbly temperament have a beneficial effect on all of them and she even inspires Georg Weerth to dedicate a poem to her. Below are several verses to give the flavour:

From Ireland she came with the flood
All the way from Tipperary
With her warm, rushing blood
What a young maid, was Mary
And as she jauntily jumped ashore
The sailors hailed her pose
"Maid Mary, thank God
Like a wild, wild Rose!

She, though, countered wild and cheeky
Even if her lips burned,
Always on the market's busy corner,
Her bearded acquaintances.
Oh, the waste of kisses galore
She had no pity
Sie swore, she cried and oh, she tore
Free of all those arms!

And with the money she took
For her juicy golden fruits
She ran quickly home
With angry mien
Took that money and locked it away
And then in January

To Ireland fast and sure
She sent it off.

That's for my people's care
That's my contribution to your coffers!
Up, and sharpen your swords and axes if you dare
And nurture the old hatreds
The shamrock of Tipperary
Longs to o'ergrow
the rose of England – Hail Mister
O'Connell from Miss Mary.[42]

Weerth clearly finds Mary attractive, and when he is again in Brussels in 1846, he is still fascinated by her personality and writes to his mother, describing her as a woman, beautiful as a wild rose, sending dark, audacious glances, and how their three-way conversations take place half in English and half in German.

The year 1845/46 is not an easy one for Engels and Mary, as there is very little money coming in. Georg Weerth helps them financially when he can, but they are living from hand to mouth most of the time. How Mary, herself, fares is not documented. Clearly, from Weerth's remarks, she doesn't lose her sense of humour, but with only English and a little Gaelic, she will have found it virtually impossible to converse with the others, apart from with Weerth and, to a limited extent, with the Marxes. But, with Marx and Engels spending most of their days and evenings locked away in intensive reading and writing, and having little money herself, she will have felt very isolated.

Early in 1846 Marx, Engels and the Belgian Philippe Gigot set up the Brussels Communist Correspondence Committee. The aim of the Committee is to form the basis of an international revolutionary workers' movement, a sort of prototypical International. It will serve as a networking and co-ordinating centre for socialist movements in the various countries. One of its members is Edgar von Westphalen, the younger brother of Marx's wife, Jenny.

Engels, always looking for practical ways of spreading their new ideas, dreams also of initiating a new system of propaganda with the establishment of a newspaper or magazine and pamphlets to propagate the ideas of the Committee. It does indeed become possible to produce a series of lithographically printed pamphlets which are distributed to their contacts in other countries. This method is largely unknown at the time in working class circles, and, when the pamphlets come out, they cause a minor sensation. It is an important breakthrough and precursor of the later proliferation of left wing printing presses, leaflets and papers.

In August 1846, when Engels leaves for Paris, where he is sent on behalf of the Brussels Communist Correspondence Committee, Mary returns to England. We don't know whether this is her own choice – very likely it is, as she will have missed her 'own people' - or whether Engels feels her presence in Paris would place restrictions on his activities or perhaps the main reason is just lack of money. Harney's letters to Mary are the only ones that give a small insight into her life, as she is unable to write, but they provide no information about this period. It will be several years before Engels returns to Manchester and they can see each other again.

Engels is a bit of a lad for the girls and although most of his life he is described as a 'bachelor', he remains far from celibate. When he returns to Brussels again from Paris, he soon finds consolation in a Flemish girl, called Joséphine, and she is the unwitting cause of one of the very few slight, if temporary, shadows to fall across his relationship with Marx. She lives with Engels in Brussels and is introduced into the German Workers' Club, but is indignantly rebuffed by Marx's wife, Jenny. One of the Club's members reports that Marx and his wife would sit in one corner of the large room and Engels with his 'woman' in the opposite one. However this does nothing to lessen the friendship between the two men. Jenny's attitude is probably not adopted out of prudery as such – she fully accepted Mary Burns – but more likely out of solidarity with Mary.

The year Engels spends in Brussels is used to undertake intensive theoretical work and he and Marx are able to lay out the basis for their new theory of historical materialism which they hope to publish as *The German Ideology*, but this proves impossible at the time, for two reasons: one, no German publisher is willing to risk the wrath of the Prussian censor and, two, because its ideas are vehemently opposed by the non-revolutionary 'true' socialists. In response, Marx then promises to present the German public with a document describing the background to the publishing ban on his work.

The German Ideology, only the second book Marx and Engels write together, is less of interest today for its polemic with contemporary

German philosophy than for the newly formulated philosophical position they adopt. Those pages of the original manuscript still extant show how closely they were already collaborating; one page is divided vertically down the middle and on one side Marx has written a text and on the other Engels, directly alongside.

In the manuscript, economic and social developments are described as historically necessary processes, and the dialectic between the productive forces and relations of production are formulated clearly for the first time, as the motors of change. The significance of revolution as the driving force for social change is emphasised, and also, for the first time, their philosophy, described as 'real humanism' in *The Holy Family*, a year before, is now termed 'theory-based' or 'scientific' communism. They formulate it thus: 'Communism is, for us, not a condition to be created, an ideal according to which reality has to shape itself. We call Communism the real movement which will supersede the present conditions...for real materialists, i.e. communists, the issue is to revolutionise the existing world, to grapple with the existing conditions and change them'.[43]

These are the ideas that lay the basis for the worldwide communist movement and form the kernel of its philosophy. That is also the reason why successive right-wing leaders of the German social democratic movement, well into the 20th century, pretended that the manuscript never existed and prevented its publication. The British Labour Party took a similar attitude and throughout its history rejected Marxist ideas. It is only in 1927, shortly after a copy of the document comes into the hands of the Soviet Communist Party, that large sections will finally be published, and only in 1932 that *The German Ideology* will be published in full – ninety years after it is written.

There is little doubt that on this project Engels is the more active in the partnership. He produces a first draft which both then discuss and which Engels then writes up once more for Marx to edit and make final revisions. This method shortens the work on the manuscript considerably, as Marx is a very meticulous and slow worker. He reveals this, humorously, in one of his letters by apologising for it being over-long, as he is 'in a hurry and lacks the time to make it brief'!

Engels arrives alone in Paris in August 1846 to take the first steps towards realising the ambitious aims of the Brussels Committee. For the time he is in Paris, he also writes articles for several newspapers, including for the Chartist, *Northern Star*, maintaining the vital network and relationships necessary if their dream of an international workers movement is to be realised. He feels very happy in Paris, which he calls, 'the heart and brain of the world...queen of all cities'. Although he is there for only a year and a half before the upcoming earthquake of the February revolution of 1848, he notes little evidence of what is simmering under the calm surface: 'as the youth of the "haute and petit bourgeoisie" still have money to squander on pleasure and even a section of the working class is well enough placed to partake in the general joviality and light heartedness'.

He takes cheap lodgings on the Left Bank, as money is still tight, and has to renounce most, if not all, creature comforts. This however probably makes it that much easier for him to immerse himself fully in revolutionary activities. He works with leaders of the Paris cells of the League of the Just, meets representatives of the radical democrats, holds discussions with the utopian communist Cabet and talks to journalists. He also visits, for the first time, the revolutionary poet Heinrich Heine. The poet already has close associations with Marx and the two have corresponded regularly. Marx also published Heine's classic, satirical epic poem, *Germany – a Winter's Tale*, which the poet wrote after his return visit to Germany after his years in exile. For Engels, a great admirer of Heine's caustic satirical works, it is undoubtedly a moving occasion. It is quite likely that he and Heine subsequently socialise together, although we have no confirmation of this. Heine, like Engels, is deeply attracted to women and the sensual pleasures of life.

Engels has no problems attracting women, as he is not only tall, slim and handsome, but also speaks excellent French. When he sometime later congratulates Paul Lafargue on his very competent English, the former, with a wink, tells him: 'the French "grisettes" (good-time girls) who taught you your French certainly earned their money honestly and to such an extent that you no longer require their services.' He makes no attempt to hide his 'carnal and erotic desires' and often castigates 'hypocritical petty bourgeois moral prudery. It is high time,' he writes, 'that at least German workers get used to things which they do daily or nightly and are not embarrassed to talk about natural, essential and exceedingly pleasurable things like the Latin peoples, like Homer and Plato, like Horace and Juvenal, like the *Old Testament* and,' he adds mischievously, 'the *Neue Rheinische Zeitung.*' In indulging his pleasures he is, though, clearly circumscribed by money: 'If I had an income of 5,000 Francs I would do nothing but work and amuse myself with the women until I was kaputt. If there were no French women, life would be not in the slightest worth the effort'. He also enjoys going to the theatre and watching the latest farces. On Sundays he goes for walks with friends into the countryside around Paris, but during the week he spends most days in earnest study.

Engels has a hard time trying to counter the social democratic arguments of the self-styled 'real' socialists, particularly those associated with Karl Grün, who becomes Proudhon's philosophy teacher and wields considerable influence over the German radicals in Paris. In a letter to Marx, he reveals his frustrations: 'Grün has really muddled the guys so profoundly that the most idiotic phrase makes more sense to them than the simplest factual economic argument. That we are obliged to exert so much effort to defeat such barbaric idiocy is vile. But one has to be patient and I'm not letting these fellows off the hook until I've defeated Grün on the field of battle and split open his stupid head'. He is at the same time trying to woo the émigrés away from the utopian Weitling's influence.

The young émigré and typesetter, Stephan Born, in his memoirs, published after Engels' death describes him at the time as not being able to find the right tone with the German artisans: 'he didn't have the character of a worker and refused to put on a pretence of being one'. Engels no doubt let his anger at their perceived backwardness come to the surface and is less tactful than would have been prudent. This is undoubtedly due more to youthful inexperience than bourgeois arrogance.

Since Marx and Engels have discovered the role played by economic development in history, they are like two evangelists, determined to convince other socialists of this vital key to both understanding the historical process and for taking control of it. It is perhaps difficult for us today, to realise what a breakthrough this discovery was and how difficult it must have been for many at the time to accept its almost bathetic truth.

Engels' second task in Paris is to develop closer relations with the French workers' movement and he does have, as with the Germans, a modest success, but it is not long lasting because as a result of unrest in the suburb of Faubourg St. Antoine, the police begin watching closely everyone in this working class suburb who is involved in socialist agitation. There have been demonstrations and violence on the part of unemployed or under-employed families, who are going hungry. Engels has been active among them, and he is reasonably certain he has been put under surveillance, as the police spies are hardly inobtrusive, but he enjoys throwing them off his tail. But life is by no means all work and no play for our intrepid revolutionary, as he himself admits: 'If they are really snitches,' he says, 'and I know for certain some are, then the préfecture will have dished out a large number of entrance tickets to the balls in Montesquieu, Valentino, Prado et al'. He also makes no secret of the fact that he is grateful to the Chief of Police for, 'the really lovely chicks I've been able to meet and the considerable pleasure I've had, because I was determined to fully utilise the days and nights in Paris that may be my last'.

He is alarmed when he hears that the Chief of Police has apparently requested that the Home Office Minister issue an expulsion order on him and other leading revolutionary foreigners. He knows, too, that, 'a massive pile of secret reports lies in the préfecture, right next door to the place where they carry out medicals on the prostitutes'.

By October 1846, Engels' father seems to have cooled his temper somewhat and begins sending money again, probably in an attempt to engineer some form of reconciliation – he needs his eldest son to help in the family firm. Engels uses the money immediately to move into more salubrious lodgings. However, with increasing police harassment, he is very soon obliged to go underground and he makes elaborate arrangements to have his post sent to 'safe' addresses, like that of a 'Monsieur A. Körner, artiste-peintre'.

In January 1847 the League of the Just sends the watchmaker Joseph Moll to Marx in Brussels and to Engels in Paris in order to persuade them to join. They agree to do so, but only if they are given the opportunity of presenting their ideas in the form of a manifesto and of proposing the League's reorganisation. This is agreed, and Engels immediately begins actively organising in the five Parisian groups of the League; Marx works with the group in Brussels. Their agitational work is at last bearing fruit, they feel and is, as Engels puts it, 'going completely according to our wishes'.

Despite being away from Britain, Engels nevertheless maintain his links with the revolutionary section of the British Chartist movement through George Harney and keeps himself fully informed of what is happening in the British Isles. Britain is at this time undergoing a deep economic crisis and Ireland is experiencing the horrors of the great famine, both conducive factors for revolution, Engels believes. He and Marx also send congratulations to the Chartist leader Fergus O'Connor on his tremendous electoral victory in Nottingham in the 1847 General Election. He is the first Chartist MP in the country.

The Manifesto of the Communist Party

The League of the Just, founded by German workers in Paris in 1836, is fundamentally a utopian Christian-communist organisation and the majority of its members are German émigrés. It is very much aware of its deficiencies, of the need to restructure and have a strong and clear leadership, and that's why it has asked Engels and Marx to become involved. Once they join, the two are determined to change it from a utopian and conspiratorial communist organisation to one based on 'scientific' or 'theory-based' socialism. One of the main conditions that he and Marx demand before joining the League is to make the new statutes free of any authoritarian superstition.

In June 1847 at its congress convened in London, it becomes duly reconstituted as a democratic organisation and renames itself the League of Communists. The old mystical and conspiratorial traditions are indeed abandoned; a new democratic structure agreed and elections organised. Marx cannot attend, but Engels is present as the representative from Paris and their comrade, Wolff from Brussels. At both its first and second congresses, Engels is given the main task of fighting their corner, with the aim of transforming the organisation from an eclectic group of utopian socialists, with disparate ideologies, into a unified party with a clear programme. In fact he and Marx find they are pushing at, if not an open door, then at least one that is ajar.

According to the newly adopted rules of the League, and the agreed new democratic procedure, the statutes and new programme are to be presented to the individual local groups for consideration, before being finally submitted to a second congress for approval. The programme, to become the basis of all future propaganda, will be in the form of a 'communist creed'. In the old League the motto had been: 'All men are brothers'; now, as proclaimed in the first (and last, as it turns out) issue of the *Communist Magazine* [*Kommunis-*

tische Zeitschrift], it becomes 'Proletarians of all countries unite'. In all likelihood, this phrase is from Marx. The magazine is published immediately after the congress finishes. It doesn't deny the former motto but removes the 'natural right' mantle, supplanting the generalised call for brotherhood with a more shrill and rebellious proletarian call to arms.

In July, Engels travels to see Marx in Brussels to discuss how to promote the League, now that it has adopted their proposals, and together they develop an ambitious programme of action. Here they also set up a new German Workers' Club and, he later relates: 'we took over the *Deutsche-Brüsseler Zeitung* [German-Brussels newspaper] and thus had a mouthpiece up until the February 1848 revolution'. This paper gives them an opportunity of communicating with a wider German readership. It is published twice weekly by Adalbert von Bornstedt, a former editor of Bernstein's *Vorwärts*, but he, it later turns out, is actually in the pay of the Austrian and Prussian governments.

Marx's and Engels' chief goal at this time – and this is the reasoning behind the *Manifesto of the Communist Party* they write later in the year – is to campaign for the formation of workers' parties wherever possible and to ensure that they adopt communist ideas. They realise that a workers' revolution is hardly feasible at the present and therefore put all their energies into supporting (bourgeois) democratic revolutions, which they see as a prerequisite for the eventual proletarian revolution, while at the same time building up the nascent communist forces.

Already by 1847 the small communist colony in Brussels has grown significantly and now includes their former colleagues from the *Rheinische Zeitung*, Wolff and Hess, two valuable and capable comrades. Marx and Engels also work closely with the organisation of 'Brussels Democrats', of which Marx is vice-president. When debates at the Brussels Club become too tedious, Engels and Marx amuse themselves by pretending to argue with each other: 'Marx would defend free trade and I protectionism, and I can still recall the amazed expressions on their faces as they watched us let loose on each other', Engels notes wryly.

In October 1847, between the two League congresses, Engels returns to Paris once more and tries to achieve the kind of success they've experienced in Brussels. He already has a very high standing among the Paris Communist League cells, and becomes secretary of the Paris Regional Committee. He is certainly an excellent socialiser and knows how to charm his way around. He manages to get himself elected as a delegate, without opposition, to the League's Second International Congress in London. While active among the Communist Leaguers, he also maintains amicable relations with the French Democratic Socialists and writes articles for their paper, *La Réforme,* and is also on good terms with Louis Blanc,[44] later to become a member of the provisional government on the wave of the 1848 revolution.

Once back in Paris, at the end of October 1847, Engels begins writing his *Principles of Communism*, as a draft programme for the League's second congress. He does this to ensure that the leaders of the young revolutionary movement will comprehend clearly what is needed to achieve their aims. But while working on these principles, he is already having serious doubts about the form. He feels strongly that a secular and rationalist programme will not sit comfortably in a quasi-religious creed format. Once formulated, these principles are presented and discussed in the Parisian cells of the League, thus making Engels the organizer of the first ever Marxist party discussions. His *Principles* become the preliminary sketch for the *Manifesto of the Communist Party* (today, better known under its more laconic title of: *The Communist Manifesto)* written by both Marx and Engels later.

In his *Principles* he sets out a list of fundamental changes that would need to be implemented by a communist government in the changeover period after the revolution, and in this list he reveals amazingly forward thinking. It is also the only attempt by either Marx or Engels to offer a glimpse of what a future communist society might look like. He calls, for instance, for the education of all children, from the moment they no longer require a mother's care, to take place in national institutions, paid for by the state; for equal inheritance rights for illegitimate and legitimate children, and for transport systems to be in the hands of the nation. He calls, among other things, for the destruction of all unhealthy and jerry-built dwellings and slum areas and the setting up of a centralised national banking system. Interestingly, it is in this same year, 1848, that John Stuart Mill publishes his *Principles of Political Economy*, in which he takes a completely opposite position, arguing in favour of free markets, albeit with limited state intervention; it becomes one of the most widely read books on economy in Britain at the time.

Mill later adopts a more socialist orientated attitude to economics.

Engels' *Principles* may not sound exceptionally revolutionary today, but they certainly are in 1847. Later, in the second section of the *Communist Manifesto* and in the *Demands of the Communist Party of Germany*, Marx incorporates Engels' *Principles* in edited form. This again reflects their almost identical thinking in so many areas. There are heated debates during the congress, but in the end Engels manages to persuade the majority of delegates to accept his draft programme, based on the *Principles*, to change the League into a propaganda society, shorn of its conspiratorial and utopian aspects and essentially under his and Marx's leadership.

In the discussions about adopting a democratic or an authoritarian organisational form, both Engels and Marx always argue for a democratic one. They admit that in a secret organisation there is a need for a central command, but as soon as you take on a more open and public profile, they argue, then elections become necessary. And this is what they want the League to do.

It is agreed that the reorganisation of the League will be undertaken on the basis of Engels *Principles*. In these, Engels reiterates that 'Communism is not a doctrine, but a movement; it isn't based on the prerequisites of certain principles but on the facts. 'Communists,' he maintains, 'don't adopt this or that philosophy, but act on the basis of the whole of history and particularly the present realities pertaining in the civilised countries'.

From now on the organisation will be known as the League of Communists and becomes the first de facto revolutionary workers' party, taking up the struggle under the slogan: 'Proletarians of all countries unite!' It is structured in branches or cells, each having to have more than three, but not more than ten, members; there would be circles, leading circles, a central committee and regular congresses. 'Democratic centralism' becomes its method of working. Everywhere, in those countries where the League has branches a similar programme of work is soon adopted: one day in the week is designated for discussion, another for social entertainment (singing, declamation etc); each branch sets up its own library and if possible organises classes for workers in elementary subjects.

'Democratic centralism' later becomes the organising principle for all the world's communist parties to date. In essence, this term should mean that after what is ideally a wide democratic debate among the membership, the issues are voted upon up to the highest

> when I then, time and time again, read the shameless lies in the Cologne paper, for example the baseness of that beggar Wachenhusen [a journalist on the paper], when I see the same people, who during the war read in the whole of the French press only lies, but who now believe every police fiction against the Commune, every slander in the most popular Parisian trash rag and trumpet it throughout Germany as if it were the Evangelium itself, it puts me in a mood that is not conducive to providing a sober response. [And, as a PS]: You can tell Emil Blank that Marx needs no money from me. I would like to see the face of that same Emil Bl. if I tried giving him advice about how to use his money.[96]

Engels' irritation is only too easy to understand. The family is attacking his friendship with Marx – the one thing that is most dear to him. There is also the bitterness left by the family's attitude to the sharing of his father's inheritance. His legitimate share was denied him and he was only given 'the right to employ' the capital tied up in the English company which, on leaving, he had to pay back to the family. In 1869 a new arrangement is made in the case of his mother dying, again to his disadvantage. It will permit him to use the interest, but not touch the capital. His relatives wish to ensure that none of the family money flows into the coffers of the communists.

His mother dies on 29 October 1873. She had fallen ill earlier in the year, but Engels manages to visit her on the day before she dies. Her death, completely unexpectedly, hits him with 'double pain', and from this moment on his links with the family virtually cease and he no longer visits his home town. Only with his brother Hermann does he maintain reasonably amicable relations.

Building the IWA

The International Workingmen's Association, sometimes called the First International, is founded in 1864 and holds its first meeting in St. Martin's Hall, London. Since the suppression of the revolutionary upsurge throughout Europe in 1849, there has been a period of quiescence in the workers' movement. With the founding of the International, largely on the initiative of foreign émigrés living in Britain, an attempt is made to re-ignite the revolutionary flame and to offer an organising focus for the disparate socialist and radical groups throughout the continent. Marx is one of the chief initiators and he keeps Engels informed of developments, as well as asking his advice. At its height, the organisation numbers over a million and a half members.

At its second Congress in Geneva in1866 and the third in Lausanne in 1867, it is dominated largely by the Proudhonists. However, at the Brussels Congress in 1868 it adopts the tactics suggested by Marx. This victory for the Marxist faction is, however, again seriously challenged at the Basle Congress in 1869, which is characterised by a serious clash between Bakunin's supporters and Marx over the organisation's tactics, but particularly over the issue of abolishing the right to inheritance.

With Marx's continued ill-health during the late sixties, Engels was invited to join the General Council of the IWA and took on increasing responsibilities in the 28-strong leadership. He is instrumental in organising its historic London conference between 17-23 September 1871. Records of attendance at General Council meetings show that Engels did not miss a single one.

During the two years which have elapsed since the Basle Congress of 1869, the General Council has been left to its own devices. The Franco-German war and suppression of the Commune served as a reason for not calling a congress in 1870; in 1871 a 'secret conference' is convened by the General Council. Engels goes about organising it so clandestinely that it appears that neither the German nor British security services are aware that the congress is to take place until quite late in the day. One of the delegates must have been a police spy, as the Prussians receive detailed reports of the congress. It is held inauspiciously in the meeting room of the German Section of the International in London – a first floor room of the Blue Post pub in Newman Street. There are 23 representatives, thirteen of whom are members of the General Council, seven of them corresponding secretaries. Engels is appointed as delegate for Saxony, as no one is able to attend in view of the impending trial for high treason of members of the International there. The trade union activist, John Hales represents Britain.

The most urgent question before the conference is the imminent threat of a split in the International between the anarchists with their supporters and the Marx-Engels faction. This struggle threatens the very survival of the organisation. Among other important issues on the agenda are measures to strengthen the International's organisation and of its General Council; the checking of the centrifugal forces which are emerging within the International and threatening its unity; and taking a definitive position on the hotly disputed topic of participation in the political struggle. Another significant topic to be discussed is whether to sanction the formation of separate working women's branches although both sexes would still be able to participate as members of ordinary branches.

The conference is characterised by its attack on Bakunin and his anarchist grouping as a 'divisive sect'. Bakunin, although declaring himself an internationalist, gives a decidedly nationalist twist to almost every political question. His negative attitude to Germans is blatantly racist; only Slavs are good. And he throws in 'the Yids' as even worse than the Germans. Marx, as a German of Jewish background, is of course the worst of all. Such attitudes colour the bitter battles between Marx and Engels on the one side and Bakunin and his supporters on the other. The core of their ideological differences is the question of power, particularly since the experience of the Commune. Marx and Engels view the anarchist position of abstention from established political processes and of opposition to the foundation of proletarian parties as fallacious and oppose this vociferously. They believe that the workers have to take control of the state in order to achieve liberation; Bakunin believes state power has to be smashed as a prerequisite for true liberation. Engels is also very much opposed to Bakunin's dismissal of organisation as 'authoritarian', arguing that 'revolution itself is an imposition of authority'. He is also convinced that Bakunin heads a secret organisation and that it is active in the International. Latter-day followers of Bakunin still dispute this, but it was widely known even then that Bakunin had founded a conspiratorial organisation already in 1864 with the aim of preparing for a social revolution.

Both factions prepare for the coming battle, which is seen as decisive. Marx and Engels are willing to use all means to defeat Bakunin and his followers and prevent them taking over the leadership of the International. Although, unlike Bakunin, they have at this time no significant following on the ground, they carry great intellectual weight on the General Council itself. They feel that, at this conference, the future of the working class movement throughout the world is at stake. Bakunin is very influential internationally, particularly in Italy and Spain, where his ideas dominate the movement. Most worker and peasant groups there warm to his demands for the immediate elimination of the state and all authority.

Engels argues that it is impossible to dismantle the state 'before you change the social relations that gave rise to it'.

This conference cannot really be said to be fully representative of the International, seeing that a number of sections, the Jura Federation among them, are not invited. Nevertheless, it passes resolutions which radically change the general rules of the organisation, resolutions tending to entrench a hierarchical and authoritarian structure, with disciplined sections entirely under the control of the General Council. The latter is very conscious of the fact that a formal defeat of the anarchists at the conference will hardly put an end to the ideological conflict and that the battle has to be won on the ground. The anarchists, of course, far from laying down their weapons after the London conference, begin to wage open war against the General Council, and this leads to a serious disruption of the organisation's work.

Marx and Engels, over many years, seriously underestimated the role of the socially less developed countries and argued that these had to reach the developmental level of the more highly industrialised nations before their workers could play a significant role in the struggle for socialism. This assessment gives Bakunin and his supporters free reign in those countries. It is an error that, in their struggle for dominance of the International, plays a key role in their ultimate defeat, despite their nominal victory at the Hague congress the following year.

The radical Italian philosopher Benedetto Croce, commenting on why Marx was not successful in winning Italian workers to his cause, says that he was 'too critical, too concentrated on economics, too sarcastic and less humanitarian'. However, the efforts of Marx and Engels are not entirely in vain, as several years later a small socialist party, based on Marxist ideas, becomes firmly established in Italy and makes slow but steady headway, following the successful example of the German Social Democratic Party. The fact that Engels' works are also now being translated into Italian and articles he contributes are published in the new party's journal, *Critica Sociale* (established in 1891) are also significant factors in aiding the growth of the new party.

Of particular interest at the 1871 conference is that it decides on a policy concerning the 'political effectiveness of the working class', largely formulated by Engels. This is also a deadly barb against the anarchists, as it emphasises the role of class struggle and the need for political organisation of the working class. As a result, the International now adds to its statutes the very significant article which states: 'In its struggle against the united power of the propertied classes, the proletariat can only present itself as a class if it constitutes itself as a political party, being in opposition to all earlier parties created by the propertied classes. It is indispensable for the triumph of the social revolution and to ensure its final goal – the eradication of classes'.

This is the first officially stated instance by the IWA of its aim of setting up specifically working class parties 'of a new type'. In his statement Engels also takes issue with those who call for abstention and for having nothing to do with 'bourgeois institutions', which is at the same time another side-swipe at the anarchists. Instead he calls on workers to defend and utilise the freedoms they have already won, like that of the press and of association. His attitude on this is strengthened by developments in Britain. This year, for the first time, sees an Act of Parliament introduced, guaranteeing legal protection for trade unions. It will give the unorganised and unskilled workers new opportunties for setting up their own unions.

Engels' work on the Commune, and in organising the conference as well as preparing contributions wins him an even higher standing internationally and he is elected as corresponding secretary for Italy, and as a member of the finance committee, then a month later also as corresponding secretary for Spain. His word gains even more weight as, in the following year, he is also given responsibility for the secretariats of Portugal and Denmark too. No doubt his linguistic facility on top of his political capabilities play a key role, but how he masters all these tasks is unimaginable. His portfolio of positions, though, also very much reflects the numerically small nature of the IWA at this time. It is still a modest organisation and largely made up of émigrés, however its political influence on left politics can not be underestimated. It does have a whole number of branches in several European countries and the USA, but in Spain and Italy, for instance, these are still dominated by the anarchists and anarchism continues to play a significant role in these two countries for many years to come, particularly Spain, up to and during the Spanish Civil War in 1936-39.

At the time of the London conference, Britain still has no federal council; the part such a body should play, is undertaken by the General Council in London. The latter has previously been against the formation of a special British federal council, because it believes an imminent social revolution in Europe will begin in industrial England. However, after the fall of the Paris Commune, it becomes clear that the first step on the road to workers taking power must be the creation of independent political workers' parties, and that the centre of gravity of the proletarian movement is being transferred to the continent. Marx is the foremost in recognising that it will be necessary to set up in Britain, as well as in other countries, a federal council, which may prove to be the germ of a British workers' party. The London conference, therefore, reversing the General Council's previous position, carries a resolution in favour of forming a British federal council.

The resolution is put into effect in October, 1871, when a temporary committee is set up in London under the chairmanship of Maltman Barry and with John Hales acting as secretary. As soon as the local branches of the International in Britain and the General Council have approved the rules drawn up by the temporary committee, a permanent federal council is elected. Many new branches are formed, and an ever increasing number of trade unionists rally to the International. In Ireland, too, the Association soon has its branches, in the defence of which the General Council takes up a decidedly militant attitude towards the British Government. However, the Irish organisations do not form a constituent part of the British Federation; they are directly under the control of the General Council.

Once the Federal Council is established it doesn't follow the path Marx and Engels have mapped out for it. Their ideological positions and domination of the General Council of the International are opposed by the leaders of the British Federal Council, which is looking for autonomy and is already adopting a reformist position, strongly opposed to Marx's and Engels' notion of class struggle. The first congress of the British Federal Council of the International meets in Nottingham on 21 July, 1872 and, perhaps surprisingly, declares, in accordance with the position of Marx and Engels, that an independent working-class party is essential to the conduct of the political struggle of the proletariat; it produces a programme which, generally speaking, is inspired by socialist ideas; and it urges trade unions to join the new workers' party and the International. But the organised workers view the International rather pragmatically. They look upon it primarily as an organisation capable of preventing the importation of cheap foreign labour, and able to assist in the struggle for electoral rights and the introduction of reform legislation. Nevertheless, certain tendencies become obvious at the Nottingham Congress which threatens to split the International. Thus, during the discussion concerning the rules for the British Federal Council, which are in general based upon those of the International as a whole, Hales proposes an amendment to the effect that the British Federal Council might enter into direct relationships with the federations of other lands and ignore the General Council. The amendment is adopted in spite of a certain amount of opposition. Another succesful resolution is aimed directly at the General Council. This motion proposes curtailing the powers of the General Council in the matter of the exclusion of such sections deemed to have infringed the rules and constitution. This is in response to the attempts by the General Council to expel the anarchists, whom a number of British trade union leaders view as allies in their opposition to Marx and Engels.

The 1871 Trade Union Act provides succour to the reform-minded faction. It gives British trade unions a legalised status for the first time, but simultaneously imposes grave penalties on those who promote strikes. It is, though, hailed by a number of trade union leaders as a tremendous victory, for it enables them to transfer their energies to peaceful organisation; it is the beginning of the era of so-called 'class-collaboration' which will characterise the whole period of working-class reformism up to the present day.

During the late 19th century British manufacturers are still continuing to flood the world market, and they find it an easy task to buy-off the working-class aristocracy, which at this time is still organised in craft unions. Engels also clearly understood that one of the reasons for the relative lack of interest in socialism during the late 1800s, after the demise of Owen's co-operative utopias and the eclipse of Chartism, was the fact that the British working classes benefited – even if only in the form of crumbs – from Britain's virtual world trade and industrial monopoly. In addition, there has also been a revival of industrial output following the banking crisis of 1866. The latter had greatly sharpened the conflict between workers and employers and led to frequent strikes, turning many workers towards the International; but then the industrial revival had the effect of sapping that new found militancy. It was felt that there was now an opportunity of gaining improvements without resorting to strikes and this provided the excuse for many leaders of the trade-union movement to abandon more militant action.

The fifth congress of the IWA is held in The Hague during September 1872 and this time Engels is delegated by the 'cleansed' section of the New York IWA. This congress becomes the venue for what proves to be the final showdown between Marx/Engels and Bakunin; the situation in the international movement is still festering and the whole IWA organisation will be jeopardised if these serious ideological differences are not settled once and for all. There had been a debate about whether to hold the congress in Switzerland, but Marx and Engels fearing such a venue would allow too many of Bakunin's delegates to be present [One of the most important centres of Bakuninist propaganda is the Jura Federation in Switzerland, and he has a strong following in Italy and Spain], they manage to persuade the General Council at its meeting on 18 June, to choose The Hague as the congress venue. Holland is easier to reach for those countries in which Marx and Engels feel sure of having strong support and they are able to persuade their comrades in the German Social Democratic Party to send a strong delegation. In response, Bakunin's supporters angrily accuse the General Council of being subservient to 'Pan-Germanic tendencies'. From June until August the General Council deliberates the proposals Engels wishes to put to the Hague congress. He hopes to take the wind out of the sails of the 'Anti-authoritarian' faction by proposing a complete re-structuring of the International, as formulated at the London conference.

The Hague congress also has to adopt a definitive position on what sort of action at a political level it wishes to advocate, and on this issue Marx and Engels and their supporters have the French Blanquists on their side. They propose that it is absolutely essential to build specific political workers' parties if workers are ever to take power, and power is essential to achieve the International's aim of social revolution and the abolition of classes. In Engels' view, if adopted, it will not only frustrate the anarchists but also the British trade unions which are advocating class reconciliation.

To begin with the prevalent feeling on the General Council is that the opposition will not even turn up in The Hague; the anarchists have already called for the holding of a special congress of their own in Switzerland. Engels is convinced that Bakunin's supporters, facing certain defeat, will not attend. But some do turn up, although the Italians are not among them. Engels clever orchestration of forces eventually wins the day and the anarchists are defeated.

The accreditation of delegates and representatives to conferences and congresses of the International had been somewhat arbitrary and this one is no exception. Many potential representatives simply cannot afford the travel costs; those that can or are geographically closer at hand, can often get themselves elected out of convenience. This leads to a lack of genuine democracy and appropriate representation for the various nations. Engels attends the congress together with Marx, his wife, his two daughters and son-in-law.

His presence at this congress is described graphically by the German Social Democrat and fellow delegate, Theodor Cuno (in his memoirs written in 1932):

> I knew Engels' face from photos, but in real life he was slimmer than he appears in his portraits. He was tall and gaunt in appearance, but with a healthy complexion, with sharply defined facial features a long, reddish beard and blue eyes. His movements and speech were quick and precise; he was able to convince those around him that he knew exactly what he wanted and what effect his words and gestures were having. In conversation with him one learnt much that was new and educational. His mind was a treasure trove of knowledge… [He goes on to add:] 'Marx was not such an effective speaker; Engels uses a conversational tone when speaking to delegates, lacing his speeches with much humour and sarcasm, reminding me more of student discussions'. [97]

Bakunin and his comrade James Guillaume are expelled from the International for 'conspiratorial activity' by a large majority decision. They respond by calling the whole process 'a comedy'. Their expulsion, though, is not the only sensation at the congress. The second one comes just as much of a shock but has deeper implications.

In his main speech, Engels calls for the headquarters of the IWA to be transferred to New York. His argument is that, although London has been a safe haven up to now, no other city on the continent can guarantee free speech and movement or provide a secure place to store documents; New York could provide that and the IWA has a strong network there. He argues that the headquarters of the International has been in London for eight years and a move will help avoid it becoming ossified.

Most delegates are dumbstruck by this seemingly perverse suggestion. The strongest opposition to it comes from the French Blanquists. They are depending on the vital support of the International in their planned attempts to lead the French working class movement and eventually, as they hope, to take power. Moving the headquarters to New York would reduce the International's influence in Europe to a token. But after a heated debate Engels' motion is carried. Both he and Marx hope that the move will ensure the survival of the International until such time as the working class movement in the various countries becomes less centrifugal and they hope the organisation can then be resuscitated in more robust form.

Moving the IWA's General Council to New York is also clearly aimed at making it exceedingly difficult for the European groups to continue their eternal debates and bickering. It is also a means of relieving both Marx and Engels of the tedium of attending long Council meetings where little of import is decided. Jenny Marx tells Liebknecht at the time that Marx is drowning in work: 'no peace day or night. How much better it would be for him if he had the tranquillity to work for those struggling by devoting his time to develop further his theory of struggle'.

Over the following years, despite the problems and effective marginalisation of the International from European struggles, Engels remains active in the General Council and writes comprehensive analyses of the European workers' movement; between the years 1869 and 1895 he writes over 14 lengthy reports for the International. On the basis of Marx's and Engels' theories, workers' parties are, over succeeding years, set up in numerous countries and help strengthen the IWA. The General Council continues its work in the USA until 1876, when its congress in Philadelphia agrees to dissolve the Association. The world situation has changed and the individual national parties need to develop and properly establish themselves; the function of the IWA as co-ordinator and promoter of those workers' parties worldwide has, it is widely felt, been fulfilled.

Already at the time of the Hague congress Engels had lost faith in the effectiveness of the International, as he writes later, in 1874, to Adolph Sorge in the USA:

> With the Hague congress it [the International] was indeed finished...For ten years, the International dominated one aspect of European history, that aspect in which the future lies,

> and it can look back on its work with pride. But in its old form it has outlived its function...The proletarian world is now too large and extended. I believe the next International will be, after Marx's writings have had several years to influence matters, decidedly communist and will, in effect, plant out our principles.[98]

Engels' role in the successful development and expansion of the various national parties can be measured by the range of his activities on the General Council. It is largely thanks to his clear sightedness, his organisational and theoretical abilities in promoting a single goal that has created the worldwide movement that will substantially shape the world during the following century.

Time for his own writing at last

Despite his increasing involvement in the day to day organising work of the IWA and advising the wider socialist movement, Engels continues his research and writing. In 1876 Wilhelm Liebknecht, the editor of the German social-democratic newspaper, begs Marx and Engels to write a fundamental riposte to the increasingly influential ideas of Professor Eugen Dühring, a blind, unsalaried lecturer at Berlin's university. Dühring is a relatively obscure intellectual whose nebulous ideas are filling the vacuum left by Lassalle's death.[99] Both Marx and Engels are angry and offended that they are being cajoled into arguing against what they see as confused and primitive thinking. Only when Liebknecht demonstrates to them how far Dühring's ideas are influencing the thinking of the social democratic rank and file, do the two realise that they have to respond.

Marx needs to devote all his time to completing the further two volumes of *Capital* and Engels has just begun to immerse himself fully in his scientific research. Reluctantly he tears himself away and sets about refuting Dühring's ideas. In a moment of rare bitterness, he upbraids Marx: 'You can thank your lucky stars,' he writes from his temporary refuge in Ramsgate, 'you can stay in your warm bed – examining specifically Russian land-owning relationships, and ground rent in general, and nothing interrupts you – but I'm supposed to sit down on the hard bench and swig the cold wine, immediately stop doing everything else and preoccupy myself with boring Dühring. Clearly I have no alternative'. Returning from

Ramsgate, he gets down to work immediately, writing his arguments straight down. The result is published as a series of articles in the social democratic paper *Vorwärts* and only later published as a book: *Herr Eugen Dühring's Revolution in Science* (1876) [known in the English-speaking world as: *Anti-Dühring*].

This polemic would be of only marginal interest today if it were not for its enormous political impact and role in promoting Marxism. Engels uses the opportunity to explain the basic ideas of dialectical materialism in a way that can be understood by all; it is a work of masterful clarity. His readers at the time are still largely unaware of the historical connections between economics, class and politics, and he puts his ideas across in a readily accessible language. In this way he breaks through the barrier that has kept his German compatriots largely in ignorance of his and Marx's theories. For the first time workers in Germany can now gain an understanding of how the on-going historical process and their own problems are interconnected and what political implications this has for the proletariat as a whole. This small work goes on to win many thousands to the ideas of Marxism, something *Capital* alone could never have achieved. However, Engels remains unhappy about taking on this hatchet job, and in a letter to his friend he says: 'They have really bludgeoned me into undertaking this thankless job – thankless, because the man [Prof. Dühring] is blind, so we are unequally armed, but then the colossal arrogance of the man prevents me taking any undue consideration'.[100]

Once he has completed this burdensome task, he returns once again to the more pleasurable pursuit of devoting himself to the natural sciences. It is in these years, from 1872 until 1882 that he begins to write the notes for what is later published in book form as *Dialectics of Nature* in 1925. Like any work dealing with natural science, it will become out of date very quickly with new discoveries and developments. Engels' would have undoubtedly revised it considerably had he had the opportunity. Much of it relates to scientific controversies of the day and, by the date of the work's publication these issues had been largely settled. Thus, the book is not significant for its insightful scientific knowledge, but rather for its holistic approach to science in general. He attempts to develop a dialectical methodology for dealing with the natural sciences. He is trying to discover the inherent laws governing material and its behaviour; his main source for this approach are the ideas of Hegel.

In essence it is an attempt to apply Marxist thinking to the natural sciences and a playdoyer for rationalism versus mysticism. It is also an attempt to demonstrate that the same dialectical laws of movement that can be applied to human history are equally applicable to all natural processes. 'Dialectics,' he writes, 'is for today's natural sciences the most important method of thinking, because it alone provides an analogue, as well as explanatory, method to comprehend the developmental processes taking place in nature, for the connectedness of all and everything, and a means of bridge-building between one research area and another'.[101]

Darwin is one of the first to elaborate the idea that nature is not a fixed entity, but in a continuous state of change, but Engels argues that this applies to all matter. In *Dialectics of Nature* he outlines the laws of movement governing the continuous process of change. Whereas Hegel saw the dialectical process as 'in our heads', Engels argues that our thinking is merely a reflection of genuine dialectical processes taking place in the material world. He defines the dialectic as 'the science of connections' or the 'general laws of all movement'. His aim in this book is to demonstrate that dialectical laws are developmental laws valid for the material world as a whole. He describes that world as in a continuous process of transformation, of becoming and dying, without fixed beginnings or ends. As the renowned biologist J.B.S. Haldane said about Engels' scientific writings in his preface to the 1940 English edition: 'Their interest lies not so much in their detailed criticism of theories, many of which have ceased to be of importance, but in showing how Engels grappled with intellectual problems'. For a man with only a formal high school education and largely self-taught, it is a tremendous achievement, not only in demonstrating the breadth of his knowledge in the natural sciences, but also in his grasp of the complex ideas that are taxing the brains of contemporary professional scientists.

However, the dialectical 'laws' he purports to find in physical and chemical processes could more accurately be termed 'principles' but even as principles they are controversial. Genuine laws allow us to interpret and understand phenomena otherwise inexplicable, but Engels' 'laws' could be more accurately characterised as descriptions of generalised observation, but not very useful in terms of their application in practice. In his attempt to apply Hegel's dialectical thinking to science rather formulaically, the result is perhaps not as illuminating or helpful as it could be. He does recognise, though, that whereas Hegel attempted to impose his thought processes on nature, it is really nature that determines our own thought processes.

His brief, unfinished essay, written in 1876 and entitled: *The part played by labour in the transition from ape to man*, is included in the *Dialectics of Nature* and is perhaps the most significant section of the book and of most relevance for us today. Engels' chief achievement in this essay is to emphasise the role of tool-making as a necessary precursor of humanity and of civilisation. He argues that the more complicated tool-making becomes, the more social interaction and co-operation becomes necessary, leading inevitably to the development of language. The physicist, J.D. Bernal felt that this essay is '...probably the most important part of the whole book because in it we find most definitely stated the view that man owes his uniqueness to the existence of society and that society in the first place is common labour'.

Although Engels' basic arguments here are undoubtedly correct in terms of the relationship between tool-making, social interaction and language development, in his supposition that adaptations by individuals are inherited by subsequent generations he reflects a Lamarckian position (i.e. believing that acquired characteristics can be inherited) rather than a Darwinian one, and it cannot be justified by scientific evidence. It is, nevertheless, an exciting piece of research which pioneers the idea that humans as intellectual and tool-making beings are products of social interaction. In this sense he not only demonstrates that society is essential in promoting individual development, but by implication that the idea of an individual without society is an oxymoron. He establishes that human beings are first and foremost co-operative animals and without co-operation our societies and civilisation would not have come about.

Dialectics of Nature is probably more of historical interest today than it is in terms of any unique scientific insights. It does, though, as Haldane says above, give us a graphic demonstration of how Engels grapples intellectually with problems and it is a classic example of the holistic approach that Marxists advocate: looking at phenomena in context and in their inter-connectedness, not studying processes in isolation.

In his authorised biography, Fidel Castro says 'I was very impressed by Engels' work on the history of the working class in England. I also remember very well...the *Dialectics of Nature*, where Engels talked about the fact that one day the sun would go out, that the fuel that feeds the fire of the star that gives us light would be exhausted, that the sun's light would cease to exist. And Engels wrote that despite the fact that he couldn't possibly have read Stephen Hawking's *A Brief History of Time* or know anything about Einstein's theory of relativity.[102]

Engels has long been a convinced atheist, seeing science as the antidote to mysticism and primitive belief. In his introduction to the English edition of his pamphlet, *The Development of Socialism from Utopia to Science*, in 1876, he writes: 'People in England believe in all sorts of impossible miracles and even geologists like Buckland and Mantell twist the facts of their science in order to avoid giving a slap in the face to the biblical creationist mythologists; it's incomprehensible that in order to find people who dare to use their intelligence in religious matters, you have to go to the uneducated, to the "unwashed hordes", as they were then called, to the workers, particularly the Owenite socialists.'

In their approach to the subject matter of social development, Marx and Engels are very much influenced by the scientific blossoming of the time and there is a steady stream of new ideas emerging on evolution, archaeology, physics and chemistry. This process began in France during the enlightenment, but is given new impetus in the 19th century by the discoveries of Darwin, Lyell, Pasteur, Koch, Bunsen and others. The ideas of creationism and faith in an omnipotent being are again, for the first time since the period of the Enlightenment, being seriously threatened by scientific investigation and rationality.

The Social Democratic Party in Germany

Certainly the biggest success internationally for Marx and Engels is the emergence of the strongest mass socialist party in the world – the Social Democratic Workers' Party of Germany. More than any other party at the time, the creation of this one in Germany and the elaboration of its political programme have been in no small part a result of their work. It is their ideas, above all others, that have been influential in forging the party ideologically. Several of its leaders over many years have also been intimate friends of the two.

Socialism and communism have always been viewed by the ruling classes as the biggest dangers to their power and privilege. In Germany the ruling class has become so alarmed by the rapid growth and influence of the social democrats that Chancellor Bismarck introduces his notorious 'Sozialistengesetz' [Socialist Laws] of October 1878, banning the party until 1891. Although this causes enormous problems for it on the ground, driving it into clandestinity, Engels sees it as positive in the long term: 'Herr Bismarck, who's worked for us for the last seven years as if we were paying him for it, now seems incapable of moderating himself in his efforts to accelerate the emergence of socialism'. He is right: In the Reichstag in 1871 there were only two representatives of the party, based on a vote of 3.2 percent, by 1890 this will rise to 35 with 19.9 percent of the vote, but by 1912, only 17 years after Engels' death, the party will win 110 seats (out of a total of around 400) with 34.8 percent of the vote.

These laws are implemented with such harshness and effectiveness that they cause complete chaos in the party. The trade union and left-wing political press is muzzled and many leaders driven into exile once again. They manage to publish newspapers, like *Die Laterne* and *Freiheit* from exile and copies are smuggled back into Germany. Social democratic candidates can still be elected to local councils or the Reichstag but only by standing as nominally independent candidates.

The government's enactment of these laws only underlines the fact that it is the socialists and their party that represent the true interests of working people. Since the suppression of the democratic aspirations of 1848/49 and the re-imposition of feudal hegemony, working people have felt unrepresented; the churches, too, have remained conservative and are largely identified with the ruling elite. In this sense, it is the socialists who have taken up the baton of the crushed 1848/49 revolution and are pointing a way forward. It is they alone who offer new hope and a vision of a society where workers will become the ruling class.

For German conservatives, the social democrats represent the 'enemy within'; they are the 'Vaterlandslosen' [those without a homeland] – a term that will be resuscitated and used again in a similar way, half a century later, by a certain Adolf Hitler. This accusation is vehemently rebuffed by Johann Jacoby, a Social Democratic member of the Reichstag, in his essay: 'The Goal of the Working class Movement': 'Your fatherland is for us only a place of misery, a prison, a hunting ground on which we're the hunted animals and where some of us don't even have a place to lay our heads. You call us scathingly 'vaterlandslos' and you yourselves have taken away our homeland'.

screeds of newsprint. He makes no bones about this urge to friends, even though he is well aware of how important the journalistic work is and carries it out diligently. He writes that his work on the paper is, 'a real pleasure. You see the impact of every word and how every article hits its target as if they were grenades exploding.' These words, though, can't hide his need to experience the excitement of real battle and real grenades, or as he resignedly puts it, 'the so-called German revolution is somewhat boring. But, for precisely this Fatherland you have to buckle down and make a sacrifice by writing leading articles for a doltish public'.

His irritation is no doubt exacerbated by arguments in the editorial board. Wilhelm Liebknecht, a close friend of Marx and Engels and later leading socialist in the German Reichstag, tells us that as long as Marx is in charge things run smoothly but with Engels in the driving seat there is invariably conflict. Why this is the case, is not revealed.

Marx, at this time, is often away, discussing the revolution with comrades in Berlin and Vienna or with radical Polish groups, and Engels is usually left in charge. It finally comes to a showdown and the other editors rebel against Engels' way of doing things. It takes all Marx's persuasive skills to calm things down again once he returns from his travels. This state of affairs is remarkable given Engels' later widely praised diplomatic skills and affability. Perhaps it can be put down to his youthful intransigence, impatience and a certain arrogance or simply the clash of very extrovert and strong personalities.

Engels comes to life in the social arena, and he soon joins the Cologne Citizens' Army and is actively involved in the Democratic Society and Cologne Workers' Club. He realises that if resistance is not organised quickly the reactionaries will succeed in their aim of rolling back the revolution. Together with others, he organises mass meetings of the people to elect a security committee to oversee the defence of the city and ensure the inviolability of the revolution. However, the middle classes see this as a step towards setting up a 'Red Republic' and seek to have it abolished. Engels then organises a new mass meeting in front of the city gates of Cologne to demonstrate the mass support for his security committee. He later reports that the meeting, estimated to be several thousand strong, has voted for the democratic-social republic, with only one vote against. They further pledge themselves to fight to the last man in any subsequent conflict between Prussia and the rest of Germany. At the end of the meeting, Henry Brisbane, a correspondent from the *New York Daily Tribune* conveys greetings and solidarity with the revolution, and while in Cologne holds talks with Marx and Engels. His is the paper for which Marx later becomes a regular correspondent during the fifties, but it is Engels who will translate and write many of the articles that will appear in Marx's name.

This mass meeting, which Engels organises, is the largest to take place anywhere in Germany during this period and not only does it once again demonstrate his great organisational skills but also indicates the path the revolution needs to take if it is to be successful in the long term. He demonstrates that masses of people can be mobilised to take into their own hands the administration and organisation of the revolutionary process, and that the second phase of the revolution can be achieved as long as the alarmed reactionaries don't intervene with force.

Encouraged by the seemingly easy victories on the level of the individual German states, a self-appointed Preliminary Parliament meets in Frankfurt. It calls for free elections to be held to nominate delegates to a National Assembly for all of Germany, and the new governments of the various states agree to this. Finally, on 18 May 1848 the resultant National Assembly opens its session. Of the 585 delegates to this first freely elected German parliament, so many are academics or university educated that it is called the 'Scholars Parliament', but it nevertheless represents an immense democratic breakthrough. The assembly starts on its ambitious plan to devise a modern, liberal constitution as the foundation for a unified Germany. By the autumn of 1848, however, the Prussian aristocrats, among them Otto von Bismarck, and the Prussian military have regained power in Berlin. They were not defeated during the March Revolution, but had merely retreated temporarilly to their country estates.

General von Wrangel leads the troops who recapture Berlin for the old regime. His troops earning the nickname 'street-sweepers' for the brutal efficiency and ruthlessness with which they clear the streets. Needless to say, Friedrich Wilhelm immediately rejoins the victorious 'Junkers'[53] who promise to restore the monarchy. In November he dissolves the new Prussian parliament and institutes a constitution of his own, which does, however, contain some liberal elements.

The Prussian bureaucracy and military view the events in

Cologne with increasing anxiety and as a significant influence on the prevailing atmosphere in the whole of Prussia. The Interior Minister's report at the time (September 1848), states clearly that he sees it as his duty to teach Cologne, as the second largest city in Prussia, a lesson for its insolence. He knows that if the situation is allowed to fester, 'the infection' will spread to other big towns.

The consolidation of the reactionary forces and their increasing belligerence alarms many in the new democratic and revolutionary organisations. In their eyes there is an urgent need for a second revolution to crush this re-emerging reaction and to safeguard the achievements of the March Revolution, as well as to press for more fundamental political and social demands. At the second Rhineland Democratic Conference at Worringen on 10 September, attended by over 10,000 people, the call for a 'social-democratic' or 'red republic' is voiced.

Once the reactionary forces of the landed aristocracy have made the necessary military arrangements, they use the holding of this Rhineland conference as a pretext for placing Cologne under a state of siege. All publications are banned and the revolutionary forces threatened with the direst of consequences. In September judicial proceedings are initiated against Engels and other members of the editorial board of the *Neue Rheinische Zeitung* for conspiring to overthrow public order. By the end of September, Cologne finds itself immersed in counter-revolutionary terror. Engels and his fellow editors go underground immediately.

Chapter Six (1848-1850)

From the barricade to guerrilla war

The early morning newspapers in Germany on 4 October 1848 are emblazoned with a 'Wanted Notice' issued by the State Prosecutor's office for one Friedrich Engels and 'his accomplice', Johannes Bürgers. But, Engels has outwitted Prussian officialdom once again and is already safely over the border in Belgium. The notice describes him, somewhat inaccurately, as a businessman, 27 years' old, 5ft 8in tall, with dark blond hair, grey eyes, a well proportioned nose and mouth in an oval face, with a healthy complexion and slim stature. He is charged with high treason – the most heinous offence on the books. He is saved from being convicted in absentia because, according to the Napoleonic justice system pertaining in the Rhineland, the case against him and his comrades cannot be opened without the accused being present.

Engels believes he is safe from extradition proceedings as long as he stays in Belgium, as the constitution of 1830 guarantees political asylum. This, though, doesn't prevent the Belgian police co-operating closely with their Prussian counterparts, and the government is certainly not keen on Belgium becoming the asylum country of choice for dangerous revolutionaries. Hardly arrived in Brussels, Engels is arrested by the Sûreté Publique, the Belgian security police, and taken immediately by prison vehicle to be dumped on the French border, from where he makes his way to Paris. So, on 5 October he finds himself, involuntarily in the city, where only a few months previously he had received such a hearty welcome. This time there are no warm embraces – he is not expected, and those revolutionaries still there are keeping their heads down. Paris is now, as he describes it, 'a dead city', and he has little desire to linger.

His report from there conjures up the depressing atmosphere:

> Between the Paris of then [Feb 1848] and now, lay the 15 May and 25 June, and the most terrible battle the world has ever seen, with a sea of blood, with 15,000 corpses. Cavaignac's grenades have blown Parisians' irrepressible jollity to smithereens, the Marseillaise and the Chant du départ could no longer be heard, only the bourgeoisie hummed their "Mourir pour la patrie", between their lips; the workers, without food and weapons, gnash their teeth with suppressed anger; under the schooling of the state of siege, the exuberant Republic soon became respectable, tame, subservient and moderate (sage et modérée). But Paris was dead, it was no longer Paris. On the boulevards only the bourgeois and police spies; the balls, the theatres desolate. The 'gamins' have disguised themselves in jackets of the mobile guard, and have now sold themselves for 30 sous a day to the "honnete republique" [respectable republic], and the more stupid they behaved, the more they were applauded by the bourgeoisie. In short, it was again the Paris of 1847 but without the spirit, without the life, without the fire and ferment that the workers then brought with them everywhere. Paris was dead and this lovely corpse was all the more horrific, the prettier it appeared. I couldn't bear to stay any longer in this dead Paris. I had to leave, it didn't matter where to.[54]

Marx has somehow managed to survive unscathed in Cologne and is able to send Engels some money, so that, with his passport already forwarded from Brussels, he is now free to leave Paris. In the short-term, though, he decides to go to Switzerland, as the nearest potentially safe haven. But the little money he now has is hardly enough for food alone, so he decides to walk there and enjoy the delights of the French countryside on the way. He doesn't mind how long it takes him; time at the moment is not his main problem.

He is, though, keen to return to join Marx again in Cologne and the fact that two of their comrades have been set free by the jury system in the Rhineland gives him new hope that he may now be able to return without fear of immediate arrest. He writes to Marx:

> How's the situation? Can I now, after the "not guilty" verdicts for G [Gottschalk] and A [Anneke], also return soon? The Prussian dogs must slowly be losing their urge to get involved in jury trials. As I said, if there were sufficient ground for me not to have to fear being remanded in custody, I'd come immediately. Afterwards, as far as I'm concerned, they can arraign me in front of 10,000 juries, but on remand you're not allowed to smoke, and I'm not prepared to be put inside under such circumstances.[55]

While in Berlin the counter-revolution is mopping up, but in Hungary and Vienna the revolutionary embers have been momentarily re-ignited. Engels, meanwhile, is sauntering through the French countryside enjoying the scenery, the wine and the girls! In his diary he gives us a graphic picture and it is clear that the turmoil and disappointments of the last months have left him debilitated and with a need to recharge the batteries. He soaks up the beauties of the landscapes, the richness and pure sensual pleasure of it all. He wanders through the Loire Valley and into Burgundy, where he relishes 'the sweetest grapes and the prettiest girls' and in Auxerre, 'the red republic of Burgundy wines'. But while he's frolicking in the meadows with the pretty Burgundy girls and savouring the rich wines, the still flickering flames of revolution are being extinguished all over Europe.

Not only in Germany, but throughout the continent the revolutions are being suppressed with gratuitous brutality. In October 1848, Field Marshal Prince Windischgratz on behalf of the Hapsburg monarchy, storms revolutionary Vienna and extinguishes the revolution there. He, together with the Croat leader Jellacic, conquers the city after a bitter struggle; the revolutionary leaders are summarily executed, countless participants arrested and judicial proceedings opened against revolutionary parliamentarians. Windischgratz had already, in June 1848, crushed the revolutionary uprising in Prague and was sent with 70,000 troops to crush the Hungarians. The Italian revolutions are likewise suppressed by the Hapsburgs.

The vacillations of the Hungarian revolutionaries and the dominance within the movement of nationalists, prevent it identifying its true allies and it too collapses; the Czech national movement turns against the Germans, linked in Czech minds with Viennese centralism. In November 1848 in Prussia, Graf Brandenburg establishes his counter-revolutionary ministry to extinguish any remaining sparks of revolution in Prussia. Thus, a short-lived revolutionary Europe is everywhere forced back into its feudal straitjacket once again.

Engels' ability to relax in the French countryside while all this is going on reveals the other side of his character; Marx is made of different metal and often gently chides his friend about dissipating his talents and not channelling them wholeheartedly into the struggle for the good of mankind. Perhaps Engels is still to a certain extent a captive of his strict Protestant upbringing and cannot see himself as a chosen individual, indispensable to the movement. Of course, once an idea takes hold of him, he can be as committed and dedicated as anybody, but he isn't driven by the same demon that Marx is, a demon that forbids him partaking of the world's richness and its sensual pleasures. Engels finds the ascetic life more difficult to contemplate.

It takes him about 14 days to walk from Paris to the Swiss border – around 500km – quite a tempo, but he is young and fit. He savours every little joy of wandering through the French countryside, the small towns and villages, leisurely soaking up the serenity and bucolic charm. He is also seduced by the rich and varied southern French wines, each of which 'takes you to a different stage of intoxication. With only a few bottles you go through all stages, from the Quadrille to the Marseillaise, from the mad desire of the can-can to the wild passion of revolutionary fervour'. Sipping his wine on the river bank, admiring the golden autumnal colours of the vines snaking up the hillsides, revolution must have felt momentarily like a distant dream.

This journey is unforgettable in many ways and he records its many facets in his *Travel Sketches*. He spends more time, he says, with the vintners and the peasant girls, eating grapes, drinking wine, chatting and laughing, and relaxing in the meadows than he does climbing the mountains. Clearly, Engels knows how to enjoy the good life as much as any gentleman of means, but even so, he isn't going to let any opportunity go by without also milking it for all it is worth in terms of its revolutionary relevance. This marathon walk is no exception; he questions and probes the peasants on their attitudes to the February revolution and subsequent events. He is keen to assess how far they can be expected to support any future revolutionary upsurge. He is sorely disappointed:

> You need to talk almost exclusively with peasants for a whole fortnight, socialise with peasants from the different areas; you need to have the opportunity to witness everywhere the same narrow-minded obtuseness, the same total ignorance of all urban, industrial and commercial situations, the same blindness in politics, the same 'crystal ball' approach to everything that lies beyond the village boundary; they use the same measuring stick for momentous historical events as they do for their peasant affairs; in a word, you have to get to know the French peasants in the year of 1848, to comprehend the totally depressing impact their stubborn stupidity has.[56]

The peasants' attitude is clearly an eye-opener for Engels, as it would be for any non-country dweller. The overwhelming majority of peasants in Europe are still living in a semi- or totally feudal state, beholden to the landowners; they are almost all illiterate and cut off from the world outside their villages as if they are living on another planet. It is little wonder Engels is sorely disappointed if he expects to come across any latent revolutionary fervour, let alone an identification of interests with the urban proletariat.

Once he arrives in Switzerland, he stops over in Geneva, but only to pick up money and clean clothes which have been sent from Germany, before continuing his journey across the country to Berne. En route, in the small towns, he establishes contact with German workers' clubs and, in chatting to the comrades, gains an understanding of the situation inside Switzerland. These workers clubs were founded by German exiles, mainly artisans and intellectuals, from the 1830s onwards. At this time their membership is no more than a thousand. Their aim is to promote education and the discussion of liberal and republican ideas as well as for socialising. After 1848 socialist and communist ideas are brought increasingly on to their agenda. The clubs are often banned as a result of interventions by the German government and their members ejected from the country.

Engels arrives in Berne on 9 November 1848, and once he's settled in, he sets about building cordial relations with the German artisans' club and with the Lausanne workers' club. He also applies officially for a temporary residence permit, explaining openly in his application that he has been involved in the 'disturbances' in Cologne, that there is a warrant out for his arrest and he is therefore a genuine political refugee. In December, he is granted a permit, but only for one year. Now, after his 'walking holiday' he loses no more time, and within days is deeply involved with the local workers' organisations and the Communist League, while also regularly attending sessions of the Berne Federal Council. He is also busy helping to organise the congress of German Clubs in Switzerland, and is the ideal person to pass on up-to-date information of what is happening in other parts of Europe from his rich experience of the revolutionary struggles in Britain, Germany, France and Belgium. To throw any police sniffers off the track, he gives an entirely different picture of his activities in his letters to Marx: 'This lazing around abroad, where I can't do anything worthwhile, and where I'm completely outside the movement – I can't stand it,' he says. Whether such letters hoodwinked the police, is debatable, but he is always aware that he is probably being watched and his letters read.

Interestingly, the congress of the German clubs takes place in the Zeuggasse 9, where Lenin, 67 years later, will also speak, during the First World War, promoting the very same ideas Engels is in the process of formulating. After the congress is over, the Berne Workers' Club elects him onto the five-man central commission of the Federation in Switzerland, and later he even stands for the vice-presidency.

He now hears from Marx that the *Neue Rheinische Zeitung* is rolling off the presses again in Cologne following the liberalisation of press restrictions and the lifting of the state of siege. Marx also informs him that he is still a member of the editorial board.

During his absence from Cologne a number of individuals have been trying very hard to break up the friendship between the two men, whether out of envy or for political reasons is not altogether clear. Even Engels' mother is mobilised in these efforts, and is led to write to him, that the paper's editorial board has declared that if he returns, they will no longer accept him as a collaborator on the paper. Marx must have got wind of these machinations, and in case Engels feels he's been abandoned, reassures him in a letter, saying that to imagine, 'I would have left you in the lurch is complete fantasy. You remain my 'intimus' and I hope the same goes for you'.

While he's been away, Marx has been defending his position vigorously at the paper, and also sends him money and clothing, requesting in return some articles on the situation in Switzerland for the paper. It is ironic that here, in a rare moment, Marx takes on

Engels' later role, as material benefactor. In response, Engels immediately begins firing off articles to the paper and this becomes his most important work during his temporary Swiss exile.

Dr. Gottschalk, the Cologne workers' leader, has been one of those attacking Engels. In an open letter to Marx and published in the paper, *Freiheit, Arbeit [Freedom, Work]*, he accuses Engels of 'having the manners and language of a boxer' and accuses both of them of expecting the workers to plunge voluntarily into 'the purgatory of a decrepit capitalist rule, in order to rise from there, 'into a nebulous heaven dreamt up by a communist profession of faith'. This is written in response to their appeal for the workers to initially support the bourgeois revolution as a pre-stage to creating a full workers' state.

During his stay in Berne, Engels also plays the role of marketing manager for the *Neue Rheinische Zeitung* and soon finds supporters. The editor of the *Berner Zeitung*, the best paper in the Canton, if not in the whole of Switzerland, is a communist and Engels manages to persuade his and other Swiss papers to reprint articles from the *Neue Rheinische Zeitung*, and quote it in their political commentaries.

In Switzerland, in the workers' movement, Engels is already viewed as 'a veteran fighter for the proletariat', despite being a mere 28 years old. Again, in just a few weeks, he manages to make a significant political impact. In fact, it is largely as a result of his intensive efforts that the Swiss Workers' and Democratic Clubs later, in 1849, become actively involved in battles to defend the revolution in Germany. Some of them enlist in Willich's guerrilla force, in which Engels becomes an adjutant, and they make up the whole of the Refugee Legion.

After sending off his last article to the *Neue Rheinische Zeitung* in January 1849, he applies for an exit permit and, once he has it, leaves for Germany, arriving in Cologne on the same day to resume his work in the editorial office of the paper. His comrades in Cologne have told him that he no longer needs to fear political persecution in Germany. The Cologne chief prosecutor also confirms to him officially that there is 'nothing more on the files against him'; he is once again free to work and live there. Clearly, as he noted earlier in his letter to Marx, the Prussian authorities have indeed, for the time being at least, given up trying to successfully prosecute the revolutionaries through the jury system pertaining in the Rhineland.

The brilliant and lively articles he writes for the *Neue Rheinische Zeitung* after his return testify to the exhilaration he feels at, being back on home soil. Particularly significant at this time are his articles on military matters, such as that on the Hungarian revolution, which was aimed at throwing off the yoke of the Hapsburg monarchy that ruled the Austro-Hungarian Empire. As Che Guevara does in the following century, in his articles on the revolutionary struggles, Engels emphasises the moral superiority of revolutionary military units over conscripted regular forces.

Wilhelm Liebknecht later relates that it was generally assumed, because of their immediacy and accuracy, that these articles had been written by a senior officer in the Hungarian revolutionary army. They are also an indication of Engels' increasing preoccupation with military matters in relation to revolutionary activity. The easy suppression of the Paris February revolution and the Cologne uprising by the Prussian army had demonstrated only too clearly how vital a military perspective and strategy was for any revolution to be victorious. As with all his published pieces at this time, the articles are still being attributed anonymously.

In view of his renewed revolutionary activity, it will only be a matter of time before the Prussian judiciary catches up with him once more. They are not prepared to take back this nest of revolutionary vipers and allow them to continue their seditious and venomous agitation unmolested. Already in February 1849, he, along with Marx and the manager, Hermann Korff, are hauled before a jury in a Cologne court, in the first such case against the press and the *Neue Rheinische Zeitung*. Like, Marx, he defends himself:

> You, honourable jury members are at this moment deciding on the freedom of the press in the Rhine province. If the press is to be forbidden from reporting what is in front of its very eyes, if it has to wait for a court decision every time before publishing any awkward fact, if it has to ask every civil servant, from the minister to the gendarme, whether the reported facts impinge on their honour or their sensibilities or that they might feel offended, irrespective of whether the facts are true or not; if the press is forced to do the opposite – either to falsify the events or remain completely silent – then, gentlemen, press freedom is finished, and if that is what you want, then pronounce us guilty! [57]

In view of the incontrovertible truth expressed in this defence of a free press, the jury does the only sensible thing and finds them not guilty; the court dismisses all charges against the paper and the defendants. This, of course, only serves to raise the profile of the paper. Such a defeat for the Prussian reactionaries infuriates them even further and increases their determination to nail these dangerous militants once and for all. This they will manage to do three years later with the notorious Cologne Communist Trial, although still the two big fish manage to slip through their nets.

Journalistic work is Engels' chief occupation, alongside delivering 'social lectures' to Cologne workers' groups. However, once revolutionary activity again reaches fever pitch during May 1849, he becomes itchy in the confines of the editorial office and longs for action. He learned a great deal during the September events of the previous year and realised that you can't lead a people's movement from the margins, you have to totally immerse yourself in the struggles. And that's what he now decides to do.

It needs to be remembered that Germany is still not a united country, but a loose confederation of nations and states. In the German-speaking world, the two most powerful states are the Kingdom of Prussia and the Austrian Empire, both of which dominate central Europe. It is only in 1871 that Germany finally becomes a unitary state. This helps explain the fragmented and divergent nature of the revolutions that take place in the autonomous statelets of Germany and in other subjugated nations of Europe.

During May, workers in Saxony begin arming themselves and drive the king and ministers from the city of Dresden, but after several days of fighting on the barricades the rebellion is suppressed. A young Richard Wagner, as well as the renowned architect Gottfried Semper, are among those who join the insurgents. After being forced to flee once the uprising is suppressed, Wagner takes refuge with Liszt in Weimar. He and Semper, though, unlike Marx and Engels, are passionate nationalists, not socialists.

The suppression of the Dresden revolt doesn't prevent similar ones breaking out elsewhere. In other areas men in the militia and the reservists are refusing to fight on behalf of the 'Prussian reactionaries' and declare that they will not 'be misused to oppress the people'. Once the old aristocratic leaders have fled, provisional governments are set up to replace them. In Baden, too, the grand duke is driven from his palace and a provincial committee has taken over the reins of government. The insurrection is also in full swing in Engels' home town of Barmen-Wuppertal.

The call to arms

On 6 May, the teacher and active Democrat,[58] Hermann Körner, from Elberfeld, turns up in the editorial office of the *Neue Rheinische Zeitung* and gives Engels a report on what is happening. A large gathering of the people has taken place in Kaiserslautern, in the Palatinate on 1 May, which declares its secession from Bavaria because the Bavarian government refuses to recognise the new Reichs Constitution agreed by the Frankfurt National Convention intended to apply to all of Germany. Engels has been expecting him and is avid to hear all the details. If the men in the Citizens' Militia in his birthplace are ready to desert the flag of Prussia, then Engels is not going to leave them in the lurch; it means there will be rebellion in this industrial heartland and he is not going to be left standing on the sidelines.

On 9 May, a spontaneous gathering of local people call for the release from the prison in Elberfeld of 69 workers from the steel-making town of Solingen who have been accused of stealing iron from a nearby fortress to make weapons. The prison is stormed and they are freed, but in the meantime the military has arrived and shot dead the last of the prisoners as he makes his escape.

The people are forced to retreat but at the same time call for the erection of barricades and in a short time the town centre is closed off. Few behind the barricades are armed. The military, led by a captain, brings up the artillery, but the rebels appeal to the ordinary soldiers: 'Don't shoot us, we only shoot at the officers'. This makes no impression on the captain who gives the order to fire, but at the same moment a shot rings out and he falls dead in the road. The platoon makes a rapid retreat.

From the whole surrounding area people stream into the town looking for excitement. The terrified mayor goes into hiding, and although troops from Düsseldorf are despatched to the town, they retreat without conflict. The town council and civil servants are driven out and a security council of leading middle class Democrats takes over the town administration. Barricades are already being erected on the streets and the mayor's home is razed to the ground. Von Eichmann, the president of the Rhine province, hysterically reports to Berlin that the 'poor have risen up against the rich'!

The May uprisings of 1849, that erupt throughout Germany, are sparked by the refusal of the majority of German provincial governments to accept the new constitution proclaimed by the first freely elected all-German Convention in Frankfurt. It begins in Dresden in May, spreading rapidly to other areas, particularly those that are chafing under the Prussian heel. It becomes the so-called 'Campaign for the Constitution'.

Engels can contain himself no longer and sets off poste-haste for Elberfeld. Immediately after his departure the following report appears in the second edition of the *Neue Rheinische Zeitung* on 17 May 1849:

> On 10 May, Friedrich Engels, an editor on the Neue Rheinische Zeitung, left Cologne for Elberfeld and took two cases of cartridges with him from Solingen. These had been requisitioned by Solingen workers after they stormed the Gräfrath town hall. Once arrived in Elberfeld, he gave the Security Committee a report on the situation in Cologne and put himself at their disposal. He was immediately given written authorisation and put in charge of the fortification work.[59]

The town's new Security Committee agrees to this authorisation, despite Engels' well-known communist views. A permit is issued for him: 'The military commission of the Security Committee herewith empowers Mr. Friedrich Engels, to inspect all barricades in the city and to ensure their strength. All sentries on the barricades are herewith requested to give the above named individual all support possible'.

At last Engels finds himself where he wants to be, in the thick of the revolution, fighting for it, agitating for it and being an integral part of it. However much he loves his journalistic work, it can't be other than marginal to the main struggle; this is the real thing. By 11 May, he is already in charge of a troop of workers from the steel-making town of Solingen, but based in Elberfeld. He hopes that this is the beginning of a revolutionary uprising throughout the whole of the Rhineland and he does his uttermost to fan the flames. Of his activity there, he says disingenuously: 'I wish to concern myself only with military matters and not get involved with the political character of the movement, because it's obvious that only a black-red-gold movement is possible here and therefore any opposition to the new

Constitution of the Reich must be avoided'. Black, red and gold are the pan-German colours and signify that the uprising is a largely nationalist, not a socialist movement.

He drafts a strategic plan of campaign in order to secure the revolution's achievements and defend it from the reaction's attempts to roll it back. Like so many such plans hatched by revolutionaries, it also fails because he overestimates the committed passion and preparedness of the majority to sacrifice in the same way as he himself is. A century later, Che Guevara makes a similar miscalculation in Bolivia.

The petty bourgeoisie is timid and the small proletariat not yet schooled in solidarity action. Many are prepared to take part in civil organisations but not to rush head-long into military confrontations. Thus Engels' hopes for a general insurrection remain unfulfilled and all that revolutionary energy is dissipated in the various unlinked groupings which rise up spontaneously, but lack an overall leadership.

He becomes frenetically active, hardly eating or sleeping, grabbing a wurst here and a cat nap there. He immediately inspects all barricades and, using his military knowledge, gives advice on how to make them more effective: recommending that they be constructed projecting forwards, wedge shaped, to better deflect any Prussian ordinance. In June he is sent to join the Elberfeld artillery and is given a permit to position the canons where he thinks best, and to requisition the necessary craftsmen to that end; all costs to be borne by the security committee. He helps set up a company of pioneers and not only commandeers the necessary craftsmen but persuades the security committee to appoint a friend and former Prussian artillery officer, Otto von Mirbach, as commander in Elberfeld. He also argues for the imposition of an obligatory tax in order to be able to pay the armed revolutionary workers. In mid-June he becomes Commander Mirbach's adjutant.

A witness at the Elberfeld court hearings, a year later, after the revolution has been defeated, tells the court that, 'a young man with glasses and a thin moustache, was pointed out to me as the editor Friedrich Engels, by a fellow irregular, and he behaved like one of the leaders, giving orders to strengthen the barricades...'[60] Elberfeld, now in the throes of rebellion, is unrecognisable to Engels. Crowds of workers, small craftsmen and children throng the streets; there is an almost festive atmosphere despite the underlying seriousness of what is happening. The upper classes have locked themselves in their homes, cowering behind their heavy lace curtains, fearful of the revolutionary waves lapping at their doors.

On the Sunday morning of 13 May, Engels decides to check the barricades on the Elberfeld–Barmen boundaries. While the good citizens of Barmen saunter to church, he is astride the gun-mounted barricade, resplendent in his red sash, giving orders on how to improve its structure. On this fateful day his father happens to stroll by and sees his son on the barricade. They exchange some strong and bitter words and the incident will dog their relationship from then on. For his father, it is the last straw. His eldest son is henceforth written off and he swears will not receive a single silver penny from him ever again. It requires his mother's considerable powers of persuasion and interventions by some of his relatives to assuage his father's outrage and at least convince him to maintain an irregular correspondence with his son. Engels can only relate to his father in a 'cool businesslike manner' thereafter, but he continues to revere and love his mother.

In his final days in Elberfeld, using his undoubted organisational and planning skills, Engels concerns himself with locating uniforms and equipment for the around a thousand strong revolutionary troop, as only very few of them have uniforms or a weapon of any kind. He later writes: 'the only thing I was able to push through, or rather with the help of several corps leaders (all of whom managed to escape and some are already in America) and on my own initiative, was to requisition, from the Kronenberg Citizen Militia, 80 rifles, held in the Council House'. Engels and his small detachment of workers from Solingen ride from town to town and village to village in their frantic search for weapons and uniforms. On 15 May he and his men again besiege the town hall in Gräfrath for this purpose.

A further witness statement at the Elberfeld court hearings, quoted above, reports on the stealing of weaponry: '...the group went to the village of Wald to fetch weapons. At the head of the column was Jansen as captain, Wohlmeiner as lieutenant and they were then joined by the editor Engels. The latter and Jansen purloined two cart horses on the way and rode on them at the head of the column until they arrived at the businessman Jung's estate, where Engels swapped his work horse for a riding horse, taking saddles too...' Yet another witness relates how Engels and his men were later joined by 6-8 sharpshooters and then, with Engels and Jansen at their head, both on horseback and flaunting sabres and pistols, the "gang" surrounded the arsenal. They placed sentries on the doors and then Engels, with pistol at the ready, strode up to the Master-at-Arms, Starke, and asked him if there were weapons in the building, demanding an answer...once inside, Engels took the uniforms and weaponry he could find and provided a written receipt for these, before sharing them out among the "gang".[61]

At the time Engels is purloining weapons, he no longer has a position in the Elberfeld military commission or in the Command. He is told that the local middle classes are so alarmed by his participation and, fearing he'll proclaim a red republic, are demanding his immediate removal. A delegation of leading Elberfeld citizens has also consulted secretly with the president of the Rhine Province, and have travelled to Berlin to brief Graf Brandenburg, a leading figure of the counter revolution.

Very soon a public notice appears on the streets, issued by the security committee, and stating, amongst other items that: 'Citizen Friedrich Engels from Barmen and latterly of Cologne, while fully commending his previous activity in this town, is requested to leave the municipal boundaries today, as his continued presence could lead to misunderstandings about the character of the movement'.

The armed workers and irregulars are outraged at this decision by the security committee and demand that Engels stay and are prepared to 'defend him with their lives'. Engels is obliged to go and calm them down, assuring them he will not be deserting his post under Commander Mirbach, in whom 'he has complete trust'.

Mirbach orders Engels to return to Cologne, i.e. into the heart of the enemy camp, but he undoubtedly does this on Engels' own suggestion. It is a face-saving way out and avoids an unnecessary confrontation. Mirbach says Elberfeld will be impossible to defend anyway in the face of the expected, imminent Prussian offensive, and promises to meet Engels later in the Palatinate region, something he is unable to do, as he is soon after arrested, but freed a year later.

Engels no doubt realises that if he has to give up his post in Elberfeld, his place is in the editorial office of the *Neue Rheinische Zeitung*, quasi the leading organ of the revolution. However, the days of the paper are now numbered; he returns just in time to help produce the last few issues. His Elberfeld experience, though, gives his last articles a sharper edge. In the issue of 19 May he regrets that, 'the armed workers haven't used their might to completely defeat a shameless cowardly, but still perfidious bourgeoisie'. Already, in an article two days before, he gave his assessment of the revolution:

> The present movement is only the preamble to another, a thousand times more serious movement, when it will be all about the workers' real interests. This new revolutionary movement will grow out of this present one and as soon as it erupts – the workers can depend on it - Engels, along with the other editors of the *Neue Rheinische Zeitung* - will be at their posts. No power on earth will force them to desert. This gigantic volcano of a European-wide revolution is not just boiling up but is on the verge of erupting. Its red flows of lava will soon bury for good the whole blessed, robber-baron economy; the whole infamous, hypocritical, rotten, cowardly and yet over confident bourgeoisie will finally be cast into the glowing crater as an unmourned sacrificial offering by the finally united and percipient proletarian masses.[62]

Florid rhetoric to fire the troops, but in fact Engels has to wait until 1871 to see the first attempt at a genuinely proletarian revolution with the Paris Commune.

The closure of the *Neue Rheinische Zeitung*, only days after his return, means the forced 'surrender of their bastion, but,' as he writes proudly 'we retreated with our weapons, equipment, to the sound of music and holding our banner high – the last red issue [of the paper which is printed in red ink]'.

Like the other editorial members, both Marx and Engels leave Cologne and Prussia immediately, not least because they are aware that further judicial measures are being prepared against them. Warrants for the arrest of all editorial board members as 'agents of social-democracy' are issued by the Prussian police only hours after their departure. Half of them could be legally prosecuted and the others, as non-Prussians, could expect to be deported.

A separate warrant for Engels' arrest is issued in connection with his military activities in Elberfeld, and all border crossing points are notified to keep an eye out for him, should he try to escape. This warrant charges Engels, along with 191 others, of serious criminal behaviour; it will remain in force until 1860: 'Engels Dr. [sic] from Cologne, rebel and leader of the Elberfeld May revolution in 1849, is also charged with rebellion and high treason in that same year, and is to be arrested for interrogation'.

In the end, only 164, already under arrest, are tried and many given lengthy sentences and substantial fines. As mentioned previously, according to the legal system current in the Rhineland, those not apprehended cannot be put on trial. However, if Engels had been caught crossing the border, or sought asylum in a country with which Prussia had an extradition agreement, his lot would not have been a happy one and world history may have taken a different course.

After the closure of the paper, most of the editors, including Engels and Marx, decamp to Frankfurt. Here the delegates to the German National Convention are gathered, but on orders from the Prussian government, all representatives from the Prussian-ruled areas have been recalled. Thus, the Convention is faced with disintegration or joining the revolution. Marx and Engels hold urgent talks with the left-orientated representatives in Frankfurt in an attempt to persuade them to support revolution. Engels argues particularly vehemently for them to support those areas still resisting the Prussian steamroller:

> ...in the Prussian Rhine area the insurrection is, it is agreed, severely threatened, but not yet defeated; in Württemberg, in Franken, in both Hessens and Nassau there is a general volatility; even in the army, it only requires a spark to cause the Baden rebellion to spread throughout the whole of southern and middle Germany...[63]

He then lays out in detail his genial military strategy to bring this about. Even in later years, he is still convinced that if his plan had been taken up, it would have saved the revolution, not only in Germany but throughout Europe. He is, though, unable to convince enough representatives, so he and Marx, disappointed, leave Frankfurt towards the end of May to join the insurgents in the Palatinate and then Baden. On arrival in the Palatinate they are seriously disappointed by the lack of organisation, leadership and clear goals. In Karlsruhe they again try to persuade the regional revolutionary government, made up largely of lower middle class Democrats, to go on the offensive and to place the National Convention under its protection. This is again rejected by the vast majority.

They are only able to tolerate this state of affairs for a few days and then decide to return to Frankfurt, but in Hessen they are summarily arrested by the military on suspicion of being party to rebellion against the provisional revolutionary government. They are taken to Darmstadt and then Frankfurt and only here are they released. In the face of yet another setback, Marx is given a mandate from the central committee of Democratic Germany to promote the interests of the revolution in Paris; Engels is to remain in the Palatinate, travelling on to Kaiserslautern. He was absolutely correct when in that last 'red' issue of the *Neue Rheinische Zeitung* he predicted that one could expect nothing more to happen on Prussian soil in terms of revolutionary progress, despite subsequently attempting to persuade the Convention to fight on.

A few days before the Prussian troops arrive in the Palatinate, Engels is meeting a group of partisans on the border. Here these 'men of action' are convinced that with a few weapons and lots of bravado, they can defeat any army that's sent against them. When he responds with a sarcastic dismissal of their naïve arrogance, he suddenly finds himself under arrest as a traitor, on the orders of the only member of the provisional government who doesn't know who he is. There is a short interrogation after which he is accused of insulting the people of the Palatinate and of attacking the provisional government.

The very next morning he is carted off in handcuffs back to Kaiserslautern. Belatedly and with acute embarrassment, the provincial government realises a mistake has been made by one of its underlings and proposes to release him on his word of honour, pending reception of a report on the incident. Engels refuses and is interned in the local prison. Once word gets out of his arrest, there are hefty protests and even members of the Rhine military corps threaten to mutiny over it. After spending 24 hours in the cells, where he 'amused himself quite well', he is released unconditionally and his former captors plead with him to remain and continue lending his support to the revolution. Then they drink a few rounds together and the incident is forgotten.

All of a sudden the Prussians enter the Palatinate, taking the government and military leadership by surprise. They have 27 battalions, new artillery and nine cavalry regiments. Engels is already aware of what is happening, as he has already read about it in the pages of the *Kölner Zeitung [Cologne Newspaper]* that arrived a few days previously, but clearly the provisional government and military are caught totally unawares. Engels, as he later tells Marx, can't resist joining the war and representing the *Neue Rheinische Zeitung* in the Baden-Palatinate army. 'The Prussian troops were approaching from Homburg,' Engels reports, 'and this gave the whole matter an interesting twist and gave me the opportunity to experience a short lesson in the school of war. I wasn't going to miss it, and as the *Neue Rheinische Zeitung* was in honour bound, at long last, to be represented in the Palatinate-Baden army, I buckled on my battle sword and went to Willich'. The latter is leading a military unit and is a member of the League of Communists. Engels now becomes a soldier in Willich's troop of irregulars – a proto-typical guerrilla army. He writes later about this experience in his brilliant 'The Campaign for the German Constitution', in which he provides a vivid, but highly accurate overview of the whole campaign and an analysis of why it finally failed.

Born in 1810 into a Prussian Junker family, Willich is no stranger to military order. The son of an officer who had served in the Napoleonic Wars, he enrolled in a military school at the age of twelve and served in the Prussian Army until he resigned his commission in 1845. Like many of his revolutionary contemporaries, he believed that the Prussian state had subverted the spirit of the people and ignored the social problems prevalent in the urbanising world of the 1840s. Rampant poverty, disease and poor living conditions for workers characterise Prussia's cities and the nation as a whole. Willich believes that democratic self-government, constitutional freedoms, education, a commitment to social reforms and the uplifting of the working classes would solve the problems of his day. He embraces the ideas of Marx and becomes a communist, but later, in London, he will fall out with both Marx and Engels over tactics and strategy.

Willich has already been involved in the revolutionary battles in Baden during 1848, when unemployed workers flocked to his unit, which became known as the 'workers' legion'. He shares his soldiers' poverty and deprivation and doesn't shirk from rolling up his sleeves and mucking in when manual labour is required. This earns him tremendous respect and loyalty from his men. Probably because of the excellent morale in his unit, it is one of the last to be defeated.

From 13 June until 12 July 1849, Willich's new unit is again active throughout the Palatinate and Baden, moving rapidly from village to village, until they are forced to retreat across the Swiss border. Because the strategic offensive by the other revolutionary forces never gets off the ground, the Baden-Palatinate operation can only be seen as a last ditch attempt to save at least the honour of the revolution. Anyone who's ever seen the Palatinate, Engels tell us, will comprehend that any movement in this wine-rich and wine-happy land will be a most light-hearted affair. At last we'd got rid of the slow-witted, pedantic, old Bavarian beer swillers, he notes, and in their place we put the loyal Palatinate wine guzzlers as administrative officers. The opening-up of the public houses is the first revolutionary act of the Palatinate people; the whole province becomes transformed into one big bar-room. And the amount drunk 'in the name of the people' during those six weeks is beyond measure. Throughout the province men are encouraged to make scythes. Engels remarks that if these had been handed out to the non-mobile citizens' militia – the so-called second line of defense – that would have been fine, but instead 'they let the lazy philistines keep their rifles and sent the young recruits into battle with scythes against the Prussian artillery'. While there is an acute shortage of guns, there is an equally curious surplus of ceremonial sabres, he tells us. 'Those who couldn't get hold of a rifle, were even more keen to get their hands on a clanking sabre, as this allowed them to call themselves officers'. These few vivid images give us some idea of the level of disorganisation and unpreparedness there is on the part of the rebellious forces. (see map on page 347)

In the first days of June the Prussians are approaching from the one side and Bavarians from the other. Engels feels that, 'with more daring' they could have won over the troops of the smaller states, but have left it too late and these are now joining the Prussians to suppress the ongoing rebellion in surrounding areas. He reports:

> A week was enough to sweep up in the Palatinate. There were 36,000 Prussian soldiers against 8-9,000 revolutionaries and both fortresses in the province were in the hands of the reactionaries. We then had to rely on the troops in Baden – 8,000 ordinary infantrymen and 12,000 irregulars and these were hard pressed by around 30,000 reactionary troops. Four big battles took place, in which the reactionaries prevailed thanks to their numerical superiority and because they used

> Württemberg territory illegally to evade our insurgent forces at a decisive juncture. After ten weeks of fighting, the remnants of the rebel army retreated to Switzerland.[64]

Engels' first battle takes place in the Rhinnthal, a picturesque, wooded area in the south of the Palatinate, on 17 June 1849. The Rhinnthal lies in a valley between the Saar basin and the Rhine plain, about 30km from the French border. He is still with the main body of Willich's corps in Annweiler when the advance guard begin fighting the Prussian 2nd division. Willich brings him up with the troops and leads them to the Rhinnthal, were the valley narrows to about 150 feet. The right-hand valley side climbs at a steepish angle, but on the left is less so to begin with, but becomes steeper and rockier towards the crest, and is impossible to ascend from the valley side. Their marksmen are ordered to take command of the crests however they can, on both sides of the valley. Engels is given command of the marksmen on the steep, rocky side on the left. He later writes a detailed report of the action:

> We'd only just climbed the shrub-covered hill and came out onto an open field surrounded by woods. From the woods the Prussians opened fire and sent their bullets flying over us. I brought up the other irregulars who were somewhat disorientated and slow clambering up the hill, and positioned them in protected places, and examined the terrain more closely. I couldn't advance with the few men I had, over a completely exposed field, about 200-250 feet wide, until the outflanking detachment had reached the Prussian flank. We could only wait as we were, in any case, not well protected as it was. Despite their modern rifles, the Prussians shot extremely badly; we were almost completely exposed during half an hour's shooting, but the enemy snipers only managed to hit a rifle barrel and someone's shirt tail. I had to find out where Willich was; my men promised to stay in position. I clambered back down the hillside...The main Prussian column on the road was under fire from our snipers on the right hand slope and were forced to retreat somewhat. Suddenly to the left of me our irregulars clambered hurriedly down the hillside and abandoned their positions...The Prussians then advanced and took our snipers in the flank, shooting on them from above, and forcing them to

> retreat. The whole hillside was soon in Prussian hands. They kept shooting at our column from above; we had no option, but to retreat.[65]

He admits that he is largely at fault for this defeat, by leaving the marksmen, who are under his command, at such a decisive moment in the battle.

On 18 June Willich's company marches to Karlsruhe to replenish their equipment and take on more volunteers. Here Engels notes that among the new volunteers are workers who had taken part in the Elberfeld rebellion. Also among the new intake is Professor Kinkel who corroborates Engels' disparaging remarks about the quality of the student recruits, who desert at the drop of a hat when conditions turn out to be more demanding than those in a boy scout camp; on the other hand he has nothing but praise for the workers, 'even though they are fully aware that this battle is not going to lead to their own liberation'. The most dedicated troops, however, are the communists, he tells us.

Once the Prussians have advanced over the Rhine, Willich's irregulars take on the vanguard role of the Palatinate revolutionary army. Their job is to stop the Prussians from cutting off the revolutionary forces in Baden where there is still fighting. On 21 June Engels has his second taste of real battle. Willich's troops continue to engage the enemy in regular skirmishes by their offensive tactics, but at this stage no decisive encounter takes place. They plan an ambush for that day. Engels says that Willich's troops now comprise around 700 men with two artillery pieces (cannons) and the men are better trained and more reliable than the other local Palatinate troops and are used to being under fire. He supports Willich's decision (as they have no idea of the strength of the enemy) to attack the Prussians at night time and to break through their lines, making their way to Bruchsal. The enemy corps they hope to attack is, though, more highly trained and contains more experienced subaltern officers than the revolutionary forces, and they have certainly no less than 4,000 men – a David versus Goliath situation. Engels takes up the story of the battle:

> We marched forward in good order through the village of Neuthardt and on to the hilltop before Karlsdorf. Once our advance guard reached the crest of the hill, they were confronted

> by the Prussians right in front of them. I heard one of the Prussians shout: "Who goes there?" and I ran forward. One of my comrades says, "He's had it; we won't see him again". But my running forward was in fact what saved me. In that moment the enemy field sentries let off a salvo and our advanced guard, instead of running at them with their bayonets, just fired back. The dragoons who were marching with me, in their usual cowardly fashion, turn and race their horses directly into our column and ride down a number of people; the first four to six sections are split apart and gallop off. At the same time, the enemy, in the fields left and right of us, begin firing and, to make matters worse, some of our idiots in the centre of the column begin firing at the head of their own troops and other idiots copy them. In no time the first half of the column is broken up, part of it dispersed into the fields, part in flight, part on the road, huddled in a confused knot. The wounded, kit bags, hats and rifles, lie scattered in the young corn. On top of it all, confused screaming, shots, whistling bullets in every direction. Once the noise subsides somewhat, I hear the sound of our own cannons being dragged away in hurried retreat. They provided the same standard of service for the second half of the column as the dragoons had for the first section. I was livid, [he writes in utter exasperation about] this childish fear that gripped our soldiers, particularly because the pathetic Prussians, despite being forewarned of our arrival, stopped shooting at us after only a few shots and retreated rapidly too. Our forward guard remained standing at their old posts and hadn't been attacked at all. An enemy squadron of cavalry or a reasonably sustained sniper fire would have sent us into the wildest flight.[66]

This, Engels' second experience of real battle, is not exactly an event to be proud of for the revolutionary army; in fact, his report again reads like a proverbial cock-up: a result of inexperience and lack of training.

For a number of days during the fighting, Engels is without a horse, but undeterred, he carries out his duties as adjutant on foot. He not only undertakes all secretarial work, but is often called by Willich to attend general staff meetings and gives advice on tactics. Willich often makes him responsible for the most difficult tasks. For example, he is given orders to requisition munitions from the town of Kaiserslautern which is about to be taken by the enemy; he is told to rescue a group of Hanauer gymnasts, who have been cut off by enemy troops, and to bring them back to the corps; the main body of their force, the Besancon soldiers, are put under his command for several days. During the battles, in which he takes part, he demonstrates a sangfroid and considerable courage even if he is not always sufficiently up to the military demands, as he has had no previous battle experience whatsoever and never been trained as an officer. He says that during the campaign he sees not a dozen individuals who behave in a cowardly manner during battle, but he does witness, where heroic courage is demonstrated individually, a whole battalion, to the last man, flee.

Only seven days later, and the men find themselves once again in the throes of battle. The revolutionary troops have marched a hundred kilometres further to the south and taken up positions on the river Murg. But this time, exceptionally, the battle goes in favour of the revolutionary forces. Opposite Willich's corps is the 29th Prussian infantry regiment from Koblenz. The Prussians fire off their bullets uselessly from 600-800 paces away, thus providing Willich with the opportunity to calmly position his guns closer to the so-called fighters. The marksmen then scramble down the wooded hillside and, supported by a few infantry troops, drive the Prussians from the opposite hill top. Unfortunately, this is not to be the final battle, and in subsequent confrontations the Prussians, with overwhelmingly superior, better trained and disciplined forces, defeat the remnants of the revolutionary forces.

Willich's irregular army in May 1849 comprises between 6-800 men and are among 'the most reliable soldiers in the whole Palatinate; most of the NCOs had served in the regular armed forces, some in Algeria, and are experienced in minor warfare'. Most of them had been involved in the Hecker coup in Baden [Hecker was a left-wing Republican who instigated an armed uprising in Baden in 1848] and, after the coup failed, they retreated into France where they received material support. Most of the soldiers are, in civilian life, ordinary workers and this leads Engels to describe the unit as having 'a definite proletarian character'.

He serves with the unit as one of about ten adjutants under colonel Willich and experiences more battles and skirmishes than those related here. He is noted for his 'passion and courage' and 'was highly praised by his fellow fighters', as reported by Mathilde Giesler-Anneke, the wife of another rebel commander. During the revolution her husband is in command of a force of 1,200 men in the central theatre. His tall, blue-eyed wife, her black hair cut short, rides alongside her husband into battle. When the Prussians capture the fortress Rastatt, the Annekes flee to Switzerland and France, and later join the exodus of German 'Forty-Eighters' to America. She is close to the communists, a friend of Marx and later, in the USA, becomes a strong feminist, educator and journalist.

It is particularly interesting to compare the official Prussian war reports of these events during the abortive uprising with Engels' own, and to find that they coincide in all relevant detail. Engels is clearly a good observer and doesn't fabricate or adorn the events. The Prussian reports also give credence to their enemy as a genuine military opponent.

He writes up his report on this campaign while in exile in Switzerland and, as a primary source, possibly uses Willich's own battle diary, but the latter has not been found. His descriptions of the military campaign reveal his considerable expertise, and it is this military know-how which leads later to his being given the moniker, 'The General'.

He can proudly say he took part in the last decisive battle of the Palatinate campaign on the River Murg. Their eventual defeat seals the fate of the revolutionary army and leaves them with only one sensible recourse, to retreat to safety over the border into Switzerland. They are able to do this unhindered by enemy pursuit, over the Black Forest hills to Wolfach, through the most glorious flower meadows, and Engels recalls the march as more akin to a 'wonderful holiday outing'. He has to be grateful for the poor marksmanship of the Prussian troops that have allowed him to emerge from the skirmishes completely unscathed. A well-aimed bullet could have changed the future course of European history and cut short what will continue to be a fascinating and eventful life.

Into exile once again

Shortly before their full retreat, on 10 June 1849, a Swiss army officer comes across the border to talk to the Willich irregulars in Rieden, in Bavaria. He warns that if they take part in any more fighting, they will be denied asylum in Switzerland. A war council is called and the men asked what they want to do. Willich himself declares he would rather die on German soil than be driven into exile, but in the end most vote for exile and so, with great relief, all the troops, with their weaponry and equipment, decamp over the Swiss border.

Engels reports that, after the decision had been taken they 'marched to the Swiss border, camped for the last time on German soil, and in the morning fired their spare munitions into the air and then, the last of the Baden-Palatinate revolutionary army crossed over into Switzerland. On the same day, simultaneously with us,' he continues, 'Constance was abandoned by the local corps; a week later Rastatt fell through betrayal, and the counter revolution had for the time being once again conquered Germany, right into the very last corner'. Battle-worn and depressed by the defeat of the revolutionary forces, he is now faced with the question of where to go. He knows he can't stay in Switzerland, as the long arm of the Prussian police can stretch even to there. However, for the time being he is left with little choice. He utilises the time to write his memoirs of the revolutionary campaign in the Palatinate while it is still fresh in his mind. These are later incorporated into his booklet, *Die Deutsche Reichsverfassungskampagne [The Campaign for the German Imperial Constitution]*. In this work he lambasts the officers who led the revolutionary forces for their incompetence; the only one who was effective, he says, is Johann Becker, who becomes a very close friend.

His experience as a rebel soldier in this revolutionary war leaves a deep imprint in his consciousness. It sparks his life-long interest in military matters and leaves him in no doubt as to the need for an effective military strategy and organisation if any future armed revolutionary uprising is to have any chance of success. He, like Che Guevara in the 20th century, sees it as vital for the revolutionary movement to learn the lessons of the armed struggle and to prepare adequately for future battles. So his 'Campaign' articles should be seen less as personal reminscence than lessons in the armed struggle.

Revolutionary aftermath

Engels is only one of around 11,000 refugees who request political asylum in Switzerland in the aftermath of the counter-revolution in Germany. Refugees from the other abortive revolutions in Europe are flooding there too, as well as to other similarly accommodating countries. Many flee to Britain, North and Latin America. There is a dreadful haemorrhaging of some of the brightest and most progressive thinkers from the continental mainland. However, many continue their revolutionary activities in their newly adopted countries, often playing significant political roles.

Twelve days after crossing the border with his comrades in Willich's small guerrilla army, and after endless time spent in registering with the Swiss authorities and marching on foot for around 200 km, they arrive in south western Switzerland, as far from the German border as the authorities can send them. Engels is granted asylum and settles temporarily in Lausanne, where he begins writing his reminiscences of the 'revolutionary farce' in Baden and the Palatinate, which is later published as a series in the *Neue Rheinische Zeitung*'s Political and Economic Review.

During his short stay in Switzerland Engels receives a little money from his family; despite everything, they clearly don't want to be made responsible for his starving to death. He renews contact with Marx, via his wife Jenny, to assure them that he is still alive and kicking. He explains how he joined Willich's irregulars once war broke out and was unable to send a letter to let them know:

> In Kaiserslautern I kept the so-called revolution at arm's length, but once the Prussians arrived, I couldn't resist the urge to join the war. Willich was the only officer worth his salt and so I joined him as his adjutant. I was in four battles, two of which were quite significant…and I found that the much lauded bravery of fighting it out is the most ordinary accomplishment one can have. The whistling of the bullets is a completely minor issue and throughout the whole campaign, despite plenty of cowardice, I saw hardly a dozen people act in a cowardly fashion during battle. However, I did see all the more "idiotic bravery". *Enfin* [in the end], I've come through it all safe and sound and *au bout du compte* [in the final reckoning] it's good that one of us from the *Neue Rheinische Zeitung* took part because all the democratic riff-raff in Baden and the Palatinate did and are now renowned for the heroic deeds they didn't perform. Again, it would have been said that the men of the *Neue Rheinische Zeitung* were too cowardly to do battle…[67]

He explains to Jenny that it has been impossible for him to write 'even a line' during the war or during the long march, after the rebel army's retreat, across Switzerland. Marx responds immediately and warns him that Switzerland will soon be hermetically sealed off and 'the mice will be caught in one fell swoop'. He tells him that he sees an opportunity for publishing a German language paper in London and urges him to travel there immediately, 'for your own safety if nothing else. The Prussians would shoot you twice, once for the Baden episode and the second time because of Elberfeld, and anyway what's the point of staying in Switzerland where you can't do a thing?'.

Engels talks the situation over with his old friend and former editorial colleague on the *Neue Rheinische Zeitung*, Wilhelm Wolff. There are signs that the Prussians are already pressurising the Swiss to extradite the German exiles, and police spying on them has been stepped up. The Prussian Consul in Berne is told about Engels' travel plans by his spies and sends a report to Berlin indicating that Engels and other exiles are planning to re-enter Germany via Constance to organise a coup in Prussia and to poison the 'enemies of the revolution'. This is certainly a concocted story, but it indicates clearly how much the Prussian authorities fear Engels and want him out of the way.

He eventually manages to make contact with Marx, who is now in Paris. Neither of them know what has happened to the other. Marx writes back and warns him about staying in Switzerland, encouraging him to go 'immediately to London' where 'I have a positive outlook for the setting up of a German journal; some of the money is already guaranteed'. Engels takes up Marx's suggestion and applies for an exit visa from the Swiss authorities. They grant him one for England and so, in September, he begins the overland trek to Genoa, from where he plans to take a boat for London. On 5 October 1849, shortly before embarking, he writes to the Chartist, George J. Harney:

> You will have got the few lines I sent you through Colonel Willich. This is to inform you, and by you Marx, that I am this morning arrived here in Genoa, and that, wind and weather favourable, I am going under sail for London to-morrow morning on board the English schooner Cornish Diamond, Capt'n Stevens. My journey will be of about 4 or 5 weeks so that by the middle of November I shall be in London. I am very happy to have found so soon an opportunity of leaving this damned police atmosphere – indeed I never saw it so organised as here in Piedmont.[68]

The boat from Genoa to London does indeed make slow progress and Engels describes it as 'a great round the world cruise'. August Willich, Engels former commander, along with several other veterans of the campaign, left Switzerland with him. They are all obliged to travel overland via Spain to Italy, as both France and Belgium would not have been as hospitable to them as on previous occasions, but they have done so separately.

Willich and his comrades arrive in London ahead of Engels. Willich, though, will only stay a short time there, after he falls out with Marx and Engels over political tactics, and emigrates to America. There, alongside other European exiles, he is to distinguish himself further by fighting for the North in the American Civil War, and will be promoted to Brigadier General.[69] He is no doubt a military man of exceeding courage, but also expertise, with a modesty and humanity rare in a soldier.

About his later experience in the Civil War, Willich says: 'The highest ambition of a commander must be satisfied by being associated with such men, who, through patriotism and a love for the free institutions of their country, have attained a degree of efficiency which professional soldiers seldom, if ever, reach.'

Marx and family are already in London when Engels eventually arrives after his long sea passage. To begin with, both he and Willich lodge with them in Anderson Street, Chelsea, in London's West End (at this time, not quite the highly expensive area it subsequently becomes, although even at this time it is a respectable middle class residential area). A short time later, they both move out, as things are a little cramped, and no doubt fraught, in the Marx house.

To begin with he finds it difficult to adapt to what is a totally different rhythm of life and a different culture. From a letter he writes some years later to Minna Kautsky (the mother of the German Socialist leader, Karl Kautsky) in Vienna we can gather how he feels after his arrival in London:

> That you didn't like London I can well understand. I felt the same years before. You adapt only with difficulty to the gloomy air and the gloomy inhabitants, to the isolation, the class differences in social life, living in closed rooms, conditioned by the climate. One has to turn down the barometer of one's own continental attitude to life...until one slowly adapts...and it

> does have its good sides that the people here are in general more direct and reliable than elsewhere, and for doing research, no city is more suitable than London, and the absence of police chicanery outweighs much of the downside. I know and love Paris, but if I had the choice I'd rather live permanently in London than there. You can only derive real pleasure from Paris if you become a Parisian with all the privileges of a Parisian and, above all, an interest only for Parisian things and an acceptance of the belief that Paris is, taken all in all, the centre of the world. London is more ugly, but more magnificent than Paris, it is the real centre of world trade and offers much more variety. London, also, allows you to adopt a complete neutrality to your surroundings, which is so necessary for unbiased artistic and scientific work. One enthuses over Paris and Vienna, one hates Berlin, but in London one maintains an indifferent and neutral objectivity. And that, too, is of value.[70]

He remains there only a month, but it is an extremely fruitful time for both Marx and himself. Together, they manage to develop a concept for the launch of the *Neue Rheinische Zeitung's* Political and Economic Review, in January 1850. They also write drafts for a series of articles that will appear in it.

The *Review* is established by Marx, shortly after his own arrival in London, but its life is short. Only six issues are published and printed in Hamburg – the final one appearing in April 1850. Copies are, though, distributed widely throughout the working class and socialist organisations.

He says he left the Marx's house only to be able to work 'in a less disturbed atmosphere'. He gives no further details, but it could be that he feels somewhat in the way of the family or perhaps Marx's wife, Jenny is finding the lodgers too much of a burden. In any case, he wants to complete his work on the campaign for the German Imperial Constitution [later published as *Die Reichsverfassungs-kampagne]* and begin work on an historical analysis of the German Peasant War, mentioned earlier, so he moves to Soho, where most of the French and German exiles are congregated.

He is still very short of money – only a small trickle comes from home, each pittance accompanied by new accusations of 'chaining yourself to Marx'; and 'do you want to ruin yourself completely?' His articles for the *Neue Rheinische Zeitung's* Political and Economic

Review bring him not a penny, and as a 'damned foreigner' he is unable to find paid work elsewhere, as it is seen as taking the bread out of the mouths of the natives.

Engels' friend, the revolutionary poet, Ferdinand Freiligrath, in his Words of Farewell penned after the defeat of the revolutionary forces in 1849, writes defiantly:

Now adieu, yet not for ever adieu!
For they cannot kill the spirit, brothers!
Soon, rattling, I will arise on high,
Soon I will return more gigantic still!

However the hopes of a new upsurge of revolutionary activity in Germany shared by many of Engels' comrades are not to be. The counter-revolution, led by the feudal Junker [German Land-owning class], has not only been victorious in its Baden-Palatinate crusade, but has been able to cement its rule throughout Germany for years to come.

The middle class is also clearly wearied by battle and shows little inclination to challenge this rule in the coming years, but probably also because it's just come through the worldwide economic crisis of 1847/48 and the new economic upturn is demanding all attention. Those among the working and middle classes who defended the revolution up to its final defeat have shed much blood and now desperately yearn for a period of peace and recuperation. So although the revolutions of 1848/49 have no tangible continuation, they remain a yardstick for all future movements. For Engels and Marx they also provide rich material for an analysis of the roles of social classes and their tendencies, as well as for a proper evaluation of the outcomes – perceived successes and failures – for Marxist revolutionary theory. These issues are covered extensively in the *Neue Rheinische Zeitung's Political and Economic Review*.

Engels' main contribution to the *Review* is a series of articles in the first three issues under the title: 'The Campaign for the German Imperial Constitution'. In the fifth and sixth issues, he writes two articles evaluating the German peasant uprisings (1524-25), 'The Peasant War in Germany'. This is the first historical work to assert that the real motivating force behind the Reformation and the 16th century Peasant War was socio-economic (class conflict) rather than 'merely' religious. In it he also emphasises the need for an alliance between peasants and workers if any future revolution is to succeed.

He goes on to write various articles, commissioned by Marx, specifically for the US public, such as the comprehensive series 'Revolution and Counter Revolution in Germany', which is carried in the *New York Daily Tribune*, at that time probably the largest circulation newspaper in the world. A number of revolutionary leaders, but particularly Lenin, will base much of their revolutionary practice on these key works by Engels. And they will play a significant role in ensuring the Bolshevik victory in 1917.

In the spring of 1850 a disaffected student attempts to assassinate the Prussian king, Friedrich Wilhelm IV; he fails, but the refugees in London feel, rightly as it turns out, that the event will be used by the Prussians to pressurise the British government to implement its moribund Aliens Act which would compel foreigners to register and make their continued presence in the country subject to their good behaviour. To deflect such action, Marx and Engels issue a declaration distancing themselves from such violent actions and emphasise that only the royalists can gain from them, not the revolutionaries. The British government, clearly little worried by any danger of anti-Royalist outbreaks in the country, sees no need to introduce measures against the émigré communities and resists Prussian entreaties.

In that same year the hated Austrian General von Haynau - the 'hyena' of Brescia and 'butcher' of Budapest, who put down the 48/49 revolutionary uprisings with unspeakable brutality – visits Britain. With a member of the Rothschild family he takes a tour of a brewery in East London, but is recognised by some of the refugees. The brewery workers, in a marvellous act of international solidarity, 'rough him up' and almost lynch him. The incident is given wide publicity and Prime Minister Palmerston, albeit reluctantly, is obliged to apologise to the Austrians. The Fraternal Democrats hold a celebratory, and well-attended, meeting where the incident took place and when Engels speaks he is given a rousing round of applause as he thanks the English workers for their action in punishing one of his compatriots.

The central committee of the League of Communists, reorganised by Marx, now sees as its main task the re-establishing of broken contacts with the radical groups still remaining in Germany and France. There is an enormous range of political and organisatorial work to be done and Engels, as an excellent organiser, is soon drafted in to help. One of his tasks is to assist in the vetting process. Among the waves of refugees, not all are genuine revolutionaries, and before letting them join the League, they are questioned in detail and assessed. Experience has taught them that police spies and agents provocateurs are continually endeavouring to infiltrate their organisations. Wilhelm Liebknecht, a leading German socialist, remembers being interviewed by Marx and Engels in the back room of a London pub, with tankards of foaming stout, and long-stemmed pipes on the table and the opportunity of eating an English beef steak, all of which reminds him of an illustration he's seen in Dickens's *Boz*.

Eugene Oswald, a republican exile who arrived in London before Marx and Engels, later becoming a regular visitor to Marx's home, states in his memoirs, that in London among the refugees 'the Communists, or advanced socialists, were not wholly absent from our numbers, but constituted no principle element'. So it can be reliably assumed that before Marx and Engels arrive in the capital, communism is hardly on the agenda.

In everything he does, Engels is fastidious and dependable. Only a week after his own arrival, he is elected on to the Social Democratic Support Committee for German Refugees, founded by Marx, and he gets down to work immediately. Largely due to his efforts, a superior lodging house in Great Windmill Street, Soho is taken over as a refugee centre, on the lines of the ones he'd experienced in Switzerland. Most of the refugees are, in the main, even more penniless than he is, and with no source of income whatsoever. He is also given the position of secretary of the Committee and is instrumental in saving many from penury.

Both he and Marx very soon become isolated ideologically from many of their compatriots, including Willich, who are convinced that the flames of revolution in Europe will soon flare up again and they can then return to complete the unfinished task. Marx and Engels are only too aware that this is wishful thinking, but their cool and rational dismissal of this possibility is not what the refugees want to hear. The discussions among the émigrés is often heated and bitter and leads to the establishment of different factions. Engels, like them, undoubtedly seethes with anger and hatred over the victorious Prussians but emotions, he is convinced, don't create revolutions. He is resigned, for the time being at least, to accept 'a certain isolation' in which he and Marx will be able to pursue their researches in tranquility. Willich and several others, themselves clearly not entirely convinced about prospects for reigniting the revolution in Europe, leave for the USA out of frustration. This moment could signal the total demise of inchoate communism in Europe and Marx's and Engels' slide into historical oblivion. The two are, though, made of sterner stuff and refuse to be elbowed so easily off the stage of history.

Engels is already high on the list of most wanted individuals in Germany, but after his military activities in 1849, his 'criminal' profile gives him quasi-star notoriety on the roll of politically dangerous agitators. His name appears in documents that circulate in the highest circles, from the Prussian Minister President, Edwin Freiherr von Manteuffel, to the most lowly police stations throughout the German lands. And the authorities are not satisfied that he is out of the country, but continue spying on him and harassing him wherever he is living. Engels is fully aware of this and often notes that his mail has been interfered with; some letters never reach their destination and end up in various police files. He is shadowed by police spies and he amuses himself immensely by leading them a merry dance, before shaking them off. However, not only the man himself is persecuted, but so are his writings. In the Cologne police files from 1854, there is a reference to the banning from lending libraries of documents written by Marx and Engels, noting the political trials against them.

The political police regularly visit Engels' father in Barmen to impound the son's property and assets. This must have seriously embarrassed and infuriated the old man and he makes no secret of his attitude to his 'wayward son'. What the relatives think of Engels can be deduced from a letter sent to him by his brother-in-law in 1849:

> You seem to me like a hounded fox who can find no place to rest...If you, by the way, had a family and worried about them like me, you would change your restless life and, in the intimate circle of your loved ones, you would have more from this short life than you will ever receive from a heartless gang of cowardly, ungrateful, loudmouths...It is as if you still harbour this thankless idea of sacrificing yourself for incorrigible mankind, to become a social Christ and to devote

> all your egoism to achieving this goal. At the moment you are unscathed and, without having to humiliate yourself, you could ensure that you don't have to stand isolated later, like a wearisome hypochondriac.[71]

Such letters do, no doubt, hurt Engels' sensibilities and underline how impossible it will be to win over his family to a different way of thinking, but there is no indication that they cause him a single moment of doubt about the correctness of his decision to devote himself to the struggle for working class emancipation and world socialism. The recipe, his family feels would cure his madness, is for him to marry and settle down. That is, though, the last thing on his mind. What now spurs him on is to analyse the reasons for the defeat of the revolutionary forces, to examine closely the strategies and tactics, in order to avoid similar mistakes next time. This project is made more difficult, because the Cologne police have confiscated most of his documents from the newspaper offices, from his flat and from friends' houses. His painstakingly collected archive is now no more, including his unfinished manuscript, The History of English Society, in which he develops his revolutionary theory. However, much of his library is saved because he left many of his books with friends in Brussels.

In his essay 'The Peasant War in Germany' Engels characterises the 1848 revolution as a class battle:

> In 1848 the interests of the opposing classes collided and each acted in its own interest. The bourgeoisie, too far developed to continue tolerating the feudal-bureaucratic absolutism, was not powerful enough to immediately subsume the demands of the other classes under its own. The proletariat was much too weak to make the rapid jump over the bourgeois period and to be sure of its own ability of assuming power within a short space of time. It had already savoured only too well the sweets of the bourgeois system under absolutism and was, in any case, far too developed to imagine its own emancipation coming about as a result of bourgeois emancipation. The majority of the nation, petit bourgeoisie, artisans and peasants, were seen at the outset, as far as their natural allies are concerned, by the bourgeoisie as too revolutionary and to a certain extent by the proletariat as not advanced enough, and were left to fend for

> themselves; divided internally, they too came to nothing and battled right and left against their fellow opponents.[72]

The 1848/49 revolutionary upsurge in continental Europe concluded in defeat for the anti-feudal forces. In Engels' revolutionary theory England should have played a decisive and active role, but in actual fact it played no part at all in the continental-wide revolution. This fact undoubtedly gave succour to the British ruling class, which had been quaking in its drawing rooms before a latent revolution. Engels is also wrong in thinking, as he expounded in 1847, that a bourgeois-liberal revolution would happen in Germany first; but it does so in France, and as a workers' revolution. On this occasion Marx is proved right, as he predicted that the revolution would break out in there first.

After this enormous defeat across the breadth of Europe, Engels realises he will not see socialism come about in the most highly developed countries of Europe either in the next few years, or perhaps even in following decades. He can see that even if a new revolution does erupt, the material conditions in these countries will not be ripe enough to sustain and see through a genuine workers' revolution. He feels, though, that in a still-to-come democratic republic, the working class would be able to exercise a generally democratic hegemony. In that vein he argues that the workers will have to set up their own revolutionary forms of government, whether in the form of municipal committees, local councils, or workers' clubs. In this way the bourgeois democratic governments would not only lose the support of the workers, but would be monitored and threatened by a competing proletarian authority. In a word: 'from the first moment of victory mistrust towards their one-time allies must be directed at the party that wishes to exploit alone the victory they have achieved together'.

This idea is of particular significance, because we can see that Lenin will follow it to the letter in Russia in 1917. After Kerensky comes to power at the head of what is, to begin with, a bourgeois democratic revolution against Tsarist absolutism, Lenin and the Bolsheviks immediately set up Soviets (workers' councils) as parallel governing structures and are able to challenge Kerensky successfully and subsequently overthrow his regime.

Engels also clearly recognises that the rural population in Europe will play little role in any future revolution. His travels through the

French countryside have helped confirm that gut feeling. He writes that it has been proved, 'by the history of all modern countries that the rural population will never bring about a successful independent movement, because it is too widely dispersed and it is difficult to reach an understanding among the majority; the impetus for it must come from the initiative of the more enlightened and flexible population concentrated in the towns'. To prepare for such an eventuality, in 1850 a number of socialists, including Engels and Harney, plan a 'World Federation of Revolutionary Socialists' whose aim would be to bring about the subjugation of the privileged classes under a dictatorship of the proletariat until the realisation of a communist society. It is envisaged as a kind of prototype communist or socialist party. It is during this period that Engels first uses the controversial term 'dictatorship of the proletariat' openly for the first time, describing it as a necessary prerequisite if the final form of organising the human community – communism – is to be achieved. It is a concept he and Marx develop as a result of the abortive revolution in France during the early part of this same year.

Revolutionary change to communism would necessitate a temporary dictatorship of the proletariat they now feel. But the concept is conceived in a flexible way by the two, as is implied in Engels' essay on the parliamentary Ten Hours' Bill (intended to limit the working day to ten hours). As two thirds of England's population is made up by industrial proletarians, he considers political rule by the working class can now be achieved alone through the ballot box.

Although both Marx and Engels write extensively about the means of creating a successful revolution, neither gives any detailed prescriptions for a future socialist society, but there are often hints or suggestions. In 1850, Engels writes that [after a successful revolution], 'The workers must demand that the confiscated feudal property becomes state property for the setting up of worker colonies, so that it can be worked together with the rural proletariat, taking advantage of large scale production and, at the same time, through this, the principle of common ownership becomes a solid basis at the centre of shaky bourgeois property relations. Just as the Democrats make alliances with the peasants, so must the workers with the rural land workers'.

Here again, we can see how the Bolshevik revolution later takes this suggestion on board, with the confiscation of feudal land, the setting up of state farms and the battles with the landowning class of rich peasants [kulaks]. The fact that these ideas will be put into practice in such an absolute and literal fashion, particularly by Stalin, means that specific national and local conditions will be ignored, resulting in widespread famine and serious social repercussions.

In writing about the goal of the revolution, Engels calls for a 'permanent revolution' until all private property has been abolished and all classes have been eradicated. We don't want merely an amelioration of the present society, but the establishment of a new one, he emphasises. Trotsky will take up this call, as will Mao when initiating his Cultural Revolution, but with catastrophic consequences.

The numbers of most recent political refugee arrivals in London in the aftermath of the 1848/49 uprisings are obediently communicated to Berlin by the Prussian envoy. Of the 300 Germans, it is estimated that 280 are artisans. It is this sector of craftsmen/artisans that is often in the forefront of revolutionary activity in most European countries. This is hardly surprising as it is the skilled craftsmen that are most threatened by industrialisation. This group is also, as a rule, better educated than the ordinary workers or rural labourers. The real proletariat is hardly represented at this time, largely because these countries do not yet have a developed manufacturing industry like Britain, and most factory workers have not enjoyed education, have little time or money to be able to play an active role, or to find the wherewithal to emigrate.

It is calculated that up to 60 million Europeans emigrate during the 19th century, largely as a result of oppression by rigid feudal hierarchies and the brutal suppression of all democratic aspirations. In the period between 1871 and 1890 almost 2 million Germans emigrate, but considerable numbers had already left before.[73] According to the British Home Office, after the suppression of the revolutionary movement on the Continent, around 300 Germans, 200 Hungarians, 100 Italians, 40 Poles and a few French came to London, but there is already a sizeable population of refugees, particularly Germans already resident. According to the census, taken a year later in 1851, there are 9,566 residents recorded in the city as having been born in Germany, but by 1891 this figure will reach 26,920. The community is very mixed, and includes businessmen, scientists, and political refugees as well as tradesmen and labourers.

Despite the meagre resources and small numbers of genuine

militants, Marx and Engels are still convinced of the potential embodied in the proletariat and the inevitable success of their campaign for worker-run states. In a conversation with Engels' fellow revolutionary soldier and former Prussian lieutenant, Gustav Techov in 1850, the two characterise themselves as leaders of a party that sooner or later will incorporate millions. He asks them how they can be so convinced and they respond, that they are only serving the 'material power of historical necessity'. Techov also reports on the division of work between the two, saying that, Marx dealt with the big political questions, while Engels occupied himself with the political-organisational issues. In this same year, 1850, the *Manifesto of The Communist Party* is published in English for the first time in Harney's *Red Republican* (in a translation by Helen Macfarlane, another extraordinary figure eclipsed by history[74]). The later English translation of the *Manifesto,* and the one we are familiar with today, is by Samuel Moore from 1888.

Marx and Engels have no illusion that a lasting united front between socialists, democrats and others can be built to last. They also dismiss the conspiratorial methods proposed for achieving the revolutionary goals. The German refugees find themselves at loggerheads over the best strategy for taking the revolution in Germany forward, and Marx and Engels very soon find themselves in a virtual minority of two. With their adamant position, they become very unpopular among many of the refugees. They put their faith in the economic factors, and continue to maintain that it is real conditions that matter, not the mere will, and that it is economics that are the historical driving force. They argue for rationality not the heart to rule decision-making. These 'dreamers', as he calls them, make Engels livid; they refuse to give credence to economic factors, no doubt because this would also involve an indeterminate wait and much patience. Engels does, though, reveal a keen perceptiveness about the specific problems of émigré work – such difficulties are revealed time and time again, and similar ones still face modern-day émigré groups. In a letter to Alexander Gurwitch he later writes:

> I know how any political emigration inevitably splits into different groups, as long as the situation remains pacific in the motherland. The passionate urge to action, despite the impossibility of doing anything effective, conjures up over-eager mental speculation in many a clever and energetic head, and

> encourages attempts to find or discover new and almost miraculous means to achieve one's aims.[75]

And again to Eduard Bernstein:

> The biggest danger for every political emigration lies in the urge for action; something has to happen; something has to be done! And thus things take place whose consequences are impossible to envision and which, as one later recognises, would have been better not attempted.[76]

Of course, it doesn't take long for the more petty bourgeois sections of the émigré community to separate from the more proletarian, and both then form their own separate refugee committees. Already by early 1850 the unity of the radical émigrés in London is irrevocably broken; a split also occurs in the central committee of the League of Communists. One of the dissidents in the League is lieutenant Techow. While recognising Marx's intellectual supremacy and the fact that he has a 'head and a heart', he castigates Engels as 'the busybody, and permanently yapping spy who by means of quarrels, lies and insolence concludes his little deals'. This is one of the very few such derogatory comments to be made on Engels' behaviour, and it is undoubtedly coloured by the bitterness of the ideological struggle being waged among the exiles at this time.

The majority in the leadership of the League, including Marx and Engels, decide to move the headquarters to Cologne, in order to distance it from the infighting. The opposition of the petty bourgeois democratic faction costs both men many hours of debilitating hassle over the succeeding months and even years. Hair-splitting arguments and debates drag on and on, as is the norm in politicised émigré communities, cut off from the real action and the realities of home. With this split comes the end of what has otherwise been a period of very fruitful work in terms of building the new party. Marx, exhausted by all the bickering, decides to bury himself in his research and Engels, who sees little choice if he is to survive, offers an olive branch to his family, expressing his willingness to return to his father's Manchester factory.

A secret Prussian police report from the time notes that the split in the Communist League forces Engels to take, what for him, is the heavy decision to return to 'slavish commerce'. Engels isn't prepared to see Marx and his family go to the dogs as victims of the refugee splits, so opts to make the sacrifice himself. Engels' links with his family back in Barmen have been maintained through his regular correspondence with his favourite sister, Marie Blank, who no doubt serves also as a go-between on behalf of their parents who are, understandably, more than somewhat sceptical of his apparent change of heart to become a businessman after all. In one of her letters Marie gives clear expression to this scepticism, saying she feels his intention of returning to the business is only to put himself financially back on his feet in order to once again return to his party work, given the opportunity. Through her words one can hear their father speaking; and, of course, these intimations are not far from the truth. Engels' father is, at the time, actually toying with the idea of sending his son to Calcutta, far away from all those European revolutionary viruses. The vehement opposition to this idea by the 30 year-old Engels stymies it. His father's second proposal, to send him to the USA where he could work as a cotton buyer for the company, is more to Engels' liking. Not that he would be happy bargaining over the price of slave-produced cotton, but the chance to undertake political work in the free atmosphere of the USA would have undoubted attractions.

Engels talks this proposal over with Marx, who declares his willingness to accompany him to the New World. But this idea, too, comes to nothing as cotton, in the interim, has become relatively cheap and plentiful, so the company doesn't need to have its own individual buyer. In the end father and son come to an agreement that he will join the firm in Manchester, that is part owned by Engels' father, and part-owned and managed by the brothers, Peter and Gottfried Ermen. In words at least, his father sympathises: 'I can imagine that your living there will not be pleasant for you, but for us and the business it would be, under these unusual circumstances, the most useful'.

CHAPTER SEVEN (1850-1870)

Two decades of purgatory

By mid-November 1850 Engels, seeing no other option, finds himself once more in Manchester. For a few months or at most a few years, he is prepared to throw himself into the hated 'jobbery' in the firm of Ermen & Engels. Little does he realise that these few months will extend to two decades. This period will be the most trying of his life, slogging away each day in a job he hates, working for a capitalist company and having to hob-nob with his sworn enemies, the mill owners of the area, and separated from his closest friend and comrade. Of course, it can be convincingly argued that life for him is hardly the purgatory that the ordinary mill workers have to endure – he has a secure job, is well paid and has the privileges accorded the son of one of the firm's partners. But for someone of Engels' intellectual calibre and vitality, sitting at a desk each day, adding up columns of figures and corresponding with trading partners, is little better than a slow death. He is prepared to do it for several reasons, the main one being that he feels it is the only way to guarantee financial security for Marx. Without his sacrifice the momentous goals they have both set themselves will be unrealisable.

As a single man with no family to support and with a ready-made business opportunity at hand, he is clearly in a much better position than Marx to earn a decent income.

During his absence abroad, Britain has undergone considerable change. The outbreak of revolution in France in 1848 gave the Chartist movement new hope and impetus, but the government, concerned about possible infection from across the Channel, seized the opportunity to brand it as a bogey of foreign revolution and clamp down. It is the 1848 revolution that saved the British bourgeoisie, Engels maintains.

However the Chartist campaign around the third petition continued and a massive gathering on Kennington Common in London in that same year was organised, with a planned march on parliament to present the petition. But the government maintaining that an armed uprising is planned, mobilises large bodies of troops and special constables in the face of which the Chartist leaders called off the march. The Charter is then presented by a small deputation. The government claims victory, and uses its advantage to implement even more violent methods to put down popular gatherings and demonstrations, and new waves of arrests take place. Engels' friend, Ernest Jones, who had in the meantime become a leading Chartist, is one of those arrested.

After 1848 Chartism dies as a national force, but its example inspires the ideas of working class organisation and of the need for unity in struggle for years to come. The six points were not won but the government had been forced to make some concessions such as the Mines Act of 1842, the Factory Act of 1844 and the Ten Hour Act of 1850. Engels is severely disappointed by the demise of what he saw as the potential party of revolution in Britain, but he recognises Chartism's achievements. He writes later, in the *Labour Standard* (No.5, June 1881):

> The working class of Great Britain for years fought ardently and even violently for the People's Charter...it was defeated but the struggle had made such an impression upon the victorious middle class that this class, since then, was only too glad to buy a prolonged armistice at the price of ever-repeated concessions to the working people.

His arrival in Manchester coincides with a renewed boom in manufacturing. Britain is at the height of its industrial might. In the decades following Waterloo, Britain had grown to become the greatest colonial power in the world with the world's strongest Navy. Its position of dominance in the mid-19th century can be compared with that of the USA today. Its technological and industrial development is far in advance of any other country and in technology it has a virtual monopoly. Even so, perhaps surprisingly, census figures from 1851 indicate that agriculture is still Britain's largest industry, although manufacturing of all kinds employs more people. So wealthy has Britain become that by the early 1850s it is exporting millions of pounds of capital, mainly to North and South America.

In the first half of the century the production of pig iron, perhaps one of the best indices of industrial development, was, in France, less than twice what it had been in 1806; in both Britain and Germany production had grown eight or nine times in the same period. By 1850 British production and consumption of iron on a per capita basis was far ahead of that of all continental countries. The same applied to cotton – the country consumed, as a comparison, nine times more than Russia.

The fifties and sixties see the most profound changes of the century not only in Britain, but in Germany too. European countries are brought increasingly closer together by modern communications systems; it is also the supreme age of railway building, with 50,000 miles of track being laid in continental Europe, as against only 15,000 before 1850. The emergence of the steamship is also revolutionising transport by sea and bringing even far-off countries closer together.

Railways and other forms of communication are much further advanced in Britain than elsewhere and make significant contributions to the expansion of the country's industry. Telegraphy also means that information and news can travel faster. The slow growth of rail networks elsewhere, particularly in France, and the resulting lack of economic integration, delays economic growth considerably. In France between 1801 and 1851 the percentage of people living in towns of over 10,000 grew from only 9.5 to 10.6 percent; in Britain by contrast, it grew from 23.3 to 39.5 percent. These advances underlie the intellectual optimism of the latter part of the century, despite the appalling social deprivations inflicted by industrial capitalism. They also have an impact on armies and military power, which become, more than ever, adjuncts of economic power.

Towards the end of June 1851, father and son see each other again for the first time since their fateful confrontation on the barricades in 1849. Engels' mother is overjoyed at what she sees as reconciliation and she persuades Peter Ermen, who runs the Victoria Mill in Salford, to invite her husband over and offer him lodgings in his house. At the same time she gives her son detailed and anxious advice on how to behave when he again meets his father, fearing that his impetuousness could ruin what is probably the last chance of reconciliation: 'I think it will perhaps be better if you don't spend too much time together and don't always talk about business, and it would be better if you avoided politics, as you both have such divergent views'. Engels clearly follows her advice, bites his lip, swallows his pride and plays the devoted son, as no altercations flare up between them. Engels briefs Marx on the new situation:

> On the whole I am quite happy with the result of my talks with the old man. He needs me here for at least three years, but I have not entered into any obligations, not even for the three years, and he didn't demand any, not in relation to my writing nor in my remaining here should the revolution break out again. He doesn't even seem to think of this eventuality, that's how secure people now feel! On the other hand, I've agreed the amount I need for representation and entertaining, right from the start – c.£200 annually, and he agreed without a problem... During the negotiations, he gave me a peek into the state of his business, both here and back home, and he's done very well, doubling his capital since 1837, so I don't feel any need to be unnecessarily parsimonious.[77]

Peter Ermen, Gottfried's brother is sent to Liverpool, where he is happy to reside, and Engels is given responsibility for the company's head office, but soon realises this ties him more than he would like:

> I suggested that this responsibility was beyond my capabilities and played modesty itself. If my old man had stayed any longer here, we'd have begun to fight. He just can't accept his luck and becomes haughty, reverting to his schoolmasterly tone and is provocative, but he's so stupid and tactless that he riles me, for instance, in the presence of the Ermens, when he thinks my gob is stopped, relying on my sense of propriety. He does this on his last day in order to sing me a hymn of praise to Prussian institutions. Of course a few words and an angry glance suffice to send him back into his lair, but that is enough to return us to the previous frozen footing...As long as it has no direct practical bearing on e.g. my financial situation, then I'm more than happy to maintain a cool businesslike relationship, better than all this emotional humbug.[78]

Engels makes a very odd businessman. Hardly begun working for the Manchester company, he tells Marx excitedly that a crisis in the markets is approaching and the revolutionary weather forecast is predicting storms in the sphere of international politics, and that he's over the moon that the battles on the continent in the coming year will coincide with a crisis. Yet his hopes that the new revolutionary upsurge will release him from his fetters are not to be fulfilled. He goes on to tell Marx that he will now begin to get down to work (not, it hardly needs to be said, for his father's company) and is thinking of moving to the outskirts of the city in order to work undisturbed. He doesn't expect his father to visit for at least another year and feels he can settle down in his own way and the money ascribed for representation can be used 'to a large extent for other purposes'.

Engels is now officially installed in the company's office as Corresponding Clerk, but as a close relative of one of the owners, is given the status of General Assistant, however, the agreement lays down that his work as General Assistant will be additional to his clerking work, which can not be neglected. In the first months his main task is to represent his father's interest in the company which gives him no status in his own right. The Ermen & Engels office is in Southgate, just behind Deansgate, in central Manchester and is, conveniently, only a ten-minute walk to the Owenite Hall of Science which opened in 1840, and where many of the big political meetings of the time take place. His new job keeps him chained to his desk for ten and later six hours a day, leaving little time at all for political activities or for research. He hates every minute of this work, compounded also by the fact that he doesn't get on with Ermen at all, nor the latter with him. His burden of work even alarms Marx, who remonstrates: 'You're surely not striving for the glory of sacrificing yourself on the altar of the Ermen-Engels office?'

He doesn't warm to Manchester anymore than he did on previous visits, and finds it very difficult coming to terms with its smoke, the damp and dinginess, where 'all the water becomes stinking sewage'. He communicates his feelings to George Harney, who replies laconically: 'I'm not surprised to find you expressing your disgust of Manchester. It is a damned dirty den of muckworms. I would rather be hanged in London than die a natural death in Manchester.' And to his friend, the poet Georg Weerth who is, at the time, in Bradford also working for a textile company, Engels writes about the mental tedium of his work, to which Weerth replies with an upbeat cliché, but hardly consoling: 'Time is costly but the future doesn't come cheap. You're doing the right thing to get yourself bored in Manchester, because boredom brings in the money, pleasure never made anyone rich...'

These are potentially the best years of a young man's life and Engels sees them dribbling away like precious water in the sand. His attitude to his 'jobbing' can be gleaned from the terms he uses in his letters to describe the business: 'shit trade', 'prison of Babylon', 'dog-eat-dog commerce' or, with bitter irony as 'sweet commerce'. Of course, he wouldn't be able to last the coming twenty years if he'd only seen the four walls in the office. He soon creates a life outside work and keeps his hours of drudgery to the absolute minimum – even though they still constitute a large chunk of his life. He begins leading a double existence and also renews his liaison with Mary Burns. After doing his daily penance at the altar of the firm, in the evenings he slinks off to see Mary or traipses with her around the working class neighbourhoods to talk with ordinary working people in their own environment and in the pubs, gathering material for a future book; the weekends he devotes to study and writing or outdoor pursuits to keep fit.

An 'official' residence in town is only rented when he expects visits from the family, otherwise he lives in cheaper furnished accommodation or at Mary's cottage. In this way he saves money, which he can then use to support Marx and the wider movement. When his father announces a visit, he rents 'fine lodgings, buys in fine cigars and wine, in order to impress. Voila la vie!' he notes. Later, when he has enough money to afford a permanent house for 'representation', his double life is played out between this and the suburban cottage he rents under a pseudonym for Mary and her sister Lydia. Only in 1869 is he finally able to give up this subterfuge.

His first accommodation in Manchester is a modest, furnished flat in Strangeways, but he leaves a short time later as his landlady moves house and, without giving him any warning, moves his things, as she assumes he will follow. In 1852 he moves out to live closer to 'Klein Deutschland' [Little Germany]. Manchester, like London, has a significant number of Germans living there, some of them radicals, and they form a vibrant community. He tells his sister that he is somewhat lonely in his flat and once he moves 'will allow myself, for a change, some amusement as far as that is at all possible in this coal smoke. For six months now,' he tells her ironically, 'I've not had the opportunity of creating my lobster salad, for which I'm a recognised expert – quelle horreur, it's enough to turn anyone sour'.

Engels knows that if he can manage to save £150 a year for the party, (that is roughly half the amount that the Social Democratic Refugee Committee has to work with for the whole year), then he'll achieve something. He feels that spending £50 on his relatives when they come, in order to put on a show of comfort, is more than enough. But if ever any one of them discovers what he is doing, he will be in a hot pickle. Although his father, suspicious as always, appears to have some inkling of what is happening, he prefers to ignore it to avoid unnecessary conflict. However, he does write a letter to his son telling him that he feels he is spending too much money and should be able to manage on £150. Engels responds that if he cuts his remuneration, he will pack his bags immediately, leave the office and return to London; a risky threat, but it pays off and his father backs down. But his father's suspicions towards 'that whole tribe of refugees' remain unallayed, reserving most of his venom for Marx, 'that ruination of my son'. It is very clear that anything more than a shaky ceasefire between son and father will be impossible to achieve; both are obliged to maintain a precarious and frosty, modus vivendi.

Engels receives a modest annual salary of £100 throughout the 1850s, but his share of the firm's profits rises from a yearly sum of around £268 in 1854 to £1078 by 1859. From his salary and expenses, he is able to siphon off enough to make regular payments to Marx. To begin with he sends him £5 per month, but by 1862, when his contract with Gottfried Ermen is confirmed and he feels materially more secure, it is raised to £10. These sums are usually sent in the form of £5 notes which he cuts in half and sends in separate envelopes, to preclude their being stolen. Presumably Marx then pastes the notes back together again to make them legal tender.

To gain some idea of what the above sums of money are worth during the 1850s a comparison can be made with workers' average earnings: a cotton mill worker, for instance, would earn between 14-17 shillings a week – c.£40 per annum, a South Wales collier would earn 24 shillings (i.e. just under one and a quarter pounds) and a farm labourer under 10 shillings (i.e. half a pound) per week. From this it becomes clear that Engels is paid a far from penurious salary and certainly sufficient to afford him a relatively comfortable existence.

In the fifties, as a most reluctant businessman, he is again longing for industrial stagnation and a deep crisis to set the scene for the coming revolution. He avidly follows the stock market figures, price changes and profit rates, not only in the cotton business, but in the whole of industry, not to see how much he is making, but in the hope that stocks are on the verge of collapse! The Great Exhibition at London's Crystal Palace in 1851 demonstrates, Britain is at the height of its industrial and military might and a severe crisis is not even on the horizon. However, Germany is catching up fast with Britain's industrial output. At the Exhibition, Krupp's company shows a block of cast steel weighing two tons, an achievement even Britain at this time can not equal. The exhibition, for the first time, also show-cases products and achievements from other countries, and in this connection Engels remarks, that it 'sounded the knell of English insular exclusiveness'. He remains highly optimistic that overproduction will eventually lead to a great crash; his own profits are of no interest to him. Cyclical crises do occur but the hoped for massive crisis leading to revolution never materialises in Engels' lifetime, so work in the office has to go on.

In 1854 he becomes a member of the Manchester stock exchange. And this so tickles Marx that he writes: 'So, you are now a member of the stock exchange and altogether respectable. My [con]gratulations. One day I'd love to hear you howling among all the wolves'. For Engels his situation is not a matter for joking. We can glean some idea of the desperate sense of imprisonment he feels in a reply he sends to his sister Marie, when she writes to him on his 32nd birthday and asks him what present he would wish for, he replies with uncharacteristic resignation: 'Ma chère soeur! For a long time now I have given up making wishes, as they are never fulfilled. Apart from that, I really have no talent for it, because when I find myself giving way to such weakness and make a wish, it is always something I can't have and that's why I'm better off if I get used to the idea once and for all of not making wishes.'

In 1856, among his other tasks in the company, he is also given responsibility for training the apprentices, and he complains to Marx about having to look after the three boys; this on top of his other work, means he is prevented from writing and editing. 'I just wish,' he writes jestingly, 'that Mr. Bonaparte would free France from himself and me from this hurly-burly'. The employment contract he was obliged to sign in 1852 means that if he neglects his work with the firm for even a few weeks, he has to work even harder in the succeeding ones. Unremittingly the company demands tribute.

Although Engels is almost never ill – he keeps himself incredibly fit with regular exercise and eats well – in the summer of 1857 he goes down with glandular fever. Not wanting to take it seriously, he still leaves his sick bed to go to the office. Marx becomes worried about him, and tells him not to be so stupid and to convalesce properly. But, in his usually flippant way, he replies to Marx that: 'The crisis [the economic, not bodily, downturn] will do me more physical good than any seaside cure; I can tell that already. In 1848 we said that our time had come, and it did in a certain sense, but this time it will come completely; now it's only a question of the head [i.e. getting the right ideas into people's heads]'. However, he does belatedly realise that something serious has hit him and in the second half of that year he goes first to Waterloo on the Lancashire coast, then to the Isle of Wight and on to Jersey in order to convalesce fully. Returning to Manchester physically restored, he is still depressed by having to return to the business, as well as by the international situation. However, the world economic crisis during the late autumn of 1857 again gives him cause for elation as he excitedly communicates to Marx:

> The general atmosphere last week here at the stock exchange was highly entertaining. The guys were livid about my sudden and unusually elated humour. Indeed the exchange is the only place where my present dullness has become transformed into a bouncing elasticity. At the same time, of course, I'm continually prophesying a black future and the donkeys become doubly angry.[79]

And again a month later:

> Today I heard that the Cookes, owners of a colossal factory on Oxford Road have sold their hunters, foxhounds, greyhounds etc., that they've sacked their servants, left the palace and put up a "To Let" sign. They're not yet kaputt, but no doubt they soon will be. Another fortnight and the ball will be in full swing. Among the philistines here the crisis has had a big effect on drinking habits. No one can bear being alone at home with the

> family and their worries; the clubs have come to life again and the consumption of alcohol has risen steeply. The deeper they sink, the more forcefully they attempt to cheer themselves up. Next morning they're then prime examples of a moral and physical hang-over.[80]

Despite Engels predictions, the crisis doesn't produce the revolutionary upsurge he and Marx hope for, and in only a few months the economy is getting back on its feet. Elsewhere the situation is no rosier. The Chartist Movement in which they have invested so much hope is also in serious decline in face of the economic upturn. The political situation in Germany is the subject of all Marx's and Engels' bitter criticism; the working class movement is virtually defunct and the Democratic Party, decried by the middle classes as 'red' has dissolved itself. The exile community is split into numerous fragments and most of its leaders are considered ideological enemies by the two. Even the few friends they have in Germany are reluctant to correspond with them for fear of retribution by the ever vigilant Prussian state. They are almost completely isolated and also subject to a spate of slanderous and vituperative attacks by erstwhile allies and comrades; they are invariably characterised as dogmatic fanatics who one should avoid at all costs. They appear to be surrounded by a world of animosity and misunderstanding. The only positive aspect of all this, is that it leaves them more time to devote to their own intellectual pursuits.

Engels is under no illusion about their predicament and is more than happy if they can discover a few individuals who share their vision and provide the illusion that they still have a party, albeit a miniscule one, behind them. Despite the seemingly impossible situation, both Marx and Engels, as we can see from their letters, remain inflexibly convinced that they alone possess the true historical insight and are able to see developments with more clarity than any of their contemporaries; they can do no other than fight on from behind the barricades.

In April 1858 Engels moves once more to a slightly more comfortable abode in Oxford Street, Chorlton and stays there, officially, for six years. However, his landlady gossips about him to the neighbours, and when cleaning mislays his letters and closes the books he is reading; she also steals into the bargain. But he puts up with all this and only decides to move again once he is made an associate in the firm and his salary improves. This will not take place until July 1864, and will also oblige him to undertake more representational responsibilities. He tries desperately to keep the hours spent on business drudgery to a minimum, so that he can devote as much time as possible to his political work and often keeps his father waiting for requested information about the company, because he is too busy doing just that. This ever constant obligation and threat hanging over him will only lift with the death of his father.

He would like to visit Germany again, but outstanding criminal charges in connection with his revolutionary activities preclude this for a decade. Then, surprisingly, in 1859, he is suddenly informed by the Prussian Justice Minister that all charges against him have been quashed largely due to interventions by his uncle, Karl Snethlage. The latter has, in the meantime, been appointed court chaplain and has the ear of King Wilhelm IV. He clearly still has a soft spot for his young nephew and appears to take the Christian principle of forgiving one's enemies to heart. The Prussian state also apparently now feels itself sufficiently stable and no longer in any danger from such subversives as Engels. This good news allows him to make plans to visit Barmen. However, the Prussian military cannot refrain from carrying out a small act of vindictiveness and, in July, they inform him that he is due to be called up for military duties. This pettiness again stymies his travel plans. Marx, who has studied law, advises him that if he refuses to return, the case can only be heard in a civil, not a military court, which means the consequences would be less onerous. This is a relief to Engels, but the civil court in Elberfeld still rules against him and imposes a large fine, and until it is paid, threatens to impound any of his assets held by the family. His father, despite his unbending loyalty to Prussia, refuses to pay a penny and denies holding any assets in the name of his son. Under these circumstances, it would not be prudent for him to travel to Germany to see his family. So, in the summer of that same year, Engels receives what will turn out to be a final visit from his father, accompanied this time by his mother. All three take a short holiday in Scotland. This will be the last time he sees his father, as he will be taken ill with typhus the following year, only to die on 20 March 1860.

While his father lies dying, his uncle again intervenes and writes a moving appeal to the Prussian Home Affairs Minister, requesting that Engels be allowed safe passage to visit his ailing father in Barmen. Other radicals, including a former editor on the *Neue*

Rheinische Zeitung, have been granted safe passages to visit ill relatives, so there appears to be a chance for Engels. However, when the travel permit does eventually come through, granting him 14 days 'arrest free' residence, it is too late - his father is already dead.

In the end the court authorities are only able to impose a modest fine of 50 Talers or, alternatively, three weeks in prison for ignoring his call-up papers. By paying the fine, Engels is able to draw a final line under the years of persecution by the Prussian government and is free to return to Germany.

For some time after his father's death his own future hangs in the balance because, according to English law at the time, a partner's assets in a company are not automatically inherited by his heirs. Everything depends on the acting partner, Gottfried Ermen, in terms of who he wants to become his new partner. Ermen would have liked to take over the firm completely, but it isn't so simple to buy out the heirs of his former partner. In May 1860 Engels' brother Emil comes to Manchester to negotiate with Ermen on behalf of the family. Although Engels' mother is recovering from typhus herself, it seems she is prepared to carry on running the firm with the help of her sons.

Towards the end of 1860 and into '61 the Engels family finds itself at loggerheads over their father's will; his siblings are not prepared to allow their elder brother too much leeway in terms of the firm or the capital, fearing, in many ways understandably, that he will not manage it in their interest. In the end a contract is drawn up which will make Herman, as the next in line of succession, the director of the company on behalf of their mother, who is nominally in charge. The business in Barmen is taken on by his brothers Rudolf and Hermann; Friedrich is to be excluded from a partnership in both the family-owned, German-based firms, and he will also be offered a poor deal as far as his father's other assets are concerned, but he is allowed to become his father's successor in the Manchester enterprise. Engels signs the agreement, but very reluctantly, as he writes to his mother:

> If it weren't for your sake, I would have found it very difficult to agree to this. It is very hard for me to exclude myself without, as it seems to me, adequate reason or justification, from the only business of father's that's left to us. I believe I had a right to it and my brothers did not have the right to expect me to

> give it up to their advantage, without so much as a murmur and without reason...Dear mother, for your sake, I have suppressed this and much else. Not for anything in the world do I want to be, in any way a cause of bitterness to sour the remaining years of your life through family arguments over the inheritance...[81]

Thus, the dutiful son submits to an agreement which robs him of his filial due. He does, though, now become the official partner in the Manchester firm on behalf of the family and is thus obligated to continue devoting much of his time to the company which will be the sole source for his future livelihood. He no doubt hoped that, with his father's inheritance, he could at last cease working for the company and live off the profits, based on his inherited shareholdings. To add insult to injury, as an official partner, he now also carries the responsibilities and the risk even though the company doesn't actually belong to him, but to the family. 'I could obtain another hundred businesses but never again a mother', he tells her sadly.

Despite not receiving his fair share of his father's inheritance, he is not left destitute by any means. He can write in 1860: 'The matter with Ermen seems to be pretty well in order. My family are leaving £10,000 in the business, something they have to do, if I'm to be a director [although this capital will have to be repaid to the family by Engels when he ceases to be a partner]. My material position will improve immediately, at least in terms of my percentage on the capital'. He is, though, unable to touch this capital even in a case of emergency, because the contract cleverly states that if even a penny of that £10,000 is withdrawn, the contract becomes invalid. We know that from 1852, for the first time, Engels has been receiving a small share of the profits: in the first four years this is 5 percent and in the following four years 7½ percent; only after a lengthier service for the company does he receive 10 percent.

The more comfortable and spacious abode he now leases lies directly opposite Manchester's Royal Infirmary. It is a villa-style house, with a large garden in a better class area, where other factory owners and businessmen live. From here he has only half an hour's walk to the office and a little longer to the stock exchange. He uses it very little though, still spending most of the time with Mary. Once he becomes an associate in the firm, he does have to live up to his new status, something he has, up to now, successfully resisted.

Convention demands that he attend receptions and accept invitations to lunch or dinner, otherwise he will draw attention to himself as an oddball. He tries to avoid reciprocating such invitations as far as possible and ducking 'this bourgeois life, which is here called the social treadmill, and only accessible to those with an excess of time on their hands; and those who want to work can't afford to be sucked into it. I refuse to do it even with the bourgeoisie in Manchester...if you need something from someone else then you go along and that's the end of it'.

During the five years between 1864 and 1869 Engels finds he is devoting an increasing amount of his time to the firm. He is now very much on his own and its continued success will depend very much on him. Fearful of being left without money, he bites into the sour apple. But every day he slaves in the office, he dreams of the day when he can give it all up and devote himself wholeheartedly to his first love, revolutionary politics. He expresses this graphically in a letter to Marx in 1867:

> In two years my contract with this pig Gottfried comes to an end and if I can arrange things here to my advantage, neither of us will have the least desire to prolong it; it could be that we go our own separate ways even earlier. In that case I'd have to leave commerce altogether, because to set up my own company would take 5-6 years of back-breaking slog with little to show for it and then another 5-6 years to earn the fruit of the first 5-6 years' work. If I did that, I'd be kaputt. I long for nothing more than release from this commercial slavery, which completely demoralises me with its time wasting. As long as I'm doing it, I'm not capable of doing anything else. Particularly since I've become a director, it means a lot work because of the greater burden of responsibility. If it weren't for the more lucrative income, I'd rather go back to clerking.[82]

Ermen would clearly like to get rid of Engels and take complete control of the company, but the partnership contract binds him, so he chooses to pick arguments and bickers with Engels in the hope that he will leave of his own accord. If Engels had decided to do this, all his sweat over the years would have been for nothing. He is determined to cling on until the contract expires and he can exit on his own terms and with a certain financial security. It will finally run out in 1869 and stipulates that on that date, Ermen has to pay Engels a one-off settlement of £1,750 for an undertaking not to set up in competition. From that date on, Engels will have the right to leave £5,000 capital in the company, for which he will receive 5% interest. He calculates that he could survive on the proceeds, together with his investments, if not in luxury, then modestly. He is overjoyed at the prospect of being a free man at last and with time to call his own. 1869 is indeed a year of celebration for him. The timing, he feels, is also ideal because, as he puts it: 'events are taking on an increasingly sharper form and the thunderstorm will break quite unexpectedly one of these fine days'. Engels realises, though, despite his earlier optimism, that he won't be able to survive without nibbling at his capital. In order to monitor and control his outgoings he keeps a household account book which he maintains scrupulously until his death. It is a valuable archive source in terms of how he spends his money and how much goes to Marx and other beneficiaries.

In 1869, out of his settlement from the company and the circa £10,000 he's been able to accumulate over the years from his salary and trading activities, he repays his mother the borrowed £10,000 capital that had been placed in the firm on his behalf. With Ermen's settlement he is left with around £10,000 and he puts this into shares immediately, mostly into the utilities, 'gas, waterworks and railways, all English companies', he tells his brother. The interest on the dividends brings him around £590 annually and he also has remaining investments in the Barmen branch of the firm which bring him in an extra £160.

On his first 'free' day, he writes to Marx: 'Dear Moor, Hurra! Today I'm finished with the doux commerce and am a free man...Tussy [Eleanor Marx who is staying with him in Manchester at the time] and I have celebrated my first free day with a long morning walk across the fields. On top of that, my eye [which has recently been causing him problems while reading] is a lot better and with care will soon be on top form again'. Once Engels has thrown off the shackles of business, on 8 December 1869, he again lets Marx know his innermost feeling: 'Yesterday Gottfried Ermen paid me the rest of my money and from now on we will both look at each other, so to speak, with our backsides'.

Although the firm Ermen & Engels is one of the more prestigious of the Lancashire cotton companies, having branches in a number of locations, and its speciality products of sewing and knitting thread and refined cottons are sold in many countries, there is little documentary evidence relating to Engels' two decades of association with it. The firm continues in existence after Engels' departure, but he keeps shares of around £2,400 in it, after withdrawing £7,500 of his family's original capital. Ermen then in 1874 establishes his own company, Ermen & Roby, which is eventually sold to the English Sewing Cotton Company in 1912.

In July 1869, he writes euphorically to his mother:

> My new freedom does me a world of good. Since yesterday I'm a man newly born and ten years younger. Instead of being stuck in the dingy town, I went this morning, in gorgeous weather, over the fields for a few hours and then sat at my desk in a comfortably furnished room, where I can have the windows open without the smoke leaving dirty marks everywhere, with flowers in the window and a few trees in front of the house. Work is now so different to what it used to be in my dingy room in the warehouse, with its outlook onto a pub courtyard. I live only ten minutes from the club [the Schiller Institute in Manchester], just far enough away from where the Germans live and from the ordinary rented quarters, to avoid being overrun. Evenings between 5 and 6 I eat at home, then go to the club to read the newspapers etc. I can do all this now I don't have to go into town anymore to check the accounts.[83]

He still suffers the psychological trauma inflicted by his two decades of working at the centre of a system he abhors, and feels the need to justify this: 'Will I ever feel I need to apologise for the fact that I was once a partner in a factory?' he asks rhetorically, 'He who wants to accuse me of that can come. And if I were certain to win a million in profit on the stock exchange tomorrow and could significantly help the party in Europe and America with the money, I'd go immediately to the stock exchange'.

During his time as a 'capitalist' he has not only supported his friend Marx materially, but also many other friends and organisations as well as the Burns family. For his many comrades in exile, simple material survival has always been the hardest task and Engels' generosity is often vital, as his comrade, Wilhelm Liebknecht informs us: he was widely known as the 'treasurer of the whole refugee tribe'. But it wasn't only material support; he also gave freely of his knowledge and advised comrades on tactics and strategy. The only thing he couldn't do during his twenty years with Ermen & Engels, was play a prominent and publicly political role and that irked him considerably. However, despite his detestation of 'sodding commer - ce' he has, during these past two decades, become a capable and respected businessman, with excellent knowledge of the market and of stocks and shares. He often carried out buying and selling for other English textile companies and also traded on the London stock exchange. This inside knowledge of how capitalism works was invaluable for Marx, too, as he is only familiar with the theory.

From now on, despite early 'retirement' and still only 49 years of age, he will be able to devote himself entirely to the movement and to his research and writing for the first time. To begin with he does so by undertaking a detailed study of the international press, to get up to speed on international developments.

The double life

Marx's son-in-law, Paul Lafargue gives us a palpable picture of Engels' daily life at this time:

> Six days a week, from 7 to 5 and, from 1857 onwards, 10 to 6, he was the businessman, dealing primarily with the firm's multi-lingual correspondence and attending the stock exchange. In the centre of town he had his official abode, where he received business acquaintances, but in his cottage on the outskirts of town he conferred with his political and scientific friends, among them the chemist, Carl Schorlemmer and Samuel Moore, the later translator of Marx's *Capital.* Here he would escape from the business slavery and in his cottage he became a free man again. During the day he didn't only take part in the business life of Manchester's industrialists, but also joined in their social life, he went to their meetings, their banquets and joined in their sports. As an excellent rider, he owned his own hunting horse, and took part in the fox hunting; he never missed a chance of joining the hunt, when the aristocracy and gentry of the area invited all riders together for the hunt in the old feudal manner. He was among the most passionate in the chase and took all the ditches, hedges and

> other obstacles. Marx commented that "I fear that one day he'll have an accident". I don't know if his bourgeois friends knew about his other life; the English are so terribly discreet and so little curious about everything that is of no concern of theirs. But in any case they knew absolutely nothing of the intellectual character of the man with whom they had daily intercourse, because Engels revealed little of his knowledge to them. He, who Marx rated as one of the most erudite men in Europe, was, for them, merely a jolly companion, who knew how to enjoy a good tipple...[84]

As a Christmas present in 1856 the 36 year-old had been given money by his father for the express purpose of buying a horse. He no doubt felt that the more his son became involved in English upper class leisure activities, the more he would be deterred from his subversive ones. Engels becomes a member of the Manchester Riding School, to which many of the young blades of the city belong. Together with other mill owners' sons and the local gentry, he takes part in fox hunts and hare coursing. What better way of venting all those frustrations and pent-up energy accumulated while bent over his desk in the dingy factory office, than charging across fields and jumping hedges on a splendid horse at weekends? The intense pleasure he gets out of this activity is expressed in a letter to Marx in 1857, after he's been out on Boxing Day with the Cheshire Hunt on Bucklow Hill:

> On Sunday I went fox hunting, seven hours in the saddle. This sort of thing gives me a devilish thrill that lasts several days. It is the most wonderful bodily pleasure that I know. In the whole field I only noticed two that rode better than me, but they had better horses. It brings my health up to scratch. At least 20 fellows fell off their horses, two horses were ruined, one fox killed – I was at the death – otherwise no other mishap. By the way, the real fox hunters were not with us, they, of course, ride much better than me.[85]

And, a year later, he again writes to Marx:

> Yesterday I allowed myself to be seduced and went to a hare coursing meeting to ride. Hares are chased by greyhounds and

> I was seven hours in the saddle. In general, it did me a world of good and kept me from working...So you don't get the wrong impression about the state of my body, I will tell you that yesterday on my nag I jumped an earthen wall and hedges, one that was about five feet – the highest jump I've ever done. Such efforts can only be undertaken if you have pretty strong limbs.[86]

Engels also, somewhat naively, attempts to justify his enjoyment of this 'aristocratic' pastime by giving it a spurious revolutionary justification: 'We need to be able to outride the Prussian cavalry when we return to Germany. We need to make it difficult for those gentlemen'. But neither this argument, nor his remarks about his health reassure Marx, who fears his tearaway activities will one day lead to a possible fatal injury. He writes to him several times, advising caution. In a suitable ironic riposte to his remarks above Marx writes (in 1858):

> I congratulate you upon your equestrial performances, but don't do too many neck-breaking jumps, as there will be more important opportunities for you to risk your neck. You seem to ride this hobby-horse somewhat hard. In any case, I don't believe that the cavalry is the specialist area of competence for which Germany most urgently needs you.[87]

In actual fact Engels does sustain a minor hernia, which will cause him pain and problems right up to the time of his death, but even that doesn't stop him pursuing his madcap hobby. He continues riding regularly until he is 65, but no longer takes part in the more strenuous fox hunts or hare coursing.

While Engels has to be scrupulous about separating his business and political activities, there is one fellow businessman with whom he can openly converse both about commerce and politics. That man is Samuel Moore. He was, during the sixties, like Engels, a cotton spinning manufacturer, but is made bankrupt in 1878. He is, though, also an intellectual with an excellent mind. He has a degree in law and mathematics and later, from 1889, earns his living as a chief judge in Asaba, in the crown colony of Nigeria, but his main passion remains economics. He is also a convinced socialist with an excellent command of German and therefore the ideal translator of Marx's *Capital* into English. Engels values him highly and calls him an 'exemplary Englishman, who incorporates all the good qualities of his nation, without any of the bad ones'. Engels will later make him one of the executors of his will, and it is Moore who will give the eulogy at his memorial service. They are to remain close friends, even during Moore's years in Africa.

He often welcomes Moore to his main abode during his two decades in Manchester, that of the Burns sisters, Mary and Lydia. Only there, in the seclusion of their cottage, can he really relax, unwind, but also carry out his party work undisturbed. The Burns sisters live in Hyde Road, Gorton, just outside Manchester proper, in a small house that lies close to fields and where he can recuperate from the 'business treadmill'. Often he stays there for weeks at a time, hardly returning to his official abode in the city. This happens particularly in the early years when money is tight, and in the colder months, when he is keen to save money on heating and general household outgoings. 'I am stone-broke and am trying to cut costs, like the Prussian government', he writes to Marx, 'I'm living most of the time with Mary to save money; sadly I can't do without my official lodgings otherwise I'd move to her's completely'.

Although in the other letters (those not later destroyed by himself) to Marx and friends, Engels puzzlingly, makes no mention of Mary. He is, nevertheless, clearly devoted to her – there is no evidence or even hearsay of any dalliance with other women in Manchester. Apart from the obvious physical attraction, he is clearly drawn to her working class values, her directness and sense of humour. During this whole period in the city, she is his companion and the person to whom he turns when he seeks relaxation and escape from the daily grind and one-dimensional company of his business associates. Of course, he will not be able to go with Mary to his clubs, to formal social gatherings or when he dines with fellow business partners; social and class codes in middle class Victorian England are particularly stringent. If he were to marry Mary, it would have been viewed by his family and peers as a terrible faux pas, and would also have meant dragging Mary into his business life, involved her in entertaining and doing the social rounds. As it is, and as a bachelor, he is largely excused such duties and is able to have a life, with Mary, outside that world.

Mary and her sister Lydia, from the little we can glean from

Engels' letters, are very involved in the Irish community and support the Fenian struggle for an independent Ireland, but there appears to be little hard evidence of how active they are. We don't even know what the two sisters do for a living, how they survive, unless solely on Engels' money. Mary arrived in Manchester as a young girl with her family from Tipperary in southern Ireland. She is virtually illiterate – she can read and write very little – so no letters of hers exist. She has now been his partner, with interruptions, for 20 years and their life may be a secretive one, but it appears to suit them both. However, in 1863, this romantic idyll is to be rudely shattered. On 8 January Engels is working alone in his city apartment, when he receives the worst news he's ever had – his beloved partner has died, aged only forty, suddenly and unexpectedly in her sleep the previous night; of 'natural causes', as it states on the death certificate. She's never been seriously ill, so her death is even more inexplicable and traumatic for him. She probably suffered a heart attack or stroke. Lydia brings him the dire news the following day. It is a devastating blow.

As he writes to Marx, 'you can't live so many years with a woman and not be profoundly shocked by her death,' and again on 26 January, after the funeral: 'I felt as if the last years of my youth were buried with her'. Marx's subsequent insensitive and abrupt response to Engels' loss almost causes a serious rift in their friendship. He remains silent for almost a week, and to avoid giving all his anger and sense of deep hurt free reign, he first writes a draft letter to Marx. In the version he sends he says: 'You'll be able to accept that this time my own misfortune and your frosty reaction to it made it absolutely impossible for me to respond to you earlier. All my friends, including our philistine acquaintances, have shown me on this occasion, which has affected me very deeply, more compassion and friendship than I could have expected. You found the occasion appropriate to communicate to me the superiority of your cool way of thinking. Savour your triumph, it won't be challenged'.

After Mary's death, Engels is unable to find his usual solace in the cottage any more and soon afterwards rents a different place, not far away, in Ardwick Green, to where Mary's sister, Lydia can move. Although the new cottage is conveniently situated, it is smaller than the Hyde Road one. The loss of Mary sends him into a minor depression, made worse by Marx's apparent lack of sympathy and he finds it difficult even to write. He desperately seeks diversion by immersing himself in a study of the Slav languages, but his loneliness

TOP: The town of Barmen in the mid-19th century
ABOVE: A pencil drawing of Engels aged 19 years
LEFT: Engels' parents

Der noble, moderne Materialismus

Zeitgeist

LEFT: Engels' sketches included in a letter to Franz Graeber, 15 June 1839. Titled: The noble, modern materialism and Zeitgeist (Spirit of the times)

RIGHT: A letter to his sister Marie in which he comments on hearing Beethoven's 5th Symphony

BELOW: His sister, Marie

LEFT: Engels' sketch of himself smoking, in a letter from Bremen to his sister Marie 9 Dec. 1840,

INSERT: Engels' Sketch of Franz Liszt in a letter to his sister, after hearing him play April 1842

TOP FAR RIGHT: Sketch of himself wearing the king's uniform in Berlin

RIGHT: A caricature by Engels of a group of Young Hegelians, 'The Free Ones' in Berlin. It ridicules their empty rhetoric and lack of deeds

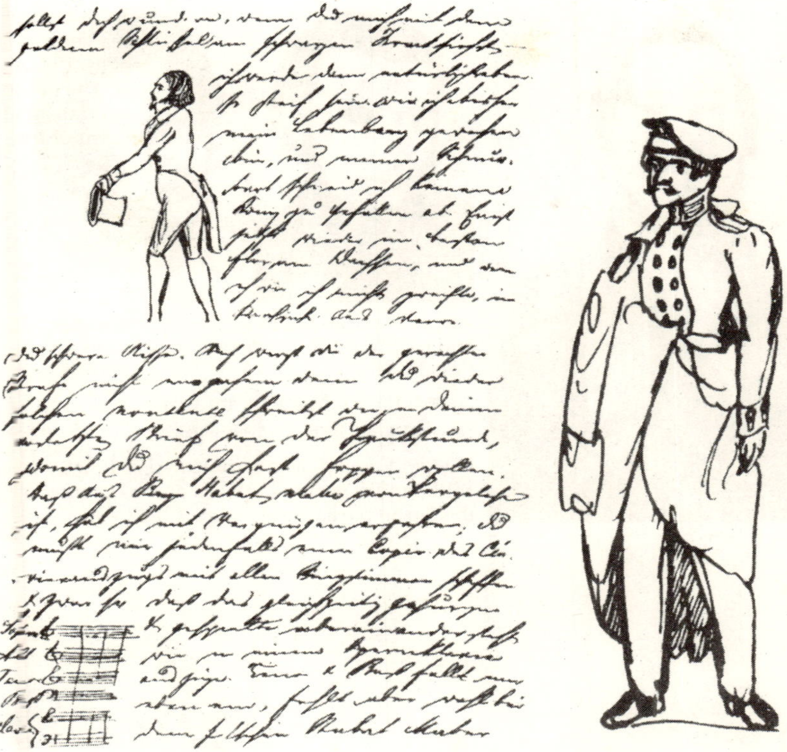

ABOVE: George Julian Harney, the Chartist and editor of the *Northern Star*, a friend of Engels

ABOVE RIGHT: Marx, as student

LEFT: Engels in the mid-forties

BELOW: Engels' cartoon of King Frederick Wilhelm IV, giving a speech at the opening of the Berlin parliament in April 1847

TOP: Suppression of the Dresden uprising in May 1849

ABOVE: Marx, Engels and Wolff examinig a copy of the Neue Rheinische Zeitung, fresh off the press. Print workers are wearing French revolutionary 'bonnets rouges'

ABOVE: Karl Marx and Engels with the former's daughters (1. to r.), Laura, Eleanor and Jenny

TOP LEFT: On the barricades in Elberfeld

LEFT: Engels' cartoon of Prussian bourgeoisie, pleading with King Friedrich Wilhelm IV, January 1849

TOP LEFT: Marx's housekeeper, Helene Demuth. Photo taken in the 1850s
TOP RIGHT: Samuel Moore, friend of Marx and Engels, and translator of *Capital*
BELOW: Engels' IWA membership card

INTERNATIONAL
Working Men's Association
Intern'le Arbeiter Assoc'n · Association Intern'le des Ouvriers · Associne Intern'le Operai
CARD OF MEMBERSHIP.

This is to Certify that Frederick Engels was admitted a Member of the above Association 18
and paid as his Annual Subscription

R. Shaw Corresponding Secretary for America.

Bernard	Cor. Sec for Belgium	Jules Johannard	Italy.
Eugene Dupont	France	Anthony Zabicki	Poland.
Karl Marx	Germany	H. Jung	Switzerland.
[illegible]	Treasurer.	J. George Eccarius	Secr Gen Council

TOP: Lydia (Lizzie) Burns in the 1870s

ABOVE: Engels sketch of Lizzie

LEFT: Engels in Barmen 1861

TOP LEFT TO RIGHT: Louise Kautsky, Engels in Manchester 1860s, Engels in London 1891, Eleanor Marx

ABOVE: Engels shortly before he dies

LEFT: Engels with August Bebel, Klara Zetkin and others during the International Socialist Workers' congress in Zurich 1893

ABOVE: Engels in London 1888 and INSERT: press pass issued to Engels for the 'Legal 8 Hours' demonstration in Hyde Park 1891

is still unbearable: 'I had to force myself to switch off. It helped; now I'm my old self again', he assures Marx, on resuming the correspondence sometime afterwards.

Several months later, the exact date is not known, Lydia replaces Mary as Engels' partner and the new situation appears to suit both of them. Once he and Lydia have become lovers, and he begins spending more and more time with her, they move once more to a larger abode, but again only a short distance further out of town. It is a two-up and two-down small terraced house in Mornington Street, Ardwick. In this house, not only Engels and Lydia Burns spend a number of happy years, but Marx comes on a number of occasions to stay and sometimes Marx's daughter Eleanor visits by herself. In fact Eleanor, Marx later reports, almost causes a spat in the family by singing the praises of her 'Manchester home' and repeatedly saying she wishes to return as soon as possible'.

Lydia is affectionately called 'Lizzie' by friends and family. Like her sister Mary, she is Irish to the core and a real firebrand. What she means to Engels is clear from a letter he writes to Bebel's wife, after Lizzie's death in 1878: 'She was of genuine Irish proletarian stock and her passionate, innate feeling for her class was of far greater importance to me and stood me in better stead at all critical moments to a greater extent than all the pseudo-intellectual and clever-clever "finely educated" and "delicate" bourgeois daughters could have done'.

She is also a member of the Fenian Society, the British section of the Irish Republican Brotherhood, founded in 1857. It is the most radical Irish nationalist organisation at this time. The Fenians are particularly active in the 1850s and, as nationalists, are battling British colonial power in Ireland.

The Fenian uprising in Ireland in 1867 is a badly organised affair and is soon suppressed, but some of its leaders hope to raise support in England, particularly in Lancashire where many Irish live and work. In Manchester, which has a large Irish community, the Fenians find ready supporters. Already in 1851, Irish immigrants comprise around 15 percent of the city's poor. Half of the people registered in Manchester's New Bridge Street Workhouse in the latter part of the century are Irish Catholics.

Two members of the Fenian, Irish Republican Brotherhood organisation and also veterans of the US civil war – Colonel Kelly and Captain Deasy – are captured in Manchester by the police, and are held in prison awaiting trial. Fenians based in Manchester resolve to rescue them and there is little doubt that Lydia Burns is involved in the plot. They attempt the rescue by stopping the prison van on the Hyde Road between Manchester and Salford, breaking it open, but inadvertently shooting a policeman in the process. They carry off their comrades under the eyes of the English authorities. Several of the conspirators are arrested shortly afterwards and three are later hanged – the so-called Manchester Martyrs: Allen, Larkin and O'Brien. Engels' friend, the Chartist and barrister, Ernest Jones conducted a spirited defence of the accused Fenians in court, but to no avail. Lizzie has been involved closely with the Fenians in Manchester for some time, but Engels is not always aware of exactly what she does, and prefers not to question her too closely, despite his undoubted sympathy for Ireland's national aspirations, if not for the Fenians as such. She may even have sheltered one or two of those involved in the ambush of the prison van, as her house is only half a mile away from the railway arch where it takes place.

Engels is an unequivocal supporter of Irish liberation, but his unflattering opinion of the Fenians is expressed succinctly in a letter to Marx[88]. He writes disparagingly: 'We shouldn't forget, despite the dirty tricks of the English, that the leaders of this sect are mostly donkeys and some are also exploiters, and we shouldn't feel in any way responsible for the idiocies committed, as they will be, in any conspiracy…I don't need to tell you that black and green [the then Irish nationalist colours] rule in my home too…'[referring to Lydia's Fenian sympathies].

The Burns sisters clearly spark Engels' imagination and a keen interest in Irish affairs and for some time they planned to take him on a visit to the 'Emerald Isle' and show him the place where their family came from. Although he does manage a short visit with Mary in 1856, he is keen to return and study the Irish situation more closely. Both Engels and Marx show a keen interest in Irish affairs, seeing its relationship with Britain as a classic case of colonial oppression. They write a number of articles, essays and letters on Ireland, examining its history, its economy and the nature of British colonial exploitation.

In August 1869 he meets his mother in Ostende and returns with her to the family home in Engelskirchen. Then, shortly afterwards, in September, a year before he finally quits the firm, Lizzie manages to organise the trip to Ireland, and they take Eleanor Marx along with them. They spend three weeks there, taking in Dublin, the Wicklow Hills, Killarney and Cork. It is now thirteen years since Engels was there with Mary, and he is amazed at the development that has taken place since that visit, but the massive depopulation of the countryside is still terribly apparent to them. The extreme poverty they witness in England's first colony is indescribable. Everywhere they see armed police and soldiers as if the country were in a state of permanent siege. Engels makes copious notes during the visit on all aspects of the country. He has plans to write a social history of Ireland, but he never finds the time to complete the project. He had planned it in four parts, the first titled 'Natural Conditions', the second, 'Ancient Ireland'; the third on the English conquest and the fourth on English domination. 'England's invasion of Ireland,' he says, 'cheated Ireland out of her whole development and threw her back hundreds of years'. Their visit there also coincides with a renewed upsurge of national liberation activity. The immediate cause is the demand for amnesty for the Fenians held in British jails. 30,000 people turn out in Limerick and 200,000 in Dublin demanding their release.

Both women return 'more Hibernian than they were beforehand', Engels reports. But it makes a deep impression on him too and helps him better understand Lizzie's deep religiosity and melancholia, her hatred of the English, her penchant for poetry and the romantic, even if he is not able to share much of it. It does, though, stimulate a new interest in British colonial history, Celtic culture and even folk song.

As hostess at Engels' gatherings of friends, Lydia Burns is always an effervescent personality, humorous as well as passionate. This fiery passion also registers clearly with Engels' friends. Referring to a large glass punch bowl he has given Engels as a gift, Paul Lafargue tells him sometime later: 'Let Mrs. Burns take a soaking in "the bath" I brought you from Bordeaux, so that she may extinguish the fire that glows inside her'.

Neither Mary nor Lizzie will be accepted by Engels' Rhine family as a de facto daughter-in-law. His aristocratic brother-in-law, Adolf von Griesheim is particularly aggrieved, and protests regularly in the name of the family about these unsanctified relationships. Engels has, though, as we know, very strong principles and feels no compulsion to marry either Mary or Lizzie because for him marriage is a bourgeois institution. A personal relationship, he feels strongly, is between two individuals and doesn't need sanction by the state, a religious institution or indeed the extended family. 'What a waste bourgeois marriage is,' he writes, 'first to get to that stage, then as long as the nonsense drags on, and then until you shake it off'.

In the meantime, he does have to keep up a certain pretence to allay suspicions and avoid embarrassment for Lizzie. When he travels with her to Bridlington for a short seaside holiday, he registers them at the hotel as Mr. and Mrs. Burns. Although, interestingly, his friend George Harney, in his letters, always sends greetings to 'Mrs. Engels'. There is some circumstantial evidence from Manchester rate book records that Engels rented the Burns sisters' residence under the name of Frederick Boardman, travelling salesman. This would explain the cryptic PS on a letter from Marx, dated 27 May 1862, in which he adds: 'My regards to Mrs Bortman and sister'. Marx's English spelling was never of the best! The fact that a well-dressed middle class gentleman is a regular visitor to a single woman in a working class neighbourhood would certainly have aroused intense curiosity. As a nominal 'travelling salesman' who lodges there this interest would be allayed. We know Engels is adept at using pseudonyms and covering his tracks, so the Frederick Boardman theory gains credence.

Engels' new-found happiness with Lizzie is very soon clouded by the sudden and unexpected onset of ill health. This fiery Fenian girl, becomes chronically ill during the sixties and, despite all Engels' efforts, she fails to make a recovery, but although her health continues to deteriorate, the two still live happily together. It is somewhat surprising that Engels, who clearly loves children as is shown by his affection for the Marx children, never has children with either Mary or Lydia. That this is a deliberate decision is unlikely given the limited knowledge, and available means of, contraception; we can only assume that either he or both women are, for some reason, infertile.

Although Engels' double life continues still into the seventies, there are increasing signs of an overlap between the two. It is in the Mornington Street house where he and Lizzie welcome his personal friends, and where Marx stays, but Lizzie seems to begin playing the role of wife also in his 'representational' house in Dover Street, at least from time to time. This is, for the stuffy Victorian citizens of Manchester, certainly provocative behaviour, but the two appear to carry it off.

In April 1869 he moves out of his 'official' residence in Dover Street and he and Lizzie move together into the Mornington Street house in Ardwick. Now that his contract with the firm is drawing to a close and the need to maintain appearances is no longer necessary, he can at last be more true to himself and publicly acknowledge his relationship with her. She is also 'over the moon' about the move. He still, though, has to maintain his bourgeois exterior for business friends and, since 1864, he has also become a 'real' capitalist, owning shares in the business.

The move is indeed a risky and courageous one for him, because if he were to be ostracised from the business world it would spell not only his own personal financial ruin but would also have severe repercussions for Marx and the whole movement. Over his two decades as businessman he is determined to give his enemies no chance at all to brand him publicly as 'a philanderer or, what would be worse, a communist'. With his two houses, he will have stirred little suspicion, as most bourgeois men have mistresses, and it will have been assumed that that is all Engels is up to. The difference is that Mary, and later Lizzie, are not mistresses – he is not a married man - and they are, successively, his genuine partners with whom he is in love.

Engels' intimate friends realise that this double life is not a matter for 'a nudge and a wink' but a serious and uncomfortable situation for him, and they treat Mary and, later, Lizzie with the respect accorded a wife. Certainly, from the Marxes there is never a disparaging remark or any underhand gossip in this connection, not even from the strictly moralistic Jenny, and they always refer to both Mary and, later, Lizzie as Mrs. Burns, not Miss Burns. In this way they all help create an atmosphere in which Engels and his common-law partner are able to behave as man and wife in a relaxed context.

The German Mancunians

Although Engels feels cut off from Marx and the heart of the movement in London, Manchester is hardly a backwater. Here there is a thriving German 'colony', and within it he has some close friends and political comrades.

By 1870, there are around 1000 Germans living in Manchester and none who would not have known Engels. They are a mixed bunch of entrepreneurs, professionals and tradesmen, plus a few political refugees. Some are already second or third generation residents. Engels is an active participant within the German community. He becomes a member of their clubs and sits on their committees. He does this not only out of a need for leisure, but he wants to influence their affairs in a democratic and progressive direction. That's why he is prepared to take on official responsibilities. He also attempts to enlighten the members and seek political allies among them and win them as allies in the creation of a future democratic Germany. He and Marx have always argued that the working class movement can work together with individual representatives of the bourgeoisie if the latter feel the 'need to emancipate themselves' and are not opposed to the working class emancipating itself. These Manchester ex-patriates, even if not revolutionary, are largely reform-minded and free-thinking individuals, characterised by the fact that they don't see their lives entirely through the monocle of business, but love books, art and, particularly, music. This legacy is palpable in Manchester still today.

As soon as he arrived in 1850, Engels joined the most prestigious club in the city, not simply to conform to bourgeois expectations, but out of an inner need for diversion and amusement, 'as far as that was possible in this coal smog'. He became a member of the Albert Club (named after Queen Victoria's consort, Prince Albert, himself a German prince). The consort's avid interest in the industrial development of his adoptive country, and his support for poor schools and better housing for workers are also reasons for their choosing his name for the club. This somewhat enlightened approach is also reflected in the fact that Ermen & Engels and Steinthal & Co, another German-owned firm, soon institute better working conditions in their factories and cheaper company housing for their workers; they employ no children and support the setting up of schools.

As an energetic and likeable young man, Engels is very soon elected onto the club committee. He must have done a good job in that position because he is not only continuously re-elected, but often with the highest number of votes. He clearly holds the members' trust and respect, and he, too, enjoys the club and the company of its members. Even after he moves to London, later, he still maintains contact, sending his contributions for their meetings and publications. He undoubtedly also helps stress the social and philanthropic role of the Albert Club during his time of membership. This concern is also evidenced by his membership of the Society for the Relief of Really Deserving Distressed Foreigners in Manchester, which no doubt also gives him the opportunity of channelling funds to radical exile friends who are in need of help.

In the 25th anniversary report of the Albert Club in 1866 it states that it has 96 members, half of them German and many of them personal friends of Engels, including Sam Moore, Edward Gumpert and Ernst Delius, wool merchant and father of Frederick Delius, the composer, and a benefactor of the Manchester Hallé Orchestra. Engels' membership of other middle class institutes is largely connected with his or Marx's political research. He joins the Manchester Subscription and Chetham Libraries so that he has ready access to books and newspapers. He is also a member of the prestigious Athenaeum, an intellectual and literary club opened in 1839, which he values for its peace and quiet and its excellent library, even though the latter is in total chaos before he manages to have it properly filed and catalogued. As a committee member of the Subscription Library, which has more modern volumes than the Athenaeum, he also recommends the purchasing of books he requires for his own research. Marx also uses the library here and describes it as 'virtually the only stall for the muses in Manchester'.

While membership of these clubs is useful in its own right, it is also invaluable as a respectable cover for Engels' activities as a political activist. The other supremely effective fig leaf, but more surprising perhaps, are his fox hunting pursuits, mentioned earlier. Since his youth he has been an avid horseman and loves nothing better than a strenuous gallop in the countryside. In order to ride to hounds, you need money and status; but as for the latter, his position as a businessman is acceptable.

During the 1860s, his club activities are largely dominated by his work in the Schiller Anstalt. It was founded in 1859, as a centennial commemoration of Schiller's birth, and becomes the intellectual and cultural focus for the German colony in Manchester, having over 300 members by 1866. Engels is a member from the beginning, but takes no active part, although he does have an 'underhand influence' he asserts. Although playing no leading role in the society, he does make efforts to combat the tendency to narrow-mindedness and middle class snobbery among the members. On one occasion, after he has been upbraided by the librarian in a pompous and bureaucratic manner for not returning a borrowed book on time, he writes a lengthy and stinging letter in reply which provides us with exemplary evidence of his sarcastic wit. It is also a devastating condemnation of small-minded bureaucracy in general:

> This tone is so far removed from that in which correspondence between educated individuals is normally conducted that I must admit I am not accustomed to receiving such letters. Indeed, as I read this tract, I felt myself transported back to the homeland and instead of holding in my hand a communication from the librarian of the Schiller Institute, I had in front of me a summons from some German police commissar, threatening a heavy penalty if the book is not returned "within 24 hours or else"...In the Schiller Institute's founding statutes it is written "that the Institute should also serve to help young Germans feel immediately at home...better looked after and protected as well as provided with moral and intellectual support, above all, to enable them to return to the fatherland unalienated". No doubt, the bureaucratic form of such an office missive is the perfect vehicle to make them feel immediately on home territory and that they are even better "welcomed and protected" here than at home in our loving patriotic police state...[89]

Engels sees himself, between the ages of 30 and 50, as a 'communist Bohemian', with no umbilical attachment 'to the middle class world and its social treadmill', but he clearly doesn't view membership of these clubs as being part of that world. On being pressed by his friend Dr. Gumpert, he does eventually become a member of the Schiller Institute's committee and, somewhat later still, even its president, devoting a great deal of time to its activities. He is largely responsible for rescuing it from becoming a stuffy, antiquated gentlemen's retreat. He ensures that its organisational structure is democratic, and that it is shielded from the debilitating virus of émigré bickering and from devolving into an exclusive upper class leisure club.

The Schiller Institute incorporates a gymnastic and choral group, and Engels participates in both. He eventually resigns his presidency of the society in 1868 after the committee invites Karl Vogt, a renowned zoologist and geologist, to address them. Vogt, it was alleged, had been a Bonapartist agent provocateur, who also wrote a pamphlet attacking Marx which the latter deemed libellous, responding with his own booklet: *Herr Vogt* (1860). Engels felt he would be betraying Marx and his other political comrades if he didn't protest at the invitation.

During his time in Manchester Engels has a number of close friends, in both the German and English communities. Perhaps the closest of them all, though, is Wilhelm Wolff or 'Lupus' as he is known to his comrades. Friedrich Wilhelm Wolff (1809-1864) was, alongside Marx and Engels, an editor on the *Neue Rheinische Zeitung* and already a firm communist in 1848. He was a delegate to the Frankfurt National Assembly, and remained one of the most resolute representatives of the 1848 revolution in Germany, and was also a co-founder of the Communist League. The son of Silesian peasants, he was imprisoned for four years being a member of a radical Breslau (today Wroclaw) students' group. His newspaper articles, exposing prison conditions and the feudal backwardness in Prussian Silesia attracted wide interest. The German playwright, Gerhard Hauptmann, later drew on these as a source for his drama *The Weavers*. In 1846 Wolff escaped renewed police persecution by travelling to Brussels to join the circle around Marx and Engels. In Manchester he ekes out a living as a private tutor.

He is intimately involved in Marx's and Engels' political lives since their common exile in Brussels. He is the one with whom Engels discusses all party matters and goes to for advice or information on political issues; they meet almost daily. He remains a loyal and intimate friend of both men until his death. Wolff and Engels in Manchester and Marx in London formed the triumvirate of the 'proletarian avant garde'. When Wolff dies in 1864, it is another big blow to Engels. 'We lost the truest friend of the German revolution and a man of irreplaceable value,' Engels states.

The communist Carl Schorlemmer, whom he gets to know intimately shortly after Mary's death, becomes another very close friend. The two also take several holidays together. Schorlemmer is also a German refugee and is a renowned chemist. He becomes an assistant to Professor Roscoe at Manchester University and later, in 1874, Professor of organic chemistry there. He is a member of the Philosophical Society (from 1870), of the Royal Society (1871) and the American Philosophical Society (1878). He gives both Engels and Marx advice on scientific subjects and is of particular help to Engels when the latter is writing his *Dialectics of Nature*. Schorlemmer's area of expertise is the classification of hydrocarbons and he is seen as one of the pioneers of the science of petro-chemicals.

Apart from holding serious conversations on science, the two men also partake of a convivial social life. The photos bequeathed us of a rather earnest-looking Engels belie his sense of humour and ability to enjoy social life to the full. He is fond of his tipple as much as anyone, and on one occasion, recalled by Eleanor Marx, Schorlemmer is visiting and they both rather overdo the drinking, and Schorlemmer is incapable of going home, so the women make up a bed for him in Engels' house. Eleanor also recalls Engels himself returning home on another occasion 'drunk as jelly'. With a few glasses of good claret inside him, Engels is also wont to burst spontaneously into song, and alongside his beloved German folk songs, he often gives voice to some English or Irish ones too. One traditional English song he particularly loves is *The Vicar of Bray*, that mock-heroic ballad about a political opportunist cleric. He even translates it into German verse for the *Vörwarts Social Democratic Song-Book*.

Dr. Eduard (later anglicised to Edward) Gumpert is Engels' GP and another close friend. He also makes distant diagnoses for the Marx family and sends prescriptions as well. He was born in Hesse, Germany, in 1834. Shortly after qualifying there, he is forced to flee after the suppression of the revolution and settles in Manchester as a general practitioner. He is attached to the Clinical Hospital for Diseases of Women and Children as an honorary consulting physician, a position he holds until his death. He, Marx and Engels also undertake several holiday trips together, and when, during these decades, Marx and family visit Manchester, they invariably stay with Gumpert. He dies in Manchester on 20 April 1893 and Engels travels up from London to attend his funeral.

This settled German community in Manchester will be severely disrupted during the early twentieth century by rising anti-German sentiment prior to the outbreak of the First World War, although by then a number, like Frederic Delius's family, had become fully integrated and anglicised.

Politics – the twilight job

Already before Engels' departure from London to Manchester in 1850, increasingly bitter ideological differences within the socialist movement were making themselves felt and there was much interpersonal slanging. As a light-hearted, if mischievous, therapeutic response to this, Marx and Engels had begun making satirical sketches of some of the leading protagonists, or 'marinating the stockfish' as Marx colourfully termed it.

A Hungarian émigré, colonel Bangya, who is introduced to Marx as a bona fide revolutionary, and who has heard about their project, suggests turning the sketches into a brochure – a sort of pioneering *Private Eye* – for which he would pay them and arrange to have printed. Short of money as always Marx is attracted by the idea of earning a few extra pounds without too much effort. He persuades Engels to help, and it is agreed that Marx, together with their friend and comrade, Ernst Dronke, will produce a first draft in London which Marx will then take to Manchester for fine tuning with Engels. Engels couldn't help to begin with because his father had just arrived in Manchester on one of his periodic visits of 'inspection'. When Marx eventually comes to Manchester with 'the draft' of the satirical sketches, to Engels' dismay work on it has hardly begun. In the extant draft of the concept, only eight pages are in Dronke's hand, but of the resultant 71, 68 are in Engels' hand and only three in Marx's! Thus, as with the *German Ideology*, it is impossible to determine exactly who wrote what. The fact that Marx's handwriting is virtually illegible, whereas Engels' is very neat, may have influenced who actually wrote their ideas down. The final document contains pen portraits of many of the leading German exiles, with whom they are in conflict, written with their usual barbed wit.

Bangya disappears with the manuscript, but no brochure materialises. It is Engels who first has suspicions and writes to Marx: 'I hope our collaborative work doesn't fall into the wrong hands. We wrote for the public, not for the private entertainment of Berlin's, or of any other, police force'. Engels proceeds to make enquiries in Germany and discovers that the printer the Hungarian had mentioned doesn't even exist. Bangya actually pays them for their work, but is subsequently unmasked as a Prussian secret agent. So, although he promised to have the brochure published in Germany, it ends up as just one more incriminating document on Marx and Engels in police files.

Already on his second visit to Manchester in 1842, Engels had established contact with the Chartists and continues to work closely with them. He immediately recognised them as one of the most significant working class movements to emerge since Britain's industrialisation. The two leaders he is most intimate with are

George Harney and Ernest Jones. Once he gets to know Jones, he hopes to win him over to his views. Jones was actually born in Berlin in 1819, one year before Engels, and only comes to England in 1838. Possibly because of his German education, with its greater emphasis on philosophy and theory, he finds it easier than most of the other British leaders to take on board much of Marx's and Engels' thinking. Jones soon becomes a supporter of the class struggle theory although most of the other Chartist leaders have agreed a peace with the employers. He is well loved and respected among rank and file Chartists. A barrister by profession, born to wealth and high standing, he throws it all aside to devote himself to the cause of the Charter. During the fifties, Jones is the only Chartist leader of any note, and of all its leaders it is he who has the clearest notion of what Marx and Engels see as the essentially international character of the working class struggle.

In January 1851, Engels tells Marx he will organise a regular meeting for working men through the auspices of Harney and Jones, to discuss the *Communist Manifesto* with them. He sees it as one of his main tasks to convince the English working class leaders of the theory of class struggle. A month later, he relates that he has set up a local Chartist group. 'These English are, within the democratic forms, far more unscrupulous than we timid Germans. There were thirteen of us and we were all elected on to the committee...' he tells Marx humorously.

Jones continues his political agitation in an attempt to awaken a new class struggle long after the massive Chartist movement has lost its impetus. He then goes on to devote his time to the renewed Reform movement which leads to the passing of the Reform Act of 1867.

Up to this time he, like Engels, doesn't believe that better conditions and income will be enough to buy off the workers and persuade them to abandon a more revolutionary struggle. However, the general economic upturn after the repeal of the Corn Laws in 1846 has led to a gradual amelioration of working conditions; militant fervour begins to ebb and the majority of workers believe it is Liberalism that has given them a better life. This sticks in the throat of Jones and Engels.

At a Chartist conference in Manchester in 1852, Jones actually argues for the creation of a working class party, but this makes little headway. On his death in Manchester in 1869, Engels tells Marx:

'he was the only educated Englishman among the politicians who was, at bottom, entirely on our side!' Jones and Harney are the first English Marxists, even though Jones later falls out with Marx after he is persuaded that reform can only come about through some form of collaboration between the working and middle classes, contradicting his earlier confidence in the working class managing it alone.

Engels complains regularly in his letters to Marx that he is plagued by visitors, many of them political exiles who have time on their hands and rob him of his valuable minutes. Then there is the daily grind at the office, his club activities and leisure pursuits, but amazingly he still finds time for research and writing. He contributes regularly to a succession of publications that Harney publishes, although he is rarely paid for these. From 1852-54 he prepares a treatise on the Hungarian revolutionary uprising of 1849. From the end of '54, he works on a brochure dealing with German and Slav history in which he attempts to demolish the 'Tsar-friendly theories of conservative German historians'. From '63, he is working with Marx on research into German-Polish relations and from '67 he begins collecting material for a light-hearted book, *The Suffering and Joys of the English Bourgeoisie*, but none of these works is completed.

In Germany the political situation is also being transformed and political agitation is on the increase once more. Engels has been receiving reports that small communist cells are being set up on the basis of discussions around the *Manifesto* –14 separate editions have already been published there. The Prussian political police are following developments with alarm and attempts are being made in the press to libel the communist leaders, particularly those living in exile. Engels writes a letter of courteous protest to Christian Carl Josias von Bunsen, the Prussian Envoy in London, about such calumnies in the *Neue Preussische Zeitung*. In what is clearly a co-ordinated plot against the English-based leadership, these accusations are picked up by the British press too.

The arrest, on the railway station in Leipzig, of a leading member of the League of Communists, who is carrying leaflets and an address book, is used to cement the case of a 'revolutionary conspiracy'. For almost a year and a half, from 1851, a big show trial against the League of Communists is being prepared. It becomes notoriously known as the '1852 Kommunistenprozess' [1852 Communist Trial], and takes place between October and November. The police have no hesitation in forging documents and minutes to give added credence to the prosecution case; confessions are forced from leading members and arrest warrants despatched in all directions. The Prussian police also have no qualms about extending their work to London as it is believed, not entirely mistakenly, that it is there where the conspiratorial centre is based. Police agents provocateurs have already tried to involve émigré communists in a plot to assassinate the Prussian king, but have been rebuffed in no uncertain terms. Intimately involved in preparing the case is Marx's arch-conservative brother-in-law, Ferdinand von Westphalen, the Prussian State Minister for Home Affairs. When the case comes to court, Engels is described as one of the ring-leaders of the 'conspiracy to mount a coup against the state government' and to be arrested on sight. Unfortunately for the conservatives, Engels cannot be formally arraigned, as the Rhineland justice system requires the presence of the accused.

Marx and Engels are very much aware of the serious repercussions that could follow such a show trial and begin preparing an international defence campaign. As we shall see, Engels proves to be not only an astute political activist, journalist and organiser, but also a veritable counter espionage expert. In a letter to Marx in 1852, he explains how to send documents in order to avoid police interception. He suggests Marx should employ a variety of business addresses and send things by the Pickford transport company, use different handwriting on the envelopes and take them to different parcels offices. 'Using all these different methods in rotation,' he explains, 'we will achieve sufficient security. But, so that it doesn't become too obvious, write a few banal letters at the same time, to me directly, as I will to you.' This concern about security is not mere paranoia on Engels' part as the wax seals on his and Marx's letters are invariably damaged or broken, clearly indicating interference.

The defence for the accused is organised by Marx from his house in London. Jenny Marx reports: 'Just now parcels came from Weerth and Engels with businessmen's addresses and mock business letters so that we can demand court documents, letters etc...two parcels are sent off immediately with business return addresses'. Despite all their work Engels is not over-optimistic about the outcome of the case; the Prussians see it as a prestige matter. He therefore presses Marx to collaborate with him on a defence document that can be widely publicised in the event of a successful prosecution. Thus the famous 'Enthüllungen über den Kommunistenprozess zu Köln' [Disclosures concerning the trial of the Communists in Cologne] comes about. It is published five days after the verdict is announced, in Marx's name alone, as Engels, since his move to Manchester, is no longer a member of the League's central committee. A fund is immediately set up in support of the prisoners and their families and an appeal is sent out to contacts in other countries.

The Prussians only get wind of this appeal when they arrest the tailor's apprentice, Bernhard Diedrich who returns to Germany from America with a copy of it. The authorities never discover where the money comes from or how it reaches the families, but they are keen to find out. The Prussians, through their efficient spy network, have detailed reports on all the active communists in London. Herr Stieber, one of the government agents who keeps them under surveillance, notes in his diary that Engels, alongside Marx, is 'one of the most zealous and active of the communists' and his 'criminal record' is one of the longest in police files.

Five days after the verdict in Cologne, the Communist League in London dissolves itself and declares the continuation of the League on the continent 'no longer in accord with the times'. This drastic action is undoubtedly undertaken to avoid further measures being taken against communists everywhere on the basis of their being part of an 'international conspiracy'. Engels, not being a member of the central committee, is not involved in the discussions that lead up to this, but is undoubtedly kept informed by Marx and will have supported the move. He attempts to draw up a balance sheet in the aftermath of the trial. In his view, it is, on the one hand, a setback but, on the other, it has given the communists a great deal of free publicity, even if not necessarily positive.

In 1855/56 the biggest strikes in Germany during the fifties take place in Elberfeld, led by the cotton mill dyers. As all the revolutionary leaders are in exile, the strike lacks real direction, but it is still a spark of rebelliousness in an otherwise bleak period and is seen as a signal that the proletariat has not been cowed. Gustav Levy, from Düsseldorf, visits Marx and gives him a report on the situation, telling him that the workers in Wuppertal still look to Engels as 'their man'. But Engels is impotently kicking his heels in the Manchester office. Disillusioned with the immediate prospects of revolution in Europe, he begins looking to America for inspiration and tells Marx: 'One of the positive aspects is that we, more than any other party of the European revolution, have been able to promote our case to the English-American public'. Both of them already write regularly for the *New York Daily Tribune*, and the New York Communist Club is one of the most active outposts of the revolutionary movement.

Although Engels is often frustrated being 'so far from the centre of activities', he is also spared the petty sniping and 'horse-trading' carried on in the exile community that Marx is obliged to endure. In a letter to him in 1859, Marx gives vent to his irritation; 'I envy you to a certain extent that you live in Manchester, cut off from all the bickering. I have to wade through this deep swamp and under conditions that are already robbing me of time for my theoretical studies. On the other hand I am pleased that you only have to deal second hand with all this dirt'.

The newspaper *Das Volk* [The People], aimed at the German exile community, which is published in weekly editions for four months during 1859 by the 'Marx Party', reflects this infighting in its columns. Engels is, of course, one of the chief financial supporters of the paper and contributes articles to it. They are both acutely aware of the need for a regular, widely distributed, socialist paper. So, when in 1861 Ferdinand Lassalle expresses the desire to publish such a daily newspaper in Berlin in collaboration with the two of them, a golden opportunity is presented, but they remain sceptical, both about the chances of this happening and about Lassalle's credentials as a bona fide socialist. They feel the party set up by Lassalle – the Allgemeiner Deutscher Abeiterverein [General Association of German Workers] – can never be more than a small sect. However, they both recognise that the period of authoritarian conservatism appears to be over and that the opportunities for a very different workers' movement are now rosier than for a long time. With this in mind, Engels formulates the tasks for a revolutionary workers' party in 1865 in his brochure: 'Die preußische Militärfrage und die deutsche Arbeiterpartei' [The Prussian Military Question and the German Workers' Party]. He sees it in terms of representing that section of the working class that has developed a class consciousness, while recognising that the class as a whole has common interests. In the small brochure he writes, he goes far beyond the immediate issues, addressing basic questions of strategy and tactics, and emphasising the need for an independent proletarian party:

> With the freedom of the press, as well as the right to hold meetings and form associations, the proletariat has won a general right to be heard...It is therefore in the interests of the workers to support the bourgeoisie in their struggle against the reactionary elements, as long as they remain true to themselves; with that caveat, every concession the bourgeoisie is able to wring from the reactionaries will, in the end, only help the working class...
> It goes without saying that in all these cases the workers' party will be active not merely as the tail of the bourgeoisie, but as a very different, independent party...In this way it will secure for itself a respected position, enlighten individual workers about their class interests and in the next revolutionary storm – and these storms are of such a regular occurrence as are the economic crises and equinoctial storms – be prepared to act.[90]

This is the first real attempt, on the basis of the Communist Manifesto, to develop a concept for a truly proletarian and revolutionary party, and it becomes the blueprint for all the world's communist parties that will be established in future decades. It also forms the basis for the programme of the International Working Men's Association (IWA), known later as the First International, which is set up in London, in 1864, with the active collaboration of Marx. This is conceived as a quasi replacement for the now defunct League of Communists. Although its name would indicate that it is a proletarian association, its general council is made up almost entirely of artisans.

Stuck in Manchester, Engels is unable to take an active part in setting up the organisation, nor does he belong to the leadership, only becoming a member with his partner Lydia early in 1865. However, he and Marx are in constant correspondence in connection with the IWA and Marx often asks him for advice and he writes reports for its meetings on aspects of the international working class movement. Despite Marx's pleading, he refuses to become directly involved, though, as his work for Ermen & Engels leaves him insufficient time. He is also aware that his position as a 'capitalist' could provide ammunition for the IWA's enemies if he were to take on a leading role at this time.

Another senior member of the IWA tries to encourage him to return to Germany, where his standing among the workers in the

Rhine area is still high, and to work for the Association there, but Engels rejects this idea too, even though he maintains close contact with the workers of the IWA section in the steel town of Solingen. The workers there inform him they have set up a co-operative for the production of steel and ironware and they immediately receive material support from him for the project.

At weekends he would often shut himself away in Mary's place, where he keeps his political archive of newspaper clippings, written articles and correspondence. He uses Mary's cottage in this way in case his workplace or main residence is raided or searched. In the wake of the big communist trial in Cologne in 1852 and the general anti-communist hysteria it engenders, this is a wise precautionary measure. This refuge became more a home to him than his official residence. By 1862 he tells Marx that 'I'm living with Mary almost all the time.'

Marx regularly sends him documents from London for 'the archive', and also often asks him for particular documents he needs in order to write his articles for the *New York Daily Tribune* or for his correspondence. During the communist trial in Cologne and for a court case Marx initiates against the *Berlin Nationalzeitung* [Berlin National Newspaper], Engels is expected to provide the necessary documentary evidence that is required. The archive takes up a lot of his time as it has to be maintained in an orderly and accessible fashion. It becomes invaluable for the journalistic work both of them undertake.

The American Civil War of 1861-65 holds a particular fascination for both men, as once again, it confirms their social analysis of the battle between the 'modern industrial forces' and the backward land-owning class structures. They also see the USA as undoubtedly the most progressive, enlightened and democratic nation, with great revolutionary potential. Some of Engels' former comrades from the German 1848/49 revolution, including his former commander Willich, as mentioned in Chapter 6, play often significant roles fighting on the side of the Yankees during the war. Together, Engels and Marx contribute seven articles to the *New York Daily Tribune* on the Civil War alone, and for such work Engels' archive is essential. He terms the American Civil War 'the first grand war of contemporaneous history'. Marx later hails it as 'the greatest event of the age'. The Civil War, or the Second American Revolution, as it is sometimes characterised, stands out as the decisive turning point of nineteenth century history. It is essentially a battle between the conservative, land- and slave-owning southern 'plantocracy' and the more democratic and industrialised north.

Marx and Engels follow the military aspects of the conflict with the closest attention. 'The General' in particular is absorbed by the tactics and strategy of the contending forces. He is impatient with the strategies of McClellan and his 'anaconda plan' for surrounding, constricting, and crushing the South, advocating instead a bold and sharp stroke launched at the middle of the Confederate forces. He thus anticipates Sherman's decisive march through Georgia two years later, in 1864. Exasperated by the manifold blunders and half-heartedness of the Union generals as well as the reluctance of the Union's middle class to use revolutionary methods in waging the war, he at one time despairs of a Union victory. But Marx, with his eye upon the superior latent powers of the North and the inherent weaknesses of the Confederacy, chides him for being 'swayed a little too much by the military aspect of things'. 'In its Civil War phase, the revolution abolished chattel slavery, and destroyed the old plantocracy,' they note. 'At the same time it insured the continuance of democracy, freedom, and progress by putting an end to the rule of an oligarchy, by preventing further suppression of civil liberties in the interests of slavery, and by paving the way for the forward movement of American labour'.

The military expert, linguist and scientist

Engels is undoubtedly a pioneer as far as the idea of military theory for the working classes is concerned. In this work, his friend and former artillery officer, Joseph Weydemeyer helps him considerably with his own detailed knowledge and experience. Although many of his ideas have since been overtaken by developments, he certainly provided some ground rules for Lenin, Trotsky, Mao, the young Che Guevara and other guerrilla leaders when seeking inspiration in his military writings. Both he and Marx feel strongly that revolutionaries should be conversant with the issues of modern warfare. They realise that social and economic relationships find their reflection in the army, and that armies play a significant role in economic developments. Engels reiterated that the complex relations of material development can be demonstrated clearly in the 'industry of death' as he explains in *Anti-Dühring*.

In response to the defeat of revolution in Europe and his own experiences of fighting in the Palatinate, he has become fascinated by the question of how to wage a successful revolutionary war and defend the revolution militarily; so, in the fifties, he begins a serious study of military theory. In letters to Marx, he often gives expert and graphic descriptions of a number of notable field commanders, such as Napoléon, Wellington and Blücher. He is also very much aware, he reveals, that it is the French Revolution that created the social preconditions for a modern military system; the bourgeoisie and wealthier peasantry were emancipated and a new officer caste created, one not based on aristocratic privilege, as used to be the norm. This, as much as anything, he argues, explains Napoléon's huge military successes. He goes on to suggest that just as modern warfare is the military expression of the liberation of citizenry and peasantry, so the emancipation of the proletariat will also create a new military strategy and tactics. He does, though, also express the hope that with the increased numerical superiority of the proletariat and the lack of an adequate opponent, such mass wars will in fact become obsolete. The US military historian, Martin Kitchen notes that, 'The notion that the French Revolution marked an important new stage in the history of warfare can scarcely be seen as highly original, [but] the consequences that Engels drew from this insight are often remarkable for their originality and prescience'.[91]

Before he leaves Manchester, Engels is also able to purchase a library of military books from a former officer in Cologne and these form an invaluable archive for his research. He examines closely all the questions of strategy and tactics, weapons categories, troop organisation, leadership and logistics. He develops many of these ideas in a series of articles, 'Revolution and Counter-revolution in Germany', followed by others on the Crimean War, wars in Asia, America and in Europe up to the Franco-German war of 1870/71. Responding to his endeavours, Marx, tongue in cheek, tells him early on that 'if there is any military action, then I will rely on immediate instructions from the War Ministry in Manchester'!

For a short time, as a result of the praise and recognition he receives for his military articles, particularly those on the Crimean War (1853-56), he entertains hopes that he may be able to earn a living as a military correspondent and give up commerce for good. In his attempts to pursue a journalistic career, Engels woos the Guardian's editor as he tells Marx: 'The editor of the *Guardian* who I've got to know is a wise man in his own mind and a sort of oracle among a number of the philistines. He's also a teller of dirty jokes and a moderate pub drinker. He's clearly heard about me, because when I mention some triviality or other he listens to me with marked respect and seeks enlightenment from me by asking penetrating questions. I'm gently letting the man come closer, so that I can then nobble him about personnel at the *Examiner* and the *Times* and can then approach these papers'.[92] But all these efforts come to nothing, although he does write several small military reports (apparently uncredited) for the *Manchester Guardian.* His articles for the American Cyclopaedia under the general heading, 'Addressed to Volunteers', include 'A Review of English Riflemen' and 'The History of the Rifle' (1861), by-lined a 'General Officer', stimulate a wide interest. He also makes attempts to obtain accreditation from a leading English paper as a war correspondent, but this also proves impossible.

He does, though, write a series entitled, 'The Armies of Europe' for *Putnam's Monthly Magazine* in New York and another series for the *New American Cyclopaedia,* alongside many for other journals. Marx tells him that a piece of his, written anonymously of course, in one of the German journals is widely believed in Prussia to be the secret work of a high-up general. His articles, of necessity written under a pseudonym, are widely considered to be written by experts in the world of military science.

Despite intensive and long hours spent in the office of the family firm, he also manages to find the time to write regular contributions for various journals dealing with the colonial struggles in China, India, Algeria and Persia. Although his views of the indigenous peoples are, commensurate with the times, somewhat clichéd and simplistic, he does expose the brutality of the colonial powers.

Alongside his military studies he also pursues his great love of 'comparative philology' and languages. Learning languages is for him no obligation, but a pleasure, and he recognises its undoubted value for an internationalist movement. To have a full grasp of events in the world, one has to be able to read the local papers and journals as well as be aware of the different cultures. His linguistic facility also allows him to maintain a direct dialogue with comrades and friends worldwide.

It is fascinating to discover how a people's culture and character is revealed in its language. If we look at words imported into English:

joie de vivre, élan and ésprit from France, Zeitgeist, Weltschmerz and Leitmotif from Germany; British cultural equivalents are, perhaps: fair play, common sense, keeping a straight bat. French passion, German philosophical rationality and English tolerance and pragmatism are reflected in these expressions. Such aspects fascinate Engels and are reflected in his correspondence. Both he and Marx pepper their letters with words and phrases in various languages to obtain nuances of meaning, impossible in one language alone.

In 1852 he has already begun an intensive study of Russian and taken conversation classes with a local Russian émigré. Despite the fact that, according to Marxian theory, socialist revolutions would break out first in the most highly developed capitalist countries, he and Marx both realise that in Tsarist Russia the brew is fermenting and revolution could soon be breaking up the old order there like spring the ice on the Volga. 'What a beautiful language is Russian! he writes, 'all the advantages of German, without the awful vulgarity'. He goes on to study Serbo-Croat and Czech. Then in the sixties, in connection with the Danish-German War of 1864, he begins looking at Scandinavian languages. By the mid 1860s, he is amazingly already familiar with 'most of the European languages', as he himself states.

Towards the end of this decade, once the Fenian movement gains a higher profile, he devotes himself to Celtic studies. The result of this has been left us only in the form of a fragment, *The History of Ireland*. No doubt Mary and Lizzie give him the impetus for this and help him from their own personal experience.

Despite these prodigious achievements, he is still dissatisfied and regrets he can't delve more into the realms of comparative philology: 'When you've spent the whole day devoted to noble commerce,' he writes, 'you are unable to reach beyond a simple dilettantism vis-à-vis such a colossal and broad subject matter, and even though I once nursed the intrepid idea of developing a comparative grammar of the Slavic languages, I've long ago put that aside...'

In order to better understand oriental affairs and the Crimean War, in the mid-fifties he begins studying Persian, His incomparable facility with languages is revealed in a letter he writes to Marx at this time: 'Since I am in any case tied up with the eastern mummery for some weeks, I have made use of the opportunity to learn Persian. I am put off Arabic...By comparison, Persian is absolute child's play. Were it not for that damned Arabic alphabet in which every half dozen letters looks like every other half dozen and the vowels are not written, I would undertake to learn the entire grammar within 48 hours...I have set myself a maximum of three weeks for Persian...' Even if he is exaggerating, the attempt alone is humbling. When, shortly after the International Workingmen's Association (IWA) is founded in 1864 and individual countries set up their own workers' parties, Engels is hardly unprepared, both in terms of linguistic skills and political nous. He becomes, almost by default, the de facto leader of the international working class movement.

After he's largely completed his studies in the military field by 1858 and assuaged his linguistic ambitions, he concentrates on the philosophical problems of the natural sciences. There seems to be no limit to his intellectual hunger and the renaissance breadth of his interests. And in a sense it is not so surprising that he now turns to the natural sciences, as these are going through a cataclysmic change during the mid 19th century. In 1827 the geologist Charles Lyell had realised from his fossil research that new species were derived from older ones, but he could not explain the mechanism. His three-volume *Principles of Geology* (1830) pictured the earth as changing over a great time span challenged orthodox religious creationism and the belief in immutable categories. The astronomer, John Nichol, in his books written from 1839 onwards also sketched an evolving universe and actually used the word 'evolution', possibly for the first time in this context.

Engels' renewed interest in the natural sciences coincides with the publication of Darwin's *Origin of Species* in 1859 which sends shock-waves through society. At the same time, Huxley and Wallace have been making parallel discoveries. In industrial processes, in chemistry and physics, enormous strides are being made too. The discovery of the cell around 1836 and the law of the conservation of energy around 1847 are also keys to Engels' interest. In Germany Bunsen and Kirchhof are conducting experiments on spectral analysis that are to have highly significant repercussions for our understanding the phenomenon of light.

An added stimulus to his studying natural sciences are the ideas of Kant and Hegel on the philosophy of nature. He requests Marx to send him some of their books, and in the same letter he says he is contemplating studying comparative anatomy and physiology. He is closely following contemporary debates and discoveries in all areas of the natural sciences.

The contemporary philosopher, Herbert Spencer is also taken

with the idea of evolution and believes a unification of scientific truth can be achieved. He, like Marx and Engels, is committed to the universality of natural law, the idea that the laws of nature apply without exception, including to the human mind. Spencer's volumes on biology, psychology, and sociology are all intended to demonstrate the existence of natural laws in these disciplines. Even in his writings on ethics, he maintains that it is possible to discover 'laws' of morality with the status of laws of nature. Where Engels and Marx disagree strongly with Spencer is in his clinging to a form of deism, which he mixes with positivism. He sees the cosmos as something designed, and the laws of nature as the creation of a transcendental being. Interestingly, although Spencer espouses Darwin's theory and even coins the phrase 'the survival of the fittest', he applies it mechanistically and, like Engels, fails to fully comprehend the underlying mechanism of evolution.

Marx himself only begins to look at natural science in any depth from the mid-sixties onwards and generously admits in a letter to Engels that: 'You know that, firstly, everything comes late with me and, secondly, that I am always following in your footsteps...' Neither of them studies the sciences with the intention of becoming expert in any particular field, but as part of their attempt to create a holistic theoretical concept, incorporating the natural sciences, the arts, sociology and economics. In this sense they are following in the tracks of the great German philosophers.

He and Marx, who is staying with him in Manchester during the summer of 1869, visit the eccentric but renowned geologist, John Dakyns who lives in Bolton Abbey, Yorkshire. With him they discuss the latest scientific discoveries as well as the ideas of socialism. Marx persuades him to join the IWA, calling him a 'natural communist'. He is such an exotic character that Marx compares him to George Eliot's *Felix Holt* and warns him that if Eliot ever encounters him she will turn him into a character in one of her novels.

During the 1860s, in view of the enormous range of scientific subject matter, they do agree a certain division of work; Marx is to take on evolution – geology and inheritance theory, while Engels will devote himself to physics and chemistry. But the philosophically explicit generalisations from their natural history research become largely Engels' task. The results of this work are contained in his *Dialectics of Nature* (first published posthumously in full in 1925) and left us only as a series of notes.

Despite undertaking this Herculean work, Engels remains dissatisfied. While working in the family firm, he is continually plagued by the consciousness that his life is remorselessly slipping away. He hasn't sufficient time to pursue his research interests and expand his knowledge as he would like and he feels that even his journalistic skills are now rusting. But what he achieves despite his 'jobbing' work is still impressive. He has been able to undertake a considerable amount of political and research work, consolidating his expertise particularly on military matters, broadening his familiarity with languages and keeping up with the latest scientific discoveries. However, he will only be able to devote the time he deems necessary to his studies once he leaves the firm of Ermen & Engels. He is, after all, in 1870 still at the height of his powers, full of energy and still champing at the bit. But he knows he will only be able to do this properly once he's moved away from Manchester, and the only place to move to is London. So, towards the end of the year 1870, that's what he and Lizzie prepare to do. Once he is free, he feels, he will be able to indulge all those research interests he has been forced to forego. Little does he envisage that the organisational demands to be made on him by the now burgeoning world working class movement and then, after Marx's death, the overseeing of Marx's legacy will eat into those dreams.

Chapter Eight (1870 - 1882)

The years of freedom

Eleanor, Marx's youngest daughter, known affectionately as 'Tussy', often stays with 'Uncle Engels' in Manchester. On one of these visits Engels takes her on a trip to Belle Vue and to Bolton Abbey, when they stay overnight at the Devonshire Arms. He also takes her along to house parties at Sam Moore's; there are picnics and shopping excursions, evenings at the theatre and tea parties of bread and treacle. No doubt, in contrast to the straitened circumstances and eternal crises at home, Eleanor relishes the relaxed atmosphere of Engels' household, his great sense of humour and his kindness. She is always happy staying with him. In fact her mother Jenny is at times quite jealous in this respect. While staying with Engels in 1870, the Prince and Princess of Wales are scheduled to come to Manchester to open the Old Trafford Royal Agricultural Show. She and Engels, with street urchin-like glee, encourage the local children to greet the royal pair with the popular chant: 'The Prince of Wales in Belle Vue jail for robbing a man of a pint of ale'.

Lizzie also plays surrogate mother and sister to Eleanor and takes her out to the markets and shows her the stall where Kelly, one of the Fenian prisoners rescued in an ambush of the police van, once sold pots. She listens transfixed to her tales of Fenian escapades and stories from Irish folklore from her niece, Mary Ellen or 'Pumps' as she is comically nicknamed. Lizzie has a lasting influence on Eleanor. 'She was quite illiterate,' she tells us, 'but she was as true, as honest and in some ways a fine-souled a woman as you could meet. She was the staunchest of friends'. Lizzie also introduces Eleanor to a freedom of behaviour, unknown in the Marx household.

At the height of that summer, Eleanor writes home that she and Lizzie, 'overcome by the heat, laid down on the floor the whole day, drinking beer, claret etc.'. And this is how Engels finds them when he comes home from work: 'Auntie [Lydia], Sarah[who helps in the house], me and Ellen[Mary Ellen or 'Pumps']', she continues, '...all lying our full length on the floor with no stays, no boots and one petticoat and a cotton dress on and that was all.'

Eleanor is holidaying with him in the same year he finally ends his servitude. He is in his 49th year, and has been negotiating his release since January. He is finally set free on 1 July 1870. This is the day he has longed for since he first began working for Ermen & Engels. When he began, he was convinced that a new revolutionary upsurge in Europe would release him from this purgatory within months, but his torment lasts much longer – 20 years. During this time he often fears that his mental capabilities will ossify and his energy dissipate.

When recalling that summer day, 21 years later, Eleanor writes:

> I was with Engels when he reached the end of this forced labour and I saw what he must have gone through all those years. I shall never forget the triumph with which he exclaimed: "For the last time!" as he put his boots on in the morning to go to the office. A few hours later we were standing at the gate waiting for him. We saw him coming over the little field opposite the house where he lived. He was swinging his stick in the air and singing, his face beaming. Then we set the table for a celebration and drank champagne and were happy...[93]

Although Engels is still under obligation to represent the company until the end of June, when his contract runs out, Lizzie is already pressing him about the proposed move to London. She is keen to move there as soon as possible. So, already in May he asks Marx to look for a house for him and, on Lizzie's urging, 'if possible without a dominating vis à vis [to Marx's own house]. We would like a place no higher up than where you live, as Lizzie has an asthmatic aversion to mountain climbing. When you find something, I will come over', he writes.

Marx, though, as in all things he undertakes, doesn't exactly rush himself with the looking, and in July, Engels has to press him again: 'We've now put a 'To Let' notice in our window. Have you still not found anything?' The matter is becoming embarrassing, until Marx's wife Jenny eventually gets involved and it is she who eventually finds the house, which for the next 25 years will become his permanent residence. Jenny, always reserved and formal, still addresses Engels as 'Mein lieber Herr Engels' [My dear Mr. Engels] despite their long years of friendship, even when she writes to tell him she has found a house for him. Without even seeing it, Engels tells her to rent it immediately. But they are only able to move to London three months after his final day at the firm, because the London house has to be thoroughly renovated before they can move in.

On 20th September 1870, he, Lizzie and her 10 year-old niece, 'Pumps', arrive in London at last. The Regent's Park Road house is a middle class family home, close to Regent's Park and Primrose Hill. The air is much better here, which is important for Lizzie, and Engels can take his daily walks through the parks. The house is only a quarter of an hour's walk from the Marxes, who live in Maitland Road, Haverstock Hill. This is just the right distance away – not too close to cause friction and not too far to prevent easy communications. When Karl Kautsky asks him why he doesn't want to live closer to Marx, Engels replies: 'It's not good when married friends live too close to each other. Their views on behaviour and habits never quite coincide'. Engels is here very perceptive; he knows how easily it is even for good friends to fall out if they begin to tread on each other's toes; it is also very possible that Lizzie, as a working class woman, feels ill at ease with the Marxes and particularly with the aristocratic Jenny. But the two men are, from now on 'one heart and one soul', and the whole next day after Engels' arrival in London 'they spent huddled together', as Jenny remarks.

In his new abode at 122 Regent's Park Road, he quickly settles in and gets down to the work he has always wanted to do. Marx's son-in-law, Paul Lafargue, in his memoirs, describes Engels' study, his attitudes and his way of working:

> In his two large and bright work rooms, the walls are stacked from floor to ceiling with books, not a scrap of paper lies on the floor and the books, with the exception of a few on his desk, are all in place on the shelves.
>
> He combined an extensive and quick-witted memory as well as an extraordinary rapid way of working and a no less amazing alacrity of comprehension. He learned quickly and effortlessly.

> Despite not having any of the usual attributes of an ivory tower autodidact, he had such a multifaceted range of knowledge that one is amazed.
> He was always carefully dressed, always straight-backed and polite; he always looked as if he were about to appear on parade as he had to when he was a volunteer in the Prussian army...I know no one who wore the same suit for so long without creasing it or pulling it out of shape. For himself and his household he only spent what he felt was absolutely necessary, but on the other side, towards the party and the party comrades, who came to him in need, he was unstintingly generous.[94]

Although this house now becomes his official residence, Engels is still super cautious, and for his political correspondence, he still prefers to use cover addresses in order to keep police spies off his tracks – he is still seen as a dangerous force by a number of European states.

After the infamous Anti-Socialist laws of 1878 are enacted in Germany by Bismarck, harassment of Engels is intensified, but he had been watched and monitored by the Prussian and other police forces from the very moment he arrived in England in 1849. This intimidation fails utterly to deter him from political activities and as soon as he settles in London, he once again throws himself wholeheartedly into political life. The surveillance will be intensified again during his efforts in the early 70s on behalf of the Paris Commune; he is permanently spied upon and harassed. But as long as he remains on British soil (and the government refrains from activating its Aliens Bill) the police forces of the continent are impotent to take further action.

The French police have maintained a substantial Engels dossier from 1871 through to 1895. French spies are despatched to London, Brussels and Geneva to follow his every move. In an instruction reminiscent of more recent police activities against those on the Left, the French 'mouchards' were told to provide as complete a picture of him as possible, about his private life, his life style, his morality and his means of existence, as well as his political connections. And again, as seems to be a pattern, what the police can't discover they concoct. Here, an example: 'he is one of the most dangerous members of the General Council of the International. He is a creature of Marx. He is fanatical; he was born in Frankfurt; he was imprisoned in Brighton for six weeks and he is attempting to complete his work "Socialism in the past and in the future"; he also has a brother of 30 or 32 years of age, born in Basle, who is also a member of the International and was twice in America', and so on in this fantastical vein. Thus, unfortunately, these police 'reports' are not exactly a mine of useful facts for any would-be biographer, reflecting more the vivid imagination of the individual spies than any reality of Engels' life. Not surprisingly, the Prussian police are even more active than the French and have spies stationed almost permanently in London. Their reports from the period between 1878 and 1895 alone fill five voluminous files on the 'Social Democratic and Communist Workers' Party (sic) in London'.

The Prussian authorities only really take note of Engels as a serious opponent again after he lambasts government polices directly in written form on their own home ground. In 'Preussische Schnapps im Deutschen Reichstag' [German Schnapps in the German Parliament], he unmercifully takes apart Prussian feudal rule. Once it is published in 1876, in *Volksstaat*, the paper of the German Social Democratic Workers' Party, it is attacked by Bismarck's paper, the *Central-Blatt für das Deutsche Reich* and other leading conservative papers. The government had reacted in a similar way only four years' earlier in response to his booklet *Zur Wohnungsfrage [The Housing Question]*. In 'German Schnapps in the German Parliament', Engels dismisses Bismarck contemptuously and with unprecedented directness as a 'man of schnapps and brown envelopes', referring to politicians who use their public office for personal gain and privilege.

The anti-socialist laws, implemented by Bismarck, are a last ditch attempt to stop the inexorable rise of the German Social Democratic Party and the further spread of socialist ideas within the country. Under these laws, all Engels' written works are banned. Their revelatory content, their mobilising agitational power and their theoretical analyses are, for the Kaiser's Empire, as dangerous as the social democratic organisations themselves. The government issues a list of twelve banned works by Engels, including his historical volume, *The German Peasant War*. Before 1878, one could quite easily buy even banned books in Germany but now they don't even have to be banned; the fear is such that any volume deemed by a bookseller to be questionable is simply not stocked. The bans also have a considerable impact on the development of the Social

Democratic Party in Germany and hinder the further dissemination of Marxist ideas there and throughout the international working class movement. These laws are never rescinded but are allowed to lapse in 1890.

It is perhaps useful to recall that between 1844 (the moment Marx and Engels fully embraced the concept of communism) and 1878 (the year the German anti-socialist laws were implemented) there are 50 authorised and published books/brochures by Marx and Engels in circulation: 33 in German, nine in English, seven in French and one in Russian. As a result of the censorship during the eighties they both begin publishing in all main European languages, to get around the bans.

Not long after his arrival in London, Engels, together with Marx and the whole IWA, are confronted with an acute dilemma and one which threatens to split the movement: what position should the working class adopt vis-à-vis the imminent war between Prussia and France? In response, Engels drafts some principles: as long as it is a question of defending Germany against invasion, then a war could be supported, but any annexation of Alsace-Lorraine by Germany must be opposed, and as soon as France has a republican, non-chauvinistic, government, all efforts to conclude a peace should be undertaken. But, the overriding common interests of the French and German working classes need to be stressed continuously.

The victory of Prussia in the decisive Battle of Königgrätz in 1866 brings the Austro-Prussian War to its conclusion and sets the stage for future international relations in late 19th century Europe. It demonstrates the incredible efficiency of the Prussian war machine and raises Prussian prestige in Europe immensely. It also means that the process of national unity in Germany becomes synonymous with Prussian conquest. Within Prussia it also serves to consolidate Prime Minister Bismarck's power.

Although during the early 1860s Germany still has five times as many men employed in workshops than in factories, this picture is already changing. The guilds and restrictions on economic freedom lingered on for more than another decade after 1848, but after 1859 most German states one after the other abolish these restrictions. This gives an enormous fillip to the development of German industry. And, by the 1860s the middle classes are vociferously demanding rationalisation on a national scale of many aspects of the economy, including a national system of commercial law and the abolition of tolls. Germany still has some way to go before becoming as fully modernised as its chief competitor, Britain, but it is ahead of France in terms of the building of railways and in steel production. Prussia's rising industrial might and its demonstrable military prowess gives it the confidence to challenge France as to which country will dominate European affairs in the future.

The Paris Commune

When the Prussian-French War (1870-71) breaks out, it comes as no surprise to Engels, even though he has actively campaigned to prevent it. His main concern is that it will undermine Franco-German worker solidarity, which has been built up painstakingly over the years, and will lead to French and German workers massacring each other on behalf of their ruling governments.

Marx and Engels have differences over their attitude to the Prussian-French War. That difference lies primarily in the fact that Marx is deeply involved in the international workers' movement and is its representative, whereas Engels is still, at this stage, somewhat of an outsider and is not a member of the General Council (he is co-opted onto the Council later in the year), and can afford to be more independent and less 'diplomatic' in his views. Marx has to remind Engels not to forget that, 'the General Council (of the IWA) has to deal with susceptibilities on all sides and cannot write as we two in our own names could do'.

As we well know from history, ordinary working people from different countries, despite having overwhelming common interests, are all too easily seduced to fight each other by nationalist and xenophobic rhetoric. The looming Franco-Prussian War of 1870 proves no exception. This fratricide, across national boundaries will take on even more horrendous proportions in the confrontation of the great European powers, during the First World War, as Engels predicts it will, when the working classes of Britain, France and Germany are to slaughter each other unnecessarily in a war which leads only to a Pyrrhic victory.

Although the *Pall Mall Gazette* is a conservative journal, the Owenite John Watts, a friend of Engels, has an editorial position there and he manages to wangle him a commission to write articles on the war, as long as he is prepared to give his proletarian sympathies a low profile. The resultant articles win much admiration. He predicts the Prussian victory, at a time when most government circles are convinced that the French will win. Engels argues that Bonaparte isn't confronting King Wilhelm of Prussia alone, but the whole German nation. In his third article for the *Gazette*, sensationally, Engels is able to disclose the secret Prussian plan of campaign. A number of continental papers, as well as British ones, including *The Times*, reproduce his articles, almost word for word, but without acknowledgement. He protests about this plagiarism but to no avail. *The Spectator* declares Engels' articles the only important ones to appear on the war. He, modest as ever, tells Marx: '...the only prophecy I made at the right moment, was published promptly and was confirmed by next day's news. That's just pure luck and impresses the philistines enormously'. He, of course, also has the good fortune that the British press is not subject to the same strict censorship rules as France and Germany are.

The Prussians eventually surround and besiege Paris during the vicious winter of 1870-1871, beating off French forces raised in the rest of the country. As a result of the siege, Parisians endure acute starvation, bombardment and the spread of disease; balloons and pigeon post provided the only contact with the outside world. With no other recourse open to it, Paris surrenders and the Prussians enter the city. Undoubtedly Germany's efficient use of its railway system and Krupp's innovative artillery are keys to its easy victory.

In January 1871 the French Prime Minister, Adolphe Thiers, signs a hasty armistice with the victorious Prussians in order to be able to turn his attention to the spreading revolution that threatens to topple his government. In the wake of the war and the chaos that ensues, the people of Paris decide to take the administration into their own hands, and the National Guard joins the insurgents. On 18 March government troops set out to disarm the Parisian National Guard and occupy the city. They attempt to seize the city's cannon, but are repulsed and the government is forced to flee to Versailles.

On the morning of 26 March 1871 the red flag is raised over Paris's Hôtel de Ville; the central committee of the French National Guard has taken power and declares its opposition to the middle class-led 'government of national defence'. The Commune is established as the legitimate Paris government. Workers dressed in red, and with tricolour cockades, parade the streets in lively groups; avid discussions take place on every corner. Demands to 'arm the people' are made and there are calls for general social reform; Paris belongs to its citizens and there are celebrations throughout the working class areas. In a short space of time the Commune introduces radical new legislation: it declares the separation of church and state, secularises education, and workers are encouraged to take over factories, where the bosses have fled, and turn them into co-operatives; it abolishes a standing army and conscription.

No event has such a profound impact on the thinking of Marx and Engels as the Paris Commune. It is the first attempt by workers to build a socialist, proletarian government. It is a beacon at the time and provides inspiration for revolutionary movements to come. Up to his death Engels was still evaluating the experiences and lessons from that short-lived, 81-day revolution.

On the 27th, one day after the raising of the red flag in Paris, the first detailed reports begin to reach Marx and Engels, who pull out all the stops to obtain a full picture and set the wheels in motion to deliver support to the Commune. A few days later, Engels presents the first comprehensive report on the Commune to a plenum of the General Council of the IWA. Then, under Engels' leadership, the General Council is transformed into a war council. Hundreds of letters are despatched around the world to provide up-to-date information and to drum up support for the Commune.

Victor Schily, a close friend of Marx and Engels, is a German émigré living in Paris, and he wins plaudits for his work in helping build and strengthen the defences of Paris, but he is also chiefly responsible for the spread and propagation of Marxist ideas throughout the Commune. This work is vital, as there is still, at this time, no independent workers' party in France, as exists in Germany. He involves Engels too and, between March and May, Engels' chief role becomes that of military adviser to the Commune. He encourages them to take strategic initiatives and to ensure a proper military defence system for the city. A realistic defence strategy is the be all and end all of any revolution, if it is to survive. Understandably, the clamour increases for Engels to be sent to Paris; time is of essence and the situation is hectic and fraught.

Paul Lafargue sends an appeal to Marx: '...I have seen the men of the Commune and they are, like the people, full of enthusiasm; they still have high hopes of taking Versailles and are working towards this goal. There is no shortage of men, but leaders are in short supply; Vaillant told me that. Couldn't Engels come over and place his expertise at the disposal of the revolution?' Engels, surprisingly, does not respond. His motives are not known, but cowardice or timidity can hardly have been the reasons, given his track record. He is however now a leading member of the General Council and this role will have overridden any personal inclinations he may have harboured. In addition, Marx is seriously ill the whole of April and, on his doctor's advice, leaves London. Engels has to substitute for him and take on much of his work in the International. Additionally, at the time the appeal reaches him, the Commune is already under siege and is unlikely to be able to break out. Engels recognises this and has reported it to the General Council. In response to this critical situation, his chief task becomes that of winning increased international solidarity for the Commune in order to strengthen its fighting spirit. He is also involved in advising negotiators who are trying to persuade Prime Minister Thiers not to use force against the Commune, but all these efforts are to little avail.

Then, on 21 May, with the connivance of the Prussians, who agree to release French prisoners of war to join government forces, Thiers again attacks the city, and after eight days' of bloody street fighting, in which thousands of civilians are butchered, his forces manage to defeat the Commune and the National Guard. On 28 May 1871 the last barricades in Paris are smashed by Thiers' forces who, in collaboration with France's erstwhile enemy, the Prussians, are able to quash the Commune; its leaders and many ordinary citizens are summarily shot or imprisoned. Government troops carry out mass executions of around 30,000 Parisians. The city is in flames but the Kaiser's Marshal MacMahon in cahoots with the French ruling elite, and on behalf of the middle class republic, announces with euphemistic banality that 'order has been restored'. Thiers, from Versailles, announces proudly to the still quaking middle classes that 'socialism in France is now dead'. Around 100,000 Parisians are deported, many condemned to hard labour and despatched to the colonies; the more fortunate just flee.

Engels now becomes the organiser of a refugee fund and launches an appeal to British workers to help those refugees from the Commune who have managed to escape the bloodbath. Eighty or ninety of them eventually make it to London and are helped by the fund. In his report to the General Council in August 1871, he clearly expresses his disappointment that British workers have shown little, if any, solidarity with the French Commune. Once again, deep-seated national attitudes appear to have dominated over any sense of international class solidarity.

As a man of stamina and with a long-term perspective, the end of the Commune does not by any means represent a coda for Engels, and he devotes considerable time to evaluating the experience and particularly looking at the military lessons so that any future attempts at building a workers' state will be more successful. This research finds expression in the introduction he writes to Marx's *Civil War in France* and which is published shortly before his death. The defeat of the Commune demonstrates, he writes, that 'the working class cannot simply take over the state machinery and set it to work in its own interests'. In this introduction he also provides an interesting definition of the contentious term 'dictatorship of the proletariat': 'Of late the Social-Democratic philistine has once more been filled with wholesome horror at the words: Dictatorship of the Proletariat. Well and good, gentlemen, do you want to know what this dictatorship looks like? Look at the Paris Commune. That was the dictatorship of the proletariat'.[95]

The events surrounding the Commune provide another excuse for his family to attack him. They have, from the very beginning of his radicalism, felt offended by his views and activities. But as long as he was working for the family firm in Manchester, they felt his 'illness' could be contained or at least subdued to a secondary symptom. Once he moved to London and became a full-time militant again, their sense of outrage turns to direct animosity. Even his mother, normally reticent in her critique, becomes overt in her accusations. The recriminations are familiar to him: as the son of an 'honourable' family he consorts with the murderers of the Commune; he has coupled himself to Marx who misuses and leaches him financially; he is completely immoral and, to cap it all, in contravention of Christian principles, he lives in sin with an uneducated factory girl.

Engels, though, is used to these accusations and has long ago given up even responding; only to those from his mother, whom he still dearly loves, is he sensitive. To her most recent and critical missive in 1871, he takes his time and a number of deep breaths before replying:

> Dear Mother,
> If I have not written to you for some time, it is only because I didn't wish to reply in an offensive manner to your recent comments about my political activity and thus hurt you. And

> when I then, time and time again, read the shameless lies in the Cologne paper, for example the baseness of that beggar Wachenhusen [a journalist on the paper], when I see the same people, who during the war read in the whole of the French press only lies, but who now believe every police fiction against the Commune, every slander in the most popular Parisian trash rag and trumpet it throughout Germany as if it were the Evangelium itself, it puts me in a mood that is not conducive to providing a sober response. [And, as a PS]: You can tell Emil Blank that Marx needs no money from me. I would like to see the face of that same Emil Bl. if I tried giving him advice about how to use his money.[96]

Engels' irritation is only too easy to understand. The family is attacking his friendship with Marx – the one thing that is most dear to him. There is also the bitterness left by the family's attitude to the sharing of his father's inheritance. His legitimate share was denied him and he was only given 'the right to employ' the capital tied up in the English company which, on leaving, he had to pay back to the family. In 1869 a new arrangement is made in the case of his mother dying, again to his disadvantage. It will permit him to use the interest, but not touch the capital. His relatives wish to ensure that none of the family money flows into the coffers of the communists.

His mother dies on 29 October 1873. She had fallen ill earlier in the year, but Engels manages to visit her on the day before she dies. Her death, completely unexpectedly, hits him with 'double pain', and from this moment on his links with the family virtually cease and he no longer visits his home town. Only with his brother Hermann does he maintain reasonably amicable relations.

Building the IWA

The International Workingmen's Association, sometimes called the First International, is founded in 1864 and holds its first meeting in St. Martin's Hall, London. Since the suppression of the revolutionary upsurge throughout Europe in 1849, there has been a period of quiescence in the workers' movement. With the founding of the International, largely on the initiative of foreign émigrés living in Britain, an attempt is made to re-ignite the revolutionary flame and to offer an organising focus for the disparate socialist and radical groups throughout the continent. Marx is one of the chief initiators and he keeps Engels informed of developments, as well as asking his advice. At its height, the organisation numbers over a million and a half members.

At its second Congress in Geneva in1866 and the third in Lausanne in 1867, it is dominated largely by the Proudhonists. However, at the Brussels Congress in 1868 it adopts the tactics suggested by Marx. This victory for the Marxist faction is, however, again seriously challenged at the Basle Congress in 1869, which is characterised by a serious clash between Bakunin's supporters and Marx over the organisation's tactics, but particularly over the issue of abolishing the right to inheritance.

With Marx's continued ill-health during the late sixties, Engels was invited to join the General Council of the IWA and took on increasing responsibilities in the 28-strong leadership. He is instrumental in organising its historic London conference between 17-23 September 1871. Records of attendance at General Council meetings show that Engels did not miss a single one.

During the two years which have elapsed since the Basle Congress of 1869, the General Council has been left to its own devices. The Franco-German war and suppression of the Commune served as a reason for not calling a congress in 1870; in 1871 a 'secret conference' is convened by the General Council. Engels goes about organising it so clandestinely that it appears that neither the German nor British security services are aware that the congress is to take place until quite late in the day. One of the delegates must have been a police spy, as the Prussians receive detailed reports of the congress. It is held inauspiciously in the meeting room of the German Section of the International in London – a first floor room of the Blue Post pub in Newman Street. There are 23 representatives, thirteen of whom are members of the General Council, seven of them corresponding secretaries. Engels is appointed as delegate for Saxony, as no one is able to attend in view of the impending trial for high treason of members of the International there. The trade union activist, John Hales represents Britain.

The most urgent question before the conference is the imminent threat of a split in the International between the anarchists with their supporters and the Marx-Engels faction. This struggle threatens the very survival of the organisation. Among other important issues on the agenda are measures to strengthen the International's organisation and of its General Council; the checking of the centrifugal forces which are emerging within the International and threatening its unity; and taking a definitive position on the hotly disputed topic of participation in the political struggle. Another significant topic to be discussed is whether to sanction the formation of separate working women's branches although both sexes would still be able to participate as members of ordinary branches.

The conference is characterised by its attack on Bakunin and his anarchist grouping as a 'divisive sect'. Bakunin, although declaring himself an internationalist, gives a decidedly nationalist twist to almost every political question. His negative attitude to Germans is blatantly racist; only Slavs are good. And he throws in 'the Yids' as even worse than the Germans. Marx, as a German of Jewish background, is of course the worst of all. Such attitudes colour the bitter battles between Marx and Engels on the one side and Bakunin and his supporters on the other. The core of their ideological differences is the question of power, particularly since the experience of the Commune. Marx and Engels view the anarchist position of abstention from established political processes and of opposition to the foundation of proletarian parties as fallacious and oppose this vociferously. They believe that the workers have to take control of the state in order to achieve liberation; Bakunin believes state power has to be smashed as a prerequisite for true liberation. Engels is also very much opposed to Bakunin's dismissal of organisation as 'authoritarian', arguing that 'revolution itself is an imposition of authority'. He is also convinced that Bakunin heads a secret organisation and that it is active in the International. Latter-day followers of Bakunin still dispute this, but it was widely known even then that Bakunin had founded a conspiratorial organisation already in 1864 with the aim of preparing for a social revolution.

Both factions prepare for the coming battle, which is seen as decisive. Marx and Engels are willing to use all means to defeat Bakunin and his followers and prevent them taking over the leadership of the International. Although, unlike Bakunin, they have at this time no significant following on the ground, they carry great intellectual weight on the General Council itself. They feel that, at this conference, the future of the working class movement throughout the world is at stake. Bakunin is very influential internationally, particularly in Italy and Spain, where his ideas dominate the movement. Most worker and peasant groups there warm to his demands for the immediate elimination of the state and all authority.

Engels argues that it is impossible to dismantle the state 'before you change the social relations that gave rise to it'.

This conference cannot really be said to be fully representative of the International, seeing that a number of sections, the Jura Federation among them, are not invited. Nevertheless, it passes resolutions which radically change the general rules of the organisation, resolutions tending to entrench a hierarchical and authoritarian structure, with disciplined sections entirely under the control of the General Council. The latter is very conscious of the fact that a formal defeat of the anarchists at the conference will hardly put an end to the ideological conflict and that the battle has to be won on the ground. The anarchists, of course, far from laying down their weapons after the London conference, begin to wage open war against the General Council, and this leads to a serious disruption of the organisation's work.

Marx and Engels, over many years, seriously underestimated the role of the socially less developed countries and argued that these had to reach the developmental level of the more highly industrialised nations before their workers could play a significant role in the struggle for socialism. This assessment gives Bakunin and his supporters free reign in those countries. It is an error that, in their struggle for dominance of the International, plays a key role in their ultimate defeat, despite their nominal victory at the Hague congress the following year.

The radical Italian philosopher Benedetto Croce, commenting on why Marx was not successful in winning Italian workers to his cause, says that he was 'too critical, too concentrated on economics, too sarcastic and less humanitarian'. However, the efforts of Marx and Engels are not entirely in vain, as several years later a small socialist party, based on Marxist ideas, becomes firmly established in Italy and makes slow but steady headway, following the successful example of the German Social Democratic Party. The fact that Engels' works are also now being translated into Italian and articles he contributes are published in the new party's journal, *Critica Sociale* (established in 1891) are also significant factors in aiding the growth of the new party.

Of particular interest at the 1871 conference is that it decides on a policy concerning the 'political effectiveness of the working class', largely formulated by Engels. This is also a deadly barb against the anarchists, as it emphasises the role of class struggle and the need for political organisation of the working class. As a result, the International now adds to its statutes the very significant article which states: 'In its struggle against the united power of the propertied classes, the proletariat can only present itself as a class if it constitutes itself as a political party, being in opposition to all earlier parties created by the propertied classes. It is indispensable for the triumph of the social revolution and to ensure its final goal – the eradication of classes'.

This is the first officially stated instance by the IWA of its aim of setting up specifically working class parties 'of a new type'. In his statement Engels also takes issue with those who call for abstention and for having nothing to do with 'bourgeois institutions', which is at the same time another side-swipe at the anarchists. Instead he calls on workers to defend and utilise the freedoms they have already won, like that of the press and of association. His attitude on this is strengthened by developments in Britain. This year, for the first time, sees an Act of Parliament introduced, guaranteeing legal protection for trade unions. It will give the unorganised and unskilled workers new opportunties for setting up their own unions.

Engels' work on the Commune, and in organising the conference as well as preparing contributions wins him an even higher standing internationally and he is elected as corresponding secretary for Italy, and as a member of the finance committee, then a month later also as corresponding secretary for Spain. His word gains even more weight as, in the following year, he is also given responsibility for the secretariats of Portugal and Denmark too. No doubt his linguistic facility on top of his political capabilities play a key role, but how he masters all these tasks is unimaginable. His portfolio of positions, though, also very much reflects the numerically small nature of the IWA at this time. It is still a modest organisation and largely made up of émigrés, however its political influence on left politics can not be underestimated. It does have a whole number of branches in several European countries and the USA, but in Spain and Italy, for instance, these are still dominated by the anarchists and anarchism continues to play a significant role in these two countries for many years to come, particularly Spain, up to and during the Spanish Civil War in 1936-39.

At the time of the London conference, Britain still has no federal council; the part such a body should play, is undertaken by the General Council in London. The latter has previously been against the formation of a special British federal council, because it believes an imminent social revolution in Europe will begin in industrial England. However, after the fall of the Paris Commune, it becomes clear that the first step on the road to workers taking power must be the creation of independent political workers' parties, and that the centre of gravity of the proletarian movement is being transferred to the continent. Marx is the foremost in recognising that it will be necessary to set up in Britain, as well as in other countries, a federal council, which may prove to be the germ of a British workers' party. The London conference, therefore, reversing the General Council's previous position, carries a resolution in favour of forming a British federal council.

The resolution is put into effect in October, 1871, when a temporary committee is set up in London under the chairmanship of Maltman Barry and with John Hales acting as secretary. As soon as the local branches of the International in Britain and the General Council have approved the rules drawn up by the temporary committee, a permanent federal council is elected. Many new branches are formed, and an ever increasing number of trade unionists rally to the International. In Ireland, too, the Association soon has its branches, in the defence of which the General Council takes up a decidedly militant attitude towards the British Government. However, the Irish organisations do not form a constituent part of the British Federation; they are directly under the control of the General Council.

Once the Federal Council is established it doesn't follow the path Marx and Engels have mapped out for it. Their ideological positions and domination of the General Council of the International are opposed by the leaders of the British Federal Council, which is looking for autonomy and is already adopting a reformist position, strongly opposed to Marx's and Engels' notion of class struggle. The first congress of the British Federal Council of the International meets in Nottingham on 21 July, 1872 and, perhaps surprisingly, declares, in accordance with the position of Marx and Engels, that an independent working-class party is essential to the conduct of the political struggle of the proletariat; it produces a programme which, generally speaking, is inspired by socialist ideas; and it urges trade unions to join the new workers' party and the International. But the organised workers view the International rather pragmatically. They look upon it primarily as an organisation capable of preventing the importation of cheap foreign labour, and able to assist in the struggle for electoral rights and the introduction of reform legislation. Nevertheless, certain tendencies become obvious at the Nottingham Congress which threatens to split the International. Thus, during the discussion concerning the rules for the British Federal Council, which are in general based upon those of the International as a whole, Hales proposes an amendment to the effect that the British Federal Council might enter into direct relationships with the federations of other lands and ignore the General Council. The amendment is adopted in spite of a certain amount of opposition. Another succesful resolution is aimed directly at the General Council. This motion proposes curtailing the powers of the General Council in the matter of the exclusion of such sections deemed to have infringed the rules and constitution. This is in response to the attempts by the General Council to expel the anarchists, whom a number of British trade union leaders view as allies in their opposition to Marx and Engels.

The 1871 Trade Union Act provides succour to the reform-minded faction. It gives British trade unions a legalised status for the first time, but simultaneously imposes grave penalties on those who promote strikes. It is, though, hailed by a number of trade union leaders as a tremendous victory, for it enables them to transfer their energies to peaceful organisation; it is the beginning of the era of so-called 'class-collaboration' which will characterise the whole period of working-class reformism up to the present day.

During the late 19th century British manufacturers are still continuing to flood the world market, and they find it an easy task to buy-off the working-class aristocracy, which at this time is still organised in craft unions. Engels also clearly understood that one of the reasons for the relative lack of interest in socialism during the late 1800s, after the demise of Owen's co-operative utopias and the eclipse of Chartism, was the fact that the British working classes benefited – even if only in the form of crumbs – from Britain's virtual world trade and industrial monopoly. In addition, there has also been a revival of industrial output following the banking crisis of 1866. The latter had greatly sharpened the conflict between workers and employers and led to frequent strikes, turning many workers towards the International; but then the industrial revival had the effect of sapping that new found militancy. It was felt that there was now an opportunity of gaining improvements without resorting to strikes and this provided the excuse for many leaders of the trade-union movement to abandon more militant action.

The fifth congress of the IWA is held in The Hague during September 1872 and this time Engels is delegated by the 'cleansed' section of the New York IWA. This congress becomes the venue for what proves to be the final showdown between Marx/Engels and Bakunin; the situation in the international movement is still festering and the whole IWA organisation will be jeopardised if these serious ideological differences are not settled once and for all. There had been a debate about whether to hold the congress in Switzerland, but Marx and Engels fearing such a venue would allow too many of Bakunin's delegates to be present [One of the most important centres of Bakuninist propaganda is the Jura Federation in Switzerland, and he has a strong following in Italy and Spain], they manage to persuade the General Council at its meeting on 18 June, to choose The Hague as the congress venue. Holland is easier to reach for those countries in which Marx and Engels feel sure of having strong support and they are able to persuade their comrades in the German Social Democratic Party to send a strong delegation. In response, Bakunin's supporters angrily accuse the General Council of being subservient to 'Pan-Germanic tendencies'. From June until August the General Council deliberates the proposals Engels wishes to put to the Hague congress. He hopes to take the wind out of the sails of the 'Anti-authoritarian' faction by proposing a complete re-structuring of the International, as formulated at the London conference.

The Hague congress also has to adopt a definitive position on what sort of action at a political level it wishes to advocate, and on this issue Marx and Engels and their supporters have the French Blanquists on their side. They propose that it is absolutely essential to build specific political workers' parties if workers are ever to take power, and power is essential to achieve the International's aim of social revolution and the abolition of classes. In Engels' view, if adopted, it will not only frustrate the anarchists but also the British trade unions which are advocating class reconciliation.

To begin with the prevalent feeling on the General Council is that the opposition will not even turn up in The Hague; the anarchists have already called for the holding of a special congress of their own in Switzerland. Engels is convinced that Bakunin's supporters, facing certain defeat, will not attend. But some do turn up, although the Italians are not among them. Engels clever orchestration of forces eventually wins the day and the anarchists are defeated.

The accreditation of delegates and representatives to conferences and congresses of the International had been somewhat arbitrary and this one is no exception. Many potential representatives simply cannot afford the travel costs; those that can or are geographically closer at hand, can often get themselves elected out of convenience. This leads to a lack of genuine democracy and appropriate representation for the various nations. Engels attends the congress together with Marx, his wife, his two daughters and son-in-law.

His presence at this congress is described graphically by the German Social Democrat and fellow delegate, Theodor Cuno (in his memoirs written in 1932):

> I knew Engels' face from photos, but in real life he was slimmer than he appears in his portraits. He was tall and gaunt in appearance, but with a healthy complexion, with sharply defined facial features a long, reddish beard and blue eyes. His movements and speech were quick and precise; he was able to convince those around him that he knew exactly what he wanted and what effect his words and gestures were having. In conversation with him one learnt much that was new and educational. His mind was a treasure trove of knowledge... [He goes on to add:] 'Marx was not such an effective speaker; Engels uses a conversational tone when speaking to delegates, lacing his speeches with much humour and sarcasm, reminding me more of student discussions'. [97]

Bakunin and his comrade James Guillaume are expelled from the International for 'conspiratorial activity' by a large majority decision. They respond by calling the whole process 'a comedy'. Their expulsion, though, is not the only sensation at the congress. The second one comes just as much of a shock but has deeper implications.

In his main speech, Engels calls for the headquarters of the IWA to be transferred to New York. His argument is that, although London has been a safe haven up to now, no other city on the continent can guarantee free speech and movement or provide a secure place to store documents; New York could provide that and the IWA has a strong network there. He argues that the headquarters of the International has been in London for eight years and a move will help avoid it becoming ossified.

Most delegates are dumbstruck by this seemingly perverse suggestion. The strongest opposition to it comes from the French Blanquists. They are depending on the vital support of the International in their planned attempts to lead the French working class movement and eventually, as they hope, to take power. Moving the headquarters to New York would reduce the International's influence in Europe to a token. But after a heated debate Engels' motion is carried. Both he and Marx hope that the move will ensure the survival of the International until such time as the working class movement in the various countries becomes less centrifugal and they hope the organisation can then be resuscitated in more robust form.

Moving the IWA's General Council to New York is also clearly aimed at making it exceedingly difficult for the European groups to continue their eternal debates and bickering. It is also a means of relieving both Marx and Engels of the tedium of attending long Council meetings where little of import is decided. Jenny Marx tells Liebknecht at the time that Marx is drowning in work: 'no peace day or night. How much better it would be for him if he had the tranquillity to work for those struggling by devoting his time to develop further his theory of struggle'.

Over the following years, despite the problems and effective marginalisation of the International from European struggles, Engels remains active in the General Council and writes comprehensive analyses of the European workers' movement; between the years 1869 and 1895 he writes over 14 lengthy reports for the International. On the basis of Marx's and Engels' theories, workers' parties are, over succeeding years, set up in numerous countries and help strengthen the IWA. The General Council continues its work in the USA until 1876, when its congress in Philadelphia agrees to dissolve the Association. The world situation has changed and the individual national parties need to develop and properly establish themselves; the function of the IWA as co-ordinator and promoter of those workers' parties worldwide has, it is widely felt, been fulfilled.

Already at the time of the Hague congress Engels had lost faith in the effectiveness of the International, as he writes later, in 1874, to Adolph Sorge in the USA:

> With the Hague congress it [the International] was indeed finished...For ten years, the International dominated one aspect of European history, that aspect in which the future lies,

> and it can look back on its work with pride. But in its old form it has outlived its function...The proletarian world is now too large and extended. I believe the next International will be, after Marx's writings have had several years to influence matters, decidedly communist and will, in effect, plant out our principles.[98]

Engels' role in the successful development and expansion of the various national parties can be measured by the range of his activities on the General Council. It is largely thanks to his clear sightedness, his organisational and theoretical abilities in promoting a single goal that has created the worldwide movement that will substantially shape the world during the following century.

Time for his own writing at last

Despite his increasing involvement in the day to day organising work of the IWA and advising the wider socialist movement, Engels continues his research and writing. In 1876 Wilhelm Liebknecht, the editor of the German social-democratic newspaper, begs Marx and Engels to write a fundamental riposte to the increasingly influential ideas of Professor Eugen Dühring, a blind, unsalaried lecturer at Berlin's university. Dühring is a relatively obscure intellectual whose nebulous ideas are filling the vacuum left by Lassalle's death.[99] Both Marx and Engels are angry and offended that they are being cajoled into arguing against what they see as confused and primitive thinking. Only when Liebknecht demonstrates to them how far Dühring's ideas are influencing the thinking of the social democratic rank and file, do the two realise that they have to respond.

Marx needs to devote all his time to completing the further two volumes of *Capital* and Engels has just begun to immerse himself fully in his scientific research. Reluctantly he tears himself away and sets about refuting Dühring's ideas. In a moment of rare bitterness, he upbraids Marx: 'You can thank your lucky stars,' he writes from his temporary refuge in Ramsgate, 'you can stay in your warm bed – examining specifically Russian land-owning relationships, and ground rent in general, and nothing interrupts you – but I'm supposed to sit down on the hard bench and swig the cold wine, immediately stop doing everything else and preoccupy myself with boring Dühring. Clearly I have no alternative'. Returning from

Ramsgate, he gets down to work immediately, writing his arguments straight down. The result is published as a series of articles in the social democratic paper *Vorwärts* and only later published as a book: *Herr Eugen Dühring's Revolution in Science* (1876) [known in the English-speaking world as: *Anti-Dühring*].

This polemic would be of only marginal interest today if it were not for its enormous political impact and role in promoting Marxism. Engels uses the opportunity to explain the basic ideas of dialectical materialism in a way that can be understood by all; it is a work of masterful clarity. His readers at the time are still largely unaware of the historical connections between economics, class and politics, and he puts his ideas across in a readily accessible language. In this way he breaks through the barrier that has kept his German compatriots largely in ignorance of his and Marx's theories. For the first time workers in Germany can now gain an understanding of how the on-going historical process and their own problems are interconnected and what political implications this has for the proletariat as a whole. This small work goes on to win many thousands to the ideas of Marxism, something *Capital* alone could never have achieved. However, Engels remains unhappy about taking on this hatchet job, and in a letter to his friend he says: 'They have really bludgeoned me into undertaking this thankless job – thankless, because the man [Prof. Dühring] is blind, so we are unequally armed, but then the colossal arrogance of the man prevents me taking any undue consideration'.[100]

Once he has completed this burdensome task, he returns once again to the more pleasurable pursuit of devoting himself to the natural sciences. It is in these years, from 1872 until 1882 that he begins to write the notes for what is later published in book form as *Dialectics of Nature* in 1925. Like any work dealing with natural science, it will become out of date very quickly with new discoveries and developments. Engels' would have undoubtedly revised it considerably had he had the opportunity. Much of it relates to scientific controversies of the day and, by the date of the work's publication these issues had been largely settled. Thus, the book is not significant for its insightful scientific knowledge, but rather for its holistic approach to science in general. He attempts to develop a dialectical methodology for dealing with the natural sciences. He is trying to discover the inherent laws governing material and its behaviour; his main source for this approach are the ideas of Hegel.

In essence it is an attempt to apply Marxist thinking to the natural sciences and a playdoyer for rationalism versus mysticism. It is also an attempt to demonstrate that the same dialectical laws of movement that can be applied to human history are equally applicable to all natural processes. 'Dialectics,' he writes, 'is for today's natural sciences the most important method of thinking, because it alone provides an analogue, as well as explanatory, method to comprehend the developmental processes taking place in nature, for the connectedness of all and everything, and a means of bridge-building between one research area and another'.[101]

Darwin is one of the first to elaborate the idea that nature is not a fixed entity, but in a continuous state of change, but Engels argues that this applies to all matter. In *Dialectics of Nature* he outlines the laws of movement governing the continuous process of change. Whereas Hegel saw the dialectical process as 'in our heads', Engels argues that our thinking is merely a reflection of genuine dialectical processes taking place in the material world. He defines the dialectic as 'the science of connections' or the 'general laws of all movement'. His aim in this book is to demonstrate that dialectical laws are developmental laws valid for the material world as a whole. He describes that world as in a continuous process of transformation, of becoming and dying, without fixed beginnings or ends. As the renowned biologist J.B.S. Haldane said about Engels' scientific writings in his preface to the 1940 English edition: 'Their interest lies not so much in their detailed criticism of theories, many of which have ceased to be of importance, but in showing how Engels grappled with intellectual problems'. For a man with only a formal high school education and largely self-taught, it is a tremendous achievement, not only in demonstrating the breadth of his knowledge in the natural sciences, but also in his grasp of the complex ideas that are taxing the brains of contemporary professional scientists.

However, the dialectical 'laws' he purports to find in physical and chemical processes could more accurately be termed 'principles' but even as principles they are controversial. Genuine laws allow us to interpret and understand phenomena otherwise inexplicable, but Engels' 'laws' could be more accurately characterised as descriptions of generalised observation, but not very useful in terms of their application in practice. In his attempt to apply Hegel's dialectical thinking to science rather formulaically, the result is perhaps not as illuminating or helpful as it could be. He does recognise, though, that whereas Hegel attempted to impose his thought processes on nature, it is really nature that determines our own thought processes.

His brief, unfinished essay, written in 1876 and entitled: *The part played by labour in the transition from ape to man*, is included in the *Dialectics of Nature* and is perhaps the most significant section of the book and of most relevance for us today. Engels' chief achievement in this essay is to emphasise the role of tool-making as a necessary precursor of humanity and of civilisation. He argues that the more complicated tool-making becomes, the more social interaction and co-operation becomes necessary, leading inevitably to the development of language. The physicist, J.D. Bernal felt that this essay is '...probably the most important part of the whole book because in it we find most definitely stated the view that man owes his uniqueness to the existence of society and that society in the first place is common labour'.

Although Engels' basic arguments here are undoubtedly correct in terms of the relationship between tool-making, social interaction and language development, in his supposition that adaptations by individuals are inherited by subsequent generations he reflects a Lamarckian position (i.e. believing that acquired characteristics can be inherited) rather than a Darwinian one, and it cannot be justified by scientific evidence. It is, nevertheless, an exciting piece of research which pioneers the idea that humans as intellectual and tool-making beings are products of social interaction. In this sense he not only demonstrates that society is essential in promoting individual development, but by implication that the idea of an individual without society is an oxymoron. He establishes that human beings are first and foremost co-operative animals and without co-operation our societies and civilisation would not have come about.

Dialectics of Nature is probably more of historical interest today than it is in terms of any unique scientific insights. It does, though, as Haldane says above, give us a graphic demonstration of how Engels grapples intellectually with problems and it is a classic example of the holistic approach that Marxists advocate: looking at phenomena in context and in their inter-connectedness, not studying processes in isolation.

In his authorised biography, Fidel Castro says 'I was very impressed by Engels' work on the history of the working class in England. I also remember very well...the *Dialectics of Nature*, where Engels talked about the fact that one day the sun would go out, that the fuel that feeds the fire of the star that gives us light would be exhausted, that the sun's light would cease to exist. And Engels wrote that despite the fact that he couldn't possibly have read Stephen Hawking's *A Brief History of Time* or know anything about Einstein's theory of relativity.[102]

Engels has long been a convinced atheist, seeing science as the antidote to mysticism and primitive belief. In his introduction to the English edition of his pamphlet, *The Development of Socialism from Utopia to Science*, in 1876, he writes: 'People in England believe in all sorts of impossible miracles and even geologists like Buckland and Mantell twist the facts of their science in order to avoid giving a slap in the face to the biblical creationist mythologists; it's incomprehensible that in order to find people who dare to use their intelligence in religious matters, you have to go to the uneducated, to the "unwashed hordes", as they were then called, to the workers, particularly the Owenite socialists.'

In their approach to the subject matter of social development, Marx and Engels are very much influenced by the scientific blossoming of the time and there is a steady stream of new ideas emerging on evolution, archaeology, physics and chemistry. This process began in France during the enlightenment, but is given new impetus in the 19th century by the discoveries of Darwin, Lyell, Pasteur, Koch, Bunsen and others. The ideas of creationism and faith in an omnipotent being are again, for the first time since the period of the Enlightenment, being seriously threatened by scientific investigation and rationality.

The Social Democratic Party in Germany

Certainly the biggest success internationally for Marx and Engels is the emergence of the strongest mass socialist party in the world – the Social Democratic Workers' Party of Germany. More than any other party at the time, the creation of this one in Germany and the elaboration of its political programme have been in no small part a result of their work. It is their ideas, above all others, that have been influential in forging the party ideologically. Several of its leaders over many years have also been intimate friends of the two.

Socialism and communism have always been viewed by the ruling classes as the biggest dangers to their power and privilege. In Germany the ruling class has become so alarmed by the rapid growth and influence of the social democrats that Chancellor Bismarck introduces his notorious 'Sozialistengesetz' [Socialist Laws] of October 1878, banning the party until 1891. Although this causes enormous problems for it on the ground, driving it into clandestinity, Engels sees it as positive in the long term: 'Herr Bismarck, who's worked for us for the last seven years as if we were paying him for it, now seems incapable of moderating himself in his efforts to accelerate the emergence of socialism'. He is right: In the Reichstag in 1871 there were only two representatives of the party, based on a vote of 3.2 percent, by 1890 this will rise to 35 with 19.9 percent of the vote, but by 1912, only 17 years after Engels' death, the party will win 110 seats (out of a total of around 400) with 34.8 percent of the vote.

These laws are implemented with such harshness and effectiveness that they cause complete chaos in the party. The trade union and left-wing political press is muzzled and many leaders driven into exile once again. They manage to publish newspapers, like *Die Laterne* and *Freiheit* from exile and copies are smuggled back into Germany. Social democratic candidates can still be elected to local councils or the Reichstag but only by standing as nominally independent candidates.

The government's enactment of these laws only underlines the fact that it is the socialists and their party that represent the true interests of working people. Since the suppression of the democratic aspirations of 1848/49 and the re-imposition of feudal hegemony, working people have felt unrepresented; the churches, too, have remained conservative and are largely identified with the ruling elite. In this sense, it is the socialists who have taken up the baton of the crushed 1848/49 revolution and are pointing a way forward. It is they alone who offer new hope and a vision of a society where workers will become the ruling class.

For German conservatives, the social democrats represent the 'enemy within'; they are the 'Vaterlandslosen' [those without a homeland] – a term that will be resuscitated and used again in a similar way, half a century later, by a certain Adolf Hitler. This accusation is vehemently rebuffed by Johann Jacoby, a Social Democratic member of the Reichstag, in his essay: 'The Goal of the Working class Movement': 'Your fatherland is for us only a place of misery, a prison, a hunting ground on which we're the hunted animals and where some of us don't even have a place to lay our heads. You call us scathingly 'vaterlandslos' and you yourselves have taken away our homeland'.

Although the anti-socialist laws banned the party and led to the ghetto-isation of the social democrats, it simultaneously strengthened their position. It forced the party to adopt new methods of working overnight. Newspapers had to be set up in exile and internally clubs and associations had to be quickly established - choirs, sports and discussion groups and funeral funds which also functioned as alternative working class social and political networks. In the party, Marxist dialectics come to replace traditional religious belief, particularly in the Protestant regions, although it is not so much the complex ideology that is the attraction, but more the idea of the 'last now going to be first' and the conviction of final victory.

The Social Democratic Workers' Party of Germany is founded in 1869, under the leadership of August Bebel and Wilhelm Liebknecht. Then, at a conference in Gotha in 1875 it merges with the Allgemeine Deutsche Arbeiterverein [General German Workers' Association], the party founded by Ferdinand Lassalle in 1863. The new party's programme is roundly criticised by Marx in his *Critique of the Gotha Programme* as being too reformist and not revolutionary enough. This is rectified at the next legal party conference in Erfurt in 1891, the first to be held on German soil after the anti-socialist laws are no longer being enforced. The programme agreed here is even more radical than the Gotha one, and more along the lines Marx and Engels are advocating, and it calls for the socialisation of all Germany's industries.

Despite the extremely difficult situation on the ground in Germany during this period, neither Engels nor Marx is sparing in their critical epistles to their friends, Wilhelm Liebknecht and August Bebel, offering advice, condemning their actions or lack of them. This infuriates Bebel and he replies acerbically to Engels: 'You living abroad have no idea of the difficulties with which almost every one of us has to struggle...' In view of their often pedantic and highly critical attitudes to their German comrades, it is amazing that Marx and Engels retain any loyalty among the social democrats there. Despite repeated overtures, begging them to write for the party, they refuse to do so on the basis that there is too much they disagree with, certainly until the Erfurt programme is adopted in 1891, but Marx is by then no longer alive. They also feel the party is coming too much under the influence of middle class elements that are diluting its proletarian character. They behave like two aged aristocratic spinsters, locked in their castle, rejecting every overture of marriage until the suitors have transformed their lives according to their wishes.

They have an almost pathological resistance to those who base their socialist convictions on a concept of justice, as a consequence of some abstract idea or principle. This attitude is odd, seeing that the early motivation of both of them was based on a hatred of injustice and the incomparable misery in which most workers lived. However, they argue forcibly that their own socialist convictions are based solely on the objective material forces driving the historical process, namely class struggle. In their intolerance of differing approaches to creating the basis for a socialist society and their vituperative lashing of those who think differently, one can see the germ of the sectarian in-fighting, the dogmatism and intolerance of dissent that will plague. communist movements of the twentieth century.

One can also detect the germ of that 'workerist' attitude that also emerges later, placing the worker on a pedestal and despising middle class and intellectual allies. Engels writes dismissively to Becker, a leading German social democrat: 'Altogether it is about time we stood up to the philanthropic haute and petit bourgeoisie, students and doctors, who are forcing their way into the German party and want to turn the class struggle of the proletariat against its oppressors into a diluted organisation for general human fraternisation'.

It is no doubt because they see the movement as a means merely of promoting and accelerating an objective process – not of procuring justice, based on abstract principles – that they refuse to be drawn into descriptions of any future 'utopia'. In all their work together they scrupulously avoid addressing in any detail what a future socialist or communist society would look like. However when their friend and leading German social democrat, August Bebel, publishes his book *Women and Socialism* in 1879, they have cause to wonder if they are perhaps wrong in their attitude. Bebel's book is an instant success and enjoys over 50 print runs, showing clearly that there is an avid desire for descriptions of the future society. Bebel in fact wins such standing in Germany that he is often referred to by friends and foes alike as the 'Gegenkanzler' [The opposition Chancellor].

Despite Engels' early profound disagreements with the German Social Democrats, his and Marx's perpetual cavilling and proffering of advice, does persuade the party eventually to adopt many of their fundamental principles. Thus, in the last years of his life, with great satisfaction, Engels follows every new victory by the party with avid interest and is fully supportive. The German Social Democratic Party of today, of course, just as the British Labour Party, has little ideologically in common with its original incarnation.

Lizzie's death

Engels' and Lizzie's move to London does little to improve her health even after several weeks, so Engels takes her on a series of spring and summer cures to Scotland, Ramsgate, Brighton and also to Germany, in the hope that it will 'see her through the winter', but even these do not achieve the hoped for results. In September Engels and Lizzie are at the coast in Ramsgate, where Marx's wife, Jenny and her children also join them. Here, despite their totally different backgrounds, Jenny and Lizzie become quite close to each other, undoubtedly assisted by Marx's youngest daughter, who has already formed a close attachment to Lizzie.

The presence in his house of Lizzie's wayward niece, Mary Ellen, who is little help or support and more of a continuous irritant, only aggravates an already difficult situation. Mary Ellen, never really settles in to London life in the Engels-Burns household. She has always been a bit of a tearaway and very egoistic. Even while in Manchester Engels tried to help her with her education. He persuaded Eleanor to teach her to play the piano and he also set her a strict course of reading, beginning, perhaps somewhat over-ambitiously, with Serbian folk ballads in translations by Goethe and then graduating to Goethe himself. These will not have been the easiest of tasks, but she is clearly bright and, despite the difficulties of the German language, masters to an admirable extent. Her general behaviour, though, remains problematic. Engels, particularly, finds her a disruptive influence and not a very helpful addition to the household. In desperation they decide to send her to a German boarding school in the hope that it will iron out her character somewhat.

In the autumn of 1875 Engels and Lizzie travel to Heidelberg and place Mary Ellen in a finishing school under a Fräulein Schupp. She is now 15 years old and is to remain in Heidelberg for a couple of years to provide her with the refinements they feel she needs. And, only a few months later, she is writing letters back home in a quite passable German. Two of Engels' German friends near Heidelberg have promised to keep an eye on the girl and give her support should she need it, and in 1876 Lizzie and Engels personally pay her a visit in Heidelberg.

Mary Ellen isn't able to complete the full two years in Heidelberg, because, despite the seaside holidays, Lizzie's health continues to deteriorate to such an extent that Engels requests Mary Ellen's help back home. On her return, relations between 'Pumps' and Engels show little improvement. She remains the somewhat tiresome girl, despite the kindness she has been shown in Heidelberg and despite her now more refined veneer. As is said of her, 'she is all sail and carries not an ounce of ballast'. Shortly after her return, she quarrels seriously with Lizzie and this offends Engels considerably, as both have been like parents to her. Ignoring their needs, she petulantly returns to Manchester to live with her own people. However, she very soon realises that even with her own immediate family, life is hardly a honey pot. She finds herself looking after three tiny children, working in her brother's fish shop and also looking after her father, who complains that he cannot afford to support her. Not long afterwards, despite refusing to apologise to Lizzie and Engels, she pops up again in London. Engels feels, though, that the salutary Manchester experience has done her 'a power of good'.

Lizzie now has 'pain everywhere' (probably rheumatism or arthritis of the joints). On walks she often holds the party back because she can only move very slowly, and housework is also a strain on her. Engels is obliged to help in the house more than he is used to: 'If you'd seen me yesterday evening making the bed and today lighting the kitchen fire, you'd have laughed', he writes to Marx. A malignant tumour in 1878 finally confines her to bed, and she realises she has not long to live. In view of her rapidly deteriorating condition, Engels finally relents and, after 16 years of living together, he officially marries her. He knows that being brought up a devout Catholic, she would be deeply fearful of 'meeting her maker as a sinner'.

A civil ceremony is impossible because the registrar cannot perform it at home and the process of posting the banns would take several days; and it is uncertain whether Lizzie will live long enough for it to take place, so she pleads with him to marry her in a religious ceremony. He sees little alternative but to organise an uncomplicated Christian wedding with a priest at home. Engels honours her feelings to the last, despite his own strongly held atheistic views.

She dies on the morning of 12 September 1878. The evening before, the Rev. W.B. Galloway from St. Marks Church marries them by special licence in their home. Lizzie is buried in St. Mary's (Roman Catholic) cemetery in Kensal Green, under a stone bearing a delicate Celtic cross and the monogram I.H.S above the words: 'In memory of Lydia wife of Frederick Engels born August 1827 died September 12th 1878 R.I.P'.

It is yet another severe blow for Engels. He lost Mary in 1862, now her sister, and with both of them he's enjoyed a comradely and mutually passionate relationship. Lizzie's death leaves a gaping hole in his life that no other woman is able to fill, but it doesn't manage to completely extinguish his optimistic nature and enjoyment of life. It does, though, represent a marked change in his personal life. He becomes even more aware of his own mortality and his slackening physical and mental resources.

Mary Ellen, to her own short-lived satisfaction, is now elevated to the head of Engels' household. 'Knighted' with the title of 'Pumpsia' as Marx puts it. Here she reigns with profound ineptitude for several years, earning Engels' affection and admiration, but not that of the Marxes.

Chapter Nine (1883-1895)
Life without Marx

Engels could not imagine that only five years after burying his partner Lizzie he would be giving another funeral oration in March 1883, this time for his life-long comrade, Marx. The year of Marx's death is also the year in which another future economic guru is born: John Maynard Keynes.

His friend's death is not simply a further blow for Engels; it is the amputation of half his being, but it also appears to reinforce his own resilience. He finds a renewed sense of determination in terms of his political work and in realising Marx's goals, as if the latter's death imposes an additional duty on him to complete his work. He does, though, often remark to friends how much he misses his old collaborator.

1883 is a significant turning point in the history of the working class movement, and the following twelve years after Marx's death are filled with an enormous amount of work for him. He now has to take on the leadership mantle alone and deal with an increasing interest in Marxist ideas as well as appeals for advice and help. He is, understandably, seen by most people in the movement as Marx's natural successor, however at no time does he attempt to portray himself thus, but always conducts himself merely as custodian of Marx's work. He never complains about the increased work load, but it clearly takes its toll. In order to master the demands, he imposes on himself a strict work regime: in the morning after waking, he breakfasts, undertakes a short walk, and from ten to five in the afternoon he works, then he eats dinner, holds 'business' discussions (which he understands as talks with comrades) and then there are visitors in the evenings; if he has a spare evening, he devotes it to correspondence and to editing Marx's unpublished manuscripts, authorising translations, as well as perusing the international press and new books.

Once the workers' movement in the USA begins its stormy upsurge, in the late eighties, he devotes Wednesday evenings solely to his 'American postbag'. On Sundays he eats his lunch at 2.30pm, after which he receives personal friends who 'must accept that on Sundays there is no opportunity for discussing business matters'.

London is the most suitable place for Engels to conduct his research work and maintain his international correspondence, and that's largely why he decides to stay put even after Lizzie's and Marx's deaths and despite urgent entreaties from his German comrades to join them in Germany as well as from Friedrich Adolph Sorge in the USA, recommending he move there. Engels also fears the uncertainty that such a move would entail. In this connection he writes:

> ...the question of emigrating to Germany, Switzerland or anywhere else on the continent, is answered by the fact that I refuse to go to any country from which I could be expelled'. [He goes on to reiterate that:] '...England has another great advantage. Since the end of the International there is absolutely no working class movement here apart from as the tail of the bourgeoisie...and now in my 63rd year with my back loaded with my own work...I'd be mad if I were to exchange my calm refuge here for a place where I would have to go to meetings and join in newspaper slanging matches, and of necessity this would muddy one's clear vision. Yes, if I were 48 or 49 I'd mount my horse again, if I had to. But now – a strict division of labour...[103]

In 1883, together with Eleanor and Marx's former housekeeper, Helene Demuth, who is now looking after Engels' household, he begins the huge undertaking of a first rough sorting of Marx's materials. 'It is an awesome task,' he complains and, 'I don't know how we are going to get through it'. They spend weeks combing through the enormous piles of papers, manuscripts, books and articles.

The lease on Marx's house at 41 Maitland Road is due to expire on 25 March 1884 and until the very last moment Engels and Helene Demuth are still rummaging through the papers. They find 'a whole lot of things that have to be kept, but about half a ton of old newspapers that it is impossible to sort'. Yet, they do manage to clear Marx's house by the deadline. It has taken a full year, twice the time envisaged, but there remains an incredible amount of sorting still to do. For Helene Demuth, too, it is a relief as Engels tells Laura: '...Nim [Helene Demuth] says that a huge weight has been lifted off her chest now that we've cleared the house; at last she can sleep soundly again. For her it was a nightmare which she couldn't even shake off by taking the occasional 'Irish' nightcap.' The six big trunks of material they save, are stowed in Engels' attic. The library is of particular value because many of the books contain Marx's notes in the margins; personal works and many of his books in English go to Eleanor, while Engels keeps the scientific and political core of the library. He is obliged to completely rearrange the furniture in his own house in order to store the trunks of Marx's voluminous papers and his books. He then pays Marx's landlord the outstanding rent and hands back the keys; the remaining furniture they put up for sale. In 1896, more than a year after Engels' death, Eleanor will write to her sister Laura: 'I believe the parcels that our dear old general piled up are still completely unsorted...'

Even with Marx's death, Engels' feelings of financial obligation to his family remain and his generous subsidy continues. In 1884 he gives Eleanor £50 for her honeymoon, but she feels uncomfortable about this, telling her sister Laura: 'Is it not too much? I feel quite unhappy about it...' Laura is probably surprised by her sister's qualms as she and her husband have no scruples about making regular demands on Engels for money, and these are always granted until they become so excessive that Engels actually feels obliged to put a stop to them after sending a last cheque for £100.

He immerses himself fully in the mountain of work Marx's death has bequeathed him. In comments he makes to friends during this time, he underlines this: 'devilishly busy'; 'for months now I've had no time'; 'enormous amount to do'; 'inundated with work' etc. He devises work plans for himself and central to these is the deciphering of Marx's writing, the editing and reworking of Marx's *Capital* manuscripts; 'The only work to which I really look forward,' he concedes.

This work is so exhausting that he takes a long holiday at his favourite resort in Eastbourne during August and September of 1883. However even here, a rest is hardly possible as he is accompanied by Helene Demuth and the Rosher family (Mary Ellen, her husband and their two children). He busies himself checking the proofs of Sam Moore's translation of *Capital* as well as trying to keep up with his correspondence. The one sitting room in the hotel where he can work is used by all the adults and Roshers' two small children. 'Just now the whole troop storms in, terribly thirsty,' he writes to Laura Lafargue, 'Jollymeier [Schorlemmer, who is visiting] has to open the Pilsner beer and you will understand that it's absolutely no use fighting such obstacles and deal with the heap of work in front of me ...the second bottle has just been opened, the little girl [Mary-Ellen's daughter] is crawling about my knees, and so I give it up in despair'.[104]

He only finishes the rough sorting of Marx's papers shortly before the lease expires on Marx's old house. Now he hopes to settle down and begin editing the second volume of *Capital* straight away, but his own landlord decides to repaint the front of the house, with the result that this work becomes impossible, as the late March winds rush in through the open windows, whipping up the papers on his desk and aggravating his rheumatism.

He realises that completing the second volume of *Capital* will take a huge amount of work as he writes to Johann Becker: 'Marx weighs every word on the gold scale, but I love this work – I am again together with my old comrade'. And later in the same letter: 'Over the last days I've been sorting the letters, 1842-1862. It quite conjures up the old times again and the fun we had with our enemies. I often laughed till the tears came, over the old stories; they could never drive the humour out of us; in between, though, some very serious things'. [105]

He no doubt finds it daunting once he discovers that his friend has completed so little of the work on Volume II. To a query from August Bebel, in 1883 as to why he wasn't aware of how far behind Marx was with the work on the second volume of *Capital*, he replies: '

> You ask how it came about that I, in particular, was kept in the dark about how far the thing was completed? Very simple, if I'd known that, I'd have given him no rest day and night until it had been completed and published. And Marx knew that better

> than anyone; he also knew that in the worst case scenario - and that has now come to pass - the manuscript would be published by me in his spirit; he even told Tussy [Marx's daughter Eleanor] that.[106]

As a result of sorting through and reading Marx's manuscripts and papers, he is stimulated to all sorts of thoughts and ideas. Some of these are developed and published as articles, letters or forewords to other works. What becomes a substantial piece of work is *The Origin of the Family, Private Property and the State*, already referred to. Much of the argument in this book is based on a comprehensive assessment of *Ancient Society*, a treatise by the North American anthropologist, Lewis H. Morgan that he finds in Marx's papers. He completes this study during the late seventies and early eighties. In fact, this will be the last substantial writing project he manages to complete before his own death. It is published in October 1884.

In his *Ancient Society*, Morgan asserted that societies develop in clear stages. This theory tied in neatly with Marx and Engels' own theory of historical development through class struggle. Marx, in his notes, and later Engels in his elaboration of them, relies almost exclusively on Morgan's accounts of the evolution of indigenous peoples and incorporates them into their own descriptions of the development of capitalist society. As a result of their work, many a left-leaning anthropologist or sociologist today will return to Morgan's writings. Within the field of anthropology his views are still controversial; some have championed his legacy while others have been vehement opponents. Undoubtedly his implicit condemnation of capitalism will have unduly influenced some to attack his theories.

Morgan's understanding of the role of property in the appearance of classes and hierarchies in society is amazingly prescient. Engels quotes him thus: "Since the advent of civilisation, the outgrowth of property has been so immense, its forms so diversified, its uses so expanding and its management so intelligent in the interests of its owners that it *has become*, on the part of the people, *an unmanageable power. The human mind stands bewildered in the presence of its own creation.*"[107] When we consider how governments and economists today are still awed and uncomprehending vis à vis sudden economic crises, trade imbalances and the vagaries of the market, this recognition of humanity's inability to control economic relations and the consequences that flow from that demonstrate the continued validity of Morgan's observations.

Alongside those like Herbert Spencer and Edward Burnett Tylor, Morgan was a proponent of social evolution. He viewed the evolution of human societies as a unilinear process, developing from primitive to modern. His evolutionary views of the three major stages of social evolution – savagery, barbarism and civilisation – are propounded in what became known as his best-known work: *Ancient Society*. These stages of social development, he argues, are divided by technological inventions, like fire, the bow and pottery during the savage era, domestication of animals, agriculture and metal working in the barbarian era and the development of an alphabet and writing during the era of civilization. Thus Morgan introduces a link between social and technological progress which also resonated strongly with Marx and Engels. He considers, as they do, that technological progress is a determining force behind social progress. Any social change, he says – in social institutions, organisations or ideologies – have their beginning in the changes of technology. His theory becomes an important milestone in the development of social Darwinism i.e. extrapolating Darwin's theory of evolution from species to societies. Engels develops Morgan's theories and incorporates them into a materialist conception of history and, building on Marx's notes, he emphasises the role of production in promoting human development.

What is particularly significant about *The Origin of the Family, Private Property and the State* is that in it Engels also pioneers an analysis of women's historical subservient role in society, how this came about and how it can be overcome. He is the first to demonstrate how an increase in wealth in society and the consequent rights of property, asserted by the physically stronger males, led to the overthrow of mother right (maternal dominance) and the emergence of patriarchy to ensure a father's sons would inherit any accumulated wealth. This accumulation of property led to strict monogamy, formal marriage and female subjugation. Increasingly, he explains, economics came to determine personal relationships; love and mutual attraction became subservient to economic factors. This understanding and his sense of outrage about 'bourgeois marriage' underlay his own refusal to marry, only acquiescing at the last minute out of deep sympathy for his dying partner.

'The overthrow of mother right *was the world-historic defeat of the female sex*,' he writes, 'The man seized the reins in the house also, the woman was degraded, enthralled, the slave of the man's lust, a mere instrument for breeding children'. He argues that only under socialism will women achieve full liberation from man's oppression.

There was, of course, already an ongoing, even if restricted, debate about the role of, and rights for, women, but no one before had attempted to explain how the denial of women's rights and their oppression had come about historically. Despite the pioneering work of Mary Wollstonecraft already in the 18th century and expounded in her book, *A Vindication of the Rights of Women* (1792), and the profound impact of John Stuart Mill's essay, 'The Subjection of Women', written almost a century later, in 1869, the rights and role of women in society had changed little. It will be, after all, almost another forty years before women eventually win the right to vote; in Engels' day they are still widely seen as the subservient and inferior gender, not capable of serious intellectual endeavour or rational behaviour. He challenges that perception.

Engels is kept from undertaking any more ambitious projects by the enormous amount of work he still has to do to complete *Capital*, on top of maintaining the numerous contacts with individual socialist parties,. After settling most of the important issues associated with Marx's legacy, he gets down to work on the manuscripts.

The two had already discussed *Capital* section by section, so Engels knows Marx's intentions and ideas better than anyone. But, nevertheless, he is appalled when he looks at the original manuscript: '...it's a total mess, with the exception of about two chapters. The illustrative quotations are not ordered, just thrown together in heaps, collected for later selection. Then there are the 'platterdings' [a form of Low German – he probably uses the expression to mean that Marx's handwriting is like a form of shorthand] that only I can read – and that only with difficulty...' He also finds that sections of Marx's text have been edited or changed by Marx himself, often several times, but it is not always clear which is intended as the final version.

Towards the end of May he begins to decipher the text and gain an overview of what it contains, but he has to do this in daylight only, to protect his eyes, which have been causing him reading problems of late. With the volume of work, he very soon realises that he won't be able to manage anymore by himself; he needs a secretary and so starts looking around for a reliable one. A social democrat émigré, Oskar Eisengarten, comes to the rescue. He is a trained printer and fled Germany after being charged under the anti-socialist laws for producing illegal leaflets. He is glad to have a job and proud to be associated with such an important task. For £2 a week, he works daily from 10.00am to 5.00pm, for almost one and a half years. Engels dictates to him and he writes it down in clean copy, and his writing is clear and legible. Engels then goes over this making last minute corrections before sending it off to the publisher in Hamburg.

'Since Easter,' he complains, 'I've slogged 8-10 hours a day, often at the lectern and as a result of my posture, my old problem has returned, but chronic this time, not in its usual sub-acute variant' [the hernia he suffered while horse riding in the sixties is now plaguing him anew]. Despite all the problems, he manages to prepare all the copy for volume two by the end of February 1885 and this is eventually published in July. Without pause, he immediately begins work on volume three. He tells friends he expects to be finished with this in a few months, as he thinks he's found Marx's finished manuscript, but this also proves to be an illusion. In actual fact this volume will occupy him for more than nine years. He is still confounded about how slow Marx worked. He writes to Laura Lafargue: 'It is incomprehensible how a man, who made such colossal discoveries, had such an extensive and complete theoretical revolution in his head could have kept them to himself for 20 years'.

By the autumn of 1888 he has completed a rough edit of volume three, but it still requires considerable fine tuning. By the end of 1893, he begins sending the manuscript to the printers in separate sections and by May 1894 the last copy is despatched. With the completion of the third volume of *Capital*, Engels leaves, as Lenin remarked, the finest monument his friend Marx could have, but it is really a monument to the work of both men.

Engels' role in building socialist parties in Europe

Throughout the work on *Capital*, he is continually distracted by demands on his time from around the world. He is asked to give advice, decide questions of dispute and become involved in debates on a myriad of issues; the international workers' press expects regular articles from him. He is, as August Bebel succinctly puts it: 'the international shop steward of the class conscious proletariat'.

Although he occupies no prominent position in any of the leading international organisations during the eighties and nineties, he is still treated by many as the de facto leader. But he never sees his role as giving orders or directives, and emphasises that 'I feel the only correct stance to take is to remain completely neutral and leave personalities completely out of the game. Otherwise it will be said that I am trying to steer the party from outside etc.' His main role is as an arbiter between the individual parties or factions. This is confirmed by Friedrich Lessner who said that 'you always got a short and clear answer from Engels, whatever question you asked, and he always spoke openly, whether one liked what he said or not. On certain proceedings in the party movement with which he was not in agreement, he would express his criticism immediately and without pulling his punches. He wanted nothing to do with suppositions and compromises. But then after you'd had a full and frank exchange of views about such uncomfortable events, he would be friendly again as if nothing had happened'.

His relationship to the various national organisations is now markedly reserved. He no longer attempts to impose his advice, giving it only when asked. Although a strong streak of intransigence is often revealed in his dealings with those who don't fully accept his interpretation of the political process. He is easily irritated by comrades who adopt a different position on general tactics, and the vitriol from his pen is allowed full flow. He is also not averse to using chicanery and occasional slander of individual activists if he feels it essential to further the cause, as he did in the International against Bakunin and the anarchists.

To gain an inkling of the intensive work Engels undertakes in the international arena, he leaves us his own description:

> I have to follow the movement in five large and a lot of small European countries and the US America. For the purpose, I receive three German, two English, one Italian dailies and from 1 January, the *Vienna Daily*, seven in all. Of weeklies I receive two from Germany, seven Austria, one France, three America (two English, one German), two Italian and one each in Polish, Bulgarian, Spanish and Bohemian; three of which in languages I'm still gradually acquiring. Besides that, calls of the most varied sorts of people...and an ever increasing crowd of correspondents, more than at the time of the International![108]

Much of the international work is now carried out behind the scenes, in the form of letters, articles and personal briefings. Engels refuses to take on leadership positions in any of the parties or to become involved in actively organising. He sees his main task as maintaining the 'doctrinal purity' of Marxist theory in those parties where it has taken a hold, and of promoting it where he sees a potential for it. Any workers' party worth its salt, he argues, has to be based on an acceptance of the class struggle and the economic realities of capitalism. Even at the risk of splits or becoming a minority group, this position must be maintained; unity 'at any price' is not an option. If the parties keep to the straight and narrow, then their time will come; patience is essential. This is the principle advice he gives all who come to him for help. In a letter to Bernstein he says, not without pride: 'we have been a minority all our lives and we have felt comfortable with it'.

During the last years of his life it gives him an immense feeling of satisfaction and achievement to witness the enormous expansion of socialist parties in Europe and the spread of socialist ideas, many based on Marxist theory. And he is, as indicated, not merely a passive observer of this process but is able to actively intervene and contribute. In all the advice and help Engels gives to European socialist parties, he refuses to be drawn into giving advice on specifically local questions or blueprints for action. In a reply to the Italian socialist leader, Filippo Turati, who is asking his advice he says: 'As far as general tactics are concerned, I have tested its [Engels' own analysis] effectiveness throughout my whole life and it hasn't let me down once. It is different in terms of its application to the contemporary situation in Italy; that can only be decided locally, on the ground by those who are in the thick of the process'.

He gives a similar reply to the American agricultural writer Isaak Hourwich, who asks him for an article on the role of the peasants in any future revolution in Russia. He tells him that, 'as an outsider' he is insufficiently acquainted with the details of agriculture and the situation of the peasantry in Russia to be able to speak authoritatively. He also complains to Hourwich about the way his and Marx's writings have been used by the émigré factions: 'If you follow the Russian émigré literature over recent years, you will yourself know how for instance sections of Marx's writing and letters have been used and interpreted in the most contradictory fashion by the various groups of Russian émigrés, exactly as if they were classical texts or from the New Testament. Whatever I could say about the issue you mention, would most probably, if it were given any attention at all, enjoy the same fate'. He also stresses that he thoroughly discards the idea of leading a revolution from abroad; it must come from inside Russia itself.

Towards the end of 1888 a Social Democratic Workers Party is also established in Austria with a Marxist programme, following the German example. The leading light behind this new party is the medical doctor, Victor Adler who soon becomes a close friend. Adler says that after his very first meeting with Engels his life took on a clear direction and purpose. When a number Austrian socialists in 1883 begin clamouring for a general strike to bring down their corrupt and reactionary government, Engels issues strict warnings not to use this dangerous weapon other than in exceptional circumstances. He advises the German party along similar lines. He stresses that all the years of hard labour, building up mass working class parties could be gambled away overnight if this tactic were to be implemented at the wrong moment, giving the rulers the excuse they need to impose draconian measures and suppress the movement.

Engels is not only intimately involved in helping the socialist parties of Germany and Austria, but also those in Switzerland, Romania, Bulgaria, Portugal, Spain, Hungary, Poland, Norway, Denmark and Sweden, as well as Russia. His role as patron, leading theoretical guru and adviser is unanimously recognised. He and Marx had long acknowledged the revolutionary potential in Russia and the impact a social revolution there could have on the rest of Europe. The lack of any meaningful agricultural reform in Russia during the eighties makes a revolution almost unavoidable he feels. The clamour of the nationalists and small groups of socialists for radical change in the country is mounting, and two of the leading Russian socialists, Leo Hartmann and Herman Lopatin are regular visitors to Engels' home in London. While he realises the potential, Engels is a little unsettled by the prospect of an attempted socialist revolution in Russia. As a backward and largely agricultural country, it is hardly an ideal place to attempt such a revolution, and according to Marxist theory, a socialist revolution can only come about on the back of a developed capitalist economy. Understandably, many adherents of the new socialist organisations are reluctant to accept the stricture that demands their country must first go through the long and painful process of building capitalism before attempting to create a socialist society. However, Engels does admit that 'their methods of struggle will be determined by their need, by the action of their enemies. As to the means they use, they are responsible to their people and to history', he stresses. He distances himself adamantly from those elements who resort to terrorism to achieve their ends: 'Those men who use this type of struggle without any need in western Europe are performing a schoolboy parody, trying to bring the revolution to its knees. They don't turn their weapons on the real enemies but against the public in general; these men are in no way successors and comrades-in-arms of the Russian revolutionaries, but their mortal enemies'. He hopes that the era of terror will give way to an open political struggle within a constitutional state, and is convinced that the continued development of capitalism in Russia will be more likely to force the Tsar to capitulate than individual acts of terror. He sees the impending Russian revolution as 'the next turning point in world history' but remains convinced that it will be a bourgeois revolution to begin with.

In 1883, the year of Marx's death, one group of Russian socialist émigrés in Geneva have set up the first real Russian socialist organisation based on the ideas of Marx and Engels. In 1892 a meeting of two of the factions of these émigrés is to take place in Engels' house in an attempt to forge unity. It is interesting that Engels tells the Russian socialists that 'The people who believe they have "made" a revolution always see by the next day that they were not conscious of what they did, and that this revolution bears no comparison with the one they intended. That is what Hegel called the irony of history'. How perspicacious in view of what will happen to the Bolshevik revolution. He is also uncannily prophetic when he writes to the Russian socialist, Nikolai Danielson in 1893, that 'the process of replacing some 500,000 farm owners and some 80 million peasants by a new class of bourgeois landowners can only be completed under terrible suffering and convulsions, but history is the most cruel of all goddesses and she rides her triumphal chariot over heaps of corpses, not only in war, but also in "more peaceful" economic developments'.[109]

Since the demise of the Chartists, his links with the British workers' movement has become tenuous. To Engels' great disappointment, this powerful mass organisation has not led to the creation of an established workers' party; most workers continue to support and vote for the established middle class parties, the Liberals and Tories.

In 1881 he is invited by the trade unionist George Shipton, the general secretary of the London Trades Council, to contribute to his new weekly, the short-lived *Labour Standard.* This he does with a series of leading articles. The paper is intended to help re-awaken an independent political workers' movement in the country. For five months, in his articles Engels tries desperately to rekindle a new politicisation of the working class in the spirit of the Chartists. He also contributes to the *Labour Elector*, a new London-based journal dedicated as an 'organ of political socialism'. On its team of collaborators are John Burns, Tom Mann and Keir Hardie. Through his articles, he attempts to win new adherents to the ideas of the *Manifesto of the Communist Party* and *Capital*, but in the end he withdraws his collaboration, realising it to be a fruitless task, as the papers are only reaching a miniscule readership.

In the early eighties, he is also wooed forcefully by Henry Hyndman, the Cambridge educated son of a wealthy businessman and founder of Britain's first socialist party, the Social Democratic Federation. Engels and Hyndman don't hit it off right from the outset. Engels finds him too full of himself and is, rightly as it turns out, sceptical of his ability to lead and promote a viable socialist party. Hyndman later refers to Engels as 'our Teutonic "Grand Llama of the Regent's Park Road," by reason of the secluded life he led and the servile deference he exacted', and went on to comment, 'though with respect to his writings I may claim on excellent grounds that I was the very first person outside Germany to give him full credit for the admirable work he had done for the movement independently of Marx. That, however, I was not wrong in my estimate of Engels' overbearing character and outrageous rudeness…'[110]

Even when the Federation inevitably splits and the Socialist League is formed under the leadership of William Morris and others, Engels remains sceptical about its potential, despite his respect for Morris as an individual. The same is true of the Fabian Society, founded in 1883. He remains aloof from the Fabians largely because they dismiss the class struggle, but he has great admiration for one of its members, Annie Besant, who plays a leading role in the East End match girls' strike. Engels realises that these organisations have been created by small groups of well-intentioned, middle-class intellectuals, but with no real connections to industrial workers and little prospect of being able to establish those essential links.

During the late eighties Keir Hardie's demands for the establishment of an independent workers' party are also gaining increasing support, and Engels, as a friend of Hardie's, is certainly fully informed of these moves. Hardie is a former miner, who rises to become secretary of the Scottish Miners' Federation. With the support of Robert Smillie, he begins actively campaigning for socialism, but soon realises that workers' interests will never be truly represented without their own representatives in parliament. In 1888 he stands, unsuccessfully, as an independent candidate in Mid-Lanark, later travelling to Europe to meet other socialists. He is also a good friend of Eleanor Marx, and she encourages him in his efforts to establish a workers' party. In 1893, as one of a small group of like-minded workers, he is instrumental in setting up the Independent Labour Party. At its opening conference, he is elected chairman and leader. In 1900, at a founding conference attended by around half of the unions affiliated to the TUC and most of the socialist groupings in the country, including Hardie's ILP, the Labour Representation Committee is formed. This eventually develops into the Labour Party. After a long battle to win a parliamentary seat, Hardie will finally become MP for Merthyr Tydfil in 1900 and will be one of only two Labour MPs in that Parliament. He becomes a champion of equality and campaigns particularly vehemently in the cause of women's suffrage. During the First World War, he is an outspoken pacifist.

Engels is certainly pleased to see the formation of the Independent Labour Party. At last, he feels, there is a party set up by workers with the prospect of becoming a mass party. He never accepted the widely held view that Britain has established a social peace between the classes. These new developments he sees as irrefutable proof that he is correct. The 'pragmatic British' are now joining the Germans and French. 'Once they know what they want, then the state, the countryside, industry and everything will belong to them', he informs various friends during the last few years of his life.

The Second International

He and Marx seriously underestimated the potential strength of the revolutionary movements in the less developed countries of Europe – as in Italy, Spain or Russia – and this mistake contributed significantly to their defeat in the First International. Engels comes to a belated realisation of this, and when a number of activists suggest resuscitating the International but on the basis of a federation of national parties, Engels is not over keen. He argues instead that it is more important for the various national parties to establish themselves on a firm footing first. Although he comes under increasing pressure from several directions to bring together a new International, in view of the rapid growth of the socialist movement throughout Europe, he is able to resist for some time. However, towards the end of 1888, he sees a danger of the movement threatened by splits, so does eventually agree to call for the setting up of the Second International. After more than a year of intensive preparatory work, with Engels drawing all the threads together, a call goes out in May and June 1889 to convene the Second International. In this work, he enjoys the close collaboration of Eleanor Marx-Aveling, who is also one of the key initiators and takes on a considerable amount of the organisation. It is she who also persuades Keir Hardie to attend the conference, which is held in Paris from 14-20 July 1889. The tremendous volume of work Engels gets through for the International alone is indicated by the fact that after his death the organisation is obliged to set up an office and employ five workers.

Despite the success of the Paris conference, it has proved impossible to heal some of the deep splits in the movement. Only in Brussels in 1891 is the rift with the (reformist) British trade unions healed, and the anarchists finally defeated. These successes are due in no small measure to Engels' intensive and persuasive lobbying, particularly of the German and French Marxists. There is, however, dissent over the idea of holding an annual international day of action on 1st May as part of the campaign for the eight hour day. The Germans and the British wish to make it the first Sunday in May, but the other delegates want it to be a day of work stoppage. A compromise is reached which recommends holding demonstrations on 1st May 'if local conditions allow'. That is why Britain, still today is one of the very few industrialised countries, that have no official May Day holiday; in true British fashion a belated compromise was reached by declaring a 'Bank Holiday' on the first Monday in May.

Engels at home

Engels' house, particularly on Sundays or on festive occasions always has visitors and conversation is entertaining and erudite. The German Social Democrat Eduard Bernstein, who is one of the regulars, writes in his recollections about a Christmas spent with Engels during the 1880s:

> Christmas was kept by Engels after the English fashion as Charles Dickens has so delightfully described it in The Pickwick Papers. The room is decorated with green boughs of every kind, between which, in suitable places, the perfidious mistletoe peeps forth, which gives every man the right to kiss any person of the opposite sex who is standing beneath it or whom he can catch in passing.
>
> At table the principal dish is a mighty turkey, and if the exchequer will run to it this is supplemented by a great cooked ham. A few additional attractions – one of which, a sweet known as tipsy-cake, is, as the name denotes, prepared with brandy or sherry – make way for the dish of honour, the plum-pudding, which is served up, the room having been darkened, with burning rum. Each guest must receive his helping of pudding, liberally christened with good spirits, before the flame dies out. This lays a foundation which may well prove hazardous to those who do not measure their consumption of the accompanying wines.
>
> In this connection I cannot help thinking of an evening at Engels' which preceded the Christmas celebrations. It was on the day when the dough, or rather paste, for the Christmas puddings was prepared. An enormous quantity was made, for there was not a single friend of the house who did not receive a Christmas pudding from 122 Regent's Park Road. Professor Karl Schorlemmer, Engels' medical adviser, Dr. Gumpert of Manchester, friend Sam Moore in Yorkshire, the old Chartist, Julian Harney in Jersey, Peter Layoff, the honoured leader of the Russian Socialists, as well as Marx's sons-in-law, Paul Lafargue and Charles Longuet in Paris, various intimate friends in London, and, if I am not mistaken, some friends in Germany as well, were always remembered...The concluding touch was given by Engels himself, who descended into the wine-cellar and brought up champagne, in which we drank to a merry Christmas and many other things as well. All this, of course, took place downstairs in the great kitchen, which enhanced the charm of the whole proceeding.[111]

Engels' home in London is a magnet for socialists and trade

unionists from all over the world. He has become the grand old man of the international movement, the man to consult, to listen to. Many come seeking advice, assistance or simply good conversation. Some of these visitors are regulars and become close friends.

Sundays in the Engels household, is a time for socialising and relaxation, the only day he doesn't work. With his close friends Sam Moore and Carl Schorlemmer he would open a few bottles of beer or go down to his well-stocked cellar for some good bottles of Moselle, Rhine or Bordeaux (which he prefers), or if there is a socialist election victory to celebrate, a bottle or two of champagne. With a few glasses downed, he would invariably break into song, recalling his old student songs or his favourite English song, The Vicar of Bray.

Most of those who gather around his table on such days are German comrades, but Edward Aveling and his partner Eleanor Marx (until she becomes estranged from Engels after Louise Kautsky moves into the house) are invariably among the guests. The leading German social Democrat, Karl Kautsky also becomes a regular visitor between 1885-90, along with his young wife Louise, mentioned above. Marx's second daughter, Laura and her partner, Paul Lafargue as well as Marx's other son-in-law, Charles Longuet come over regularly from France. Charles Bonnier, a lecturer in languages at Oxford, is also often seen at the house. He is a passionate Marxist, but an equally passionate Wagnerian and he and Engels have lively arguments about the importance of Wagner; Engels abhors this 'Music of the future' as he terms it.

The number of British visitors to his home is small and this is a sore point with Engels. But what he doesn't realise is that one of the chief reasons many from the British labour movement now avoid his house, is because of his closeness to Aveling, who they see, correctly, as vain and untrustworthy. The Webbs once remarked to Eduard Bernstein that in attacking Marxism they were really aiming at Aveling. Aveling was a smooth operator, a philanderer, not trustworthy in financial matters and not well liked in the wider socialist movement. He also double-timed Eleanor and secretly married someone else while still living with her. This will lead directly to Eleanor's suicide in 1898.

William Morris, the distinguished poet and artist, and leader of the Socialist League, is also an occasional visitor at the house, and Engels tolerates his infatuation with the medieval with patience and humour, because he recognises his other outstanding qualities and his genuine commitment to the socialist cause.

Among other British socialists who visit or consult him is Belfort Bax[112], a leading light in the emerging British socialist movement, with whom he enjoys hour-long discussions on the philosophy of history. The trade unionist Tom Mann, and the Fabians, Beatrice and Sidney Webb as well as George Bernard Shaw make occasional visits. His laconic view of the latter's political insight is contained in a letter to his friend Kautsky: 'The paradoxical belletrist Shaw – very talented and witty as a belletrist but absolutely useless as an economist and politician, although honest and not a careerist – wrote to Bebel that if they did not follow this policy [referring to the Fabians' call for workers to affiliate to the Liberal Party rather than form their own party] of forcing their candidates on the Liberals they would reap nothing but defeat and disgrace (as if defeat were not often more honourable than victory) and now they have pursued their policy and have reaped both'.[113] But to be fair, this comment was made before Shaw adopted a Marxist outlook and before he had written books like *An Unsocial Socialist* (1914) – an eloquent argument for socialism.

Engels, probably through Eleanor, gets to know the leader of the gas workers' union, Will Thorne. He is excited by the movement of New Unionism which Thorne represents because it is organising unskilled workers for the first time. He actively encourages Eleanor and her partner, Edward Aveling to involve themselves in this movement and inject some socialist politics into it.

Thorne was a barely literate gas worker, a member of the Social Democratic Federation, later becoming a branch secretary. He improved his reading skills with the help of Eleanor Marx, and in 1889, was instrumental in founding the National Gas Workers' Union (a forerunner of today's GMB), one of the prominent New Unions, later becoming its general secretary. He will also help organise the massive London dock strike of 1889. Thorne is a very welcome visitor. He later becomes a Member of Parliament for the Labour Party. Both Eleanor Marx and Engels think very highly of him. Engels gives him a copy of, the English edition of *Capital*, with a long personal dedication, and only the distance of his place of residence – the outskirts of London's East End – prevents him becoming one of Engels' regular guests. Another trade unionist who visits on a number of occasions is the engineer, John Burns. He is one of the first British artisans to join the socialist movement, later becoming a government Cabinet Minister. Engels is very well aware of his superior capacities and admires his proletarian 'instincts', but he bemoans the vanity of this undoubtedly gifted worker and trade unionist-turned-politician.

Engels is particularly enthused by the mass strike movement unfolding in Britain towards the end of the century, like the big dock strike, and the increasing involvement of new sections of unskilled workers. Skilled workers had been organised for some time, but clung to their reformist politics; the new unions were, it seems, made of stronger metal and were prepared to fight. Through Eleanor, who is intimately involved in the dock strike, he readily gives advice to the leaders. He writes that 'there is a completely new streak in them'. The old unionism still 'believes in harmony' [but] the young ones laugh at those who talk of an identity of interests between capital and work'.[114] He sees this new movement and its preparedness to fight and strike as an essential means of overcoming reformism in the British working class movement.

In 1891 he is emotionally overwhelmed by the enormous May Day demonstration in London. He is present on one of the wagons in Hyde Park, watching the massed columns of workers parading past with their colourful banners. He feels, somewhat prematurely, that the 'sleeping colossus' is at last stirring and that it will soon 'join the large international army' that is already marching on the Continent. 'What would I give if Marx could have witnessed this awakening,' he tells his comrade August Bebel, 'I carried my head two inches higher, as I clambered down from the wagon...The grandchildren of the Chartists are now joining the front line'.

Seeing that the international socialist movement is now more firmly established than ever and with a whole new generation of capable leaders, Engels feels he can take more of a back seat. He can now indulge more personal desires and decides to undertake, what he has always wanted to do but never allowed himself the time: foreign travel.

In the summer of 1888, together with Carl Schorlemmer and the Avelings he takes his first trip to the United States, where they spend a whole month. It is to be a short private tour of both the USA and Canada, and he demands total secrecy from all his friends, as he doesn't want to end up being besieged by socialists in America demanding his attention. He seeks primarily relaxation and diversion, but hopes to see a select few old friends too. During this trip Eleanor comments that she has 'never known him to be so well, or so lazy!' He spends five days at Niagara Falls and takes a short trip into Canada where he notes that the country is already 'half annexed [by the USA] in terms of its social relations – hotels, newspapers, advertising etc all following the American example'. Most of his time is spent in and around New York, where he also meets his 'nephew' Willie Burns (in fact one of Lizzie Burns' nephews from Manchester) who is enjoying the new life there. He also visits a prison in Concord, where he is impressed by the highly civilised standards he encounters: 'the inmates dressed like ordinary workers look you straight in the face without that "hang dog look" of your usual criminal prisoner'. He is suprised to find that the prison has a library, workshops, running water and paintings on the walls, conditions 'the like of which you won't see in the whole of Europe'.

Engels' observations are those of a very perceptive tourist and are certainly apposite, if sometimes very generalised. The Americans are 'more approachable than the English, but sometimes too direct,' he notes. He finds New York bubbling with its sense of destiny as the future centre of the industrialised world, but everywhere he sees 'advertising, intrusion, croupier types'. And Americans' down-to-earth pragmatic approach to life at the expense of aesthetic pleasures offends his European sensibilities. The primal drive for immediate profit, he feels, determines all else. The 'parvenu is the national character', he states. What is most alien to him, though, is that 'the Americans don't know how to take delight in things'. Despite these drawbacks, he recognises clearly that this will be the dominant nation of the coming century. In 1890, again with Schorlemmer, he visits Scandinavia and the Arctic Circle, and apparently Denmark on another occasion, but we have no detail of these visits. They are undoubtedly primarily for relaxation and enjoyment.

On 4 November 1890, with the death of Helene Demut, Engels loses an old friend and housekeeper. In the obituary he writes for her he says: 'By the death during the past week of Helene Demuth the Socialist Party has lost a remarkable member. Born on New Year's Day, 1823 [In fact New Years' Eve 1820], of peasant parents, at St. Wendel, she came, at the age of 14, into the family of the von Westphalens of Trier. Jenny von Westphalen in 1843 became the wife of Karl Marx. From 1837 to the death of Mrs. Marx in 1881, with the exception of the first few months of the married life, the two women were constant companions. After the death of Marx's wife and then of Marx himself on 14 March, 1883, Helene Demuth went to keep house for Friedrich Engels. The leaders of the Socialist movement bore testimony to "her strong common-sense, her absolute rectitude of character, her ceaseless thoughtfulness for others, her reliability, and the essential truthfulness of her nature".' In her will, she leaves everything (£95) to 'my son Frederick Lewis Demuth', born Henry Frederick, according to his birth certificate, on which no father's name is given.

Engels is not only someone who loves women as feminine and sexual beings, but despite his early youthful 'machismo', he later develops considerable respect for their abilities in the political field, as revealed in his valediction for Helene Demuth. At her funeral he tells the assembled mourners that Marx took counsel of Helene Demuth, not only in difficult and intricate party matters, but even in respect of his writings on economics. [He doesn't of course mention that he also took her to his bed] 'As for me,' Engels said, 'what work I have been able to do since the death of Marx has been largely due to the sunshine and support of her presence in the house.' Helene is buried at Highgate in the same grave as Marx and his wife.

During his youth, as reflected in his letters at that time, with their patronising attitude, to his sister Marie, Engels had little faith in women's political nous. This changed dramatically as he matured, no doubt also as a result of his contact with strong women like Mary, Lizzie, Helene and particularly the Marx daughters. Earlier, during an election to the London Schools Board in 1876, Engels, encouraged by Eleanor, 'casts all his seven votes' for the successful candidate, Mrs. Westlake. He declares that he thoroughly approves of women's entry into public office. Shortly after the Reichstag elections of 1877 he writes to a German lady: 'When we take power, not only will women vote, but they will be voted for and make speeches, which at last has already come to pass on the School Boards...moreover, the ladies on these School Boards distinguish themselves by talking very little and working very hard, each of them doing on average as much as three men'.

Engels, the charmer and lover of women, is clearly smitten by the young Louise Kautsky's élan and political passion. When she and her husband stay with him in London for a short time, he is immediately taken with her. When she, in 1890, tells him that she has separated from her husband, Karl and wishes to come and work for him, he is overwhelmed. She is only 30 years-old – 41 years his junior. She comes from an upper class family, but appears to have no qualms about taking on the lowly role of secretary-cum-housekeeper with Engels.

Once she communicates her desire to come and work for him and live in his house, he replies warning her of the possible repercussions. For a young single woman, other than a servant, to live in the house of an eligible widower would be viewed askance at this time. He urges her to take advice and think the whole thing over before finalising her decision. 'I love you far too much as to wish that you would make a sacrifice for me,' he writes. He signs the letter, 'in eternal love', an unusually passionate and 'unfatherly' expression one might feel. She ignores his warnings and is determined to come to London.

Louise arrives in the Engels household on 18th November, exactly a fortnight after the death of Helene Demuth. On 3 January 1891 he tells his comrade, Sorge, 'I can now work in peace again and better than ever, as she's also taken on the role of secretary for me'. Louise will stay with him for the rest of his life. He relishes her presence and they get on supremely well: 'she superintends the house and does my secretary's work which saves my eyes and enables me to make it worth her while to give up her career,' he writes. We have no real indication of how intimate the relationship between Louise and Engels is, and given the huge difference in their ages, it is most probably a platonic one only, but they clearly find each other's personality attractive and enjoy the other's company. The relationship appears to be more of that between surrogate father and daughter, as well as political comrades, than of lovers. Three years after arriving in Engels' house, she changes her name to Freyberger after her marriage to Dr. Freyberger in 1894 and her new husband also becomes one of Engels' firm friends.

In the short inter-regnum between Helene Demuth's death and Louise Kautsky's arrival on the scene, Engels' niece, Mary-Ellen or 'Pumps' again resurfaces and takes over the running of his house, but not to Engels' satisfaction; relations between the two, as ever, are fraught. She remains the wilful, undisciplined and manipulative woman she always has been, despite his generosity towards her, and with Helene now gone she sees her chance to take things over, only to be frustrated by Louise's coming.

On 28 November 1890 Engels celebrates his 70th birthday, and the house is inundated with greetings from around the world, but he dislikes being the centre of such attention and much prefers the role of 'backroom boy'. On this occasion 'Pumps' is drunk again. She is frightened that someone else could perhaps oust her and, as she confides to Louise Kautsky (before the latter is living permanently with Engels), that he may cut her out of his will if she oversteps the mark. She is manipulative and exploits Engels' sense of obligation to her unmercifully and in the house he is completely dominated by this 'drunken enchanter' as Eleanor describes her to her sister Laura. A few days after the birthday celebrations, Eleanor writes: 'He *does* love the tipsy Pumps, but for all that distance lends enchantment even to the tipsiness...He rages against Pumps - & loves her...How can I be friends with her when you say she is only counting on your death?' Louise asks. The love hate relationship is acted out against Engels' increasing attachment to Louise and he even gives stern lectures to 'Pumps' threatening to expel her from the house if she doesn't mend her ways.' But this never happens. Once 'Pumps' realises Louise is there to stay, she is spoiling for a fight, determined to get her out of the way. In this she fails miserably, and it is she who goes in the end.

In celebration of this 70th birthday, Eleanor is invited by an Austrian social democratic magazine to write a short essay about the 'acknowledged head of the present party'. This she does and writes with loving admiration of his unimpaired vigour of body and spirit, his lack of grey hairs and that 'he carries his six foot-odd so lightly...and although Engels looks young, he is even younger than he looks. He is really the youngest man I know. As far as I can remember he has not grown any older in the last twenty hard years...'

He later tells friends how excruciatingly embarrassing and unpleasant he found Eleanor's effusive paean, with its 'ghastly, nauseous adulation'.

Eleanor's sense of debt to Engels and her admiration for him is expressed above in perhaps hyperbolic terms. However, her description is probably not such an exaggeration as Engels himself writes to his brother around the same time boasting of his fitness: he has regained his maximum weight of twelve stone, and says he is 'all healthy firm muscular brawn, no flabby fat...'

Eleanor's close relationship with Engels – he is virtually a second father to her – is fractured in the last year of his life and both of them suffer under the resulting alienation. Eleanor doesn't get on at all with Louise, Engels' new secretary and housekeeper, who she feels is influencing Engels negatively and spreading gossip, although this has not been substantiated. Her perceptions are more likely to be the result of jealousy as much as anything.

In 1881 'Pumps' has an affair with a certain Percy Rosher, a flighty, accountant and would-be small businessman, and becomes pregnant. Engels pressures Rosher to marry her. Such action contradicts his known dismissive attitude to marriage as a bourgeois institution, but his own personal interest may have triumphed here over his principles – he doesn't want to be lumbered with his niece plus an illegitimate baby. But if this is his intention, it back-fires. Once Rosher's business attempts end in failure, the whole family ends up moving in with Engels anyway. He accepts the situation with stoicism, even though it is also a financial burden and causes considerable friction in the crowded house, but he enjoys playing the devoted 'grandparent' to their young daughter, whose conversation, Marx acerbically remarked at the time, is more interesting than her mother's.

Some time afterwards the Rosher family emigrates to Canada, but soon returns again to London, unable to establish themselves there and 'Pumps' once again attempts to ingratiate herself with Engels, relying still on his generosity. She remains ungrateful though, despite his continual indulgence of her whims. She even complains bitterly after his death that she has not inherited more of his money, despite his generous endowment [In actual fact he leaves her £3,000, a not insubstantial sum at the time]. She was clearly always more interested in his pecuniary potential than in his person.

Engels' changing views

There is still much debate and confusion among Marxists as well as non-Marxists as to interpretations of Marxist theory. This is not surprising, as all great thinkers change and modify their ideas over their lifetime. Does one take as definitive an early interpretation or a later one? Engels is no exception and a number of his statements in the last decade of his life could be seen as contradicting, or at least qualifying, earlier positions. While Marx and Engels clearly established a new way of analysing society and of understanding the historical process, they subsumed into their thinking ideas from many of their forerunners and contemporaries. Clearly Hegel provided the fundamentals, but the utopianism of St. Simon and Fourier, Proudhon's ideas on the role of the state, Owen's co-operative concepts, all find a place within their overall theory. These different elements are stressed at different times.

It needs emphasising that Engels doesn't see communism as the final and utopian end of human development as many of his followers have implied. In *Anti-Dühring*, he stresses that the process of becoming is endless; there is no final stadium of human development. He fully accepts Hegel's dictum that there can be no final and absolute truth and no absolute or final stage of human development. In accordance with his understanding of science, he is also certain that the world as we know it will eventually become uninhabitable and reach a 'pretty certain end'. Here we can discern in Engels a certain contradiction between the political optimist and the scientific pessimist. His materialist outlook though convinces him that if life can be created once, then it can, and will be, created again and again.

When he talks about communism, in no way does he envision the sort of centralised and authoritarian states that characterised the 20th century attempt at building a communist society. He views communism as an era in which everyone will take responsibility for their own socialisation and control those alien forces that have ruled their lives until now. He describes it thus: 'Only from then on will mankind be able to create its own history in a fully conscious manner and those social causes it sets in motion will, by and large and to an increasing extent, achieve the effects it desires. It will be mankind's leap from an era of necessity into an era of freedom'. Without the knowledge to consciously forge our own societies, he argues, we remain victims of outside forces and career from one crisis to the next, unable to predict or correct what is happening to us. His vision is of an all-embracing liberation, an end to exploitation of man by man and a form of co-operative justice in which humans finally take control of their own destinies. He also polemicises against those who are attempting to suggest that the economic basis of a society determines everything else in a mechanistic one-way process. As Marxist theory is increasingly finding new adherents around the world, he already detects a certain dogmatism creeping in and an oversimplification of the ideas he and Marx have developed –

arguments about 'correct' interpretations of the texts and an increasing preparedness of their followers to apply the theories as eternal truths. In a letter to Joseph Block he writes:

> We make our own history, but first under very specific preconditions and circumstances. Among them the economic ones are, in the long run, decisive. But also the political etc., yes even the traditions that have hold on people's minds play a role, even though not a decisive one...
> The laying of undue weight on the economic side than is its due, is something the younger ones are doing nowadays, Marx and I are ourselves partly to blame. We had to emphasise this main principle in the face of our opponents' denial of it, and there was not always the time, place or opportunity to do justice to the other interacting moments involved...
> According to a material understanding of history, the determining moment in the history of production and reproduction is, *in the last instance,* real life.
> Now if anyone distorts that sentence to the extent of making the economic moment the only determining factor, then they transform it into a meaningless abstract and absurd phrase. The economic situation is the basis, but the various moments of the superstructure – political forms of class struggle and their results – constitutions established, after battles won by the victorious class etc. – forms of justice and even the reflections of all these real struggles in the minds of those taking part in them, political, juridical, philosophic theories, religious beliefs and their further development into systems of dogma, also have their impacts on the unfolding of historical struggles, and in many cases will largely determine their form. It is a recipricocity of all these moments. In the end it is through all these myriad incidentals (i.e. from things and events, whose inner connected - ness may be so distant or unprovable, that we can take them as not there or ignore them) that the economic movement, as a necessary force, asserts itself. Otherwise applying the theory to any arbitrary historical period would become more facile than solving a simple algebraic equation.[115]

In these later writings, Engels gives his clearest views on how he feels the theory of economic materialism should be understood. In so doing, he grants that he and Marx probably overemphasised their most contentious central principle of the role played by economic forces in history. This they had to do in order to gain credence for their new theory against the widespread scepticism and hostility they encountered; they emphasised too strongly the emergence of ideological positions from economic fundamentals. In doing so, he admits they 'stressed content to the neglect of the formal side': how and why these ideas come about was not sufficiently considered. He becomes increasingly worried that his and Marx's ideas are being interpreted as gospel truth and are, by some, being applied like ready made templates to contemporary reality, according to which that reality has to conform, rather than using the ideas as tools of interpretation.[116]

We can also find in Engels the seed of what will come to characterise prevalent attitudes in many communist and socialist parties in later years – a distrust of intellectuals. He clearly expresses his fears of the increasing influence of 'Literatentum' [the literary world] [117] as he calls it on the proletarian parties. He feels the influence of this group to be more motivated by personality than by a view of themselves as servants of the working class.

Inner party democracy is another issue that begins to concern him at this time, particularly in the now successfully growing Social Democratic Party of Germany. To Wilhelm Liebknecht he writes: 'If one has to expel anyone [from the party] then only in those glaring cases where there is clear and provable evidence of deep treachery'. And at the same time he is also concerned about moves to create a monolithic thinking in the party: 'The largest party in the Reich cannot flourish without all tonal nuances finding full expression in it', he says.[118]

Engels takes an active part, through letters, articles and advice, in the drafting of the new German Social Democratic Party's programme adopted at its conference in Halle in 1890, when Marxist theory is formally adopted. In this same year the party – now able to contest elections as a party again – gains 27.2 percent of the votes. In the discussions around the draft programme he refutes one section in which it states that 'the number and misery of the proletariat will steadily increase'. He argues that such a statement is too absolute and that because of the increasing strength of working class organisations in Europe, the workers will be able to wrest concessions from the factory owners. What he does stress though is that there will be an increasing insecurity of employment.

He also wishes to see emphasised in the document that in France, America or Britain, where there is a greater degree of constitutional democracy, it should be possible to build socialism peacefully. He wishes to have it noted that workers could only assume power from within a democratic society, but at the same time he rejects the reformist argument that working class power could be achieved through a slow infiltration of the system or by piece-meal dismantling of the old.

With the perceived danger of the rulers in Germany and even in France using force to clamp down on the growing workers' organisations, there is an undercurrent of murmurings calling for a pre-emptive strike by the workers and taking power by force. Although Engels is still convinced that the ruling class will resist the revolution with all means possible and that armed resistance on the part of working class organisations may become necessary, he dismisses romantic ideas of fighting on the barricades as in the past, particularly in those cities, like Paris and Berlin with wide, open avenues, ideal for well-drilled state troops, but not for irregular soldiers. He also knows full well that weaponry has advanced considerably since he was involved in the revolutionary struggle in 1849. 'The revolutionary would have to be crazy to choose to involve himself in a battle of the barricades in one of Berlin's new working class districts', he tells his comrades in the German Social Democratic Party. This caution on Engels' part leads some on the left to accuse him of going soft and becoming a reformist himself. His chief concern, though, is to prevent the socialists from taking a fatal step which could set the movement back decades. He is sure a rash and adventurous move would be just what the conservative forces are waiting for in order to strike back with an iron fist.

In the nineties, one of his chief concerns is to ensure the implementation of resolutions carried at the Second International. In his correspondence with socialist parties, he emphasises the need to fight on issues such as the demand for an eight-hour-day, international solidarity and the establishment of 1st May as an international holiday of the working class. He attends every big rally for the eight hour day in London, and reports with pride that on the London May Day demonstration of 1891, when he is present on one of the podiums, that 500,000 people are gathered in Hyde Park in a magnificent show of working class strength. Such demonstrations convince him more than ever that the working class is now in a position to impose genuine social change if it wishes to do so.

Increasingly, during the last years of his life, he also dedicates considerable effort to the struggle for peace, which he now views as an essential prerequisite for the emancipation of working people. The last book he writes, two years before his death, *Can Europe disarm?* puts forward disarmament proposals, exceptional for the time, and still valid today:

> I am writing this on the assumption that it is increasingly gaining recognition that the system of standing armies in the whole of Europe has been taken to such an extreme that whole peoples face economic ruin as a result of the military burden or it will certainly degenerate into a war of general extermination, unless the standing armies are transformed beforehand into a general armed people's militia. I am attempting to prove that this transformation is already possible, even for today's governments and in today's political circumstances...if these armies remain in place, it will not be for military reasons, but for political ones, in other words the armies are not there to defend against an outside enemy but the enemy internally...The gradual reduction of conscription periods by means of an international treaty is the cornerstone of my proposal, and I believe it is the simplest and shortest route to achieve the gradual change from standing army to an armed people's militia.[119]

Such a proposal is revolutionary for its time, but is also far-sighted and prophetic. He proposes a disarmament conference between the great European powers, but his appeal, unsurprisingly, falls on deaf ears. Of one thing he is certain: any new European war will result in 'mass killing of unbelievable. proportions and finally lead to the collapse of the old system'. He realises that the nations would battle to total exhaustion in their fight for economic supremacy. Less than three decades later Europe is indeed confronted with the senseless slaughter of the First World War and the use of troops to quell workers' revolts in a whole number of countries, including Britain. The First World War is fought over the spoils of the colonies and economic domination of world trade, not for national defence purposes.

In notes he makes at this time he also predicts that after such a war: 'American industry would be victorious everywhere and confront all of us with the alternative: either retreat into pure agricultural production for the home market (any other would be prevented by American wheat) or social transformation'. In view of what he sees as the danger of a pan-European war, Engels undertakes a frenetic campaign to promote disarmament and the dissolution of standing armies. He still hopes that international worker solidarity will bring down remaining feudal systems in Europe and thus hinder an all-out war between nations. The former does come about, but not the latter.

The looming military threat to Europe also encourages him to return to his military studies in order to examine possible outcomes. Although he would like to think that out of the carnage of such a war the workers' movement would emerge all the stronger, he nevertheless hopes passionately that it can be avoided. He vacillates between seeing war as conducive to a rapid demise of the capitalist system, to one of scepticism about the immediate repurcussions and the virulent nationalism it would undoubtedly unleash. On 22 December 1882 he writes to Bebel:

> I'd see a European war as a catastrophe. This time it would be dreadfully serious. Chauvinism would be everywhere enflamed for years, because each nation would be fighting for its own survival. The whole work of the revolutionaries in Russia, who are now perched on the cusp of victory, would be destroyed for nothing; our party in Germany would be inundated by a flood of chauvinism and fragmented; the same would happen in France.[120]

He sees that the workers' movement across all European countries is growing and gaining strength; war, he feels strongly, could only be retrogressive and push the movement back to the margins again for years to come, and also mean that it would have to be built from scratch again.

In 1887, in an introduction to Sigismund Borkheim's brochure: *Zur Erinnerung für die deutschen Mordspatrioten 1806-1807 [In memory of the German Arch-Patriots 1806-1807]*, Engels writes with prophetic vision about the coming war:

> Germany will have allies, but Germany and its allies will ditch each other at the earliest opportunity. And finally there will be

> no other war possible for Prussia-Germany than a world war, and it will be, in fact, a war of such inconceivable extension and fury than we have ever known. Eight to ten million soldiers will murder each other and at the same time the whole of Europe will be turned into a desert, worse than a locust swarm could accomplish...

He goes on to describe the horrors of past wars and concludes:

> That is the prospect if this system, taken to its extreme, of each nation outdoing each other in arming for war, finally bears its unavoidable fruits. That's the way it is dear Lords and statesmen, that's where, in your wisdom, you've brought old Europe. And when you have no other alternative than to begin the last great war dance – it's alright with us. The war may push us into the background for a short while, may tear from us some achievements. But when you have unleashed the forces that you can no longer control, may it go as it will: at the conclusion of the tragedy you'll be ruined and the victory of the proletariat will be either achieved already or will be unavoidable.[121]

No one else is predicting this sort of development. In fact some contemporaries accuse him of being unnecessarily negative and actually call him a 19th century Cassandra. He feels strongly, however, that if the workers' parties in the various countries can unite around a common position, as proposed by the International, then war can still be avoided.

At the same time he is savouring every small victory for socialist parties everywhere, but particularly in Germany where the party is most successful. He celebrates at home with friends each election win and he takes personal delivery of each telegram that arrives, reading them aloud to the assembled company. In his papers there are, from the parliamentary elections of 1893 alone, 83 telegrams from the main electoral districts. As he has to respond to these, he remarks, jokingly: 'This whole thing is becoming too expensive for me; the Social Democrats are now having too many electoral victories'. This flippant comment belies his unbounded generosity; most payments he receives from articles published in the various countries, he donates to the individual parties. Only five months before his death, he is able to view the future with equanimity, convinced of the certain victory for the Social Democrats in Germany. He believes that as long as the party can continue organising and growing within even a limited democratic framework, there is nothing that can stop its onward march; only an act of adventurous stupidity, followed by a coup by the feudal oligarchy could do that.

As Engels understands the centralisation of capital and the continuous cycle of economic crises, he is sure the capitalist system will be plunged into ruin in the short or longer term. The proletariat, as a result of the increasing impoverishment and ruin of the middle classes, will increase geometrically, he argues, and towards the end only a few millionaires will exist and the rest of the population will be proletarians and will easily take control, and the lever for the proletariat to take power is the class struggle.

Apart from his prediction of the workers taking power (which of course did happen in Russia in 1917, but did not outlast the century), much of Engels' prediction is being validated, when we view the increasing wealth disparities in today's world and the trend to global monopolisation. He is, though, unlike many of the so-called Marxists who follow in his and Marx's wake, not a dyed-in-the-wool determinist. He reconciles this brutal and historically necessary truth with his own deep-seated and almost instinctive classical idealism in that he believes the working classes can either remain subservient to the system and descend into a more profound barbarity or fight for their own dignity and humanity. In this sense, he sees class struggle as the only means of preventing such a descent into barbarity, but nothing is a foregone conclusion. Certainly it makes more sense than 'philanthropy and charity', he argues.

When Engels, a few years before his death, writes a new foreword to the second edition of his youthful work *The Condition of the Working Class in England*, it is aimed at a new unphilosophical generation and he feels he has to justify the fact that the book emphasises that the roots of modern socialism lie in German classical philosophy and he lays great weight on the fact that communism is not simply a party doctrine of the working class, but has as its goal the freeing of the whole of society.

Modest to the end

In 1892 Engels' great companion, Prof. Schorlemmer dies and early the following year, his friend and GP, Dr. Gumpert. Apart from Sam Moore, these are the last of his intimate friends and contemporaries.

Their departure underlines once more his own tenuous mortality, particularly as his own health is becoming increasingly fragile. He is also seemingly isolated; his closest friends are now gone and he has very few links anymore with the British working class or with the newly emerging trade union movement. He is also cut off geographically from what is happening in Germany. The comrades there have repeatedly tried to coax him to return to Germany, but he has resisted.

Now the anti-socialist laws are no longer in force in Germany, his close comrades begin pressurising him once more to return to see for himself how the country has changed in the intervening decades. He had planned such a trip in 1892 but his old hernia still plagued him so he postponed it. In 1893 he is fit enough, and travels there with Louise and her husband Dr. Freyberger. Beforehand, he convalesces in his favourite resort at Eastbourne, to recuperate and gain strength for the long trip. The last visit to his homeland was in 1876, when, with Lizzie Burns, he visited 'Pumps' in Heidelberg.

As the train travels towards the Rhine and the steeples of Cologne's cathedral rise above the horizon, he no doubt recalls Heine's poignant verses describing his own emotional return to Germany in *Wintermärchen* [*Winter's Tale*], and particularly the stanza:

'But see! There in moonlight
The colossal fellow
Soars upwards, devilishly black
That's Cologne's cathedral'

Engels is also overcome by the emotion of this return journey. 'This beautiful land, if only one could live in it', he exclaims nostalgically. He is met in Cologne by the leading Social Democrat, August Bebel who escorts him for the rest of his trip. 'The continent has undergone a complete revolution since I was last here,' he remarks after his first few days. After his whistle-stop tour of Germany, he spends a fortnight in Switzerland, where he also meets his brother Hermann, before going on to Zurich. He arrives there in mid-August, towards the end of the International Socialist Congress taking place there. He is greeted with a standing ovation by the delegates and celebrated as the 'founding father' of the international socialist movement. Some of the delegates have corresponded with him over the years or read his works, but have never met him before.

During his stay he also meets up with Eleanor Marx who is one of the delegates.

Despite his age – he is now 73 – he still retains a keen eye for vivacious young women. He is obliged to give an audience to a group of Russian women comrades, several of whom have 'wonderfully beautiful eyes' and he is given a warm kiss by Vera Sassulitsch, a fiery revolutionary figure who gained fame (or notoriety) by shooting a despotic Tsarist governor. 'But my real darling', he admits, in a letter to his brother Hermann on16 August, is 'a lovely Viennese factory girl, exceedingly attractive to look at and charming in her manner'. This is Adelheid Dvorak, later Popp, who goes on to play a leading role in the Austrian workers' movement. He regrets, he says jokingly, that Bismarck did not annex Austria as part of Germany, 'if for nothing else, then for the Viennese girls!'

He is made honorary chairman of the congress and can't resist closing the final session himself. He is jubilantly cheered as a legendary figure by the delegates from all the countries represented. But all this adulation and attention, as usual, causes him considerable discomfort, and as ever, in his final address, he emphasises that he was only a mere collaborator of the real founder of the movement: 'Out of miniscule sects at that time, socialism has grown into an all-powerful party, which now causes the whole world to quake. Marx is dead, but if he were alive today, there wouldn't be another man in Europe and America who could look back on his life's work with such justified pride. We are now a great power,' he concludes and 'that is my pride - we haven't wasted our lives'. After the emotionally uplifting, but also draining, travels around Germany and then the euphoria of the Zurich congress, he is happy to return to his tranquil refuge in Regent's Park Road at the end of September.

If I go to the continent again, he writes to his friend Adolph Sorge, I will demand written assurances that I won't have to be paraded before the public. While he is amazed at the generosity of his welcome, he prefers to leave such public shows to 'parliamentarians and professional public speakers': 'that's part of their role, but hardly part of my work'. Once back home, he immediately gets down to work on the third volume of *Capital* again, and then he hopes to return to his research on the German Peasants' War.

Even during the late eighties, although his health and his strength are slowly ebbing, his behaviour and temperament are still those of a young man and remain so almost to the end. Only about a year before his death does ill-health take its toll, and he ages rapidly. Even then, he doesn't want to recognise or accept it, as he writes on 18 December 1894: 'As to myself, I have nothing to complain about, but I realise that I am 74 and not 47 anymore.' And in January 1895 he admits: 'that I can't take all the liberties with food, drinking etc anymore; I'm not as weatherproof as I used to be'.

He is still determined to witness the 'big collapse' and the working class taking power, at least in the most significant European countries. 'The events must help us,' he tells the Russian philosopher, Piotr Lavrov, in December 1894, 'to keep our vitality; the whole of Europe is in fermentation; everywhere the crisis is maturing, particularly in Russia. It can't continue much longer there'. And in a similar vein, on 3 January 1895 he writes to the old Mainz communist Paul Stumpf: 'I crave just to be allowed to peek into the new century, around 1 January 1901, but I'll be totally worn out by then and it can take me away'.

Engels has withstood the normal ravages of ageing, but is unprepared for the fatal cancer that eventually takes him away. In May 1895 he becomes aware of the first indications of this, and begins to complain about splitting headaches, sleeplessness and an inability to work. The tumour on his neck is growing but he still imagines (or vainly hopes) it to be benign and can be dealt with by a small operation. Despite the cancer that will end his life in only a few months, he remains amazingly sprightly. Those who visit him at this time speak of him still as the 'jovial Rhineländer', full of humour, vivacity and mental acuity. In February he reported that 'my health is better than ever...I sleep my seven hours during the night and work gives me pleasure'. Even when he realises that he has a tumour, he doesn't let it depress him – his doctor keeps its terminal condition from him – but bears it with stoicism and even humour, calling it 'the potato field in my neck'.

In an effort to recuperate and avoid the busy life in London, in June Engels takes a break in Eastbourne on the recommendation of Dr. Ludwig Freyberger, who keeps a close watch on him and visits daily in Eastbourne, but the sea air brings no betterment. In the end, Freyberger finds it impossible to keep up the pretence that the tumour is a minor matter. Although he doesn't give Engels the full and dire dianosis, he states later that it is cancer of the oesophagus in the final stages, a diagnosis confirmed by Dr. Victor

Adler, the renowned Viennese doctor and leader of the Austrian social democrats.

Samuel Moore writes with deep concern to Eleanor on 21 July 1895:

> I felt very anxious about how the General was getting on, so I went to Victoria Station to await the train that leaves Eastbourne at 7.15pm and the one usually taken by Dr. Freyberger. I met him and I'm sorry to say that his report is anything but cheering; he says that the disease has attained such a hold that, considering the General's age, his state is precarious. Apart from the diseased glands of the neck, there is a danger either from weakness of the heart or from pneumonia – and in either of these two cases the end would be sudden. He may go on for some weeks if pneumonia does not intervene, but if it does then it will be a question of a few hours. In spite of it all, however, the General is quite hopeful and is certain he will recover – he intends, and has arranged with two doctors, to return to London on Wednesday evening – so that if you want to see him you had better go to 41 Regents Park Road on Thursday. This is sad news and I trust the doctors may be mistaken. There is so much work to be done which the General alone is capable of doing; that his loss will be irreparable from a public point of view – to his friends it will be a calamity.[122]

In the last letter Engels is known to write, and in his usual flippant way of dealing with his own ailments, he tells Laura on 23 July that they are returning to London the next day and that 'there seems to be at last a crisis approaching in the potato field in my neck, so that the swellings may be opened and relief secured. At last!' before going on to report on the British elections and the loss of Keir Hardie's seat. On 26 July, with apparent total peace of mind, he adds the final codicil to his will.

On 29 July 1893, in the company of his old comrade Friedrich Lessner, his new GP, Dr. Ludwig Freyberger, the second husband of his secretary and 'lady of the house', Louise Kautsky-Freyberger, he draws up his final will. In it he makes generous provision for Marx's two remaining daughters and their children, as well as support for other friends and comrades. The will is written while he still has full control over his faculties, but he is very aware that his days are now numbered, as he writes in a note to Marx's daughters: 'And now farewell my dear, dear girls. May you live long, in bodily and mental freshness and enjoy these.' And to Bebel and Singer in Germany, he writes: 'Make sure that you get the money and when you have it don't let the Prussians get their hands on it. And when you've decided what to do with it, open a bottle of good wine to my memory'. In leaving the money to Bebel for the Social Democratic Party, he describes it as a 'donation for electoral expenses' to avoid the payment of inheritance tax.

At the time of his death, his whole estate is valued at a little over £25,000. The royalties from his most successful work, *The Condition of the Working Class in England*, he leaves to its translator into English, the American, Florence Kelley. Kelley is the daughter of a US Congressman, a leading socialist and early feminist writer. And although he was unhappy with her rather wooden translation and had to rewrite much of it himself, he is clearly grateful for her efforts. Perhaps surprisingly, he leaves nothing to Marx's illegitimate son Freddy Demuth.

Only on his death bed does Engels confide in his friend and the executor of his will, Sam Moore, that Marx is actually the father of Freddy Demuth. Among Marx's and Engels' intimate circle it has been assumed that Engels is the father of Helene Demuth's illegitimate son. He hasn't disabused them of this belief in order to save Marx's marriage and protect his reputation. However, he clearly doesn't wish to die and have accusations bandied around later, of his supposed dalliance and abandonment of 'his son'. Moore feels obliged to tell Eleanor, who is flabbergasted by the news, and refuses to believe it, demanding that he asks Engels once more to confirm this, which he does. Still not convinced, she insists on hearing it from Engels' own lips. This becomes her first visit to his house for several months. She became estranged from him during the last year of his life, largely due to the influence over him, as she saw it, of his secretary and housekeeper, Louise Kautsky-Freyberger with whom she does not get on.

Louise, in a letter she will write three years later to August Bebel in 1898 recounts the episode:

> On Sunday, the day before he died, General himself wrote on his slate that Marx was Freddy Demuth's father. Tussy broke down

> when she left the room. All her hatred of me was forgotten and she wept bitterly on my shoulder. Moore, after Engels told him, went to Eleanor – she sent him back and he reconfirmed; she demanded to hear it herself but Engels was no longer able to speak. General authorised us (Mr. Moore, Ludwig [Louise's husband] and myself) to reveal the facts only if he were accused of having treated Freddy badly.[123]

Doubts were cast on the truth of Louise's statement for some time, before it could be corroborated. She knew Freddy (but not his parentage) as a weekly visitor to see Helene Demuth in Engels' house – he always used the back entrance, so as not to attract attention. Helene told Louise that he was 'her admirer'.

Eleanor can hardly believe that her beloved father had been involved in an adulterous relationship and kept it secret from them. However, she does go on to develop a close and warm relationship with Freddy and he reciprocates with fraternal fidelity. It is questionable whether they would have hit it off so intimately if they hadn't been closely related, as their cultural backgrounds and intellectual levels were very different.

Thankfully, Engels' suffering is relatively short and he dies peacefully in his bed at home in London on 5 August 1895. As he has requested, the funeral is strictly private. The executors of his will and family Freyberger maintain a strict secrecy and invite only personal friends from the international workers' movement and his relatives. Around 80 people come to the Necropolis near Westminster Bridge where a short ceremony is held. Despite the summer warmth and sunshine, the mood is one of deep sadness. Everyone is acutely aware that with Engels' death, not only has a colossal individual being been lost to humanity, but a whole era has come to an end.

Eduard Bernstein, the leading German Social Democrat, describes Engels' subsequent cremation in his recollections: 'His body was reduced to ashes at the Woking crematorium, which lies about an hour's distance by rail from London [at that time, crematoria were still few and far between – burial being the usual option]. It was decided that the funeral procession should accompany the body only as far as the Waterloo terminus. It was a gloomy day on which the burial took place, and only about a thousand mourners, the great majority of whom were Russian-Jewish workers, took part in the procession...I spoke on behalf of the German, and Peter Kropotkin on behalf of the Russian Socialists.' Among the 60 odd guests, Will Thorne, Harrry Quelch, Eleanor Marx and Edward Aveling represented the British socialist movement.'

In 1895 obituaries for Friedrich Engels are carried in 150 different European newspapers, condolences flood in from around the world. Two weeks before he dies, a young Russian social democrat is on his way via Paris to visit the great man in London. The latter's deteriorating health makes it impossible for him to do so. Thus history lost the chance of recording a meeting between Vladimir Illych Ulyanov, known as Lenin, and the man who, with Marx, was the inspiration for the successful revolution he led.

Engels' literary legacy is, to begin with, given to August Bebel to look after and it is kept for a long time in the archives of the German Social Democratic Party and then, a few years after Bebel's death, in the house of Eduard Bernstein. After the latter's death in 1932 it goes to the party archive of the German SPD, but then, just before the Nazi attack in 1933, it is taken abroad to safety. In 1935 the Prague party executive sold all the papers to the International Institute for Social History in Amsterdam. It survives the Second World War and Nazi occupation and is still held there today. Unfortunately the materials in the possession of Eleanor Marx-Aveling were not kept together after her suicide in 1912 and are now scattered in various collections. Most of the original documents relating to both Marx and Engels are now held either in the International Institute for Social History in Amsterdam or the former Institute of Marxism-Leninism in Moscow.

In his will Engels expressly wished, 'that my corpse be cremated and my ashes, at the first opportunity, be buried at sea.' He wanted to avoid the danger of any hero cult developing around a grave, and this wish accords with his conviction that the only life after death is as free molecular building blocks for other organisms. He wants no posthumous glory and no shrine. His close comrades carry out his wishes. On a blustery morning on Tuesday 27 August, Eleanor, Aveling, Lessner and Bernstein travel to Eastbourne, 'the pleasantest seaside place', as Engels described it. There they hire a small boat and row through the grey choppy waters almost straight out from Beachy Head, to consign his ashes to the ocean. Even in death his self-effacing modesty is upheld: he wanted no monument other than the coming socialist revolution.

Chapter Ten

The terrible twins

Marx and Engels were both physically impressive in very different ways: Marx thick set and swarthy with full beard, Engels tall and slim with a military bearing. Seeing the black and white images of these stern-looking Victorians, or even delving into one or two of their dense tomes you could gain the impression that they were both dour and impenetrable German academics.

In the *Communist Manifesto* they talk of a 'spectre haunting Europe, the spectre of communism', but they too became spectres haunting the sleep of capitalists and unnerving the comfortable and monied middle classes everywhere. They are indeed, for their putative enemies the 'terrible twins'. That image has also been compounded by their many humourless and sometimes ruthless followers. Yet, this assessment would be far from the truth. Both men had an immense sense of humour, enjoyed a good laugh, a childish prank and risqué jokes, as revealed in their letters and recollections of their contemporaries. When Eleanor was only 14, she recalled that Engels 'was the life and soul of every party and every group in which he found himself.' Marx's son in law, Paul Lafargue, refers to Engels as 'my ever laughing Engels'.

Since their second meeting in Paris in 1844 until Marx dies in 1883 – 39 years – they remain on the most intimate of terms, collaborating politically and in literary matters as well as socialising with gusto. This friendship, with one small but important episode, is never shattered or disrupted. They are like Siamese twins; one without the other is unthinkable. History has scarce an example of such a friendship and collaboration. There are none of the usual petty envies, competition or jockeying for leadership. In terms of their approach to research and writing, as well as style, there was, though, a considerable difference.

Both are linguists and masters of language. Engels, though, is impulsive, energetic and sometimes hot-headed and gives the impression that he hasn't spent undue time cogitating over an idea or style; he works quickly and without reticence; his writing is flowing, elegant and translucent, easily comprehended. Marx, on the other hand, is slow and meticulous; he will spend hours thinking before setting pen to paper and then incessantly edits and re-edits what he has written. Marx attempts to incorporate his whole intellectual store cupboard in what he writes; he thinks on the page, revealing a bumper harvest of ideas and concepts; he writes epigrammatically and structures his ideas dialectically, making few concessions to the reader. This makes translating his works adequately an almost impossible task. Engels admits to his German socialist friend Bebel that he learnt first from Marx 'how to work methodologically'.

Engels picks up concepts and ideas quickly; he immediately puts pen to paper in the heat of his discoveries. For a man of action, this is often a positive attribute. Marx on the other hand, needs time to cogitate and will often ask Engels' advice before finally writing his thoughts down. Engels' advice on the political level is undoubtedly more useful than any philosophic advice he might have given, as Marx has, in this area, a more profound knowledge and understanding. Engels has an advantage over Marx in that he is fully conversant with politics and commerce. He has first hand experience of large industrial processes and has been able to make detailed observations of a modern proletariat, how it actually exists as a class. In this sense, he is the ideal partner for Marx, who brings the ability of abstract thinking, generalising and systematic rigour to refine the ideas and goals they both have. Even in the area where Marx achieves his greatest fulfilment – political economy – it is Engels who, certainly to begin with, is very much the feeder. It is undoubtedly he also who pushes Marx in the direction of investigating the role of private property and the contradiction between the humane phraseology of capitalism's apologists and the inhuman practice of the free market system. It is Engels who explains to him how economic crises occur and the minutiae of capital accumulation and concentration. In a certain sense Engels is the activist who takes his struggle into the study; whereas Marx begins in the study, only to join the street fighting later. Engels' rebelliousness and thirst for freedom could be detected already during his youth, ignited in the first instance by religious conviction and classical literature. His sense of justice turns him into a man of action.

Considerable evidence of the depth and intimacy of their friendship is contained in the extensive correspondence between the two – over 2000 letters have been saved, but there was probably double that number originally. Unfortunately, in terms of acquiring a complete picture of their relationship, we have lost a considerable amount of more personal correspondence, in the letters destroyed by both Engels and Eleanor Marx to avoid hurt to living persons or damage reputations. Barely a week went by during their friendship without at least one exchange of letters between the two. This correspondence was their elixir. Eleanor remembers how her father 'spoke to the letters as if the writer were present...but most of all,' she says, 'I remember how Moor sometimes laughed over the letters, until the tears poured down his cheeks'. Engels and Eleanor herself also correspond avidly, particularly after Marx's death, but these letters too have disappeared.

In the example Eleanor describes above, the correspondence certainly offers a clear antidote to the idea of the two being 'humourless lefties', as their letters are littered with jokes and humorous remarks. Many are written in that linguistic mish-mash typical of bi-lingual expatriates, but with these two it is not just the two languages, English and German, but Latin, French and occasionally with Italian or Spanish phrases. Many of their letters are concerned with gossip about fellow émigrés and political associates or enemies and here both of them are invariably derogatory and sarcastic when writing about any of them, apart from their few very close comrades.

They both suffer if more than a day passes without hearing from the other. Engels writes on 29 Jan 1851:

> Your silence and your astonishment at my silence became suddenly explicable to me when today my old witch of a landlady, after some sharp cross-examination hunted out your letter of 7 inst. from among a pile of books in my room where it had been peacefully slumbering since 8 January. I happened to be out that evening, and this person had simply placed the letter

> on top of the books; later, when tidying up, she had in her haste put another book on top of it, and as that pile of books has remained untouched all this while, the letter might, without your reminder, have gone on slumbering there till Doomsday. Had I been studying Russian this month instead of physiology, this wouldn't have happened.[124]

Marx responds flippantly: 'Is it on Mary you're studying physiology, or elsewhere? If the first, I can understand that this *n'est pas de l'hébreux* [isn't Hebrew] nor even *Russian'*. Some sense of their visceral need for each other and reliance on the other's thoughts and ideas is contained in the following short extracts:

Marx writing to Engels (24 Feb 1857): 'Dear Engels, are you crying or laughing and are you sleeping or are you awake? To the various letters I've despatched to Manchester over the last three weeks I've had no response. I am assuming they arrived.'

Engels to Marx (20 May 1863): 'Moro viejo, Moro viejo, el de la vellida barba (Old Moor, old Moor, with the bushy beard) What's happening with you, seeing as I hear nothing either about you or your fate or deeds? Are you ill or locked in the depths of economics? Or have you appointed little Tussy as your correspondence secretary? Or what?'

On the death of his beloved son, Edgar, or 'Musch' as he is affectionately known, Marx writes (12 April 1855): 'Under all the terrible tortures I've gone through these last days, the thought of you and your friendship has kept me on my feet and the hope that, together, we can do something to bring a little sense into the world'. Or again, later: 'I can't thank you enough for the friendship with which you do my work for me and for your sympathy for the child'. And a final example: 'Dear boy, under all these circumstances, one feels more than ever, the good fortune of having such a friendship, as the one we have. You know, from your side, that, for me, no other relationship is more important'.

Their correspondence also reveals the enormous range of interests and knowledge they both had, from politics, science, anthropology, fine art to Celtic folk song and philology. After Marx's death, Engels himself hopes to write his own biography of the man, but he never finds the time to do so, as his main goal is to order and edit Marx's manuscript of the second and third volumes of *Capital* (before he dies Marx expressly indicates that Engels should take this on). A biography would 'demand that people stop interrupting me,' Engels notes despairingly, 'but when will that be?' The answer is, sadly, never, so even this potential source of intimate detail is lost to us.

Paul Lafargue, in his reminiscences writes:

> It was a celebration for family Marx when Engels signalled a visit from Manchester. They would speak about it for some time beforehand and on the day of his arrival Marx became so impatient, that he was unable to work. The two friends then sat smoking and drinking the whole night together and spoke through everything that had taken place since their last get-together. Marx respected Engels' opinion more than anyone's, because Engels was the man he saw as capable of being his collaborator...Marx is proud of Engels. He speaks with satisfaction about all the moral and intellectual qualities of his friend...he admired the extraordinary multi-faceted range of his scientific knowledge; he is worried about the smallest accident that could befall him. "I always shudder," he said to me, "when I think that he could have an accident on one of his hunting outings, in which he takes part with such passion, galloping across the fields, taking every obstacle".[125]

Engels, though, takes no heed of Marx's concerns and continues hunting with the Cheshire Hunt and riding well into his sixties. He even, on one occasion when Marx is visiting, persuades the latter to join him in the saddle. Afterwards he writes to Jenny: 'Moor has been riding for two hours and has been so invigorated by it that he is beginning to feel enthusiastic about the cause'. There is no record, however, of Marx riding again; physical exercise is for him a waste of valuable time and not his idea of fun.

Engels' nature, certainly in the early years, is not of the sort that allows him to sit for hours in the library, even though he loves books and study; he is more interested in people and discussion, in forging contacts and organising. Despite his lack of formal academic training compared with Marx, his intellectual breadth is phenomenal and his ability to immerse himself in new areas of learning seems infinite; he can make more use out of a few spare hours than others could with a whole week.

He always maintains that he is not a great theoretician and doesn't possess the necessary patience and endurance for detailed and long-term research that Marx does; the latter also has an ability to synthesise facts and ideas. Engels knows that he can deliver useful building blocks and help in defining the fundamentals, but he could never alone build the whole edifice. He says of Marxist theory: 'without him [Marx] the theory would not be what it is by far. That's why it justifiably carries his name'. But he goes on to say that 'both during the establishment and in the elaboration of the theory I had a certain independent input'.[126]

Engels' immense admiration for Marx may have caused him to exaggerate the latter's contribution; it is difficult to know. He invariably hides his own light under the bushel: 'That which I was able to contribute – with the exception of in a few specialised areas – Marx would have managed to do without my input. What Marx achieved, I would have been unable to do'. Despite Engels' generosity here, it is unlikely that Marx's achievements would have been possible without his friend's input.

While Marx is writing *Capital*, they correspond, exchange views and discuss every aspect of the work, from the nature of surplus value, profit to ground rents and agricultural processes. Engels often harries Marx to get the work published, demanding to know why it's taking so long. He realises the urgent need for the burgeoning socialist movement to have a sound theoretical basis that, he hopes, *Capital* will provide. The letters also document the continual and steady financial support Engels provides for Marx and his family, but also the vital assistance he gives Marx in his journalistic activity, particularly in terms of specialised research.

Despite his material help, the Marx family still endure a life on the edge of destitution throughout their lives and stumble from one crisis to another. Some idea of Marx's often desperate straits can be garnered from the several letters where he begs Engels to send him some stamps so that he can write or send him papers he can't afford.

Marx's wife, Jenny von Westphalen, comes from an aristocratic family; the half-sister of the Prussian Minister for Internal Affairs. She finds it exceedingly difficult, if not impossible, to run a household along working class lines, commensurate with the reality of her husband's financial situation. She has never had to live like a working class woman; her desire to maintain some kind of status and standards are understandable, but are to an extent also responsible for Marx's continuous indebtedness. His income just can't pay the bills for a family even with only modest middle class aspirations.

In 1855 the situation can hardly worsen. In November Marx's son, Edgar, dies; the landlord is threatening to withdraw the lease on the house, as the rent is badly in arrears; Laura is ill and rapidly losing weight; Tussy has a severe bout of measles; Jenny has diphtheria and there is no coal! Only one person can rescue the situation. Engels immediately sends £15, some bottles of port, sherry and claret – the usual medicines, regarded by both of them at the time as the supreme remedy for all kinds of bodily ills. In order to economise, the Marx family moves to a more modest house at 9 Grafton Terrace in Kentish Town – a 'mean little house' according to Mrs. Marx, but actually a substantial town house on four floors – but the family's debts continue to mount. In January 1857 Engels agrees to provide the family £5 a month to ensure a modest, but regular income – an amount that is soon increased as yet one more crisis follows the other in the Marx household.[127]

Engels continues to provide this support despite being sued in that same year by an outraged Manchester citizen (see below). He not only helps the Marx family with cash but with regular crates of wine too. He manages to do this on top of the financial help he also gives to Mary and Lizzie and the extended Burns family.

Despite all the help, the Marx family fortunes are still at a low ebb and in December 1859 they gather around an imaginary Christmas tree, with hardly any food to grace the table, to drink the champagne Engels has sent them. Engels himself, while certainly having a materially easier life than Marx, is not living in luxury either and in his letters he often expresses regret that his purse is empty and he will only be able to send funds at a later date. But he appears to have given all this support unstintingly and willingly.

There is no evidence we have, either from friends or enemies to indicate that he ever resents Marx's reliance on his financial support. And in an early version of a will Engels writes, he leaves all he owns to Marx, should he die first. Never is there a reticence about asking for help, nor is there ever a reprimand for making too many demands – such sacrifice and support is taken for granted in their friendship.

Through letters and documents it is estimated that Engels gave Marx around £3,000 between the years 1851-69 alone, and that is on top of contributions he gave to other individuals and to organisations. Between 1854 and 1859, he tries to ensure that he at least maintains the monthly £5 to supplement the Marx family budget. Once his contract with the firm is placed on a more secure footing in 1862, he increases the sum to £10 per month.

From 1865, he makes sure that Marx has enough money to enable him to finish his work on *Capital*, whose completion has been delayed time and again. It is only in this period, and in connection with the completion of *Capital*, that their letters indicate any sort of agreed division of work. And, towards the end of 1868, when he is certain his contract with the company is drawing to a close, he arranges for Marx to receive an annual sum of £350.

The British founder of the Social Democratic Federation, Henry Hyndman, stated maliciously that Engels based his relations with people on money: 'Engels was rich, Marx very poor', and he loved 'to obtain the full exchange value of his money'. It is, though, well documented how much Engels despised not only the money-making business, but also money itself and such a characterisation as Hyndman gives us here, hardly fits the evidence. Hyndman's comments are undoubtedly a reflection of his embitterment because Engels refuses to support his Federation.

At this stage in Marx's life, during the fifties and sixties, Engels is one of the very few people who recognise his exceptional qualities. This is also partly due to Marx's relative isolation, working for many hours a day in the British Museum library or arguing in poky and smoky rooms with small groups of émigrés. Apart from Engels' vital material support, without his intellectual and moral support as well, *Capital* would never have been written. Irrespective of whether Marx is exhorting Engels' views on philosophy, economics, politics or domestics, he is always unstinting in his advice and encouragement. Their correspondence at this time is often daily, if not twice daily. There are six postal deliveries on weekdays in Kentish Town and they make full use of these.

Their friendship is, though, severely tested in 1863. In the night of the 6-7 January 1863 Mary Burns, Engels' partner for more than twenty years, dies suddenly at the age of 40 of 'natural causes', as the coroner establishes. On being informed of this, Marx's response is a short, laconic sentence, before going on to complain about his own dire financial situation. For Engels, traumatised by the loss, his friend's dismissive condolence is like a kick in the teeth. Now, on one of the very few occasions in his life when *he* needs support, Marx fails him. This insensitivity hurts Engels deeply and could have severely strained, if not broken, their friendship, but he bites his tongue and responds immediately to Marx's concerns, despatching £25 and offering advice on obtaining a loan. However, there does follow a short, but significant break in their correspondence after Mary's death by which Engels clearly signals to Marx that he is deeply offended by his lack of sympathy. Marx fully accepts that his response was inappropriate and insensitive, expressing genuine remorse. For many weeks afterwards, Engels feels his new loneliness intensely. He begins to study the Slavonic languages, but he finds small consolation in this, and he soon turns to less exacting diversions. He collects postage stamps and sends parcels of them to Tussy, Marx's youngest daughter, for her collection. He clearly never forgets this injury for when his own, beloved sister, Marie Blank, dies of scarlet fever in 1869, he writes to her husband: 'No condolences can help in such cases...and I do not write to condole but simply because I know it does one good to be shown the sympathy of those from whom one can allow oneself to expect it.'

Marx and Engels appear to have no secrets from each other, each knows in the smallest detail about the other's personal situation and they counsel each other, even about the most intimate family relationships. When Jenny has just given birth to their latest offspring, Marx writes: 'The circumstances that accompanied my wife's giving birth have unnerved me for some days, I can only tell you face to face. I can't write these things.' And Engels similarly: 'A few days before my old man came to visit, I had the most awful bad luck. At a gathering in a pub, an unknown English man insulted me [calling him a "bloody foreigner"]. I had my umbrella to hand and struck out at him, and the point caught him in the eye. The man then went to his lawyer; I took the necessary counter steps and, to begin with, the affair seemed to be settled, since his eye was not seriously damaged and he was fully recovered, although it still cost me. Now the swine has suddenly changed his mind and is threatening me with an action and if it comes to that, the whole affair will cost me over £200 and on top there would be the public scandal and a row with my old man, who would have to pay the costs'.

Their intimate friendship does not preclude conflict situations, and they often have their differences, but these are resolved in the manner of friends, even if it sometimes takes time and effort. They are both strong personalities in their own right and unwilling to compromise for the sake of it, but the strength of their friendship and immense respect for each other, manages to re-cement any fractures.

Such a case arises when Marx sends a mutual acquaintance to Engels for money. This infuriates him, and he lets Marx know his feelings. With regard to an appeal from Ernst Dronke (a fellow exile and erstwhile comrade who is now involved in making money by blockade-running to the Confederate States in the USA, and who wants to use Engels to guarantee a bank overdraft), he writes to Marx: '...You know best of all why I can't help – but it seems to him that I am being extremely stingy. I can assure you, if it was not for your sake, I'd have given the little twerp a kick up the arse. I was so angry, I got pissed and wrote to you in that pissed state a furious letter about it, and I probably included some pretty strong stuff, but I have absolutely no recall about what I wrote. So that you understand the whole context, I mention it here again'.

Engels is almost certainly the only person Marx confides in over the latter's dalliance with his housekeeper, Helene Demuth, and about the son they produced together, although any letters between the two men referring to the matter have, it seems, been destroyed. Frederick is the son of Helene Demuth, the faithful 'Nimmy' who is as a second mother to the children of Marx. Freddy Demuth or Henry Frederick, as he is registered, is given away for adoption to a local family, called Lewis, shortly after his birth and even Marx's other children, born in wedlock, are unaware of his existence. Freddy becomes an ordinary workman, to whom life is not over kind. Interestingly, he becomes a member of the Amalgamated Engineering Union and a founder member of the Hackney Labour Party, as well as a close friend to his half-sister, Eleanor, after Engels' death, so some of Marx's political genes, it seems, must have been passed on. For a long time, some of their acquaintances who know about Freddy's existence, are convinced that Engels is his father, not least perhaps because of the common name, and there is controversy and doubt about his true paternity until Engels' revelation of the truth on his death bed. During his lifetime Engels never let on to anyone about Freddy's true paternity, despite such rumours, so concerned was he of protecting Marx's reputation at all costs.

Marx, in London, daily beavers away almost illegibly on *Capital* for twenty years, while Engels is bent over his office desk in Manchester adding up figures. However, Sundays, by mutual agreement, are days of relaxation and 'business' is banned. The Marx family takes walks and family picnics on Hampstead Heath, when they are sometimes joined by Engels if he is in London. On one occasion, to the hilarity of all, Marx rides one of the donkeys on the Heath and looks, they all agree, like a rotund Jesus Christ on the road to Jerusalem. Afterwards they would retire to Jack Straw's Castle for a draught of ale, and here they may even have encountered a scribbling Charles Dickens, as he is also fond of a pint in the same watering hole. George Harney, in his reminiscences, also tells us about such picnics organised by the German Democratic Society on the Heath. He describes swimming in the ponds in a heat haze, beside them enormous piles of German sausages, bread and a butt of beer; there is much banter and jollity.

Marx, despite the long hours spent alone in the British Library, takes great delight in his family. He reads the *Arabian Nights*, Dante, Homer and especially Shakespeare to Eleanor, his youngest daughter, as he has done to her sisters. He prances around the room with her on his shoulders, while she screams with delight. He ties convolvulus flowers in her hair, and keeps up a steady stream of banter with her. She is clearly the darling of the family, being the more effusive and lively of the girls. Engels, too, enjoys the company of his surrogate family and, of the children, he establishes particularly close bonds with 'Tussy'. Both as a child and young woman she also corresponds with him and pays several visits on her own to Manchester, which she describes as her 'second home'.

Shakespeare is the dramatist most admired in the Marx household and their admiration is shared by Engels. He and Marx go as often as they can to peformances of Shakespeare's plays in London, especially to the Lyceum, where they see Henry Irving in his acclaimed roles as Hamlet, Shylock or King Lear. Eleanor is later instrumental in setting up a Shakespearean club that invariably meets at Marx's house; the two men are enthusiastic members of the group which undertakes readings of the plays together.

Whenever he is asked if he has been happy playing second fiddle to Marx or if he has had other ambitions, Engels testily dismisses such questions. There is no evidence in his own writings or from acquaintances that would suggest that he is other than fully satisfied in his relationship with Marx. Just as he easily came to terms, as an eighteen-year old, with the fact that he was not destined to be a great poet, he seems to have accepted his role as Marx's lieutenant with similar equanimity. He can't understand, he writes in 1880 to

Bernstein, concerning Marx, how one could be envious of genius: 'It's such a peculiar thing, that we, who don't have it, know from the start that it is unattainable'.

In May 1867, as Marx at last has the completion of his great work in sight, he writes to Engels: '...Without you I would never have been able to finish the work and I assure you it has been like a nightmare on my conscience that your amazing energy has been largely squandered in commercial activity and allowed to rust, and into the bargain you've had to share with me all my little miseries. On the other hand, I can't hide from you that I still have a year of trial ahead of me'. His optimism is however unrealistic. He only manages to complete the first volume, published in that same year, but for which he receives only a nominal payment. He remarks bitterly: '*Capital* will not even bring me in enough to cover the cost of the cigars I smoked while writing it'.

Some have suggested that Marx and Engels agreed early on to take on different responsibilities, rather as Che Guevara and Fidel Castro did after the victory of the Cuban revolution. Engels, so the argument goes, would take on the task of getting the money in while Marx would devote himself to research and theory. There is no basis whatsoever for this suggestion, and it is highly doubtful if Marx would have agreed to such an imbalanced deal.

It is often forgotten that, after the defeat of the '48 revolution, Marx becomes London correspondent for the *New York Daily Tribune* and for some time in this way earns a modest, but regular, livelihood. He could, no doubt, have continued to eke out a living with various freelance journalistic or teaching jobs had it been absolutely necessary. Although when he first obtains the contract as correspondent for the paper in 1851 his English is so basic that Engels has to translate the articles into English for him.

Over the next 12 years, until 1862, he and Engels write almost 500 articles for the paper. Marx repeatedly asks Engels to write on his behalf, as is revealed in his letters from January 1852 onwards. Engels writes the whole series of 15 articles on 'Revolution and counter-revolution in Germany' and several others. Marx relies on him particularly if he hasn't the time or thinks Engels has more expertise in a particular area. Engels also edits many of his articles, but all are published under Marx's name and neither Charles Dana, the commissioning editor at the paper, nor its founder and owner Horace Greeley, ever suspect that they aren't all from the pen of their prolific correspondent in London. In a letter to Marx about the *Tribune*, on 2 March 1852, Engels actually refers to 'our articles'. Engels essays are always clear, precise and contain a wealth of technical detail, making them highly successful with both editors and readers of the *Tribune*. Some of his military articles are also published in the form of unsigned editorials and therefore attributed to Dana, leading Marx to quip to Engels: 'Mr. Dana will make his reputation as Field Marshal in America'. Later, Engels also writes occasionally for the *Manchester Guardian*, including a series of articles on the perspectives for the Franco-Prussian War of 1870-71. His journalism reveals him to be one of the period's most original and sharpest observers of the contemporary scene.

Marx is amazed how, despite his daily grind at the office and the usual ups and downs in temperament and élan, Engels is 'capable of working at any time of the day or night, drunk or sober, he writes rapidly and is incomparably quick on the uptake.' He scans the international press and incorporates the relevant material with ease into the articles and reports he writes. Marx would easily spend a day on a single article and even that is often not enough time. His friend remarks, discouragingly, that he is clearly not cut out for a journalistic career, but is, he acknowledges, clearly the better political strategist.

Both men also maintain a keen interest in events beyond Britain and Europe and show a particular interest in Britain's colonial empire. During 1857 and into 1858, a large scale mutiny erupts and spreads throughout India; its target is the rapacious East India Company which is plundering the country unmercifully. This mutiny eventually leads to the end of the company's domination of the sub-continent and to direct rule by the British government in the form of the British Raj. Marx and Engels together write around 30 articles about the revolt for the *New York Daily Tribune* between July 1857 and October the following year. In their articles they attempt to refute the contention that the revolt is a minor mutiny by native East India Company soldiers with no involvement of broader sections of society. In 1858 Engels writes: 'The great rebellion, stirred up by the mutiny of the Bengal army, is indeed, it appears, dying out. But this second conquest has not increased England's hold upon the mind of the Indian people. The cruelty of the retribution dealt out by the British troops, goaded on by exaggerated and false reports of the atrocities attributed to the natives have not created any particular fondness for the victors'.[128] His dire prediction does not materialise and the Raj maintains British hold over India for almost another century. Engels also gives perceptive military evaluations of the Indian struggles and his suggestion for guerrilla-style attacks on the British forces is amazingly forward-looking at a time when military thinking is still very traditional:

> If it was the interest of the British to rest during the hot weather, it was in the interest of the insurgents to disturb them as much as possible. But instead of organizing an active guerrilla warfare, intercepting the communications between the towns held by the enemy, of waylaying small parties, harassing the foragers, of rendering impassable the supply of victuals, without which no large town held by the British could live – instead of this, the natives have been satisfied with levying revenue and enjoying the leisure left to them by their opponents.[129]

Together again

Once Engels is finally free of his company responsibilities and moves to London in 1870, he and Marx become inseparable and spend more time in each other's company than most happily married couples. A short time after his arrival in the metropolis, Ludwig Kugelmann, the German doctor with whom Marx is normally in regular correspondence, enquires worriedly whether Marx is ill, as he has heard nothing from him for some time. Marx's daughter, Jenny replies:

> I can happily inform you that illness is not the reason for his silence. All in all, his health is better than it usually is at this time of the year, and the reason, without a doubt, is that our good "doctor" Engels has arrived. Engels or "General Staff", a title we have awarded him [the "General" title was awarded because of his great military achievements in the *Pall Mall Gazette* and the title "Staff" from the comical mistake made in *Figaro*, when this great paper demonstrated its base ignorance by translating General Staff as if it were a person]. He lives close by and he does Moor more good than any amount of medicines and takes him on long walks. We see "the General" every day and spend very enjoyable evenings together. A few evenings ago a great

> patriotic event took place at our house. As well as other songs, Moor and "Staff" sang together "Die Wacht am Rhein" [Watch on the Rhine – a popular patriotic song from the period of the Franco-Prussian War] to the tune of "Krambambuli".[130]

From the late seventies onwards, Engels becomes increasingly concerned about a real deterioration in his friend's health. Marx, already fragile, is particularly hard hit by the successive deaths of his beloved wife, Jenny in December 1881 and then, a little over a year later, his daughter Jenny (Longuet) in January 1883. Already in early 1882 Engels is resigned to the fact that he alone has to take on 'the immense correspondence that we earlier shared between us'. Early in the year, on the advice of his doctor, and paid for by Engels, Marx takes a lengthy holiday of recuperation, first to the Isle of Wight, before beginning a year of peregrination, first to Algiers, then Monte Carlo, France and Switzerland, before finally returning to Ventnor on the Isle of Wight. This results in a temporary improvement just before his total collapse and death on 14 March 1883. Engels has been very much aware of Marx's slow deterioration as he is obliged, during the seventies and early eighties, to take on more and more of his work, but it is not this extra burden that is his chief worry, but Marx's slow demise. Even the regular social get-togethers and the jovial Sunday lunches in Engels' house no longer take place towards the end of the seventies.

After receiving news of Marx's death, George Harney in a very moving and sensitive letter to Engels writes:

> But your grief! For you it is no ordinary loss or a loss of a family member. Your friendship and attachment, his warmth and his trust made the fraternal bond of Karl Marx and Friedrich Engels something that stood above anything I've ever experienced in other people. For that bond between you (two) was one "stronger than the love of a woman" – that is only the truth. I seek unsuccessfully for words to express my feeling for the painful loss that has smitten you and also for my deepest sympathy for your suffering and with your sorrow.[131]

Engels receives numerous such letters of condolence and many ordinary working people throughout the world grieve with him. On 17 March 1883 he gives the short valedictory oration 'on behalf of the international proletariat', as Marx's remains are interred in the family grave in an unconsecrated corner of Highgate Cemetery, in the shadow of Whittington Hospital. It is a very private affair, with only 11 mourners:

> On the 14 of March, at a quarter to three in the afternoon, the greatest living thinker ceased to think. He had been left alone for scarcely two minutes, and when we came back we found him in his armchair, peacefully gone to sleep – but for ever.
> What the fighting proletariat of Europe and America, what historical research have lost with the death of this man is immeasurable. Soon enough the gap that has been torn open by the death of this mighty man will make itself felt.
> Just as Darwin discovered the evolutionary law of organic nature, so Marx discovered the developmental law of human history: the simple fact, hitherto concealed by an overgrowth of ideology, is that mankind must first of all eat, drink, have shelter and clothing, before it can pursue politics, science, art, religion, etc.; that therefore the production of the immediate material means, and consequently the degree of economic development attained by a given people or during a given epoch, form the foundation upon which the state institutions, the legal conceptions, art, and even the ideas on religion, of the people concerned have been evolved, and in the light of which they must, therefore, be explained, instead of vice versa, as had hitherto been the case.
> But that is not all. Marx also discovered the special law of motion governing the present-day capitalist mode of production, and the bourgeois society it creates. With the discovery of surplus value, light was suddenly shed, while all previous investigations, of both bourgeois economists and socialist critics had been groping in the dark.
> Two such discoveries would be enough for one lifetime. Happy the man to whom it is granted to make even one such discovery. But in every single field which Marx investigated – and he investigated very many fields, none of them superficially – in every field, even in that of mathematics, he made independent discoveries.
> So was this man of science. But this doesn't make up even half the man. Research, for Marx, was a historically dynamic,

revolutionary force. However great the joy with which he welcomed a new discovery in some theoretical area of research, whose practical application perhaps it was as yet quite impossible to envisage, he experienced quite another kind of joy when the discovery involved immediate revolutionary changes in industry and in historical development in general. For example, he followed closely the development of the discoveries made in the field of electricity and recently those of Marcel Deprez.

For Marx was, above all else, a revolutionary. His real calling in life was to contribute, in one way or another, to the fall of capitalist society and the state institutions it created, to contribute to the liberation of the modern proletariat, of which he was the first to make it conscious of the necessary conditions for its own emancipation.

Fighting was his element. And he fought with a passion, tenacity and a success that few could rival. His work on the first *Rheinische Zeitung* (1842), the Paris *Vorwärts* (1844), the *Deutsche Brüsseler Zeitung* (1847), *The Neue Rheinische Zeitung* (1848-49), the *New York Tribune* (1852-61), and, in addition to these, a host of militant pamphlets, work in organisations in Paris, Brussels and London, and finally, crowning all, the formation of the great International Working Men's Association – this was indeed an achievement of which its founder might well have been proud even if he had done nothing else.

And, consequently, Marx was the most hated and most slandered man of his time. Governments, both absolutist and republican, expelled him. Bourgeois, conservative or ultra-democratic, vied with each other in defaming him. All this he brushed aside like cobwebs, ignoring it, responding only when he was compelled to. And he dies revered, loved and mourned by millions of revolutionary fellow workers, from the mines of Siberia, through the whole of Europe and to California in America – and I make bold to say that, though he may have the odd opponent, he hardly has a single personal enemy.

His name will live on through the ages, and so also will his work.[132]

There is no doubt that Marx's ideas were already finding firm footholds in the working class movements and socialist parties in many countries even before his death, but afterwards they find even greater purchase and lead directly to the creation of the Soviet Union and other socialist countries.

Engels has already seen the potential in Russia, when he writes prophetically in 1882: 'Russia represents the advanced guard of revolutionary action in Europe; the Russian revolution has all the potential to be the signal for a proletarian revolution in the west'.

Ironically, it is in Britain, where Engels and Marx carry out most of their research and organising activity, that revolution still seems farthest away. According to Marxist theory, though, it should have been one of the countries closest to revolution, having the most highly developed capitalist industrial base and a large, experienced proletariat. However, towards the end of 1881, after the long economic depression, there is a short upsurge of renewed interest in socialist ideas in the country. In the following years New Unionism and the organisation of unskilled workers, gives a new fillip to the working class movement, and some perceive a revolutionary potential, which, however, is not realised.

Both Engels and Marx are asked in 1868 by the latter's daughter Jenny to write their 'confessions' in her album. Below are the results. Although a humorous parlour game at the time, it does reveal significant differences in attitude between the two friends.

Engels

Your favourite virtue	– jollity
Your favourite quality in man	– to mind his own business
Your favourite quality in woman	– not to mislay things
Your chief characteristic	– knowing everything by halves
Your idea of happiness	– Château Margaux 1848
Your idea of misery	– to go to a dentist
The vice you excuse	– excess of any sort
The vice you detest	– cant
Your aversion	– affected, stuck-up women
The character you most dislike	– Spurgeon*
Your favourite occupation	– chaffing and being chaffed**
Your favourite hero	– none
Your favourite heroine	– too many to name one
Your favourite poet	– Reineke de Vos,

	Shakespeare, Ariosto etc.
Your favourite prose writer	– Goethe, Lessing, Dr. Samelson
Your favourite flower	– Blue Bell
Your favourite colour	– any one, not aniline
Your favourite dish	– cold: salad, hot: Irish Stew
Your favourite maxim	– not to have any
Your favourite motto	– take it easy.

* Charles Haddon Spurgeon (1834-92) England's best-known preacher for most of the second half of the nineteenth century

** taking the piss or having the piss taken!

Marx

Your favourite virtue	– simplicity
Your favourite quality in man	– strength
Your favourite quality in woman	– weakness
Your chief characteristic	– singleness of purpose
Your idea of happiness	– to fight
Your idea of misery	– submission
The vice you excuse	– gullibility
The vice you detest	– servility
Your aversion	– Martin Tupper*
Your favourite occupation	– book worming
Your favourite hero	– Spartacus, Kepler
Your favourite heroine	– Gretchen [heroine in Goethe's Faust]
Your favourite poet	– Shakespeare, Aeschylus, Goethe
Your favourite prose	– writer Diderot
Your favourite flower	– Daphne
Your favourite colour	– red
Your favourite dish	– fish
Your favourite maxim	– nihil humani a me alienum puto [nothing human is alien to me]
Your favourite motto	– de omnibus dubitandum [doubt everything]
Your favourite names	– Jenny, Laura[133]

Chapter Eleven
The Legacy

What makes any attempt at an objective evaluation of Engels' work particularly difficult is trying to separate his contribution from that of Marx. I would argue that his work and life can only be evaluated meaningfully by examining those of both men as part of a whole. This is true also because we can never be completely certain who the real originator is of what has been written in either of their names. Rarely, if ever, in the history of intellectual endeavour, has there been such a close and long-term collaboration, and such an apparently perfect symbiosis between two men as there was between these two. No doubt Marx was the more academic and with a deeper understanding of philosophy and theory, whereas Engels certainly had a better grasp of economic practice and the realities of working class life. Any difference between their individual achievements and the extent and import of their writing also needs to be seen from the perspective that Marx was, thanks to Engels' financial support, a full-time academic, whereas Engels had a day job for a significant part of his life and could only carry out research and write in his limited free time. It is also clear that with any two individuals, there will undoubtedly be differences of opinion, different approaches and perspectives. In the case of Marx and Engels these are not easy to tease out, but there are those who claim to recognise significant and far-reaching differences between the thinking of the two men.

It is certainly difficult to comprehend how someone as passionate and politically active as Engels was prepared to devote a large chunk of his life to a hated office job as a merchant in order to support the Marx family, so that his friend could devote all his time to research, writing and organising, exactly the work Engels himself would love to have done full-time. Whatever the motivation for this unique relationship, it bore surprising fruit.

The two men were living during a time of unprecedented change; the old feudal order in large parts of Europe was being rapidly replaced by a new industrial capitalism. This was sending strong tremors through its societies. The iniquities of the new capitalism and the human degradation it brought with it made searing impressions on both men. It affronted their deep sense of humanity, of culture and justice. It is no wonder that they, like many of their contemporaries in their individual ways – a Christian soldier like William Booth, novelists like Charles Dickens, Elizabeth Gaskell, George Eliot, playwrights like Shaw or poets like Shelley – railed against the system. They realised that the dysfunctional and exploitive society they lived in could never deliver real emancipation or true happiness.

Marx and Engels thought that with their theories of economic development and class struggle they'd found the key to human progress, just as Darwin had found the key of evolution to explain how human beings originated or Mendel discovered the genetic formula to our heredity. They were obsessional in promoting the building of strong, centralised and united communist parties in each country based on their theory of dialectical materialism, because they realised that without such an organisation to rally and lead the working masses, from a strong theoretical basis, there would be little progress. Their ideas had more impact on social developments throughout the late nineteenth and twentieth centuries than any other body of thought.

There were, of course, a whole number of philosophers, like Marx and Engels, who were attempting to offer explanations and solutions to the challenges and upheavals of the 19th century. These ranged from Malthusian fatalism, biological determinism through utopian socialism, salvation through religion, co-operative settlements and anarchism to pseudo-scientific panaceas. Marx and Engels were convinced that working people could take control of their own lives and change the society they lived in; they were not fated to be the eternal victims of an oppressive system. But in order to be able to do this they had to first understand how their class had been formed during the process of historical change, and then to harness that knowledge to a strategy for changing the process in their favour; they would need to become fully conscious of themselves as a class. In their numerous writings this is, in essence, what Marx and Engels attempted to explain and promote.

Undoubtedly one of their chief achievements has been to demonstrate to us that the history of humankind is first and foremost the history of evolving economic relations. This may sound like a banality today, but for pre-nineteenth century historians it was far from obvious, and there are still those who dispute the centrality of these relations. Marx and Engels argued that it is economic or property relations that have largely determined the course of social progress. From the earliest farming tribes who produced a food surplus, enabling a non-working elite to emerge, to the battles between a conservative feudalism and bourgeois mercantilism up to the continuing battles today between workers and the owners of the means of production and by nation states against globalised finance, economic relations are central.

However one chooses to evaluate their theoretical contribution to the science of human development, they did provide arguably one of the most comprehensive, rational and plausible theories as well as a useful analytical tool – dialectical materialism – for understanding society. This theory, over time, has captured the imagination of untold thousands throughout the world, led to the establishment of communist parties in almost every country and to communist revolutions, even though not in those countries where they had most expected such revolutions. Although in Germany at the close of the First World War a country-wide socialist revolution was brought very close: short-lived 'Soviets' were set up in Munich on 7 November 1918, in Berlin on 9 November and also in Bremen, in the wake of the Spartacist uprisings, but these were brutally suppressed.

The question is often raised, why the ideas of Marx and Engels failed to find fertile ground in the countries they are most associated with, but particularly in Britain, where they both spent most of their lives. The reasons are complex, but one strong factor is perhaps the national characters of these countries, a factor that does not slot easily into Marxist theory. National character is a nebulous, but nevertheless tangible attribute of nations, and it certainly contributed to frustrate their vision.

Expressed succinctly, the British are a pragmatic nation, not to be set alight easily by abstract ideas or philosophies; the French are emotional and impetuous, whereas the Germans are devotees of the big idea, and respond to appeals to their rationality. Thus it is not surprising that the British remained largely indifferent to Marxism, the French flirted with it and the Germans took it readily into their heads. It was eventually defeated in Germany by a combination of traditional conservativism, subservience to authority and a virulent fascism promoted by a capitalist class in fear of communism.

Any intellectual movement, if it is to remain a live option for generations beyond the time of its original formation, one that wishes to address newly emerging realities, must be adaptable, have the ability to take on board new knowledge. Marxism has this potential and this is what probably explains its amazing longevity and influence.

Undoubtedly the most important achievement of these two friends is to be the originators and leaders of a mass movement that would sweep the world. In the mid-nineteenth century they were two oddball émigrés who had fallen out with virtually everyone else in the wider progressive and socialist movement – they were literally 'a party of two' – and few were in the slightest interested in their ideas. They could easily have become simply minor footnotes to 19th century history. How this transformation came about is complex, but their social and economic discoveries and the theories they elaborated clearly had a validity and resonated with the zeitgeist.

The *Manifesto of the Communist Party* – a slim booklet containing a mere 10,000 words – is one of the most succinct analyses of the historical process and struggle for human emancipation ever written. It was drafted by Engels and Marx together. In its brevity, its compact sentences redolent of meaning, its barbed wit, it is a masterpiece of agitational prose. It is one of the most vivid, excoriating condemnations of social oppression and injustice, combined with a fervent demand for emancipation. In its description of society and the process of social development it has an uncanny contemporary feel; much of it is just as applicable today as it was in the mid 19th century when it was written.

If one replaced the archaic term 'bourgeoisie' by 'modern capitalism', it could, in places, be a description of society today:

> The bourgeoisie cannot exist without constantly revolutionising the instruments of production, and thereby the relations of production and with them the whole relations of society…The need of a constantly expanding market for its products chases

> the bourgeoisie over the whole surface of the globe. It must nestle everywhere, settle everywhere, establish connexions everywhere...All old-established national industries have been destroyed or are daily being destroyed. They are dislodged by new industries, whose introduction becomes a life and death question for all civilised nations...National one-sidedness and narrow mindedness becomes more and more impossible and from the numerous national and local literatures, there arises a world literature.

Or again, on individual relationships:

> [it] has left remaining no other nexus between man and man than naked self-interest, than callous "cash payment". The modern state is but a committee for managing the common affairs of the whole bourgeoisie...The bourgeoisie has stripped of its halo every occupation hitherto honoured and looked up to with reverent awe. It has converted the physician, the lawyer, the priest, the poet, the man of science, into paid wage-labourers.[134]

It is not surprising that the *Communist Manifesto* became one of the most read and influential books ever written. It captures the essence of the capitalist system and its socially corrosive essence. It can still provide an answer to individual fears of social instability, unemployment, homelessness, pension uncertainty and social breakdown, by explaining that their causes are intrinsic to the system and do not lie in individual inadequacy. It is, perhaps, difficult today to envisage what an apocalyptical era the industrial transformation in 19th century Europe represented. After a century or more of barely noticeable change, people suddenly found themselves as passengers riding an ever faster train lurching through a dark tunnel to an unknown and frightening destination. Marx and Engels offered them a manual that would help them take control of that train and determine its route. Those looking for a solution grasped it with alacrity.

Engels' particular contribution to the worldwide socialist movement, especially in his later years, was to be the de facto co-ordinating and communications centre for the various national movements. It was he who advised, cajoled and assisted the exchange of experience between the different parties, and helped them maintain a clear ideology and internationalist outlook. Unfortunately, Engels has been seen by many as merely Marx's lieutenant or by some as the less intellectual practitioner who turned Marx's great theoretical work into a political dogma. Such points of view do both men an injustice. In his 1880 preface to the French edition of Engels' *Socialism: Utopian and Scientific*, Marx writes that Friedrich Engels is 'one of the most outstanding representatives of modern socialism'. He readily admitted that some of his own economic ideas were triggered by Engels' *Outline of a Critique of Political Economy* (1844). Engels' first published book, *The Condition of the Working Class in England* is still held up as a model of investigative social reporting. UNESCO included it high on their list of all time influential works of sociology. For that one work alone he deserves to be honoured and remembered.

Engels' rhetorical phraseology, particularly in his youth, did at times betray a certain pugilistic ruthlessness. When he complained for instance, in 1848, about the bourgeoisie not giving the real militants weaponry to wage the struggle, he admitted that they realised 'the guns will be subsequently turned on them'! But this is said by a young man in the heat of revolutionary battle; he certainly moderated his views in later life. Such phraseology and attitudes are uncannily similar to those of Che Guevara at a similar age, but Che, of course, didn't have the luxury (or misfortune) of growing old. There is, though, little in the writings of either Engels or Marx that reveals callousness, cynicism or lack of humanity. Their motivation was always to facilitate the liberation of the most exploited and oppressed and their whole lives were devoted to the pursuit of that goal. Neither Marx nor Engels was the fanatic they are sometimes portrayed to be; obsessional maybe, determined and committed, yes, undoubtedly; but these qualities can be better understood in the context of 19th century industrialisation, the misery, crass inequality, extreme class conflict and revolutionary turmoil.

A new orthodoxy has been proclaimed, particularly in the English-speaking world, that argues that there is a clear distinction between Marx's and Engels' thought. Their basic argument is that Marx's Marxism is a humanistic philosophy whereas Engels' version is mechanistic materialism. George Lichtheim in his book, *Marxism: an*

Historical and Critical Study (1967), began the process and he was followed by Norman Levine (*The Tragic Deception: Marx contra Engels* 1975) and Terrell Carver (*Marx and Engels, the Intellectual Relationship* 1983).

Levine represents this position most forcefully. He argued that Engels and Marx 'suppressed their major differences in thinking'. And that it is the vulgarisation of Marxist thought by Engels that led directly to Lenin and Stalin. He wrote his polemic, as he states in the introduction to his book, as a response to the student movement during the 1960s and the eagerness among students [in the United States] for knowledge of Marx. He maintains that a misinterpretation of Marx begins with Engels. This difference between the two men, he argues, was already recognised by Gramsci and Lukács among others, but not developed further by them. He argues that 'pure' Marxism has been muddied by what he calls 'Engelsism'. Marx, Levine says, rather contradictorily, 'saw man as basically a being of praxis, a being who through his activity modified the natural world, humanized that world...Engels was a metaphysical materialist. The elemental forces in the universe, for Engels, were matter and motion. Marx didn't see history as inevitable process, didn't see it as unilinear...Engels did see history as a unilinear process. Engels believed that macrocosmic forces determined the inevitable path of history'.

He even argues that Marx and Engels had divergent views on the future communistic society, and of the evolutionary process of history: 'Marx saw communism as the end of human alienation, the end of dehumanisation, the beginning of free human history, when man would be one with praxis. Engels envisioned communist society as an enormous factory. It would be regimented, highly supervised, devoted to the work ethic, but highly productive of the necessities and luxuries of life'.

This supposed dichotomy and dystopic image is surely a figment of Levine's, not Engels' imagination and he provides not a shred of evidence to support it. Neither Marx nor Engels said very much in terms of what a future communistic society would or could look like. There is nothing in the extant writings of either of the two men or in accounts by others to even hint at, never mind justify, this suggestion. Levine compounds his attempts to drive a wedge between the two thinkers by describing Engels in condescending terms: 'I conclude that his [Engels] mind was of a second order when compared with that of Marx'; 'He was a commentator rather than an originator'. Do we detect here an element of academic snobbery towards Engels, the self-taught intellectual, as against Marx, the 'true academic'?

He avows that 'Engels was really the founder of the view that Marxism was predestinarian economic determinism.' He even tries to justify his arguments on spurious psychological grounds. Engels, he says, was motivated by rebellion against the pietism and hypocrisy of his family and the provincial environment in Barmen. He also had 'a touch of dilettantism' about him; Marx is the great abstract thinker, Engels is largely motivated by psychological factors.

A chief plank of Levine's argument appears to be that Engels has had the effrontery to apply the dialectical method to the natural world, not just to human society, thus bringing the method into disrepute.

Engels' attempts to apply dialectics to the natural world were bequeathed us in a series of notes which were only published posthumously, as one volume, in 1925. While developing a dialectical approach to nature, and researching the natural sciences, Engels shared his ideas regularly with Marx, and we have no evidence that the latter gave any intimation of disagreement. In fact, he rarely responded to Engels' comments. This could have been because Marx felt out of his depth in the natural sciences, particularly physics and chemistry, but it may also be that letters in which he makes comments have been lost or destroyed. We don't know. However, most of this work was carried out while Engels was in London, so the two would have discussed the issues, but not corresponded.

Engels was undoubtedly more steeped in the natural sciences than Marx who hadn't begun to examine them in terms of applying the dialectical method. Whether Marx would have agreed with Engels elaboration of his 'Laws of Dialectics' as applied to the natural world, we can never know, but the fact that they both envisioned the method as a holistic one, applicable to all life, can hardly be doubted. Indeed Levine, in his opening chapter admits that, 'Nature for Marx was a totality'.

There has always been heated debate about whether Marx himself was a determinist and indeed whether Marxism itself is a determinist philosophy. Both Engels and Marx were somewhat equivocal on this issue. There is enough documentary evidence to show that both certainly viewed history in a unilinear and determinist way in the early years after they had begun to elaborate a materialist view of history, but in their later years, the evidence points to their moving away from such a rigid position. The *Manifesto of the Communist Party* actually states unequivocally that 'Its [the bourgeoisie] fall and the victory of the proletariat are equally inevitable'. But this early document was after all a propagandistic and agitational tool for the newly emerging communist movement, not a philosophical treatise. They are, though, undoubtedly determinist in the sense that most scientists are: recognising that events and developments are not arbitrary, have specific, material-based causes and that these can be comprehended as well as changed by human intervention.

There have certainly been continuous and egregious attempts to denigrate Engels and saddle him with the full responsibility for how Marxist ideas were later implemented in the attempts to build communist societies in Eastern Europe and elsewhere, but it is difficult to make the mud stick in the face of ample contrary evidence. The Marxist historian, Eric Hobsbawm has distanced himself from a position like that taken by Levine and others and remains firmly of the opinion that the work of the two men cannot be viewed in separation.

Engels and Marx are clearly as much products of their times as any other great thinkers. Their understanding and interpretation of their era is based on the realities of the industrial revolution, of the emergence of a new working or proletarian class and of the new economic forces stamping their imprint on history. That era has now changed for good, in fundamental ways, but many of their ideas remain valid, even if their revolutionary predictions do not, precisely because capitalism is still the hegemonic world system and is still accompanied by injustice, exploitation, class differences and crises. These injustices might have shifted in the 20th and 21st centuries from the industrial cities of England, Germany and the USA to the Philippines, India, Africa and Latin America, and the system itself evolved and adapted to new circumstances, but the injustices and inequality remain essentially the same. Engels' lurid descriptions of working and housing conditions in mid-nineteenth century England could apply equally today in areas of Bangladesh, China or Latin America.

Before Marx and Engels developed Hegel's philosophy of

dialectics, history had been seen as a confusion of battles, of defeats and victories, of vying monarchs and imperial conquests. The underlying mechanisms of historical change were occluded by the accretion of a myriad of seemingly incidental and unconnected events.

Historical materialism, although Marx prefers the term philosophical/dialectical materialism, is the intellectual approach developed in order to achieve a better understanding of historical processes. It is also an attempt to provide us all with the intellectual tools to learn from our common history and take control of our future. Engels defines it as: 'That view of the course of history which seeks the ultimate cause and the great moving power of all important historic events in the economic development of society, in the changes in the modes of production and exchange, in the consequent division of society into distinct classes, and in the struggles of these classes against one another'.[135] Historical materialism views the causes of developments and change in human society, in the way humans collectively live together, as based in economic relationships, which largely determine all the other characteristics of society (the superstructure) e.g. social classes, political formations, ideologies and culture.

Few could deny the impact historical materialism has had on thinking in almost every field and still has, from economics to the arts and culture. However, while dialectical materialism has been taken on board by a significant number of thinkers and become part of the mainstream philosophic discourse, even if the idea of a communist utopia at the core of their thinking has often been rejected.

One of Engels' contemporaries, Bernard Shaw was introduced by the social democratic leader, H.H. Hyndman to the works of Marx and Engels, and he met Engels on a number of occasions. Shaw became convinced by the economic theories in *Capital* but felt they would have little impact on the working classes. Although the treatise had been written in the cause of liberating the working man, Shaw felt, 'Marx never got hold of him for a moment.' And with typical Shavian contrariness and perspicacity, he went on, 'It was the revolting sons of the bourgeoisie itself – Lassalle, Marx, Liebknecht, Morris, Hyndman, Bax, all like myself, crossed with squirearchy – that painted the flag red. The middle and upper classes are the revolutionary element in society; the proletariat is the conservative element.' Shaw firmly believed, with Proudhon, that 'property was theft' and, like Engels, that capitalism was deeply flawed, but unlike him, Shaw, the Fabian, favoured gradualism to revolution.

Another of Engels' contemporaries, albeit 34 years' younger, wrote in 1891:

> A map of the world that does not include Utopia is not even worth glancing at, for it leaves out the one country at which Humanity is always landing. And when Humanity lands there, it looks out, and seeing a better country, sets sail! Progress is the realization of Utopias.[136]

That contemporary was Oscar Wilde. In his essay, *The Soul of Man under Socialism*, he also writes: 'Socialism, Communism, or whatever one chooses to call it, by converting private property into public wealth, and substituting co-operation for competition, will restore society to its proper condition of a thoroughly healthy organism, and ensure the material well-being of each member of the community.' Utopia will always be on mankind's map of the future in some form or other. Although both Marx and Engels were influenced by the early utopian socialists, they later fought tooth and nail against their ideas and would have vehemently denied that they were utopians; however their commitment and sacrifice for a communist future belies that. In fact, in Engels' early work *Outlines of a Critique of Political Economy* he mounts a critique of bourgeois society in several passages from the standpoint of abstract principles of a universal morality and humanitarianism. With the increasing conviction that their theories of social development were scientific, this utopian aspect was occluded.

The reason they both attacked the utopians was because they saw their ideas as rooted in a nebulous Christian ethos, with little relevance to the real world; appealing to men's and women's goodness, they felt, would hardly bring about the social changes they felt were essential. Socialism could only be achieved, they argued, if the struggle were based on rationality and an understanding of historical reality. They were determined to place socialism/communism on such a rational foundation and, for that reason, both consciously avoided describing a future utopia, as earlier socialists had done, considering such exercises the realm of fantasy and not grounded in reality. Significantly, Fidel Castro, a great admirer of

Engels' work and a self-avowed Marxist, nevertheless describes himself as a 'utopian socialist'.[137]

Throughout his life Engels wrote an enormous amount on an extraordinary range of subjects. In his younger years these included poems, a play, opera libretto and various essays, literary criticisms and newspaper articles. He went on to write polemical brochures and pamphlets, books and numerous articles on military science, philology, the natural sciences and economics. Clearly a great deal of what he wrote is of minor historical interest today, but, I would argue, several of his chief works are much more than that. Even though human knowledge has progressed considerably since he died, his methods of working and, indeed, many of his ideas are still revolutionary.

Of those works he wrote entirely by himself, the significant ones are: The *Condition of the Working Class in England* (1845), *Herr Dühring's Revolution in Science* (1876) (commonly known as *Anti-Dühring*), which includes the seminal three chapters which Engels had reprinted as a separate brochure in 1880, titled: *Socialism: Utopian and Scientific, The Origins of the Family, Private Property and the State* (1884) and *Dialectics of Nature* (1883). These texts, as well as the numerous articles he wrote for newspapers in Britain, Germany, the USA and elsewhere are now largely accessible in the *Collected Works of Marx and Engels*, published in English. And, of course, it shouldn't be forgotten that Engels actually wrote the last two volumes of *Capital*, albeit from Marx's copious notes.

One important cause of misunderstanding, and rejection, of Marxism has been the interpretation of the German term 'Wissenschaft', translated into English as 'Scientific'. The idea of a 'scientific' socialism appears to be somewhat of a contradiction or illogicality for many subsequent adherents as well as critics of Marxism. In its German meaning it relates to methods of investigation and is connected with theory; it is not synonymous with the more narrow definition in English, which refers to the natural sciences only. The inadequate translation of this word has led to the alienation of many, who otherwise may have been more amenable to the theory– that is the conflating of science with the struggle towards a utopian goal. The idea of creating a better society is something many of us would subscribe to, but many would reject the idea that seeking this could be seen as a scientific process. Science per se, as the word is understood in English, cannot have goals or aims; it can only provide an analysis of objective reality, and its findings must be demonstrable. The problem with history and economics is that developments in these fields are only demonstrable retrospectively and there can be no controlled experiments to test various hypotheses. One can't turn history back and try it a different way. Marx and Engels could be, feasibly, correct that the logic of human development and the conflict between classes will irresistibly lead to a socialist society, and they were determined to use their theory to make it come about, but whether they believed categorically that such a development was a scientific necessity i.e. a certainty, is doubtful.

The later creation of a belief system and dogma out of Marxist theory, turning it into a quasi-determinist project, particularly in the Soviet Union, together with the Cold War propaganda by the West, led to a subsequent and unfortunate rejection by many of Marxist ideas. Marx's unforgettable words: 'The philosophers have only interpreted the world in various ways; the point, however, is to change it' were taken seriously by many of their followers who did change the world. That is what both Marx and Engels endeavoured to achieve, but it is doubtful if they would have been happy with many of the consequences.

The most cataclysmic social upheaval of the twentieth century – the Bolshevik Revolution of 1917 – was implemented and carried out based on the ideas developed by Engels and Marx. In examining the way Lenin and the Bolsheviks steered the revolutionary process in Russia one can see this clearly. Marx and Engels had concluded, logically according to their own historical analysis, that a successful socialist revolution could only come about in a country with a highly developed capitalist system and with a large industrial proletariat. Ironically their theory was undermined by the influence and success of their own ideas, as well as a conducive historical constellation of forces on a backward and feudal Russia, where the first socialist revolution took place. The attempt to build a utopia, which became seriously flawed does not, however, invalidate their main argument that to consciously build our own future, we need to understand our past and the causative elements in the historical process and take control of the chief forces responsible for social change.

Of course, we cannot make Engels or Marx posthumously responsible for what happened in their name. Irrespective of whether you see the Bolshevik Revolution and subsequent upsurge of communism throughout the world as something positive or negative, they did not provide the blueprint for the erection of communist states; they only argued for the necessity of changing the capitalist system and provided guidance on how to carry out a successful revolution. However, we can't let them off the hook entirely. It was after all their ideas that laid the basis and made possible the building of communism as a force and led to the subsequent revolutions.

The strategy that Engels and Marx promulgated was, though, in a sense proved correct: without disciplined organisation, clear political and social goals, creating a new society is hardly possible. But this goal, for all sorts of reasons, failed. The main one being the enormous and combined economic, political and even armed pressure that was brought to bear on that first fragile communist state by the capitalist world. The Soviet Union, even in its infancy, represented a dire threat to the whole capitalist system. But the communist utopia also turned sour due to a number of factors, among them: Russian historical and autocratic traditions; human inadequacy on the part of some of the revolution's leaders and, of course, the armed interventions, sabotage and blockades of the young Soviet Union by the capitalist countries.

Engels deserves to be not only remembered, but his works re-examined. Our society, on a global scale, is still divided into rich and poor, we still have rapacious capitalism, now on a much more globalised scale than in his day. In many countries of the world we still have slum housing, child labour and social conflict. His vision of a better and more just world and his understanding of history have not lost their relevance, even though we are chastened by the first, unsuccessful experiments in trying to build socialism.

Engels enjoyed nothing more than a lively debate, the clash of ideas and argument. He would have been the first to find a monolithic ideology and dogmatism anathema. In his concluding speech to the International Socialist Workers' Congress in Zurich in October 1893 he said: 'We must allow discussion in order to avoid becoming a sect, but maintaining our common position. The loose ties, the voluntary unity, supported by congresses, are sufficient to achieve our victory and no power on earth can take that away from us.' And again, a comment which certainly contradicts the sort of centralisation that the Communist International attempted to impose on communist parties worldwide: 'It's a nonsense to want to form a uniform movement in all countries...the party needs socialist theory and this cannot live without freedom of the movement.' Although many of the followers of Marx and Engels have interpreted their works in a dogmatic and quasi-religious way, this was far from their intention or their own way of working. To quote Engels: 'The workers' movement is based on the sharpest critique of contemporary society, critique is its life element, how can it exclude itself from criticism?'

Contrary to the way he has often been portrayed, as a devotee of violent revolution, certainly in his later years, and with the visible success of the German socialists, Engels increasingly believed a working class victory could be achieved through the ballot box as he made clear in 1893:

> Today we can already count on 2¼ million voters. If that growth continues, by the end of the century we will have won over the majority of the middle classes in society, the petty bourgeoisie and small peasants, and grow to become the decisive force in the country, before which all other powers will have to defer, whether they like it or not. To maintain this momentum until it engulfs the present government system, that is our main task.[138]

Engels' faith in the ability of working people to vote their way to power would perhaps have been tempered had he been able to foresee the role played by modern media and, given their ownership, to manipulate mass consciousness.

If much of what Engels raised and discussed in his writings appears familiar to us today, it is of course partly because he was one of the 19th century's leading thinkers. The concepts and language which many of us now take for granted when discussing social issues had first to be developed and elaborated by Marx and Engels. He and Marx offered their generation and future generations an alternative vision, making many realise that they don't have to accept given social relations or the capitalist system as the final and absolute one; there are alternatives. Like the radical ideas in Thomas Paine's *Rights of Man,* little over half a century before, their ideas, too, as succinctly expressed in the *Communist Manifesto*, shook the very foundations of their own society and resonate still today. The question is whether the demise of 20th century communism signifies the end of the whole concept and whether the ideas of Engels and Marx still have something useful to say about creating a truly democratic and socialist society in the 21st or future centuries?

The eminent historian Eric Hobsbawm emphasises that in order to properly understand the present, we have to understand history, and Marxism provides the most useful tool with which to attempt this. It offers us a methodolgical approach to history as a whole; something no other approach does.

Certainly, the grave problems facing our own generation can be tackled and solutions found; whether they be global warming, environmental degradation, mass economic migration, shortages of raw materials or the dilemma of science and technology as enslaving or liberating forces. All these challenges are surmountable, but only by means of a rational approach based on a comprehensive understanding of social history, on genuine solidarity and co-operation. They will certainly not be solved if the market and the profit motive continue reigning supreme. And whether one calls the possible alternatives socialism, communism or some other -ism is not of importance. In the sense that we have to consciously seek and work for an alternative to the present capitalist system, one which appears devoid of an ethical or moral base and is incapable of providing solutions to the great problems we face, then the ideas of Marx and Engels cannot be written off. Their ideas can still challenge social ossification. They believed in humanity's ability to control those social forces that shape our lives, they gave hope to those without hope and also provided us with an intellectual tool with which to challenge hierarchical societies.

In his authorised biography, Fidel Castro says: 'Marxism taught me what society was. I was like a blindfolded man in a forest, who doesn't even know where north and south is. If you don't eventually come to truly understand the history of the class struggle, or at least have a clear idea that society is divided between the rich and the poor, and that some people subjugate and exploit other people, you're lost in a forest, not knowing anything'.[139] This statement is symptomatic of so many who have discovered the ideas of Marx and Engels – it transforms their lives. Marxism certainly doesn't hold all the answers to our existential questions – nor does any one system of ideas or belief – but it is one of the best tools for understanding if used as such, rather than treated as a religious dogma.

Guevara was certainly familiar with at least some of Engels' military writings beyond the well-known political tracts. In his 'Guerra de guerrillas: un método' [Guerrilla War – a Method] he quotes from Engels' *The Civil War in France* in which the latter draws lessons from the street battles of the Commune.[140]

Interestingly, the renowned North American journalist, I.F. Stone puts his finger on the contradictory forces driving Che Guevara: a deep humanity marred by an element of ruthlessness; it is an observation that could equally apply to Engels: 'Che will live with Bolivar and Juarez among the heroes of the Latin hemisphere. But I have always felt,' he writes, 'there was something anachronistic in his mission to build a new and bigger Sierra Maestra in the Andes. It had all the naïve hopefulness and humanitarian faith of the 19th century…I recognise the Shelleyan purity of Che's intentions. I welcome the fact that new Ches will spring up to carry on his work – for without revolutionary challenges neither the Latin oligarchy nor Washington will make peaceful change possible. But I believe their success would be out of all proportion to the terrible cost…' This apparently contradictory assessment is equally applicable to Engels and to most, if not all, revolutionary visionaries.

There is no doubt that continued social progress and stability will depend on a better understanding of the forces shaping our societies and our ability to control them. We need to be able to comprehend change, to grasp the ways in which it can be managed, so that we can mould our history rather than be steam-rollered by it – and offering a key to such an understanding is the true legacy of Engels and of Marx.

29 Engels, Foreword to the *Condition of the Working Class in England*, 'To the Workers of Great Britain' (Barmen 1845) (*MEW*, Vol 2).

30 Georg Weerth, "The Cannon Forger", in *A young revolutionary in nineteenth century England – selected writngs of Georg Weerth*, Peter and Ingrid Kuczynski (ed.) (Seven Seas Books Berlin, 1971).

31 Engels, "Outlines of a Critique of National Economy" (Umrisse zu einer Kritik der Nationalökonomie in *Deutsch-Französische Jahrbücher*,) 1844, reprinted (*MEW*, Dietz Verlag, Berlin. Vol. 1, Berlin 1976. pp. 499-524).

32 ibid.

33 Feuerbach: studied under Hegel in Berlin and became a leading light among the Young Hegelians. His most famous work *The Essence of Christianity* was translated into English by Engels' contemporary, the English novelist, George Eliot.

34 Engels, letter to Marx, 20 Jan 1845 (*MEW*, Vol 27 p.14). In this letter Engels' use of the word 'page', or 'Bogen' in German, undoubtedly refers to a 'printer's running sheet' which would contain a number of pages. *The Holy Family* is a book of 220 pages.

35 Engels, letter to Marx, 20 January 1845 (*MEW*, Vol. 27 p.18).

36 Engels, letter to Marx, 20 Jan 1845 (MEW Vol 27 p.14).

37 Engels, letter to Marx 19 November 1844, in: *Letters of the Young Engels, 1838-1845* (Progress Publishers Moscow, 1976).

38 Dr. Wesendonk: is, as a matter of minor interest, the brother of the Wesendonk whose name was to be immortalised by Wagner in his Wesendonk Songs. Wagner like so many intellectuals is later caught up in Germany's revolutionary turmoil of 1848/9 and is forced to flee the country.

39 Engels, letter to Marx in Brussels (MEW, Vol. 27, 26pp).

40 Marx, Foreword to *A Contribution to the Critique of Political Economy*, Progress Publishers Moscow, 1977.

41 Ernesto 'Che' Guevara, letter to Julio Castro, in *Che Guevara – a revolutionary life*, John Lee Anderson (Grove Press, New York, 1997, p.424).

42 Klaus-Dieter Sommer, (ed.) *Georg Weerth.* Poesiealbum 37 (Neues Leben, Berlin 1970).

43 Communism: From Engels' time onwards there has been much confusion between the terms 'communist' and 'socialist' and the two have often been used interchangeably. For both Engels and Marx, the terms are essentially interchangeable, but for them 'communist' signified a socialist outlook based on their materialist theory of society; a future society without private property or a capitalist economic system would be a Communist one.

For the 'communist' countries of eastern Europe 'socialism' came to be defined as that pre-communist stage of society, during the construction of communism, i.e. a perfected society, with no money relations and where everyone would be 'rewarded according to their need' and not according to their work.

After the death of Marx and Engels, most socialist or social democratic parties (at that time the two terms were also identical) split into Marxist wings (most later becoming communist parties) and reformist (socialist/ social democratic) wings, like the British Labour Party.

44 Louis Blanc: born in Madrid, the son of Joseph Bonarparte's Inspector General of Finance; he became a radical thinker and writer. He pioneered the idea of social workshops, equality of wages and of a society based on the concept of 'from each according to his abilities, to each according to his needs'. He became a socialist and a minister in the provisional revolutionary government created by the revolution of 1848.

45 Engels, Introduction to Karl Marx's "The Class Struggles in France 1848 to 1850", March 6, 1895 (*MECW*, Vol 27, pp. 506-524).

46 Engels, letter to Marx, 24 November 1847 (*MEW*, Vol. 4, pp. 361).

47 Engels, in the *Deutsch-Brüsseler Zetiung*, 1848.

48 Engels,"Die Bewegungen von 1847" (*MEW*, Vol 4, pp. 494 – 503).

49 Gen. Cavaignac: Minister of War, with dictatorial powers, who put down the Parisian insurrection of 1848, on behalf of the French Assembly, with extreme brutality and enormous loss of life.

50 Engels, Reminiscences (*MEW*, Vol 21).

51 Engels, letter to Marx 25 April 1848 (*MEW*, Vol.27 p.125).

52 V.E. Kunina (ed): *Frederick Engels – his life and work* (Progress Publishers Moscow, 1987).

53 The Junkers: landed aristocrats who traditionally provided the officer class for the Prussian army.

54 Engels, "Von Paris nach Bern" (*MEW*, Vol. 5, pp. 463-480).

55 Engels, letter to Marx, 28 December 1848 (*MEW*, Vol 27, p.132).

56 Engels, "Von Paris nach Bern" (*MEW*, Vol. 5, p. 463-480).

57 Manfred Kliem, *Friedrich Engels – Dokumente seines Lebens,* (Reklam Leipzig 1977, p. 239).

58 The Democratic Germany movement: established by largely middle class intellectuals and progressive artisans and businessmen to fight for a united Germany with a democratic constitution. In its early formation it included a broad spectrum of political viewpoints, from liberal-democratic and pure nationalist to socialist.

59 Report in *Neue Rheinische Zeitung* Nr. 300 (17 May 1849).

60 Prosecution statement against the accused involved in the Elberfeld rebellion in 1849, in: Kliem, *Friedrich Engels – Dokumente seines Lebens*, p. 246.

61 opus cit

62 Engels, article in Neue Rheinische Zeitung (*MEW*, Vol. 6, pp. 500-502).

63 Engels, "Report to leftist delegates at the Frankfurt Constitutional Assembly", in Kliem, *Engels – Dokumente seines Lebens*, p.254.

64 Ibid. p. 258.

65 Engels, "Die deutsche Reichsverfassungskampagne" (*MEW*, Vol.7, p.169).

66 Ibid. pp. 169.

67 Engels, letter to Jenny Marx (*MEW*, Vol.27 p.501).

68 Engels, Letter to G.J. Harney, 5 October 1849 (*MEW*, Vol 49 p.513).

69 Willich: In a *Newsletter of the Friends of the Max Kade Institute* (Vol 6, Fall

1997), there is a report on Willich's contribution to the American Civil War. The author writes: 'Glorious feats of military daring pepper any account of US Civil War battles. In almost all of these, readers will surely find an anecdote describing what Lew Wallace, author of Ben Hur, described as the "most audacious" act of any Union commander during the war. In his account of the Battle of Shiloh, Wallace relates the "magical" calming effect of a Prussian colonel coolly drilling his regiment of Turner volunteers in the manual of arms in the middle of battle as a shower of bullets rained down around them'. That Prussian colonel was Willich. He was only one of many revolutionaries of this period who distinguished themselves as revolutionaries and freedom fighters in the USA and other parts of the world.

70 Engels, letter to Minna Kautsky, Nov 1885, (*MEW,* Vol. 36, p.392).

71 Adolf von Griesheim, letter to Engels May 1849 in Engels' family archive in Engelskirchen; Kliem, *Friedrich Engels – Dokumente seines Lebens, p. 280.*

72 Engels, *Der deutsche Bauernkrieg - Klassiker der Sozialrevolte (Vol. 10,* Unrast Verlag, Münster, 2004).

73 Graf von Krokow, *Die Deutschen in Ihrem Jahrhundert 1890-1990 (*Rowohlt Hamburg, 1990).

74 Helen MacFarlane: a leading socialist from Burnley. She is mentioned by George Harney in a letter to Engels, 16 December 1850.

75 Engels, letter to Gurwitsch, 27 May 1893 (*MEW,* Vol. 39, p. 75).

76 Engels, letter to E. Bernstein, 4 November 1882 (*MEW,* Vol. 35, p.394).

77 Engels, letter to Marx (*MEW,* Vol. 27, p. 276).

78 *ibid.*

79 Engels, letter to Marx, 15 Nov 1857 (*MEW,* Vol 29).

80 Engels, letter to Marx, 7 December 1857 (*MEW,* Vol 29).

81 Engels, letter to his mother (*MEW,* Vol. 30, p.663).

82 Engels, letter to Marx (*MEW,* Vol. 31, p.293).

183 Engels, letter to his mother (*MEW,* Vol. 32, p.617).

84 Paul Lafargue, "Personal Reminiscences of Karl Marx", reprinted in *Mohr und General (*Dietz Berlin, 1983, pp.286).

85 Engels, letter to Marx, 31 December 1857 (*MEW,* Vol. 29, p.244).

86 Engels, letter to Marx, 11 February 1858 (*MEW,* Vol. 29, p.473).

87 Marx: letter to Engels (14 February 1858 (*MEW,* Vol 29 p.280).

88 Engels, letter to Marx, 29 November 1867 (*MEW,* Vol 31 p.396).

89 Engels, draft letter to Marx (MEW Vol.30 pp.596).

90 Engels, *Die preussische Militärfrage und die deutsche Arbeiterpartei* (The Prussian Military Question and the German Workers' Party) (*MEW,* Vol.16).

91 Martin Kitchen, 'Friedrich Engels' Theory of War', *Military Affairs (*Vol. 41, No. 3, Oct., 1977, pp. 119-124).

92 Engels, letter to Marx, 12 December 1855 (*MEW,* Vol 29).

93 Yvonne Kapp, *Eleanor Marx* (Virago London, 1972).

94 Paul Lafargue, "Personal Reminiscences of Friedrich Engels", reprinted in *Mohr und General (*Dietz Berlin, 1983, pp.429).

[95] Engels, Introduction to *The Civil War in France* by Karl Marx, March 1891 (MECW, Volume 27, p. 506-524).

[96] Engels, letter to his mother (*MEW*, Vol. 33, pp. 299).

[97] Theodor Cuno, 'biographical papers' (Originals held in Moscow).

[98] Engels, letter to Adolph Sorge, 12-17 September 1874 (*MEW*, Vol.33).

[99] Lassalle: Like Marx, Lassalle came from a prosperous Jewish family. He took part in the revolutions of 1848-49 and was imprisoned as a result. Although Lassalle was a member of the Communist League, his politics were strongly opposed by Marx and Engels. He, secretly, directly influenced and advised Bismarck's government on some of its reforms. He founded the Allgemeiner Deutscher Arbeiterverein (General German Workers' Association) which was the first German workers' party. It later merged to become the Social Democratic Party of Germany (SPD).

[100] Engels, Letter to Johann Phillip Becker, 20 November 1876 (*MECW*, Vol. 45).

[101] Engels, *Dialectics of Nature* (*MEW*, Vol.20, Dietz Verlag Berlin, 1972).

[102] Ignacio Ramonet (ed.), *Fidel Castro - My Life* (Allen Lane London, 2007).

[103] Engels, letter to August Bebel, 30 April 1883 (*MEW*, Vol.36).

[104] Engels, letter to Laura Lafargue, 19 August 1883 (*MECW*, Vol.47 p.46).

[105] Johann Philip Becker: Becker (1809-1886) was a brush maker, who first came to prominence during the Hambacher Convention (the first mass meeting of nationalists to be held in Germany), in the Palatinate, during the 1832 revolutionary upsurge, when he was twenty-three years old. From 1833 onwards, he carried out propaganda and agitation, arranged escapes and armed attacks to liberate comrades from prison. He aided many of his comrades in this way. In 1833 a group, with which Becker was closely connected (he himself was then in prison), made an armed attack on a Frankfurt guard-house, in an attempt to get hold of the arms. One of the most daring participants in this uprising was Karl Schapper, who also later became a close comrade of both Marx and Engels. He spent several spells in prison as a result of his revolutionary activities. He is one of the very few people Engels, in his letters, addresses with genuine warmth and intimacy. Becker joined the Baden revolution in 1849. He was one of the main organisers of the Baden People's Militia. He was a leading member of the First International and became a close friend of Engels and Marx.

During the 1849 revolution, with hardly 1000 men, Becker held the line at Pfinz for over four hours against a whole Prussian division and forced them to bring up another two divisions as reinforcement. He was covering the retreat of the revolutionary army from Karlsruhe. Engels called it 'one of the most glorious episodes of the Baden-Palatinate conflict'. When Garibaldi began his struggle for Italian unity, Becker went to Genoa for two years to set up a German volunteer legion to support him. Engels made use of his History of *The South German May Revolution of 1849* when writing his own *The Campaign for the German Constitution* (Reichsverfassungskampagne). An able man, he later became a writer, though never an outstanding theoretician. He was much more the practical revolutionary.

[106] Engels, Letter to Bebel 30 August 1883 (*MEW*, Vol. 36 p.56).

[107] Engels, *The Origin of the Family, Private Property and the State* (Progress Publishers Moscow, 1977, p.174).

[108] Engels, letter to Laura Lafargue, 17 December 1894 (*MECW,* Vol. 50, p.386).

[109] Engels, letter to Nikolai Danielson, 24 February 1893 (*MEW* , Vol.39).

[110] Henry Mayer, *HM Hyndman - The Record of an Adventurous Life (*The Macmillan Company London, 1911).

[111] Eduard Bernstein, *My Years of Exile - Reminiscences of a Socialist,* originally published in German (Erich Reiss, Berlin 1918); English translation by Bernard Maill, published 1921.

[112] Ernest Belfort Bax (1854-1926): socialist, journalist and philosopher. Leading member of the Social Democratic Federation, later joining William Morris's Socialist League, then rejoined SDF. Studied in Germany and developed interest in Marxism. He opposed setting up of Labour Representation Committee and was an ardent opponent of women's rights.

[113] Engels, letter to Karl Kautsky, 4 September 1892, in: *Marx/ Engels on Britain,* Progress Publishers Moscow, 1953.

[114] Engels, letter to Conrad Schmidt, 9 December 1889 (*MEW,* Vol. 37).

[115] Engels, letter to Joseph Block, 21 September 1890 (*MEW,* Vol 37 p.462).

[116] Engels, letter to Paul Ernst, 5 June 1890 (*MEW,* Vol 37 p.441).

[117] 'Literatentum': an unusual expression to use, as it signifies literally 'the world of the men and women of letters' i.e. intellectuals.

[118] Engels, letter to Liebknecht, 10 August 1890 (*MEW,* Vol 37 p.444).

[119] From Engels: "Can Europe disarm?" (*MEW,* Vol.21, pp.350).

[120] Engels, letter to Bebel, 22 December 1882 (*MEW,* Vol. 35 p.415).

[121] Engels, Introduction written in 1887 to Sigismund Borkheim's brochure: *Zur Erinnerung für die deutschen Mordspatrioten 1806-1807 (In memory of the German Arch-Patriots 1806-1807) (MEW* , Vol.36, p.379).

[122] Samuel Moore, letter to Eleanor Marx, 21 July 1895 (*MECW,* Vol.49, p.535).

[123] Louise Freyberger, letter to August Bebel, 2 and 4 September 1898, Bebel Papers held in International Institute of Social History, Amsterdam.

[124] Engels, letter to Marx, 29 January 1851 (*MEW,* Vol.27).

[125] Lafargue, Paul: *Reminiscences of Karl Marx,* op.cit.

[126] Engels, *Ludwig Feuerbach and the End of Classical German Philosophy,* (1887) (Progress Pubishers, Moscow,1973).

[127] As a comparison: in the 1850s, a governess in a middle class household earned around £15 per annum, a cook around £40 and a GP, with a fairly fashionable practice, between £1000 and £2000. An average family's expenditure per week in the 1840s was around 13 shillings 9 pence or, in today's terms, just over £35.

[128] Engels, Article on the Indian mutiny (*New-York Daily Tribune,* 1 October, 1858).

[129] ibid.

[130] Kliem, *Engels – Dokumente seines Lebens,* opus cit. p.434.

[131] *The Harney Papers,* Black, Gees Frank & Renee Metivier Black (ed.) (Van Gorcum, Prakke & Prakke, Assen, 1969, p.295).

[132] Engels, Oration at Marx's Grave, Highgate Cemetery 17 March 1883 (*MEGA* Vol 25 p.415).

[133] Confessions: in Jenny Marx's album 1868 (*MECW*, Vol. 43, p. 541).

[134] Marx and Engels, Manifesto of the Communist Party (Cosimo Classics, New York 2006).

[135] Engels, *Socialism: Utopian and Scientific* (Foreign Languages Press, Peking, 1975).

[136] Oscar Wilde, "The Soul of Man under Socialism" in: *de Profundis* (Penguin Classics, 2003).

[137] Ramonet, Ignacio ed., *Fidel Castro: My Life,* (Allen Lane, London 2007).

[138] Engels: Einleitung zu Marx's *Klassenkämpfe in Frankreich,* March 1895 (*MEW,* Vol. 22, p.524).

[139] Ramonet, Ignacio, *op cit*

[140] Che Guevara, "Guerra de guerrillas: un metodo" (*Cuba Socialista,* Vol.11/Nr. 26, 1963).

FRIEDRICH ENGELS (1820-1895)

A Brief Chronology

1820 28 November: Born in the small textile town of Barmen in the Rhineland.

1828 October: Begins primary school in Barmen.

1830 July: Revolution in France.

1834 October: Attends the Gymnasium (grammar school) in the neighbouring town of Elberfeld.

1837 September: Leaves secondary school and begins work in the family's Barmen textile mill as a junior clerk.

1838-41 July - March: In Bremen to continue his training with the businessman and consul Heinrich Leupold.

1841 March: Returns from Bremen to Barmen. During the second half of the year, he studies Ludwig Feuerbach's *Essence of Christianity*.

1841 2 September: He begins his obligatory military service as a one-year volunteer with the artillery in Berlin. Here he grasps the opportunity to sit in on lectures at the University of Berlin

1842 12 April: Starts writing for the *Rheinische Zeitung*. On 10 October he returns to Barmen making a short stop-over in Cologne.

1842-44 End of November: First longer stay England to complete his management training in the Manchester cotton spinning mill of Ermen & Engels. Here he makes contact with Julian Harney, the editor, of the *Northern Star,* and a member of the more radical wing of the Chartist Movement. Towards the end of October, he begins writing for *The New Moral World,* the paper of the English Owenites.

1842 December: Meets the German revolutionary and writer, Georg Weerth; and they become friends.

1843 Beginning of long-term relationship with Mary Burns Makes

	contact, in London, with leaders of the underground German workers' organisation, Bund der Gerechten (Federation of the Just), Karl Schapper, Joseph Moll und Heinrich Bauer.
1844	January: He writes articles for the Deutsch-Französischen Jahrbüchern (German-French Almanacs) and by the end of February has begun corresponding with Karl Marx as a result of his contributions to the Jahrbüchern
	End August: He returns to Germany via a short stopover in Paris where he meets up with Marx.
1844-45	In Barmen where he completes his book *The Condition of the Working Class in England.*
1845-46	Exile in Brussels.
1846-48	Continued exile in Paris, then expulsion from there in January, moves to Brussels to join Marx.
1847	Joins League of the Just. He and Marx persuade its members to change the name to League of Communists and adopt their principles.
1848-49	Is at various times in Brussels, Paris, Germany and Switzerland
1848	Revolution in Paris and revolutionary clashes in Germany. Marx becomes President of the Bund der Kommunisten (League of Communists); *Manifesto of the Communist Party* published.
1850	Marx and Engels address the League of Communists.
1857	The year of a world economic crisis starting in November in North America.
1851	Founding of the Amalgamated Society of Engineers in England – the prototype for a new model of trade union.
1851	May: The World Exhibition in London takes place and demonstrates Britain's leading economic strength.
1852	Drawn out but unsuccessful strike of engineering workers in England.
1854	The Labour Parliament convened – in essence represents the end of the Chartist Movement.
1857-58	Widespread economic crisis and the suppression of the Indian uprising.
1859	Darwin publishes *Origin of Species.*
1859-60	Big Building workers' strike in England.
1860	Engels' father dies in Barmen.
	May: Visits his seriously ill mother in Barmen.
1861-65	US Civil War.
	Amnesty in Germany for those who took part in the 1848 revolution

1861 George Eliot completes her novel *Silas Marner*.

1862 Herbert Spencer (leading positivist philosopher) publishes his *First Principles*.

1863 January: Death of Engels' first partner, Mary Burns.

1864 May: Engels' comrade Wilhelm Wolff dies.

Founding of the International Workingmen's Association (IWA).

1865 Engels and his partner, Lydia become members of the IWA.

Reform League established in Britain with the leading participation of the General Council of the International. It is the biggest organisation involved in the struggle for electoral reform.

1866 May: Beginning of the national economic crisis of 66/67

July: several mass demonstrations.

1867 First volume of *Capital* published.

1869 Engels officially finishes working for the Ermen & Engels company, but has to act as advisor for another year, as he is still a partner.

1869 August: Founding of the German Social-Democratic Workers Party in Eisenach.

1870 September: Engels and Lydia move to London

1870-71 Franco-Prussian War. Between July and Feb 1871 he writes 59 articles on the war for the *Pall Mall Gazette*.

1871 March – May: Paris Commune. Engels occupied with international campaign to defend Commune and then in support of the refugees.

1872 Engels is a delegate to the Hague congress of the IWA.

1873 Work on the concept for *Dialectics of Nature*.

Last visit to family in Engelskirchen.

1875 Writes his critique of the German Social Democratic Workers Party Gotha programme.

Firm of Ermen & Engels is taken over and ceases to exist under the old name.

1876 Works on *Anti-Dühring*.

1878 11 September: marries Lydia Burns.

12 September: death of Lydia Burns.

1878-90 Anti-socialist laws in force in Germany, making all socialist activity there illegal.

1880 Writes his booklet *Socialism: Utopian and Scientific*.

1881 Marx's wife, Jenny dies.

1883 March: Karl Marx dies..

1884 Publication of *Origin of the Family, Private Property and the State*.

1885 *Capital* (Vol 2) published and prepared for publication by Engels.

1888	Travels to the USA and Canada with Carl Schorlemmer, Edward Aveling and Eleanor Marx .
1889	Founding of the Second International.
1890	Engels joins the big May Day demonstration in London
	Helene Demuth dies.
	August: Uniting of Lasalle's General Workers' Association and the Social Democratic Workers Party of Germany into one party: German Socialist Workers' Party of Germany.
1893	Writes his series of articles promoting world disarmament: 'Can Europe Disarm?'.
	Tours Germany and Switzerland and attends the International Socialist conference in Zurich.
1894	Finishes work on the third volume of Marx's *Capital* which is published that year.
1895	5 August: Engels dies.

ENGELS' PRINCIPAL WORKS

1844 Feb.	*Outlines of a Critique of National Economy* (Umrisse zu einer Kritik der Nationalökonomie).
1844 Nov.	*The Holy Family or a critique of critical criticism* (Die heilige Familie oder Kritik der kritischen Kritik).
1845	*The Condition of the Working Class in England* (Die Lage der arbeitenden Klasse in England.
1846	*The German Ideology* (Die deutsche Ideologie) with Marx.
1847 Nov.	*Principles of Communism* (Grundsätze des Kommunismus).
1848	*Manifesto of the Communist Party* (Manifest der Kommunistischen Partei) with Marx.
1850	*The German Constitutional Campaign* (Die deutsche Reichsverfassungskampagne).
	The German Peasant War (Der deutsche Bauernkrieg).
1852 Sept.	*Revolution and Counterrevolution in Germany* (Revolution und Konterevolution in Deutschland).
1865 Feb.	*The Prussian military Question and the German Workers' Party* (Die preußische Militärfrage und die deutsche Arbeiterpartei).
1866	*Observations on the War in Germany* (Betrachtungen über den Krieg in Deutschland).
1870 May	*The History of Ireland* (sketches) (Die Geschichte Irlands).
	On War (Über den Krieg) Article.
1871	*On War* (Über den Krieg) Article.
1873	*On Authority* (Von der Autorität).
1873 Feb.	*The Housing Question* (Zur Wohnungsfrage).
	The Civil War in France.
	Writings on the Paris Commune with Marx.

1876 *The Part Played by Labour in the Transformation of Ape to Man* (Anteil der Arbeit an der Menschwerdung des Affen.

1878 Herr Eugen Dühring's Revolution in Science (Herrn Eugen Dühring's Umwälzung der Wissenschaft).

1880 *The Development of Socialism from Utopia to Science* (Die Entwicklung des Sozialismus von der Utopie zur Wissenschaft).

1884 *The Origin of the Family, Private Property and the State* (Der Ursprung der Familie, des Privateigentums und des Staats).

1886 *Dialectics of Nature* (Dialektik der Natur).

1888 *The Role of Force in History* (Die Rolle der Gewalt in der Geschichte).

SELECT BIBLIOGRAPHY

Adler, Max: "Engels als Denker Zum 100. Geburtstag Friedrich Engels", in: *Freiheit*, (1920)

Black, Gees Frank & Renee Metivier Black (eds.): *The Harney Papers* (Van Gorcum, Prakke & Prakke, Assen, 1969)

Carlton, Grace: *Friedrich Engels – the shadow prophet* (Pall Mall Press, London 1965)

Carver, Terrell: *Engels* (Oxford University Press, Oxford 1981)

Cole, G.D.H.: *Chartist Portraits* (Macmillan, London 1965) [1941]

Easton, Loyd D: *Hegel's First American Followers* (Ohio University Press, Ohio 1966)

Frow, Ruth & Eddie: *Karl Marx in Manchester* (Working Class Movement Library, Manchester 1985)

German, Lindsey: 'Friedrich Engels – the life of a revolutionary', in *International Socialism*, No.65, 1994)

Gemkov, H. (ed): *Friedrich Engels. Eine Biografie* (Dietz, Berlin 1970)

Heine, Heinrich: *It will be a lovely day* (Seven Seas Books, Berlin 1965)

Henderson, W.O.: *The Life of Friedrich Engels*, 2 vols (Routledge, London 1976).

Hirsch, Helmut: *Engels* (Rowohlt, Hamburg 2002)

Hobsbawm, Eric: *On History* (Weidenfeld & Nicholson, London 1997)

Hunley J.D: *The Life and Thought of Friedrich Engels: A Reinterpretation* (Yale University Press 1991)

Jenkins, Mick: "Friedrich Engels in Manchester" (Lancashire and Cheshire Communist Party 1951)

Kapp, Yvonne: *Eleanor Marx*, 2 vols. (Virago, London 1972)

Kautsky B: *Friedrich Engels' Briefwechsel mit Karl Kautsky* (B. Kautsky, Vienna 1955)

Kitchen, Martin: 'Friedrich Engels' Theory of War', *Military Affairs,* Vol. 41, No. 3 (Oct. 1977)

Kliem, Manfred (ed): *Friedrich Engels. Dokumente seines Lebens* (Philipp Reklam, Leipzig 1977)

Levine, Norman: *The Tragic Deception: Marx contra Engels* (Clio Books, Sta Barbara 1975)

Marcus, Steven: *Engels, Manchester, and the Working Class* (Weidenfeld and Nicolson, London 1974)

McLellan, David: *Engels* (Fontana, London 1977)

Marx-Engels Collected Works, in 50 vols. (published jointly by Progress Publishers, Moscow, Lawrence & Wishart, London and International Publishers, New York 1975-2004)

Marx, Karl: 'Enthullungen über den Kommunistenprozess zu Köln' (Berlin: Buchandlung Vorwärts, 1914)

Marx/Engels: *On literature and Art* (Progress Publishers, Moscow, 1976)

Marx/Engels: *Irland Insel in Aufruhr* (Dietz Verlag, Berlin 1975)

Mayer, Gustav: *Friedrich Engels: a Biography* (translated by G. and H. Highet) (Chapman, London 1936)

Mehring, Franz: *Karl Marx. Geschichte seines Lebens, in: Gesammelte Schriften,* Band 3 (Dietz Berlin, 1979)

Oswald, Eugène: *Reminiscences of a Busy Life* (Alexander Moring, London 1911)

Ramm T. Engels, Friedrich. In: Sills DL, ed. *International Encyclopedia of the Social Sciences* New York, Macmillan; 1968)

Schoyen, A. R.: *The Chartist Challenge – a portrait of Geroge Julian Harney,* (Heinemann, London 1958)

Stepanova E.A.: *Friedrich Engels. Sein leben und Werk* (Progress, Moscow 1989)

Riazanov, David: *Karl Marx and Frederick Engels - An Introduction to Their Lives and Work* (International Publishers, New York 1927)

Ullrich Horst: *Der Junge Engels. Eine historisch-biographische Studie seiner weltanschaulichen Entwicklung in den Jahren 1834-1845,* 2 Vols. (Deutscher Verlag der Wissenschaften, Berlin 1961- 1966)

Whitfield, Roy: *Engels in Manchester: the search for a shadow* (Working Class Movement Library, Manchester 1988)

Woolfson, Charles: *The Labour Theory of Culture* (Routledge & Kegan Paul, London 1982

Index